# dancing at the PITY PARTY

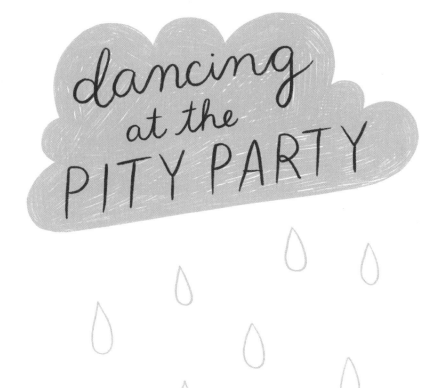

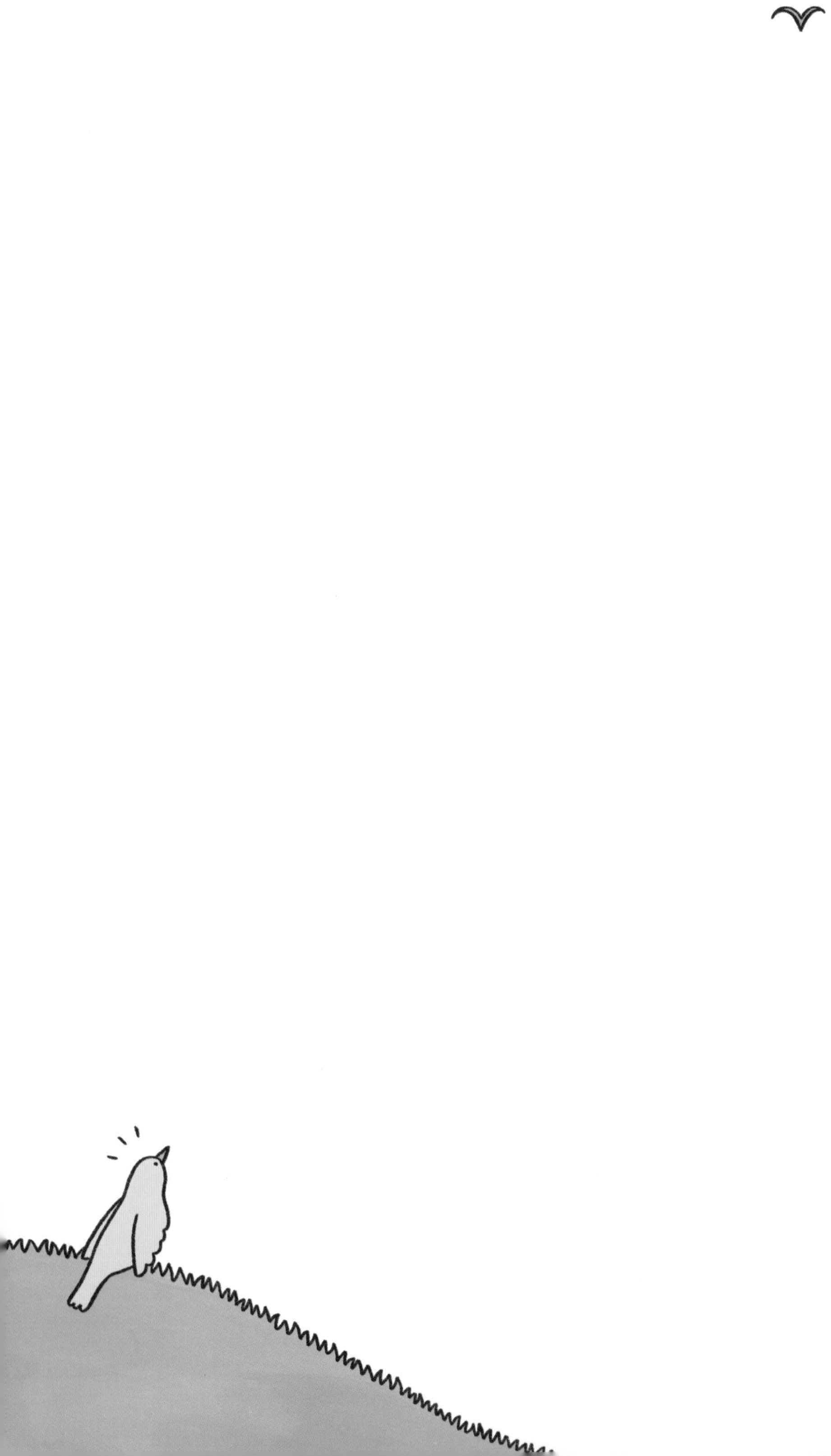

# dancing at the PITY PARTY

## a dead mom graphic memoir

by
TYLER FEDER

Dial Books

Dial Books
An imprint of Penguin Random House LLC, New York

First published in the United States of America by Dial Books, 2020
First paperback edition published 2022


Visit us online at penguinrandomhouse.com.

THE LIBRARY OF CONGRESS HAS CATALOGED THE HARDCOVER EDITION AS FOLLOWS:
Library of Congress Cataloging-in-Publication Data
Names: Feder, Tyler, author, illustrator.
Title: Dancing at the pity party: a dead mom graphic memoir / by Tyler Feder.
Description: New York: Dial Books, [2020] | Summary: "Tyler Feder shares her story of her mother's first oncology appointment to facing reality as a motherless daughter in this frank and refreshingly funny graphic memoir"—Provided by publisher. | Identifiers: LCCN 2019050647 (print) | LCCN 2019050648 (ebook) | ISBN 9780525553021 (hardcover) | ISBN 9780525556350 (ebook) | ISBN 9780525556367 (kindle edition) | Subjects: LCSH: Feder, Tyler—Comic books, strips, etc.—Juvenile literature. | Feder, Tyler—Family—Comic books, strips, etc.—Juvenile literature. | Children of cancer patients—United States—Biography—Comic books, strips, etc.—Juvenile literature. | Mothers and daughters—United States—Comic books, strips, etc.—Juvenile literature. | Terminally ill parents—United States—Comic books, strips, etc.—Juvenile literature. | Death—Comic books, strips, etc.—Juvenile literature. | Grief—Comic books, strips, etc.—Juvenile literature.
Classification: LCC RC265.6.F44 A3 2020 (print) | LCC RC265.6.F44 (ebook) | DDC 362.17/5—dc23
LC record available at https://lccn.loc.gov/2019050647
LC ebook record available at https://lccn.loc.gov/2019050648

Manufactured in China
ISBN 9780525553038
1 3 5 7 9 10 8 6 4 2
TOPL

Design by Jennifer Kelly and Tyler Feder | Text handlettered by Tyler Feder for my mom

(obviously)

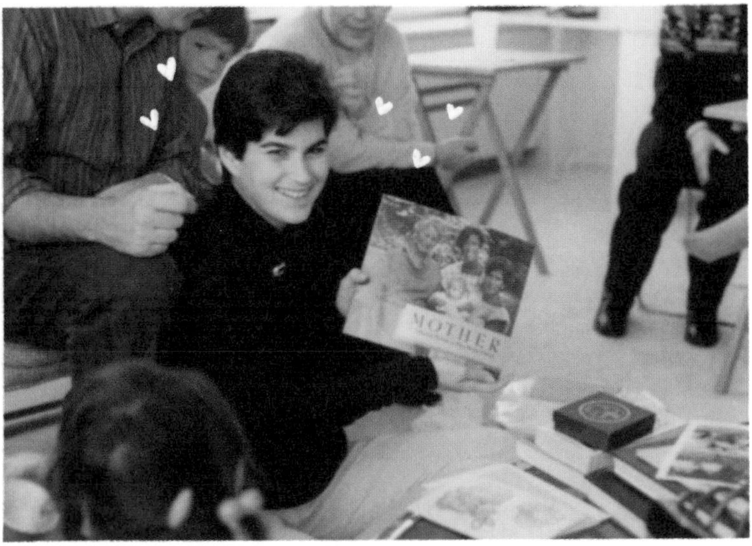
MOTHER

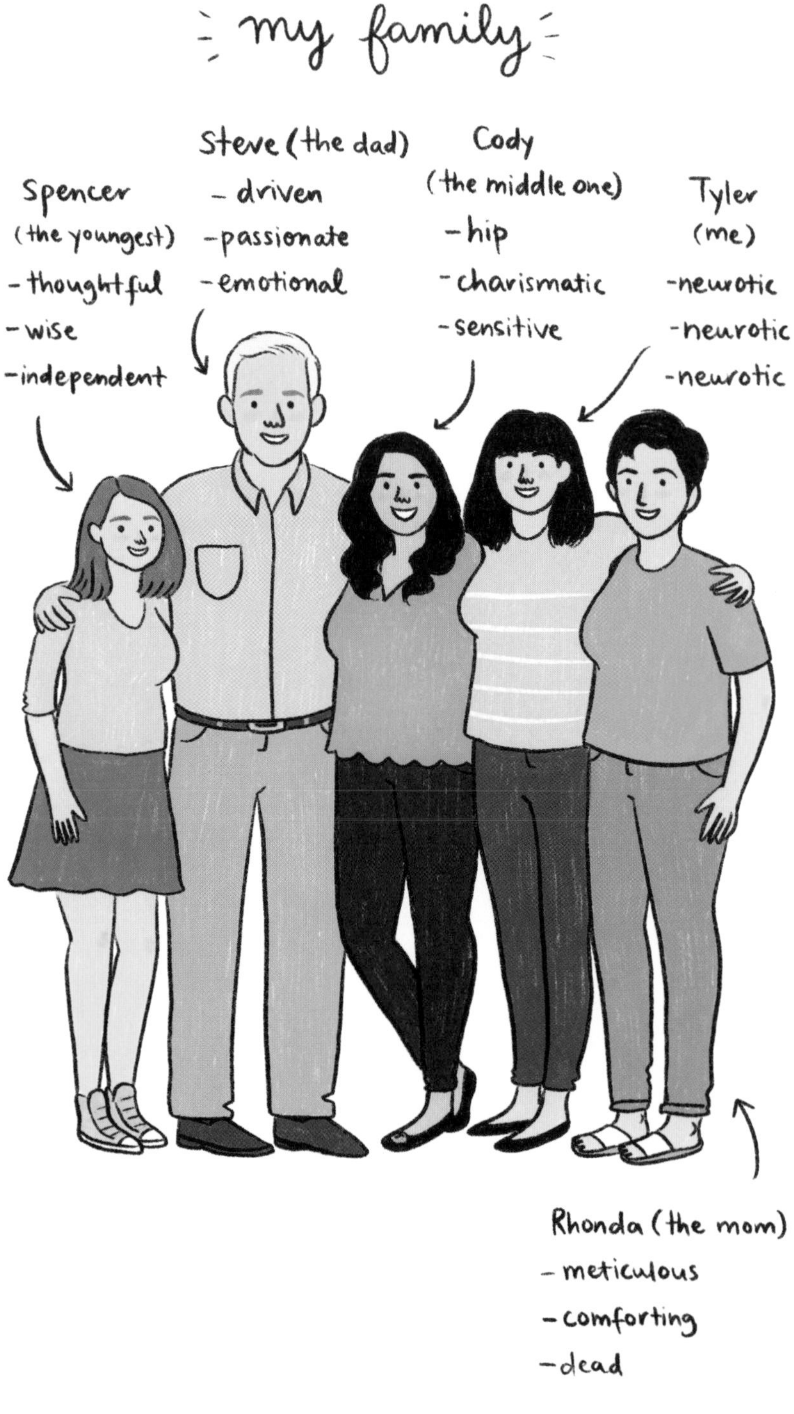
my family
Steve (the dad)
- driven
- passionate
- emotional
Cody
(the middle one)
- hip
- charismatic
- sensitive
Spencer
(the youngest)
- thoughtful
- wise
- independent
Tyler
(me)
- neurotic
- neurotic
- neurotic
Rhonda (the mom)
- meticulous
- comforting
- dead

# introduction

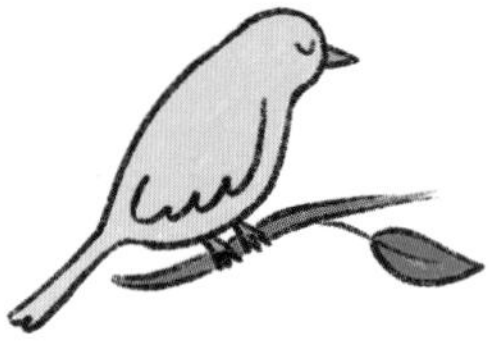

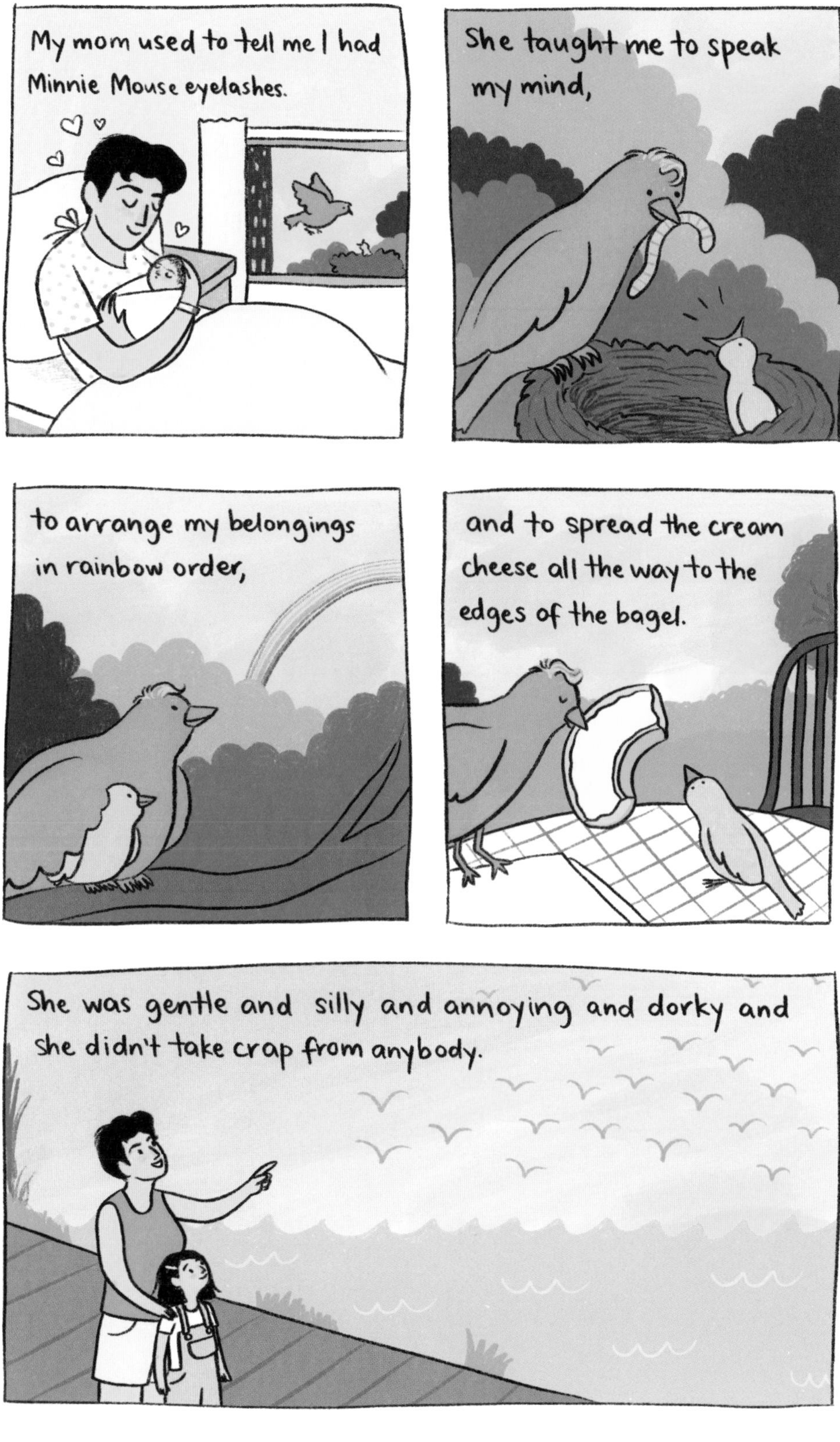
My mom used to tell me I had Minnie Mouse eyelashes.
She taught me to speak my mind,
to arrange my belongings in rainbow order,
and to spread the cream cheese all the way to the edges of the bagel.
She was gentle and silly and annoying and dorky and she didn't take crap from anybody.

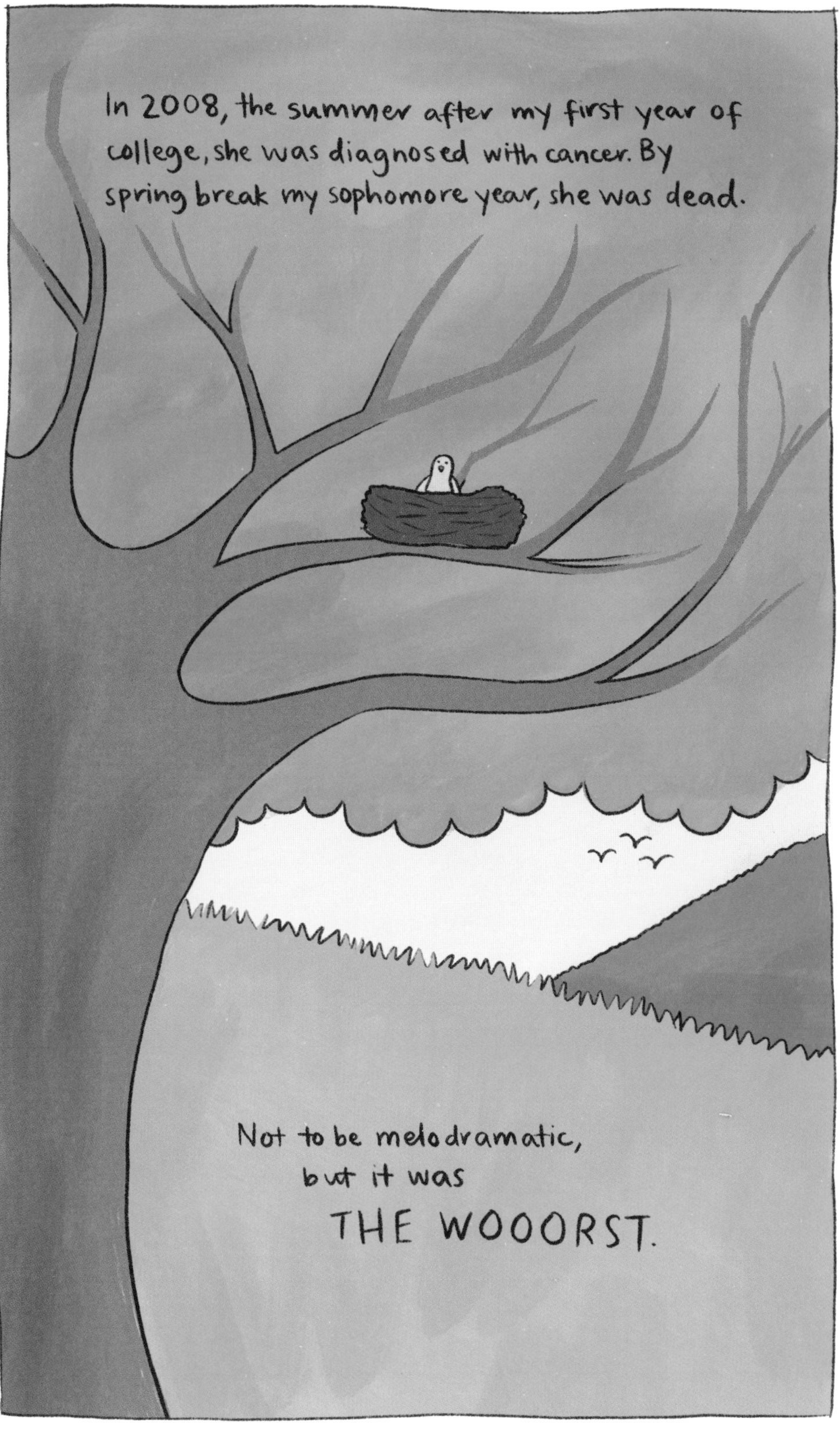
In 2008, the summer after my first year of college, she was diagnosed with cancer. By spring break my sophomore year, she was dead.
Not to be melodramatic, but it was
THE WOOORST.

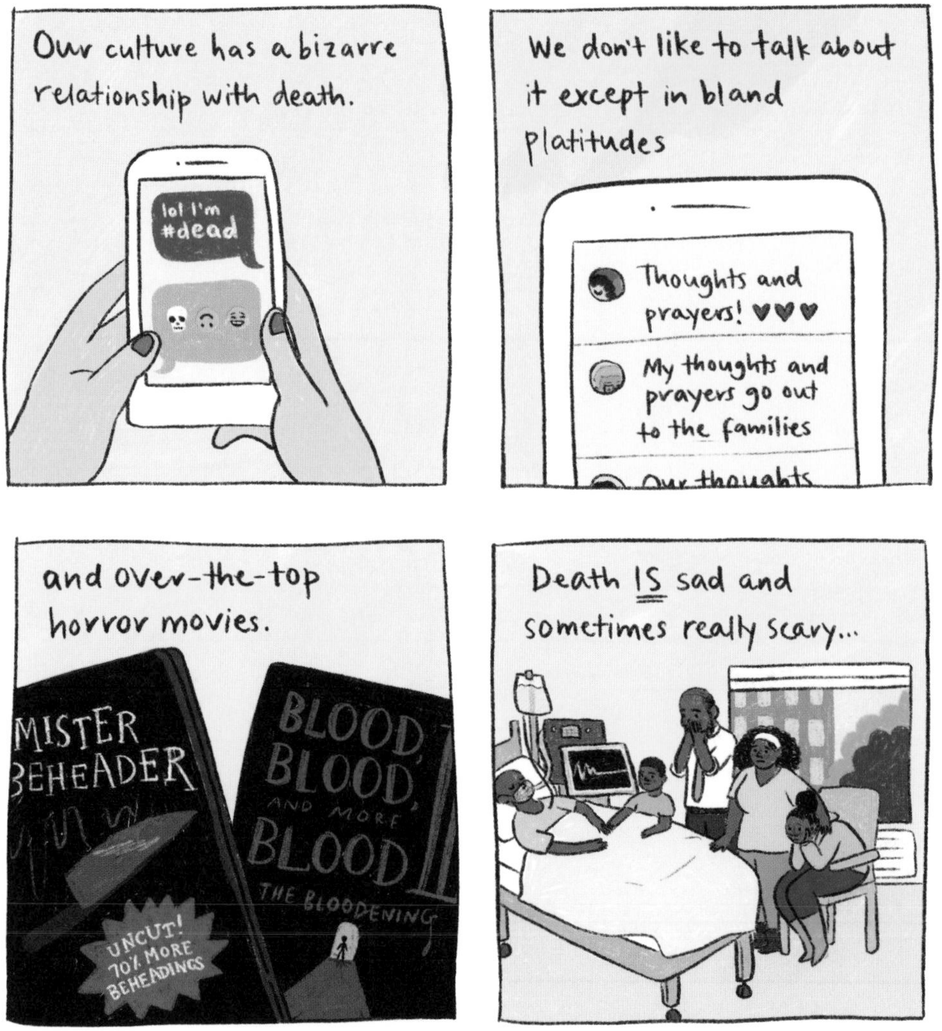
Our culture has a bizarre relationship with death.
lol I'm #dead
We don't like to talk about it except in bland platitudes
Thoughts and prayers! ♥♥♥
My thoughts and prayers go out to the families
and over-the-top horror movies.
MISTER BEHEADER
UNCUT! 70% MORE BEHEADINGS
BLOOD, BLOOD, AND MORE BLOOD
THE BLOODENING
Death IS sad and sometimes really scary...

but oscillating between euphemisms and torture porn does not a healthy relationship with mortality make!

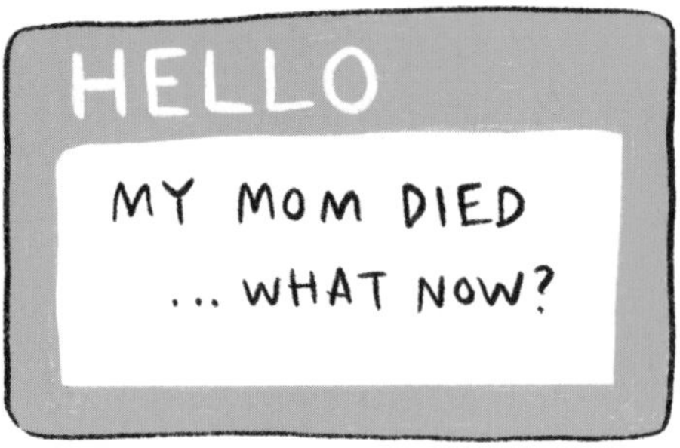
HELLO
MY MOM DIED
... WHAT NOW?

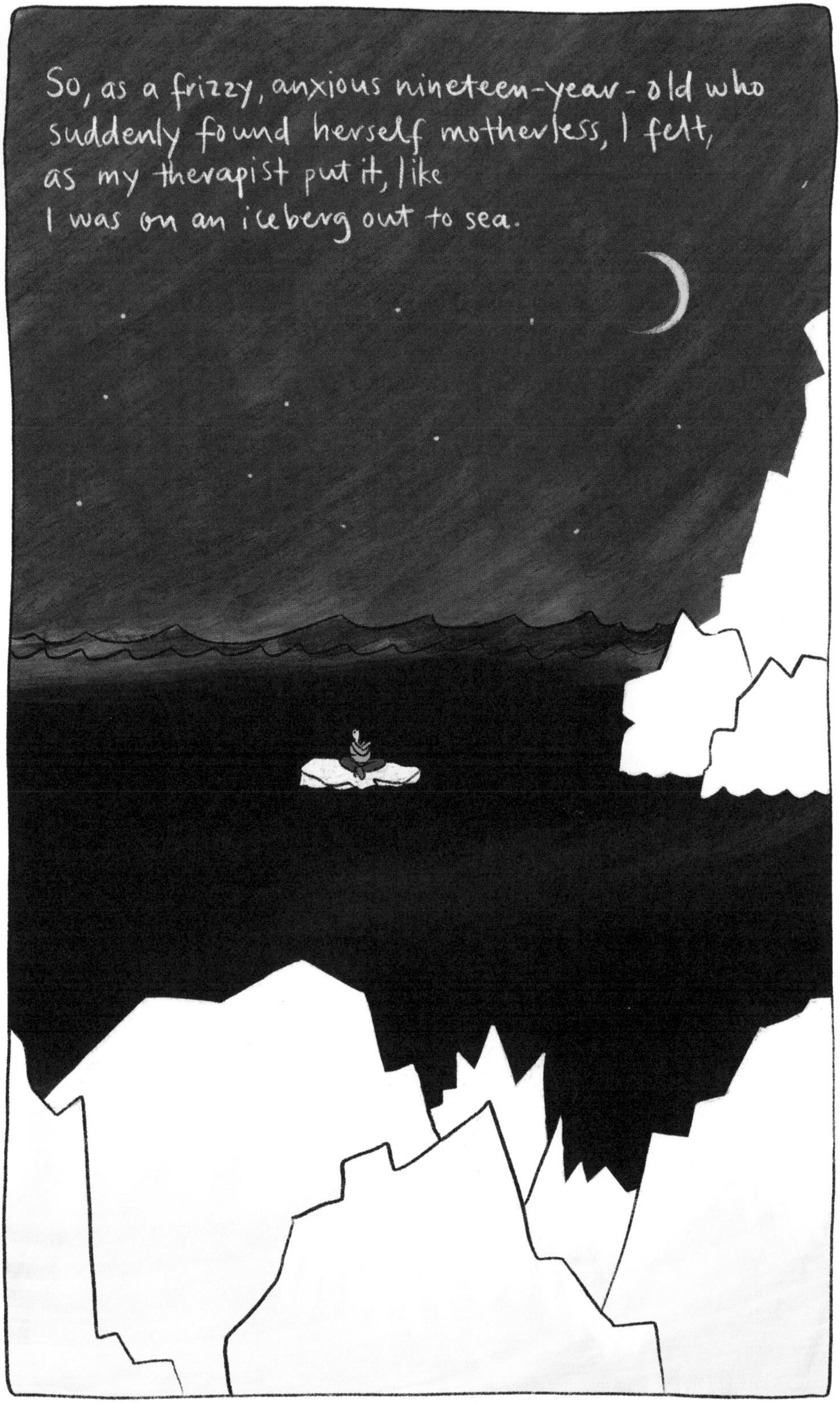
So, as a frizzy, anxious nineteen-year-old who suddenly found herself motherless, I felt, as my therapist put it, like I was on an iceberg out to sea.

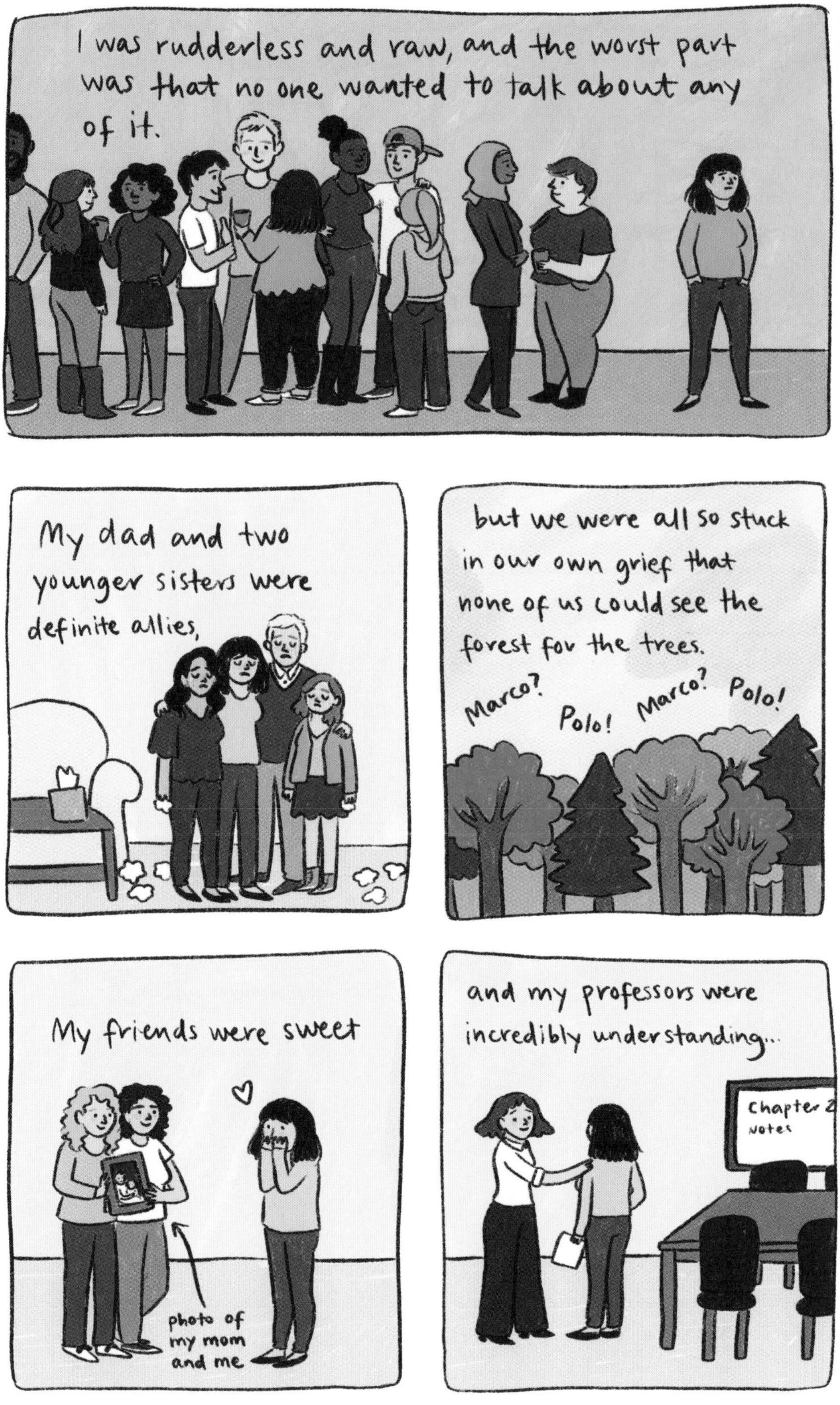
I was rudderless and raw, and the worst part was that no one wanted to talk about any of it.
My dad and two younger sisters were definite allies,
but we were all so stuck in our own grief that none of us could see the forest for the trees.
Marco?
Polo!
Marco?
Polo!
My friends were sweet
photo of my mom and me
and my professors were incredibly understanding...
Chapter 2 Notes

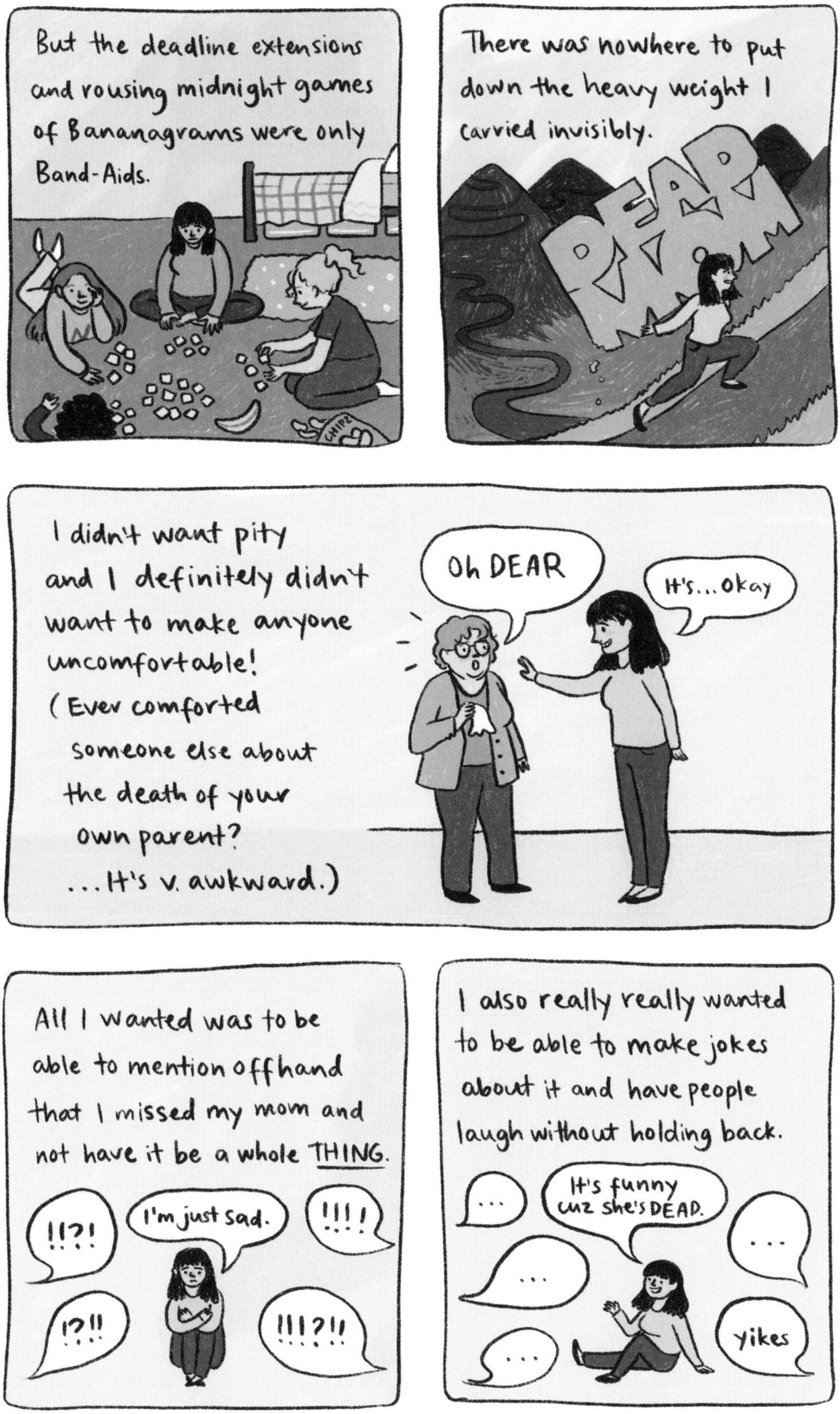

But the deadline extensions and rousing midnight games of Bananagrams were only Band-Aids.
There was nowhere to put down the heavy weight I carried invisibly.
I didn't want pity and I definitely didn't want to make anyone uncomfortable! (Ever comforted someone else about the death of your own parent? ...It's v. awkward.)
Oh DEAR
It's...Okay
All I wanted was to be able to mention offhand that I missed my mom and not have it be a whole THING.
!!?!
I'm just sad.
!!!!
!?!!
!!!?!!
I also really really wanted to be able to make jokes about it and have people laugh without holding back.
...
It's funny cuz she's DEAD.
...
...
...
yikes

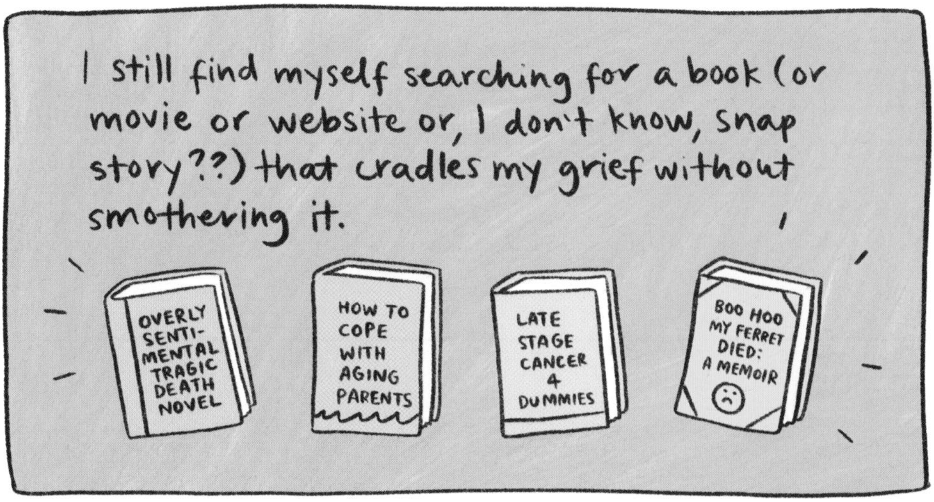
I still find myself searching for a book (or movie or website or, I don't know, snap story??) that cradles my grief without smothering it.
OVERLY SENTI-MENTAL TRAGIC DEATH NOVEL
HOW TO COPE WITH AGING PARENTS
LATE STAGE CANCER 4 DUMMIES
BOO HOO MY FERRET DIED: A MEMOIR

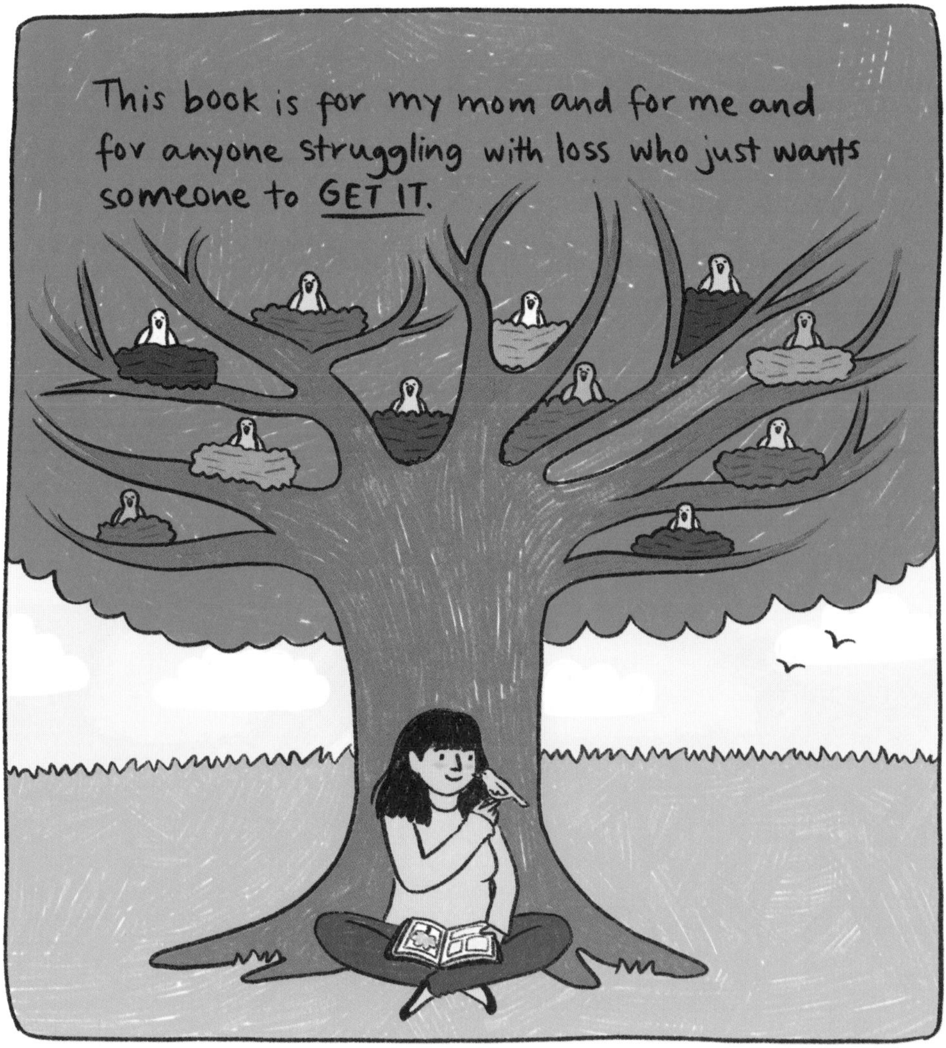
This book is for my mom and for me and for anyone struggling with loss who just wants someone to GET IT.

# chapter one

# MAW

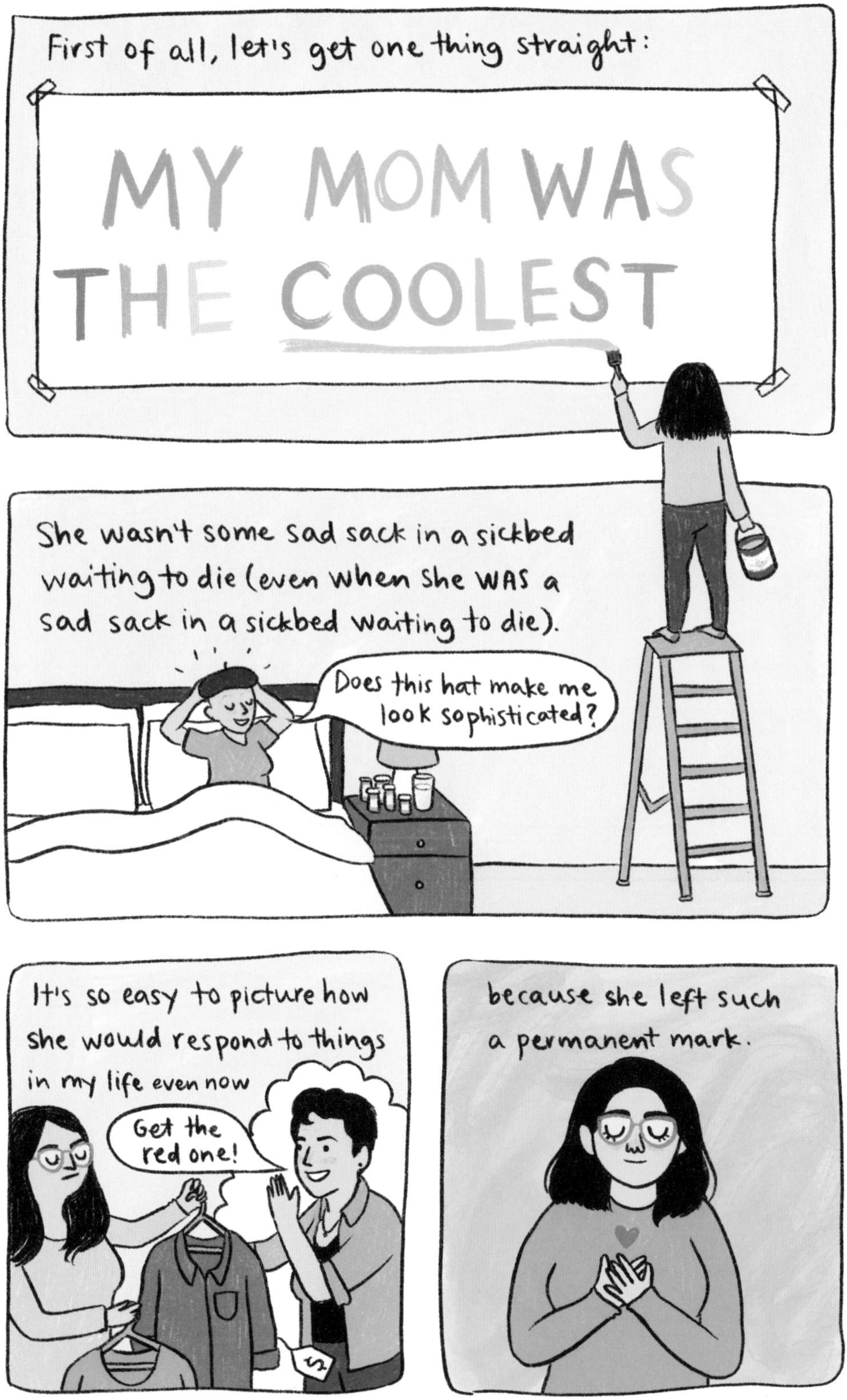
First of all, let's get one thing straight:
MY MOM WAS THE COOLEST
She wasn't some sad sack in a sickbed waiting to die (even when she WAS a sad sack in a sickbed waiting to die).
Does this hat make me look sophisticated?
It's so easy to picture how she would respond to things in my life even now
Get the red one!
because she left such a permanent mark.

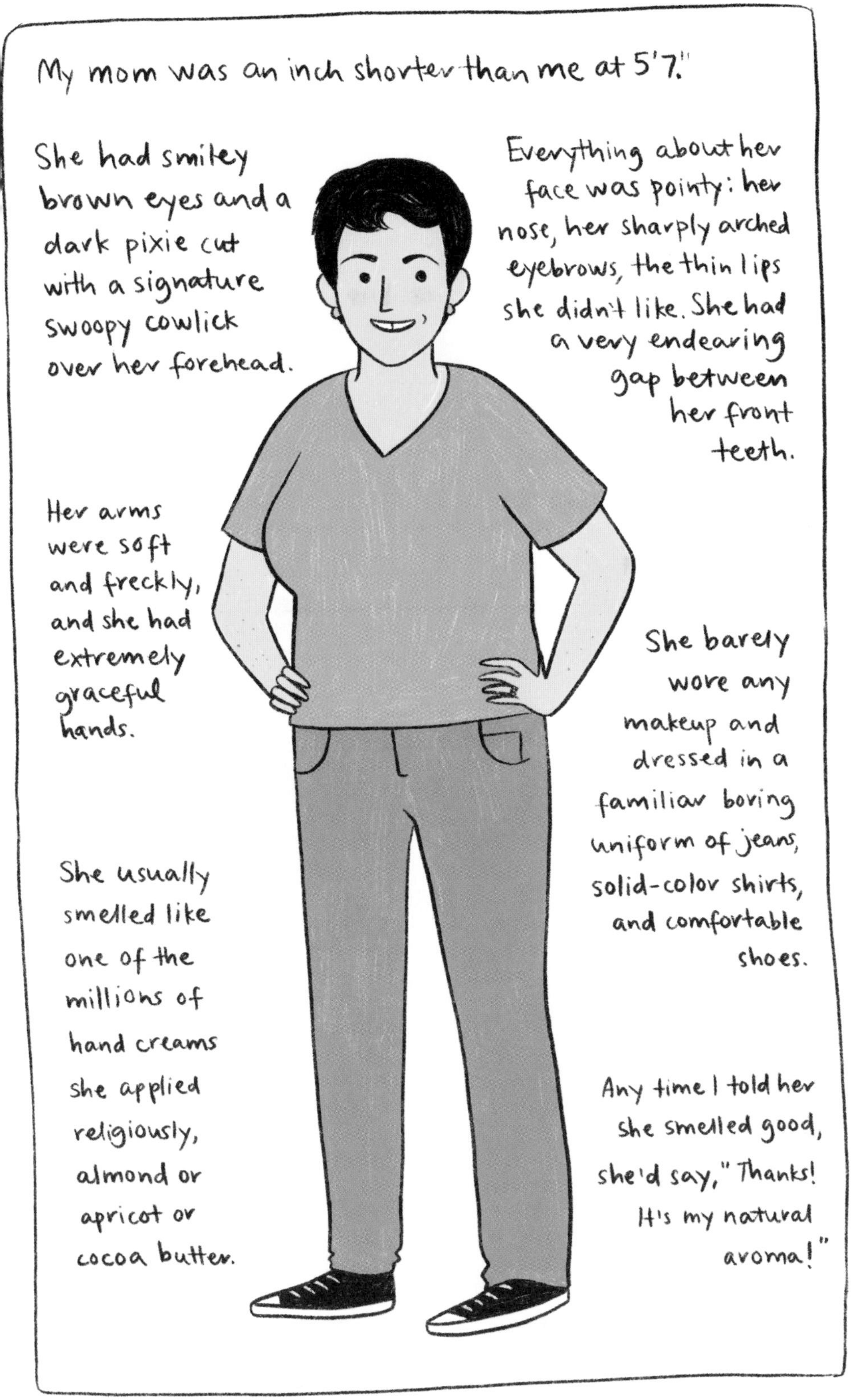
My mom was an inch shorter than me at 5'7."
She had smiley brown eyes and a dark pixie cut with a signature swoopy cowlick over her forehead.
Everything about her face was pointy: her nose, her sharply arched eyebrows, the thin lips she didn't like. She had a very endearing gap between her front teeth.
Her arms were soft and freckly, and she had extremely graceful hands.
She barely wore any makeup and dressed in a familiar boring uniform of jeans, solid-color shirts, and comfortable shoes.
She usually smelled like one of the millions of hand creams she applied religiously, almond or apricot or cocoa butter.
Any time I told her she smelled good, she'd say, "Thanks! It's my natural aroma!"

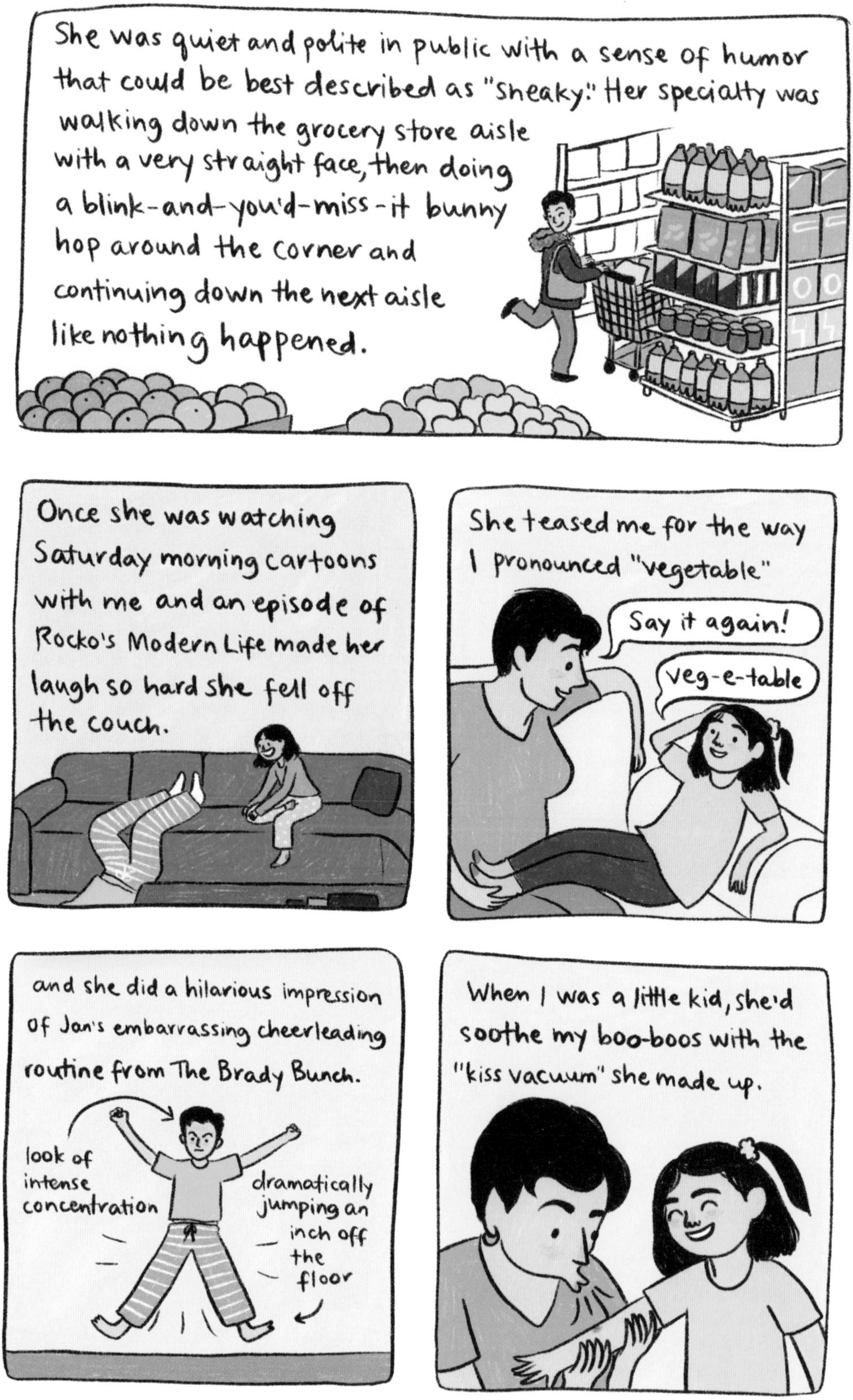

She was quiet and polite in public with a sense of humor that could be best described as "sneaky." Her specialty was walking down the grocery store aisle with a very straight face, then doing a blink-and-you'd-miss-it bunny hop around the corner and continuing down the next aisle like nothing happened.
Once she was watching Saturday morning cartoons with me and an episode of Rocko's Modern Life made her laugh so hard she fell off the couch.
She teased me for the way I pronounced "vegetable"
Say it again!
veg-e-table
and she did a hilarious impression of Jan's embarrassing cheerleading routine from The Brady Bunch.
look of intense concentration
dramatically jumping an inch off the floor
When I was a little kid, she'd soothe my boo-boos with the "kiss vacuum" she made up.

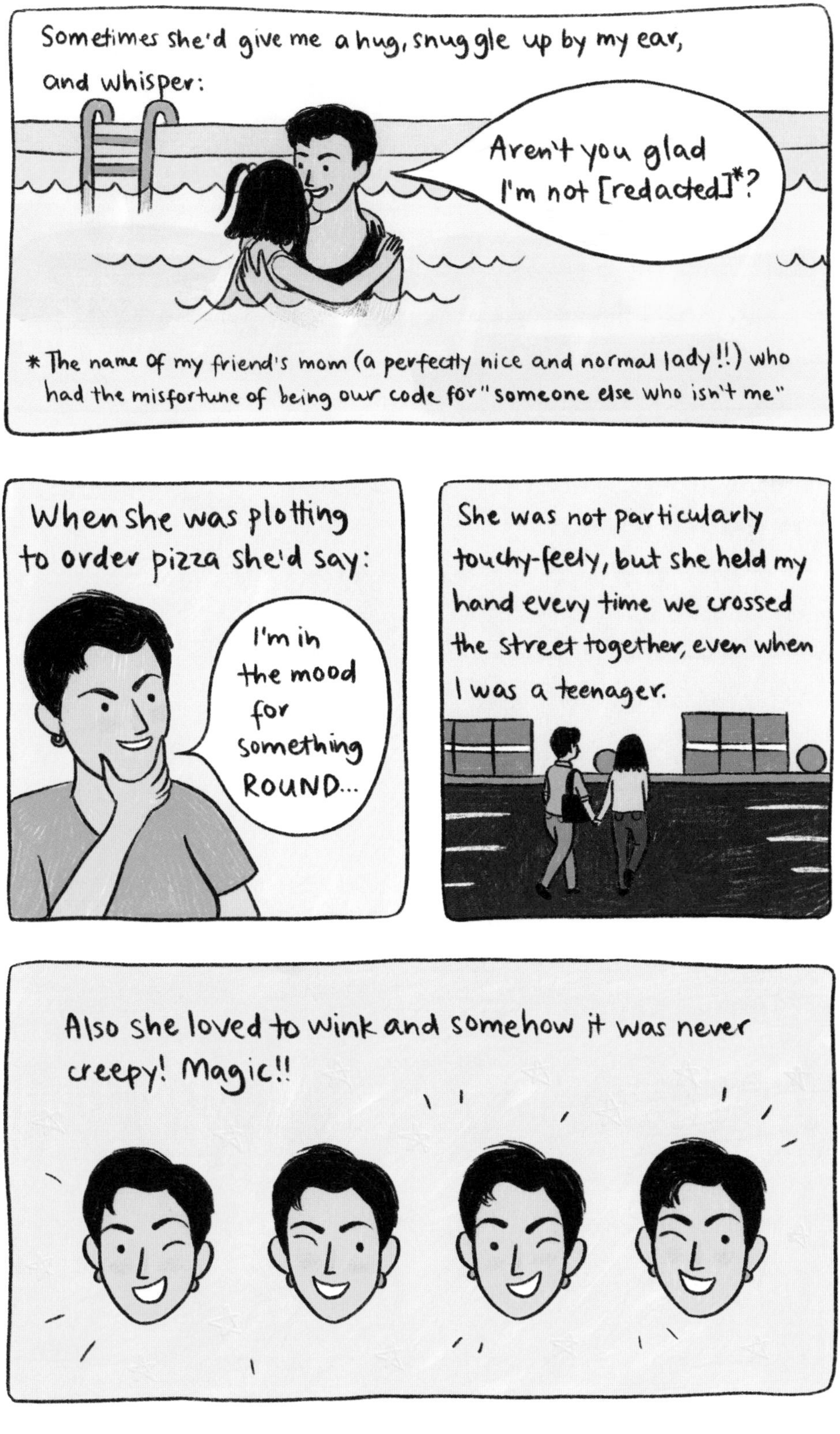
Sometimes she'd give me a hug, snuggle up by my ear, and whisper:
Aren't you glad I'm not [redacted]*?
* The name of my friend's mom (a perfectly nice and normal lady!!) who had the misfortune of being our code for "someone else who isn't me"
When she was plotting to order pizza she'd say:
I'm in the mood for something ROUND...
She was not particularly touchy-feely, but she held my hand every time we crossed the street together, even when I was a teenager.
Also she loved to wink and somehow it was never creepy! Magic!!

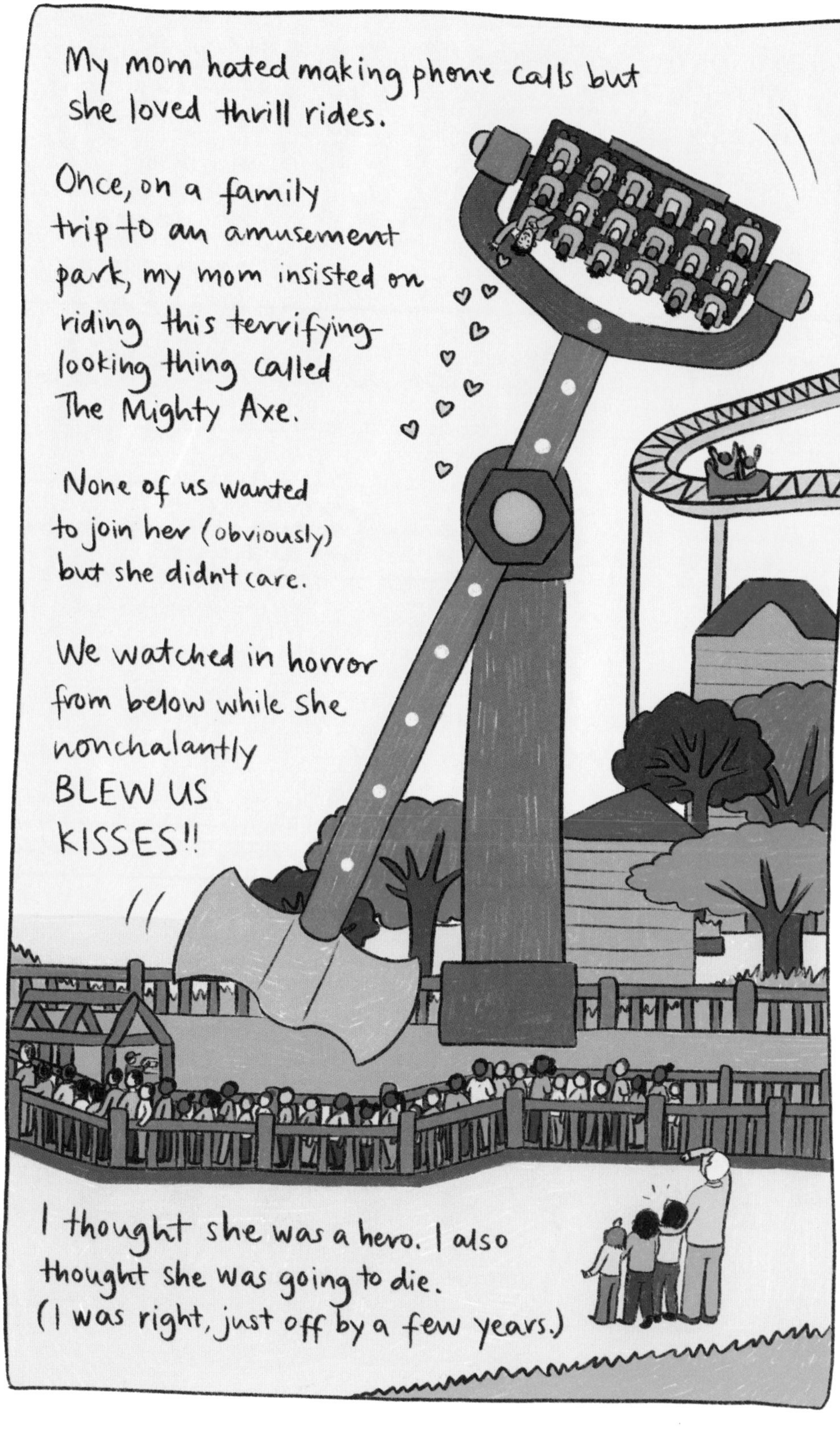
My mom hated making phone calls but she loved thrill rides.
Once, on a family trip to an amusement park, my mom insisted on riding this terrifying-looking thing called The Mighty Axe.
None of us wanted to join her (obviously) but she didn't care.
We watched in horror from below while she nonchalantly BLEW US KISSES!!
I thought she was a hero. I also thought she was going to die.
(I was right, just off by a few years.)

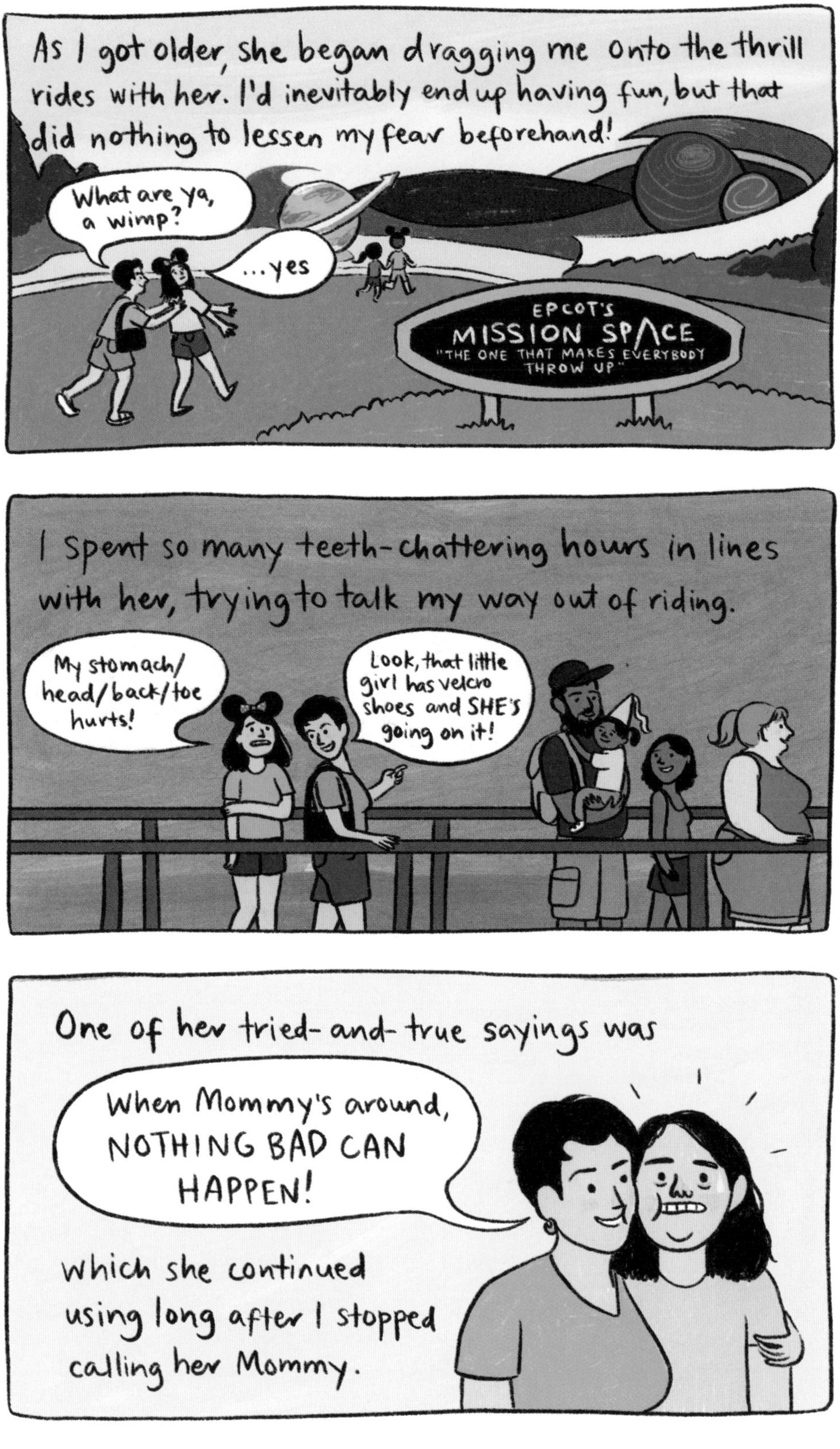
As I got older, she began dragging me onto the thrill rides with her. I'd inevitably end up having fun, but that did nothing to lessen my fear beforehand!
What are ya, a wimp?
...yes
EPCOT'S
MISSION SPACE
"THE ONE THAT MAKES EVERYBODY THROW UP"
I spent so many teeth-chattering hours in lines with her, trying to talk my way out of riding.
My stomach/head/back/toe hurts!
Look, that little girl has velcro shoes and SHE'S going on it!
One of her tried-and-true sayings was
When Mommy's around, NOTHING BAD CAN HAPPEN!
which she continued using long after I stopped calling her Mommy.

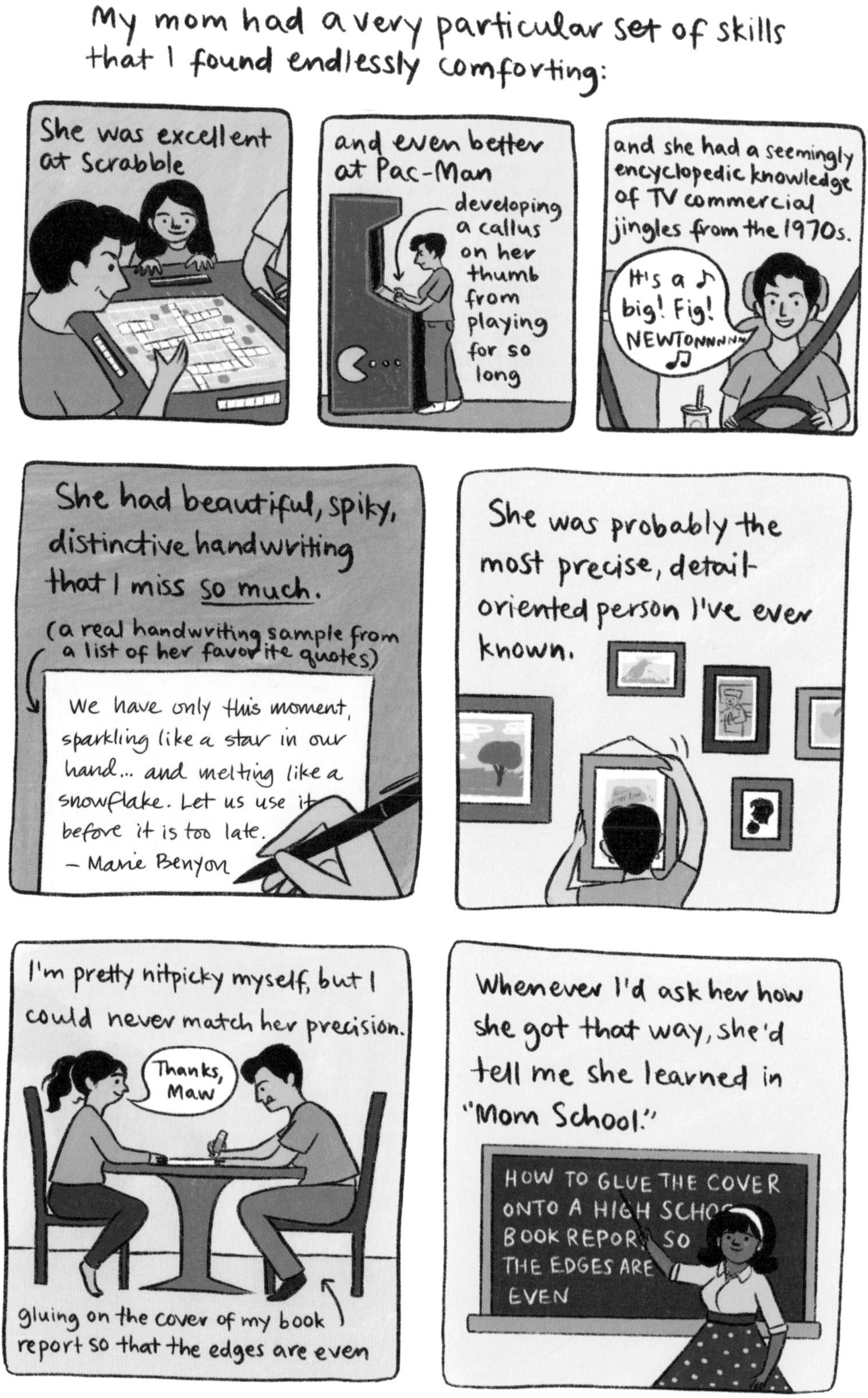
My mom had a very particular set of skills that I found endlessly comforting:
She was excellent at Scrabble
and even better at Pac-Man
developing a callus on her thumb from playing for so long
and she had a seemingly encyclopedic knowledge of TV commercial jingles from the 1970s.
It's a big! Fig! NEWTONNNNN
She had beautiful, spiky, distinctive handwriting that I miss so much.
(a real handwriting sample from a list of her favorite quotes)
We have only this moment, sparkling like a star in our hand... and melting like a snowflake. Let us use it before it is too late.
– Marie Benyon
She was probably the most precise, detail-oriented person I've ever known.
I'm pretty nitpicky myself, but I could never match her precision.
Thanks, Maw
gluing on the cover of my book report so that the edges are even
Whenever I'd ask her how she got that way, she'd tell me she learned in "Mom School."
HOW TO GLUE THE COVER ONTO A HIGH SCHO BOOK REPOR SO THE EDGES ARE EVEN

My mom's precision extended to every part of her life, including some very specific food preferences.

| LOVES | | | INTENSE DISLIKES | | |
|---|---|---|---|---|---|
| key lime pie | vegetarian faux Buffalo wings | milky coffee | tea | cheesecake (or any sweet cheese thing) | sugar in coffee |
| caprese of all sorts | mushroom everything | calamari tentacles | celery | all olives | strawberry jam |

I have so many memories of eating yogurt or pudding as a kid and handing the cup to her when I was done so she could scrape the last bits into one last spoonful for me.

I always thought it looked like hair on a face

My mom was also an ABSOLUTE FANATIC about eyebrow maintenance.

For a long time she insisted on tweezing mine herself.

If you would JUST tweeze a FEW hairs every day, we wouldn't have to do all of this at ONCE!

OW

She was very artsy growing up, and in high school, she and a friend were named Most Creative in their class.

RHONDA HOFFMAN, coolest future mom

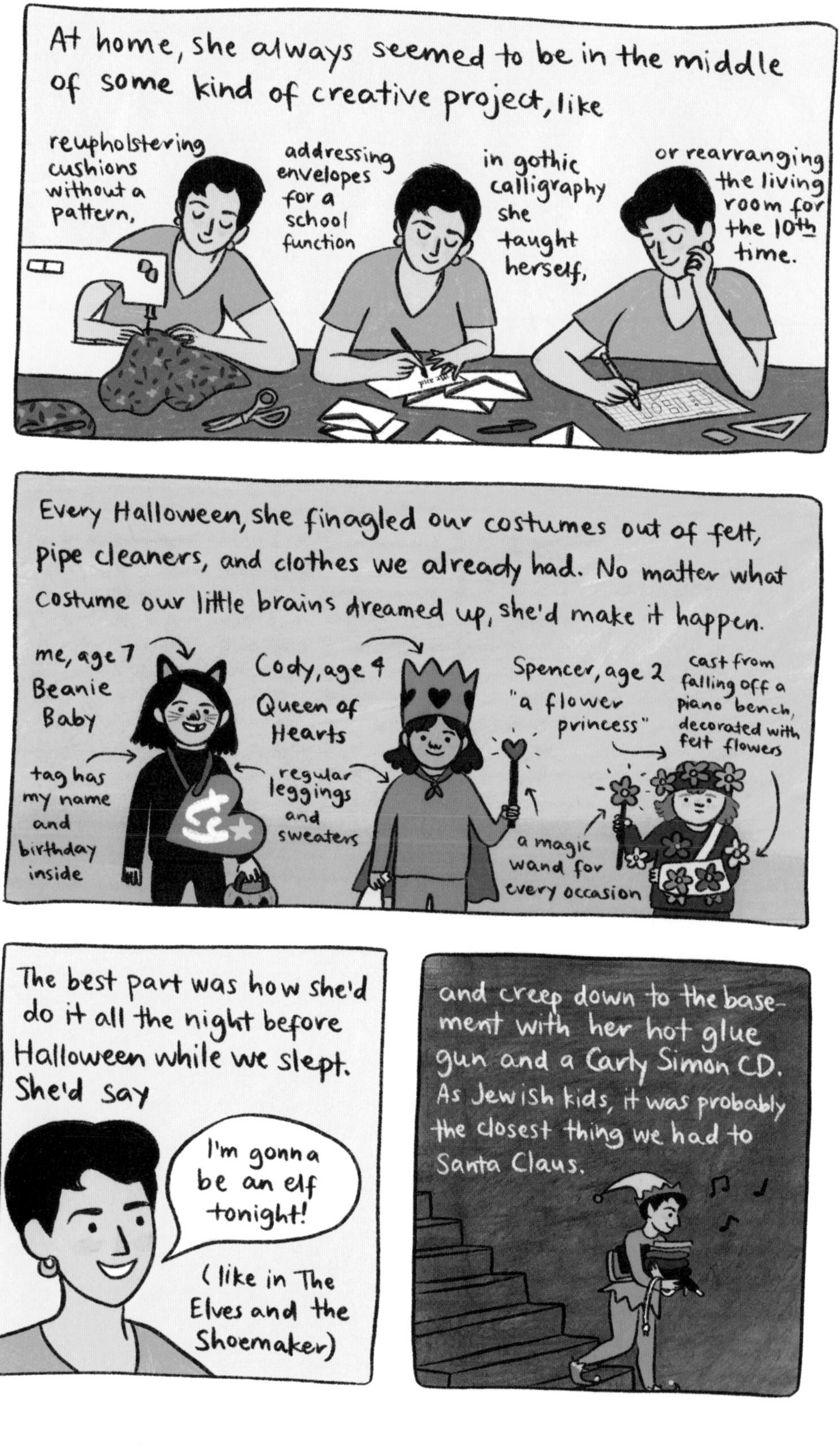
At home, she always seemed to be in the middle of some kind of creative project, like
reupholstering cushions without a pattern,
addressing envelopes for a school function
in gothic calligraphy she taught herself,
or rearranging the living room for the 10th time.
Every Halloween, she finagled our costumes out of felt, pipe cleaners, and clothes we already had. No matter what costume our little brains dreamed up, she'd make it happen.
me, age 7
Beanie Baby
tag has my name and birthday inside
Cody, age 4
Queen of Hearts
regular leggings and sweaters
Spencer, age 2
"a flower princess"
a magic wand for every occasion
cast from falling off a piano bench, decorated with felt flowers
The best part was how she'd do it all the night before Halloween while we slept. She'd say
I'm gonna be an elf tonight!
(like in The Elves and the Shoemaker)
and creep down to the basement with her hot glue gun and a Carly Simon CD. As Jewish kids, it was probably the closest thing we had to Santa Claus.

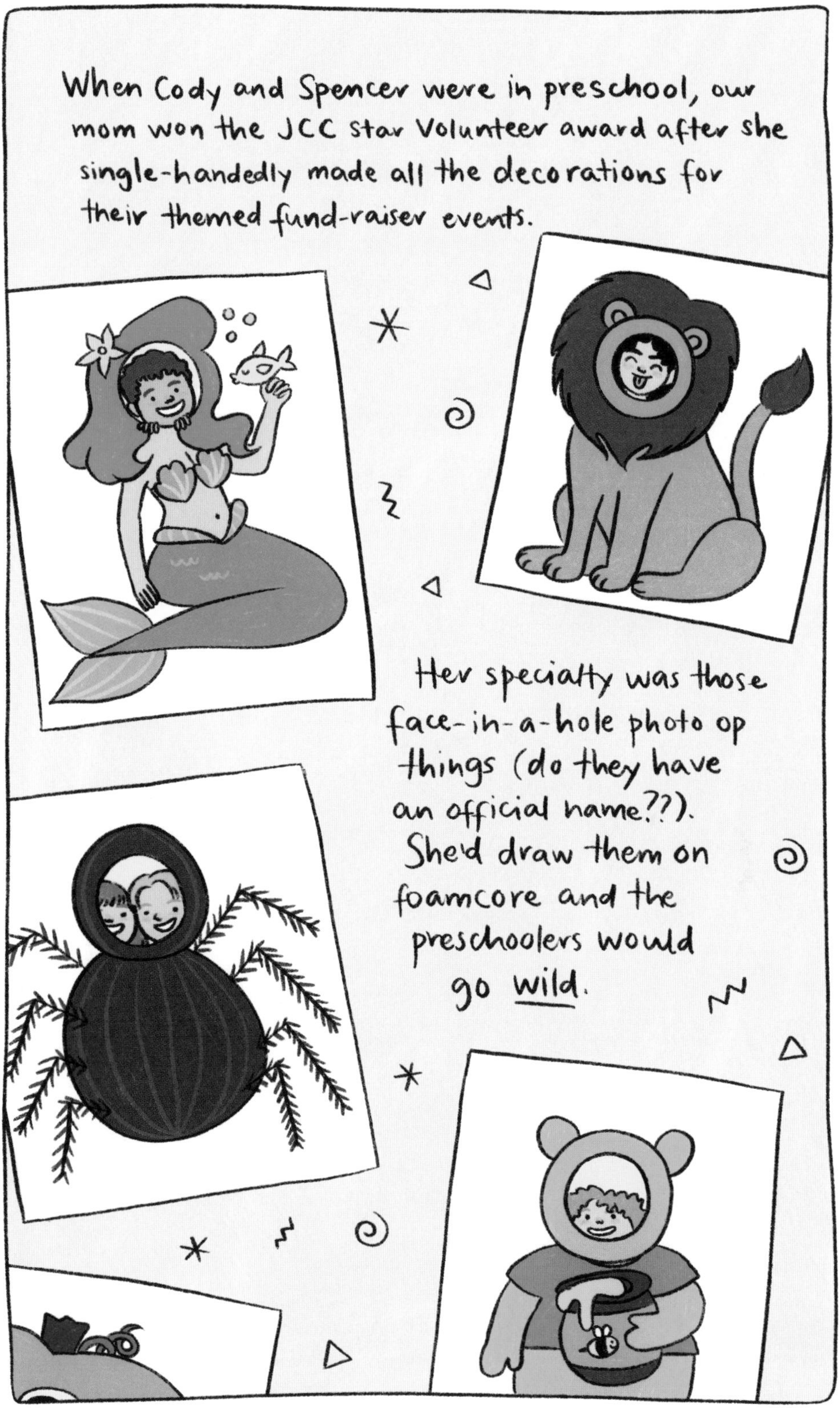
When Cody and Spencer were in preschool, our mom won the JCC Star Volunteer award after she single-handedly made all the decorations for their themed fund-raiser events.
Her specialty was those face-in-a-hole photo op things (do they have an official name??). She'd draw them on foamcore and the preschoolers would go wild.

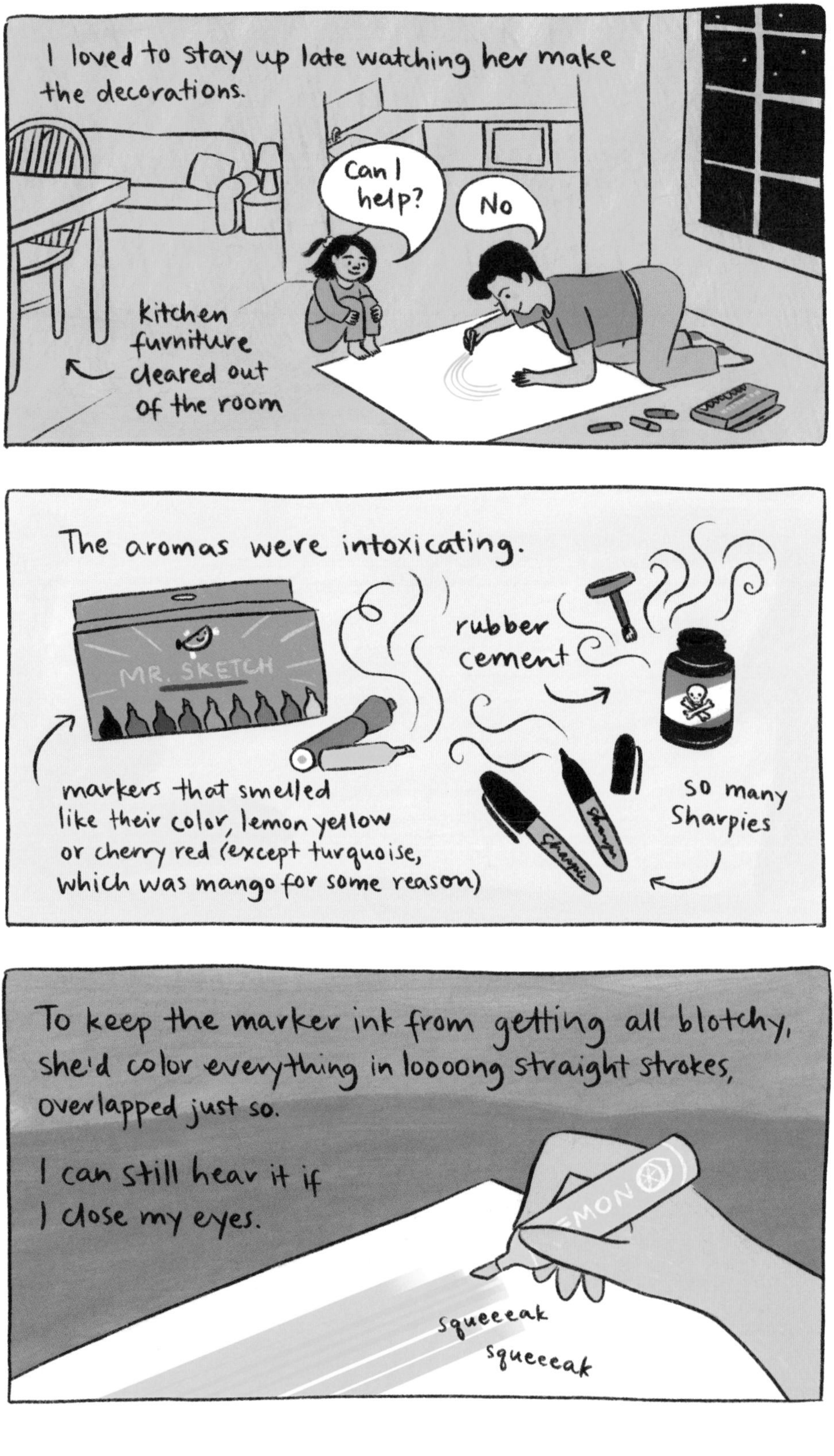
I loved to stay up late watching her make the decorations.
Can I help?
No
kitchen furniture cleared out of the room
The aromas were intoxicating.
MR. SKETCH
rubber cement
markers that smelled like their color, lemon yellow or cherry red (except turquoise, which was mango for some reason)
so many Sharpies
Sharpie
Sharpie
To keep the marker ink from getting all blotchy, she'd color everything in loooong straight strokes, overlapped just so.
I can still hear it if I close my eyes.
LEMON
squeeeak
squeeeak

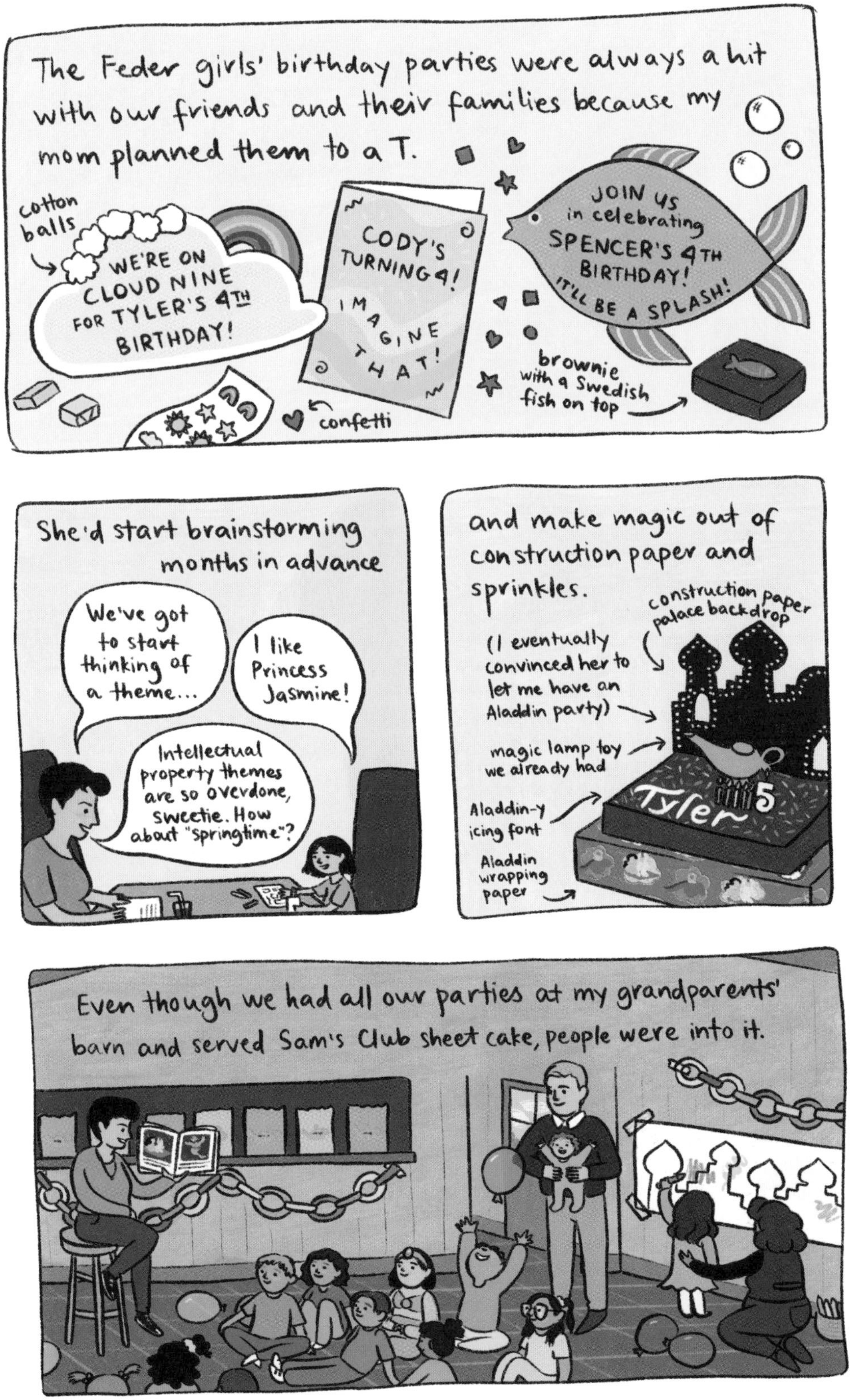

The Feder girls' birthday parties were always a hit with our friends and their families because my mom planned them to a T.
cotton balls
WE'RE ON CLOUD NINE FOR TYLER'S 4TH BIRTHDAY!
CODY'S TURNING 4! IMAGINE THAT!
JOIN US in celebrating SPENCER'S 4TH BIRTHDAY! IT'LL BE A SPLASH!
brownie with a Swedish fish on top
confetti
She'd start brainstorming months in advance
We've got to start thinking of a theme...
I like Princess Jasmine!
Intellectual property themes are so overdone, sweetie. How about "springtime"?
and make magic out of construction paper and sprinkles.
construction paper palace backdrop
(I eventually convinced her to let me have an Aladdin party)
magic lamp toy we already had
Aladdin-y icing font
Tyler 5
Aladdin wrapping paper
Even though we had all our parties at my grandparents' barn and served Sam's Club sheet cake, people were into it.

One of my favorite memories of my mom is the little morning routine we developed when I was in sixth grade. It was the only year I was in middle school while both my sisters were still in elementary school and I had to get up super early.

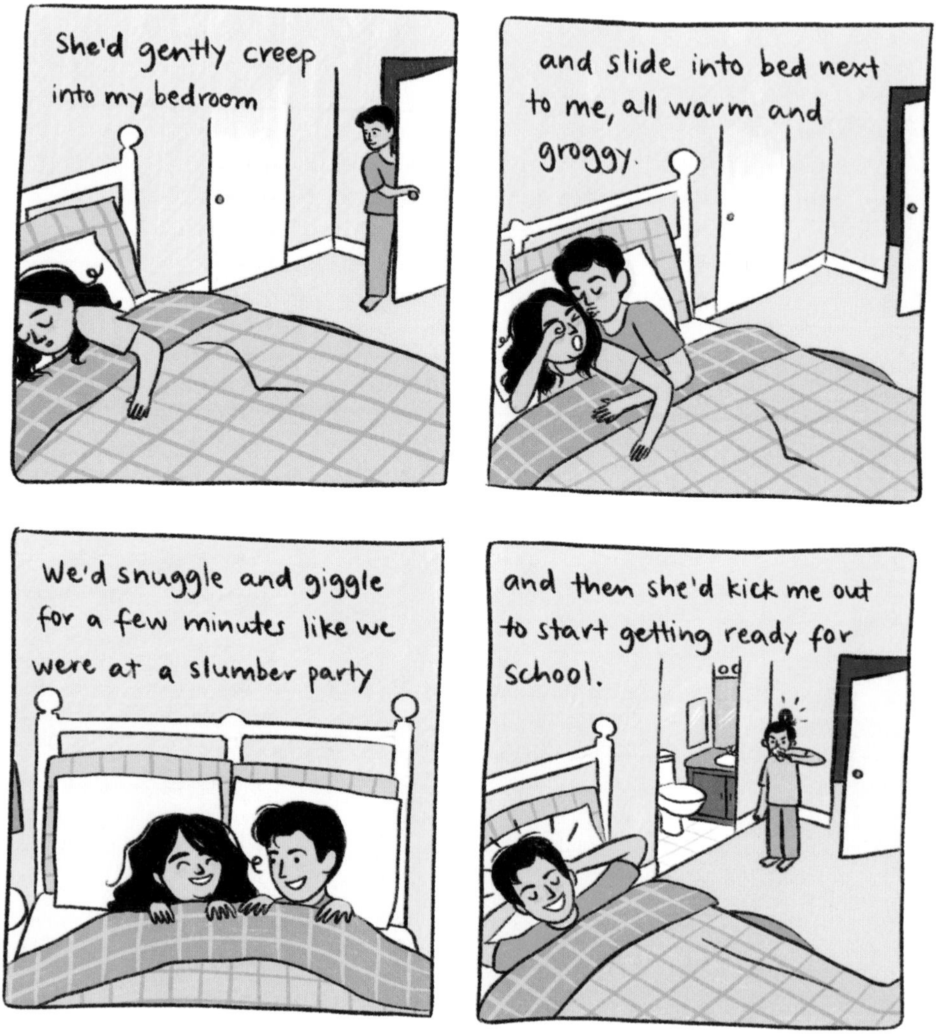
She'd gently creep into my bedroom
and slide into bed next to me, all warm and groggy.
We'd snuggle and giggle for a few minutes like we were at a slumber party
and then she'd kick me out to start getting ready for school.

It used to drive me bonkers but now it feels like a one-way train to METAPHOR CITY. ☹

My mom was mysterious and reassuring and so much fun and I would give anything to climb back under the covers with her. Ughhhhh!

# PEOPLE, REAL AND FICTIONAL (plus one cat), WHO REMIND ME OF MY MOM

WHO: Elizabeth James
(the mom from the 1998 Parent Trap)

actor Natasha Richardson died the same week as my mom!

WHY: she's elegant, creative, and a little mischievous

WHO: Duchess from The Aristocats

I'm Marie

WHY: she's gentle and comforting with 3 babies

WHO: Jamie Lee Curtis

my mom would have been so cute with this haircut

WHY: same spunky, short-haired vibe

WHO: Princess Diana

also died young!

WHY: she had a quiet warmth that put people at ease

WHO: Tina Fey

especially in old Second City photos omg

WHY: her dark eyes, pointy face, and sharp wit

WHO: Mary Poppins

my mom's favorite movie!

WHY: she's no-nonsense and silly at the same time

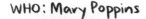

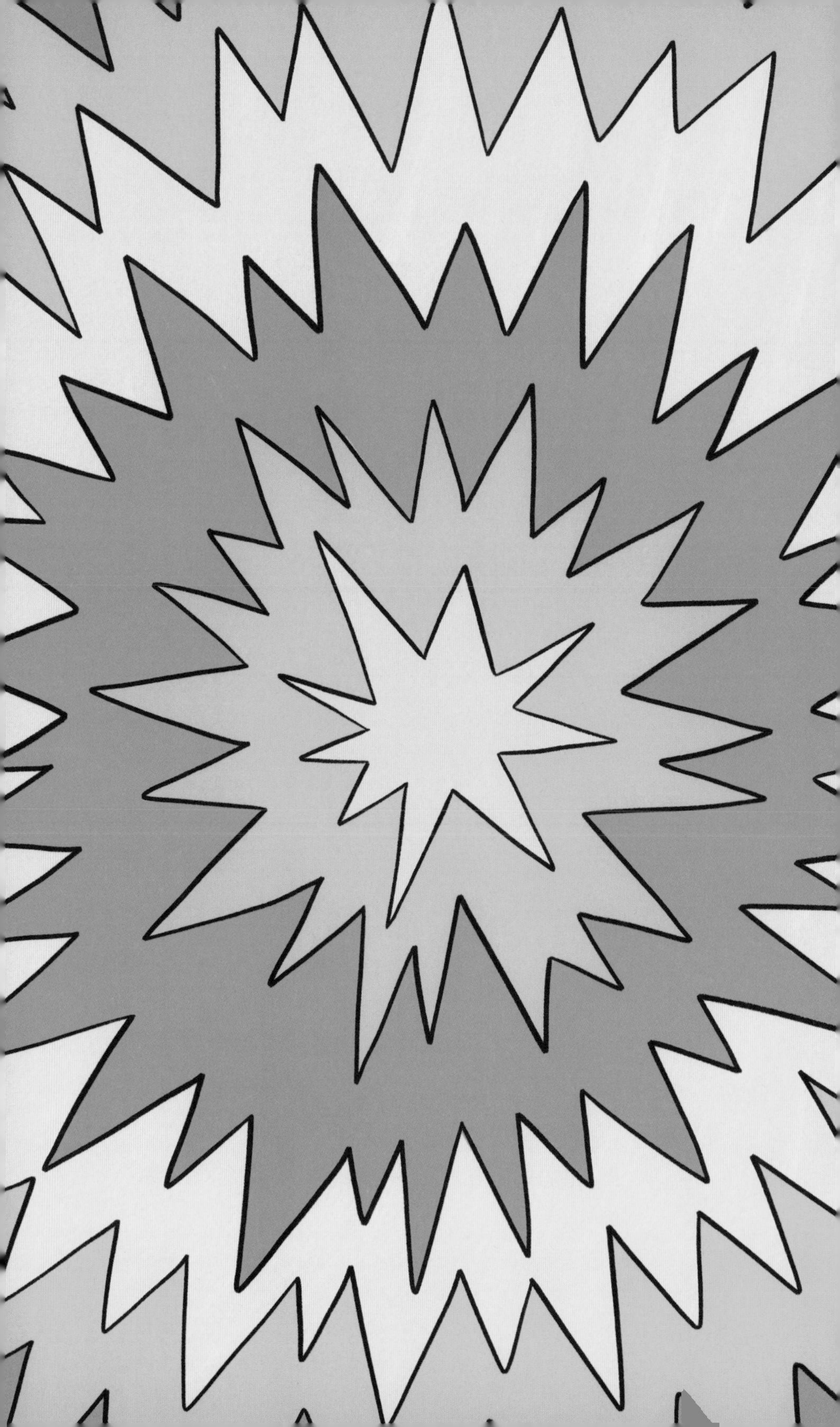

chapter two

UH-OH

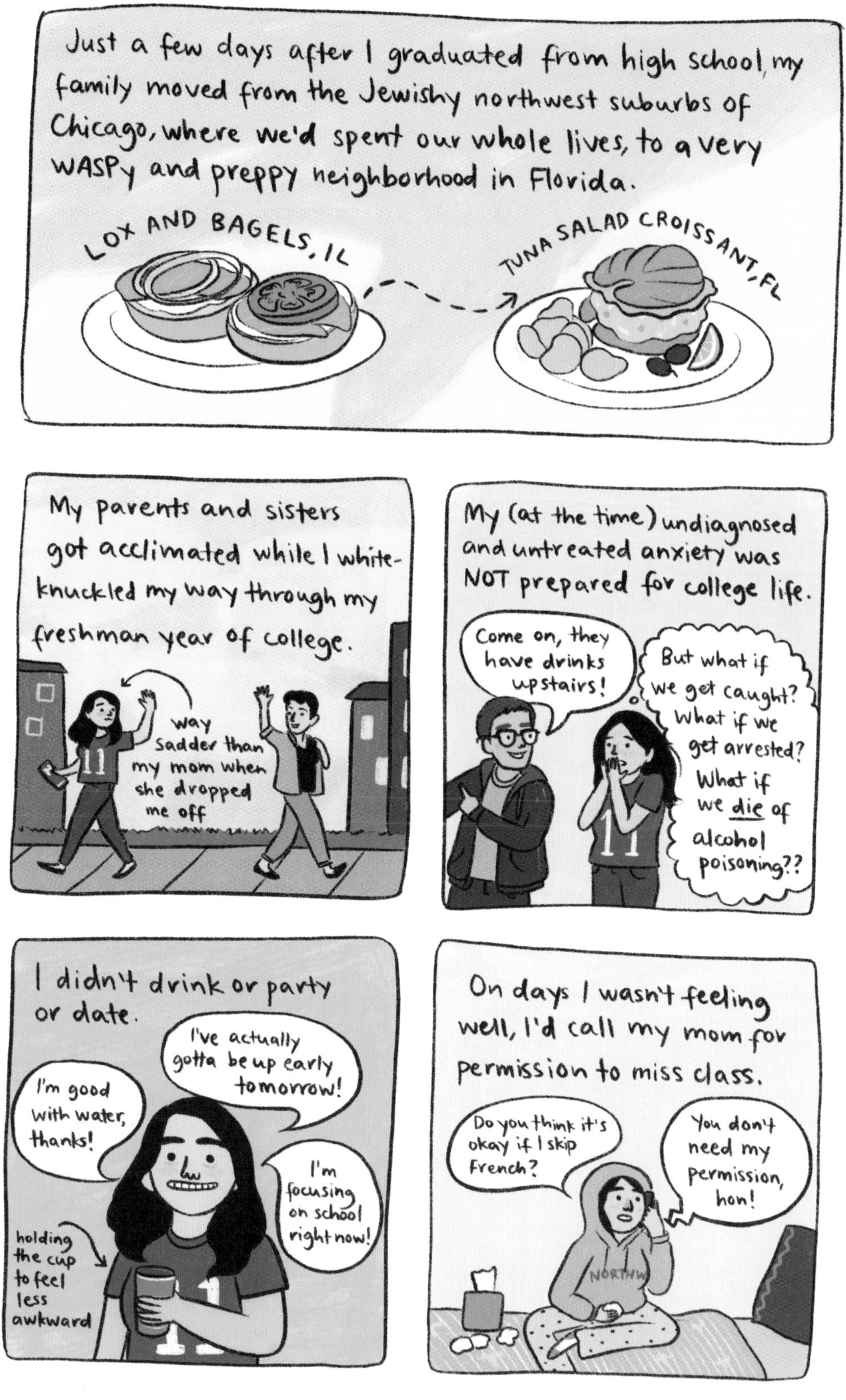
Just a few days after I graduated from high school, my family moved from the Jewishy northwest suburbs of Chicago, where we'd spent our whole lives, to a very WASPy and preppy neighborhood in Florida.
LOX AND BAGELS, IL
TUNA SALAD CROISSANT, FL
My parents and sisters got acclimated while I white-knuckled my way through my freshman year of college.
way sadder than my mom when she dropped me off
My (at the time) undiagnosed and untreated anxiety was NOT prepared for college life.
Come on, they have drinks upstairs!
But what if we get caught? What if we get arrested? What if we die of alcohol poisoning??
I didn't drink or party or date.
I've actually gotta be up early tomorrow!
I'm good with water, thanks!
I'm focusing on school right now!
holding the cup to feel less awkward
On days I wasn't feeling well, I'd call my mom for permission to miss class.
Do you think it's okay if I skip French?
You don't need my permission, hon!
NORTHW

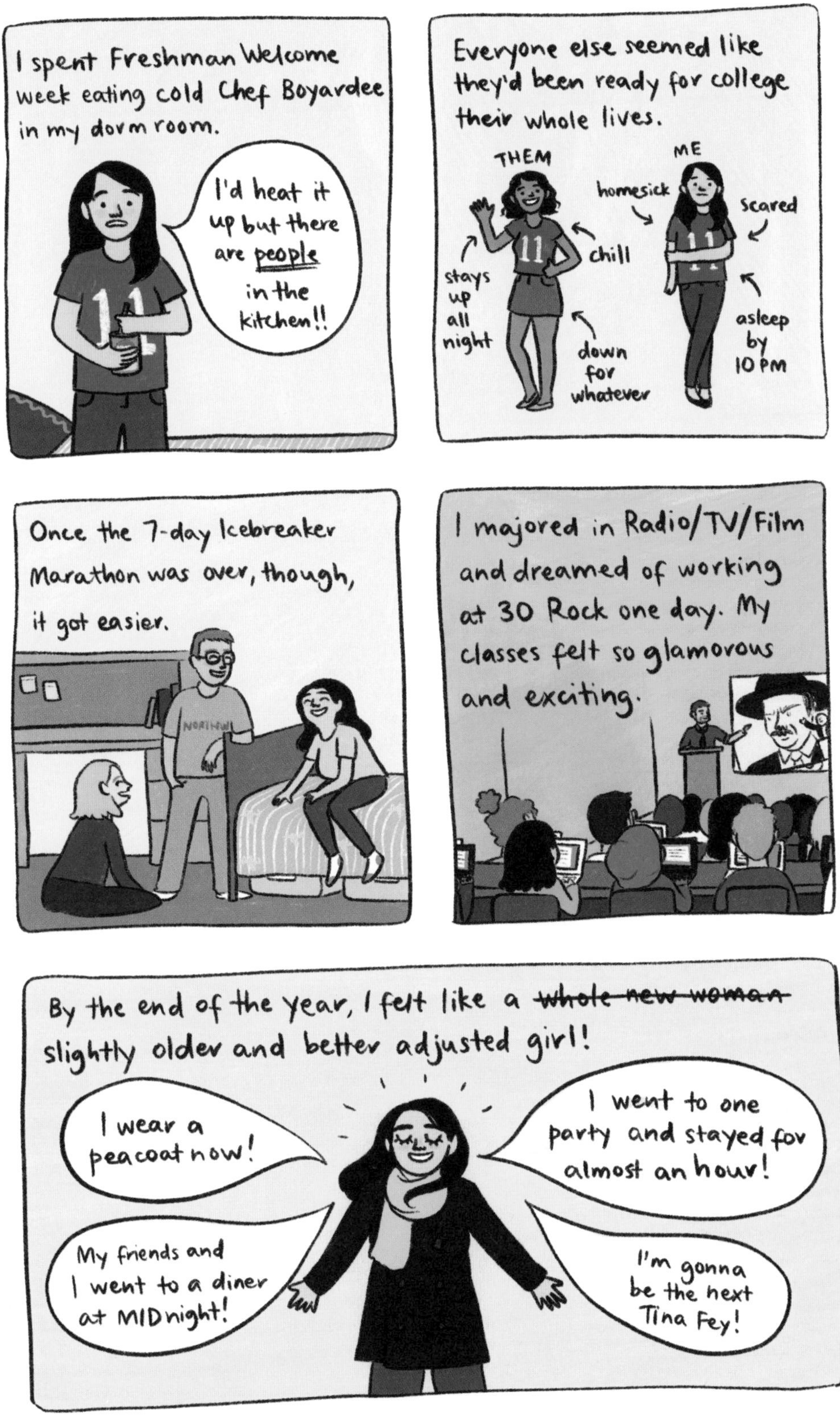

I spent Freshman Welcome week eating cold Chef Boyardee in my dorm room.
I'd heat it up but there are people in the kitchen!!
Everyone else seemed like they'd been ready for college their whole lives.
THEM
ME
stays up all night
chill
down for whatever
homesick
scared
asleep by 10 PM
Once the 7-day Icebreaker Marathon was over, though, it got easier.
I majored in Radio/TV/Film and dreamed of working at 30 Rock one day. My classes felt so glamorous and exciting.
By the end of the year, I felt like a ~~whole new woman~~ slightly older and better adjusted girl!
I wear a peacoat now!
I went to one party and stayed for almost an hour!
My friends and I went to a diner at MIDnight!
I'm gonna be the next Tina Fey!

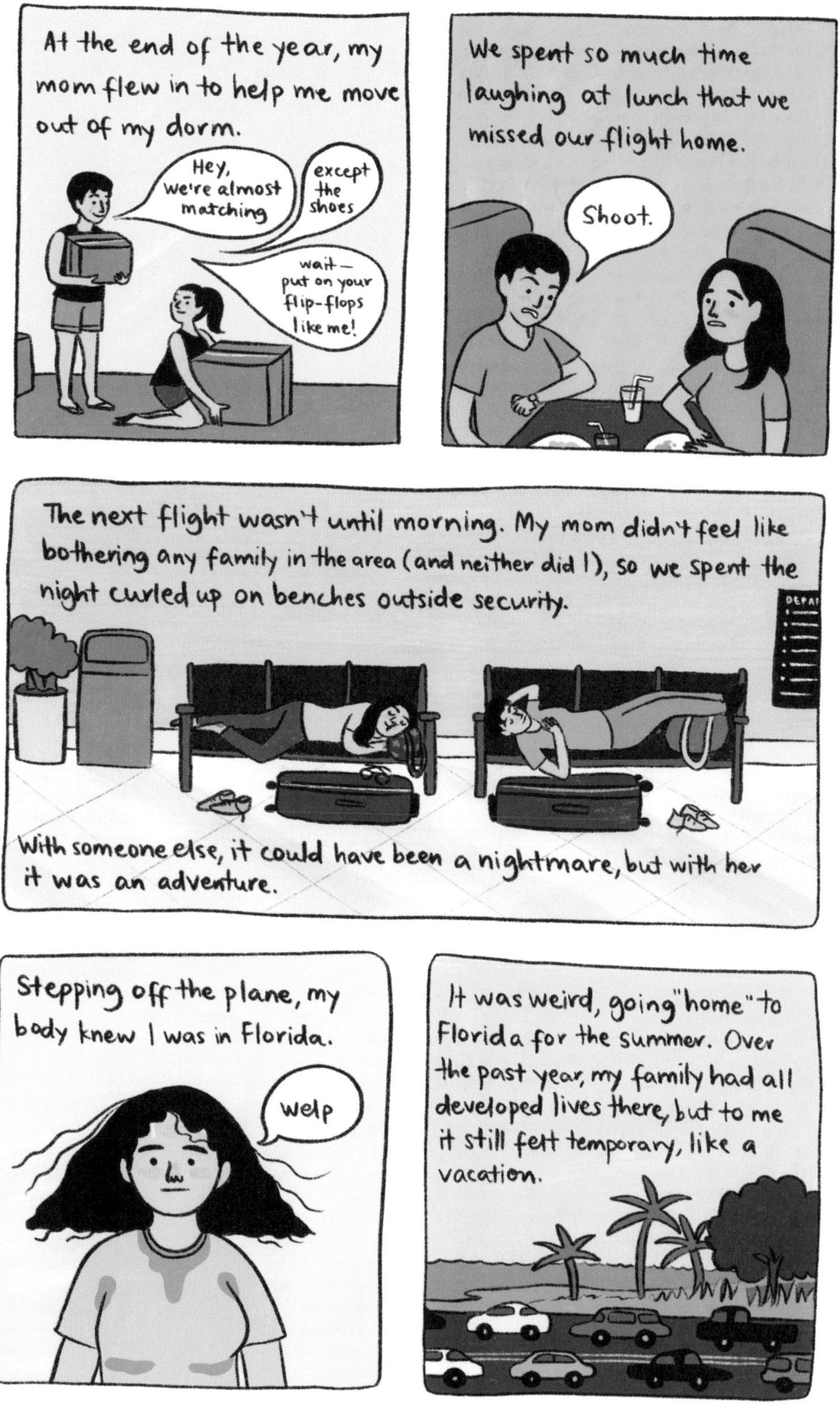
At the end of the year, my mom flew in to help me move out of my dorm.
Hey, we're almost matching
except the shoes
wait— put on your flip-flops like me!
We spent so much time laughing at lunch that we missed our flight home.
Shoot.
The next flight wasn't until morning. My mom didn't feel like bothering any family in the area (and neither did I), so we spent the night curled up on benches outside security.
With someone else, it could have been a nightmare, but with her it was an adventure.
Stepping off the plane, my body knew I was in Florida.
welp
It was weird, going "home" to Florida for the summer. Over the past year, my family had all developed lives there, but to me it still felt temporary, like a vacation.

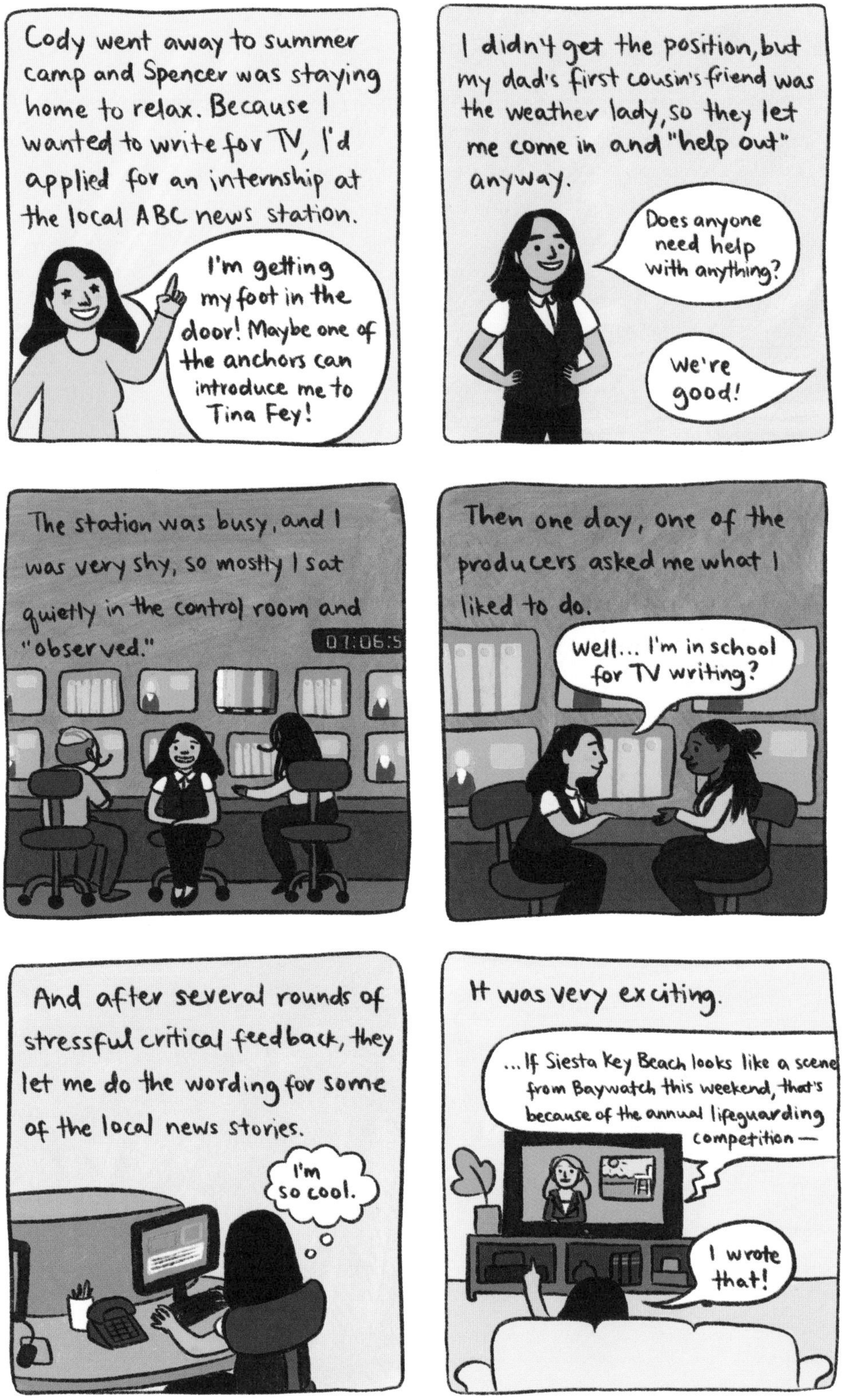
Cody went away to summer camp and Spencer was staying home to relax. Because I wanted to write for TV, I'd applied for an internship at the local ABC news station.
I'm getting my foot in the door! Maybe one of the anchors can introduce me to Tina Fey!
I didn't get the position, but my dad's first cousin's friend was the weather lady, so they let me come in and "help out" anyway.
Does anyone need help with anything?
We're good!
The station was busy, and I was very shy, so mostly I sat quietly in the control room and "observed."
Then one day, one of the producers asked me what I liked to do.
Well... I'm in school for TV writing?
And after several rounds of stressful critical feedback, they let me do the wording for some of the local news stories.
I'm so cool.
It was very exciting.
...If Siesta Key Beach looks like a scene from Baywatch this weekend, that's because of the annual lifeguarding competition—
I wrote that!

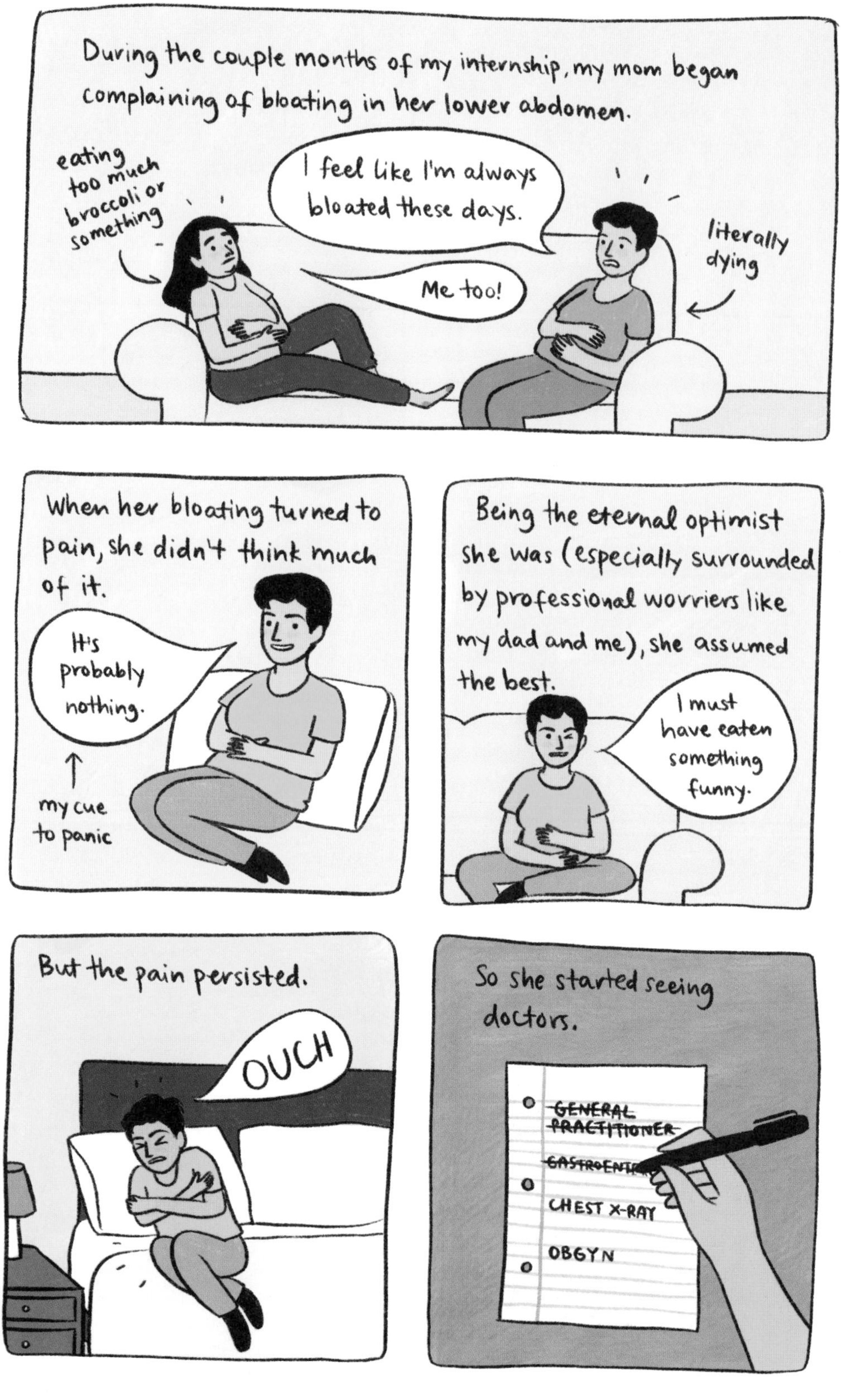
During the couple months of my internship, my mom began complaining of bloating in her lower abdomen.
I feel like I'm always bloated these days.
eating too much broccoli or something
Me too!
literally dying
When her bloating turned to pain, she didn't think much of it.
It's probably nothing.
my cue to panic
Being the eternal optimist she was (especially surrounded by professional worriers like my dad and me), she assumed the best.
I must have eaten something funny.
But the pain persisted.
OUCH
So she started seeing doctors.
GENERAL PRACTITIONER
GASTROENT
CHEST X-RAY
OBGYN

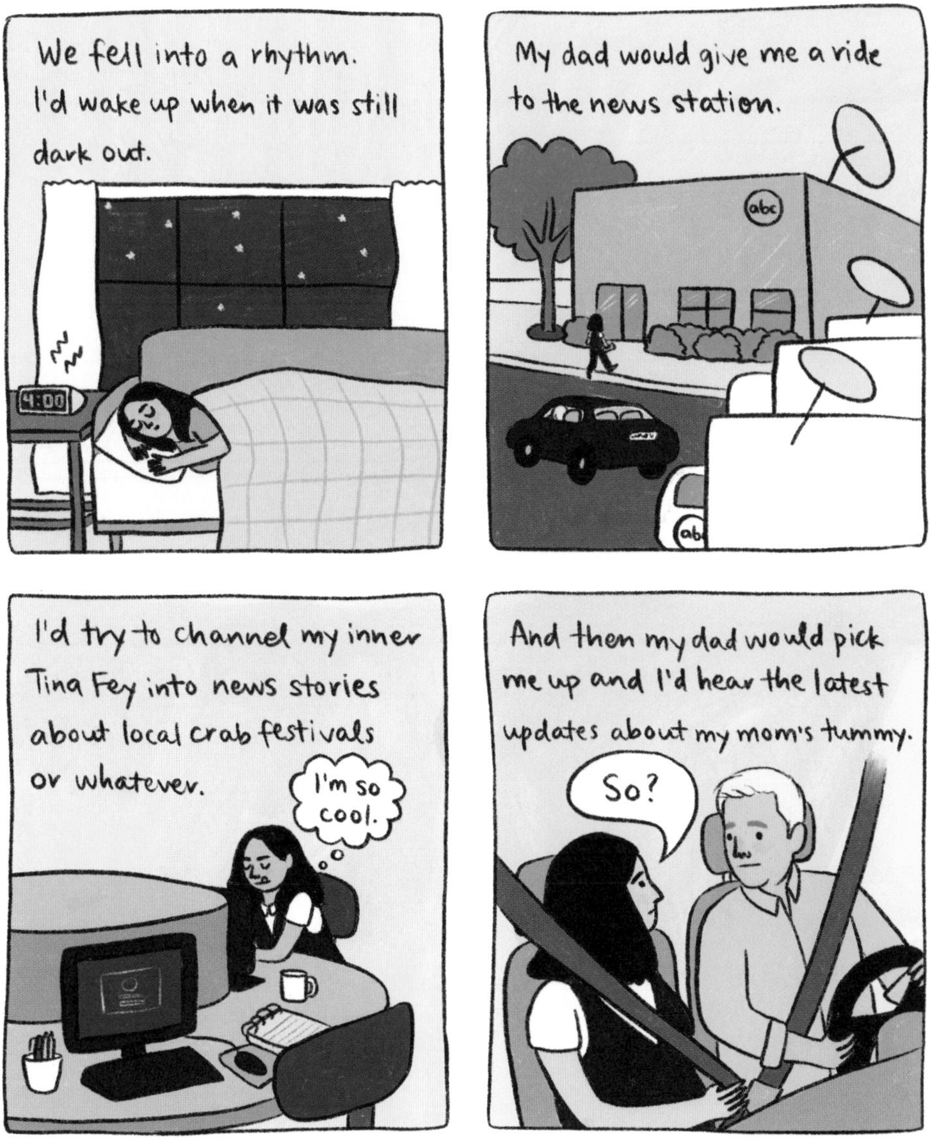
We fell into a rhythm. I'd wake up when it was still dark out.
4:00
My dad would give me a ride to the news station.
abc
I'd try to channel my inner Tina Fey into news stories about local crab festivals or whatever.
I'm so cool.
And then my dad would pick me up and I'd hear the latest updates about my mom's tummy.
So?

First, a doctor thought she had some sort of digestive problem. Then a different doctor wondered if she'd broken a rib somehow.

It was all white noise, you know? Maybe it was just an infection. Maybe she was allergic to this or that. Maybe she had an easily manageable condition.

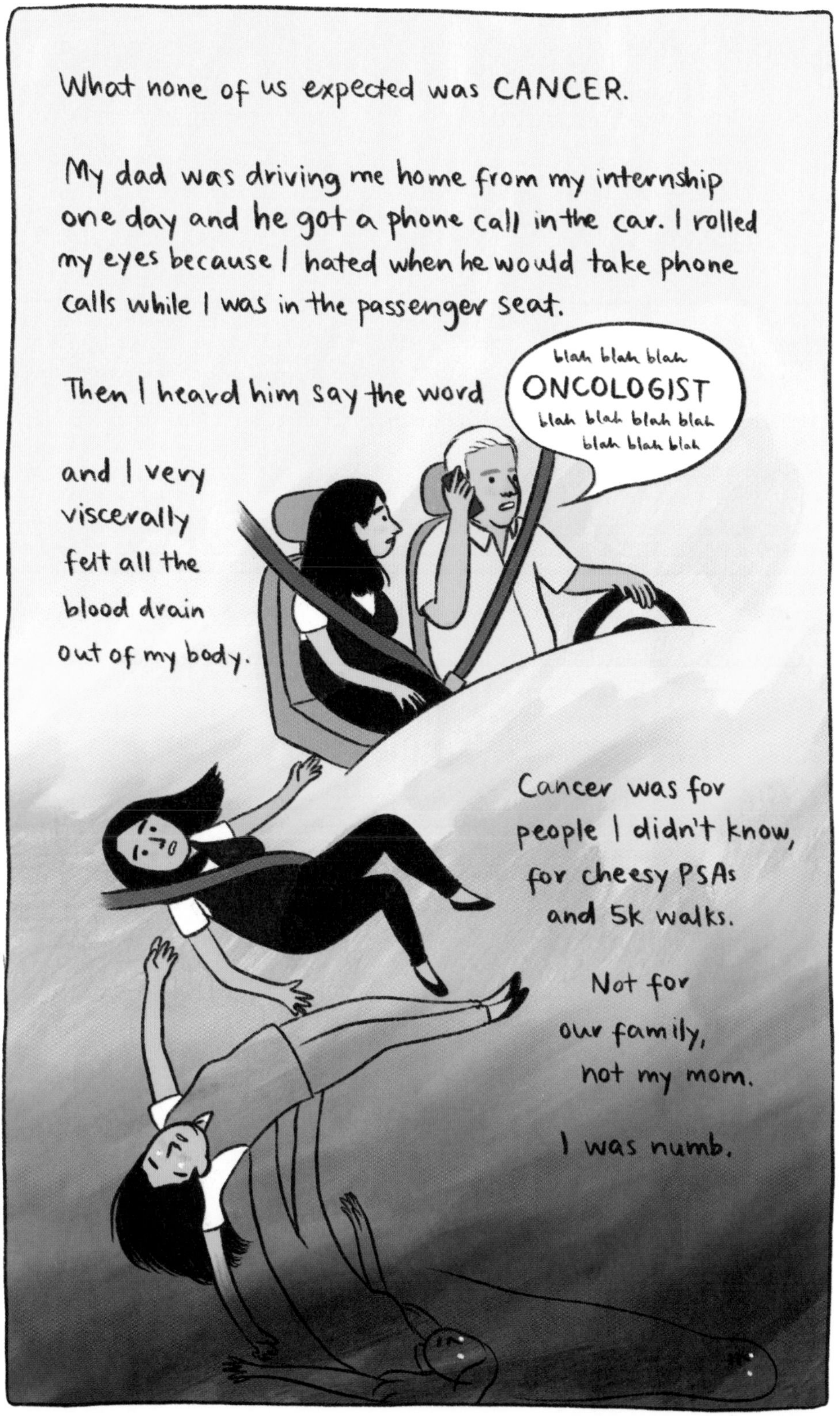
What none of us expected was CANCER.
My dad was driving me home from my internship one day and he got a phone call in the car. I rolled my eyes because I hated when he would take phone calls while I was in the passenger seat.
Then I heard him say the word
blah blah blah ONCOLOGIST blah blah blah blah blah blah blah
and I very viscerally felt all the blood drain out of my body.
Cancer was for people I didn't know, for cheesy PSAs and 5k walks.
Not for our family, not my mom.
I was numb.

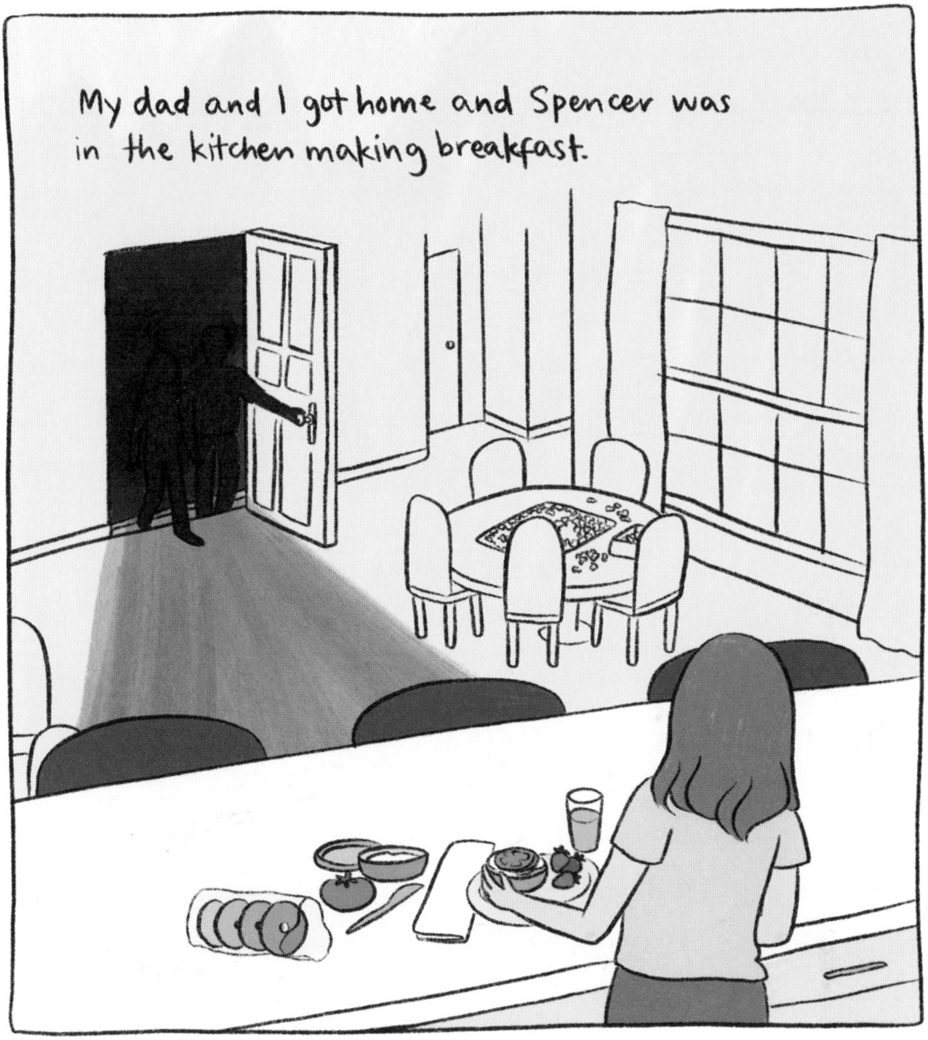
My dad and I got home and Spencer was in the kitchen making breakfast.

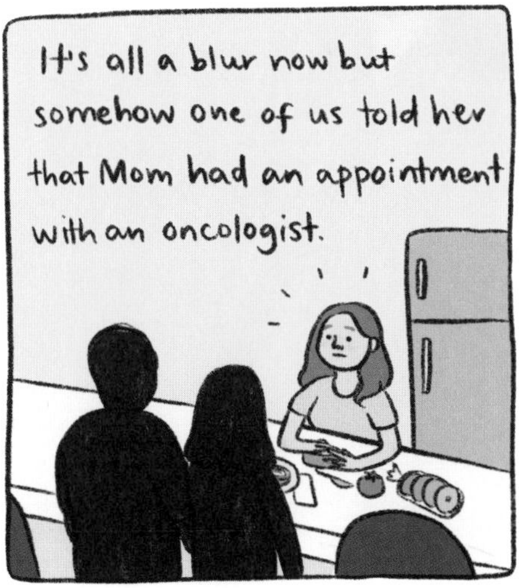
It's all a blur now but somehow one of us told her that Mom had an appointment with an oncologist.

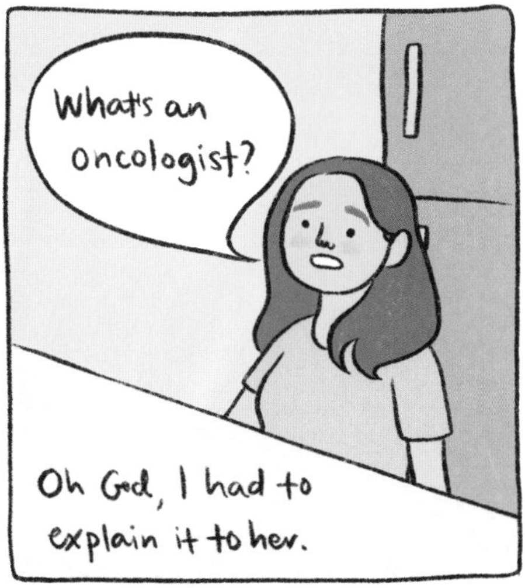
What's an oncologist?
Oh God, I had to explain it to her.

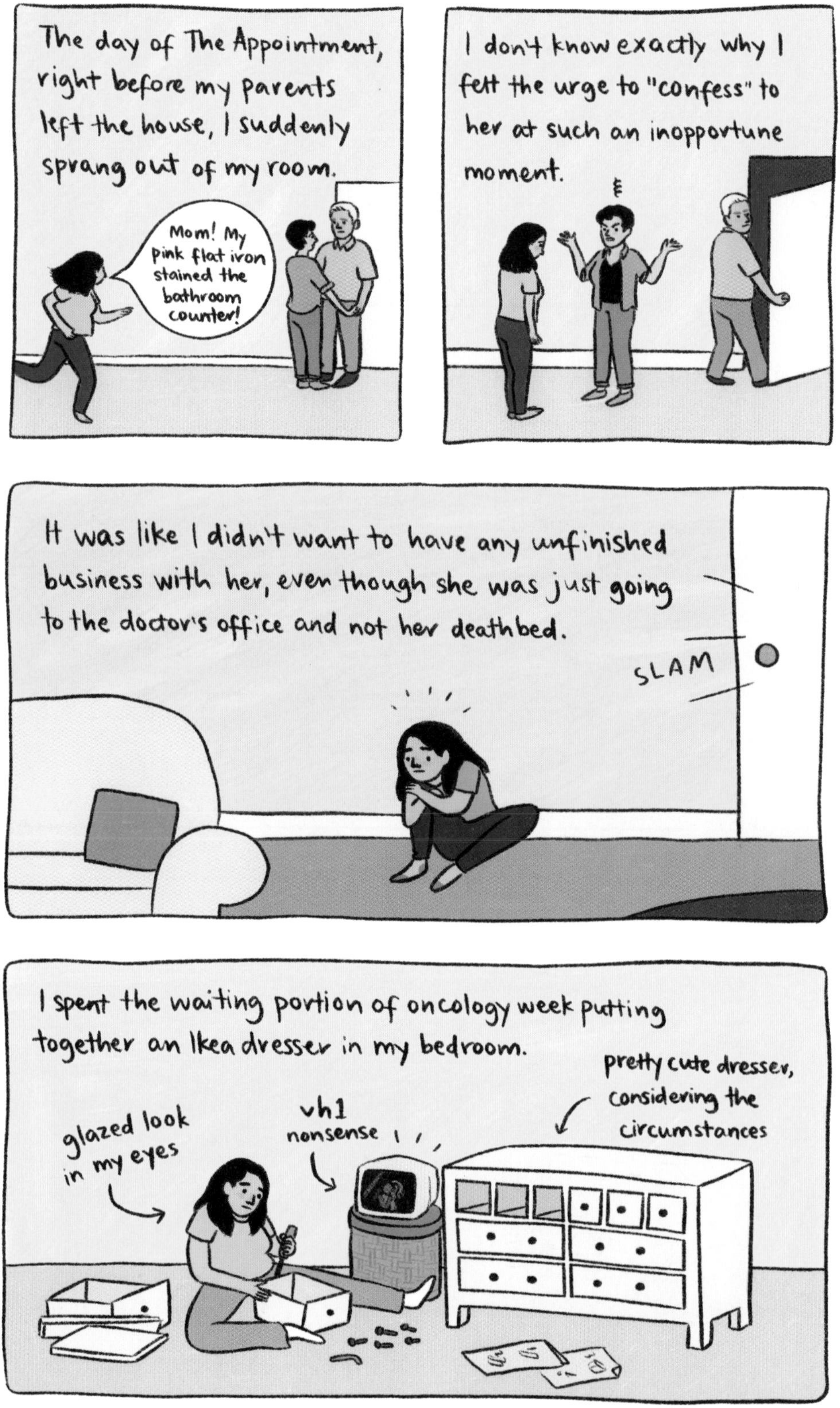
The day of The Appointment, right before my parents left the house, I suddenly sprang out of my room.
Mom! My pink flat iron stained the bathroom counter!
I don't know exactly why I felt the urge to "confess" to her at such an inopportune moment.
It was like I didn't want to have any unfinished business with her, even though she was just going to the doctor's office and not her deathbed.
SLAM
I spent the waiting portion of oncology week putting together an Ikea dresser in my bedroom.
glazed look in my eyes
vh1 nonsense
pretty cute dresser, considering the circumstances

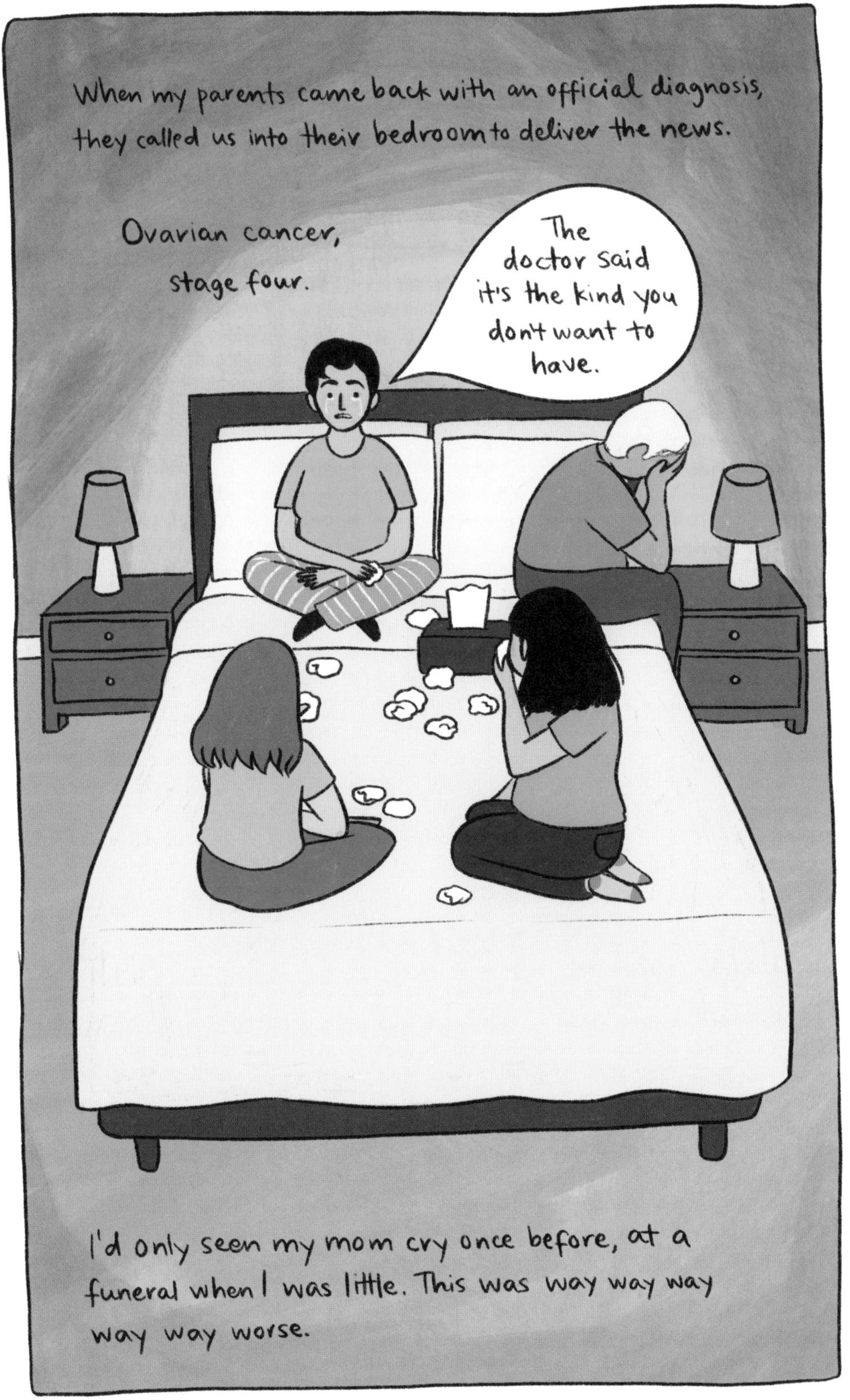
When my parents came back with an official diagnosis, they called us into their bedroom to deliver the news.
Ovarian cancer, stage four.
The doctor said it's the kind you don't want to have.
I'd only seen my mom cry once before, at a funeral when I was little. This was way way way way way worse.

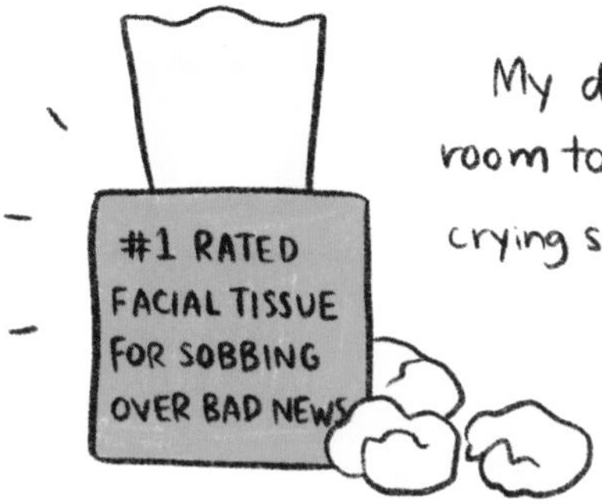
#1 RATED
FACIAL TISSUE
FOR SOBBING
OVER BAD NEWS

My dad and Spencer left the room to process, and I stayed behind, crying softly into my mom's shoulder.

We sat there in silence for a while.

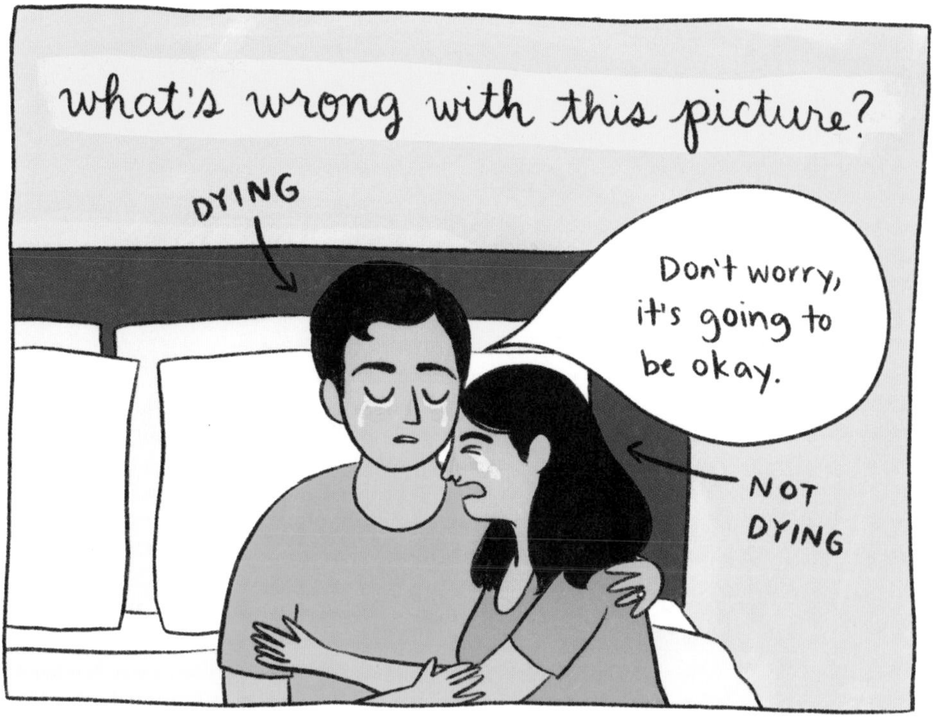
what's wrong with this picture?
DYING
Don't worry, it's going to be okay.
NOT DYING

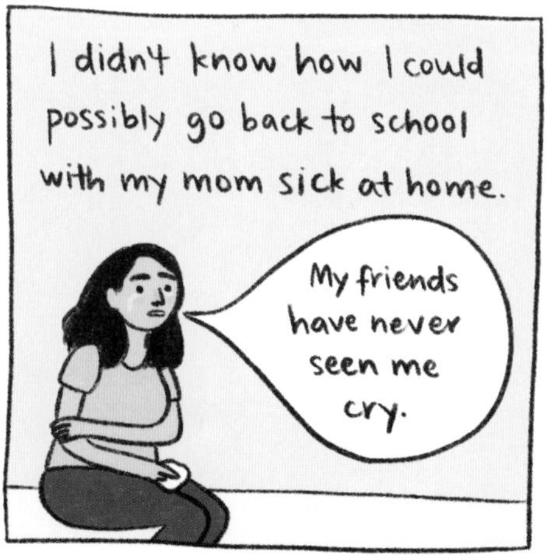
I didn't know how I could possibly go back to school with my mom sick at home.
My friends have never seen me cry.

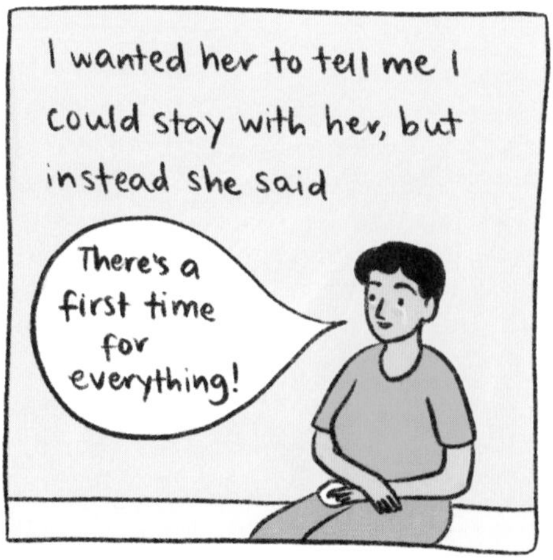
I wanted her to tell me I could stay with her, but instead she said
There's a first time for everything!

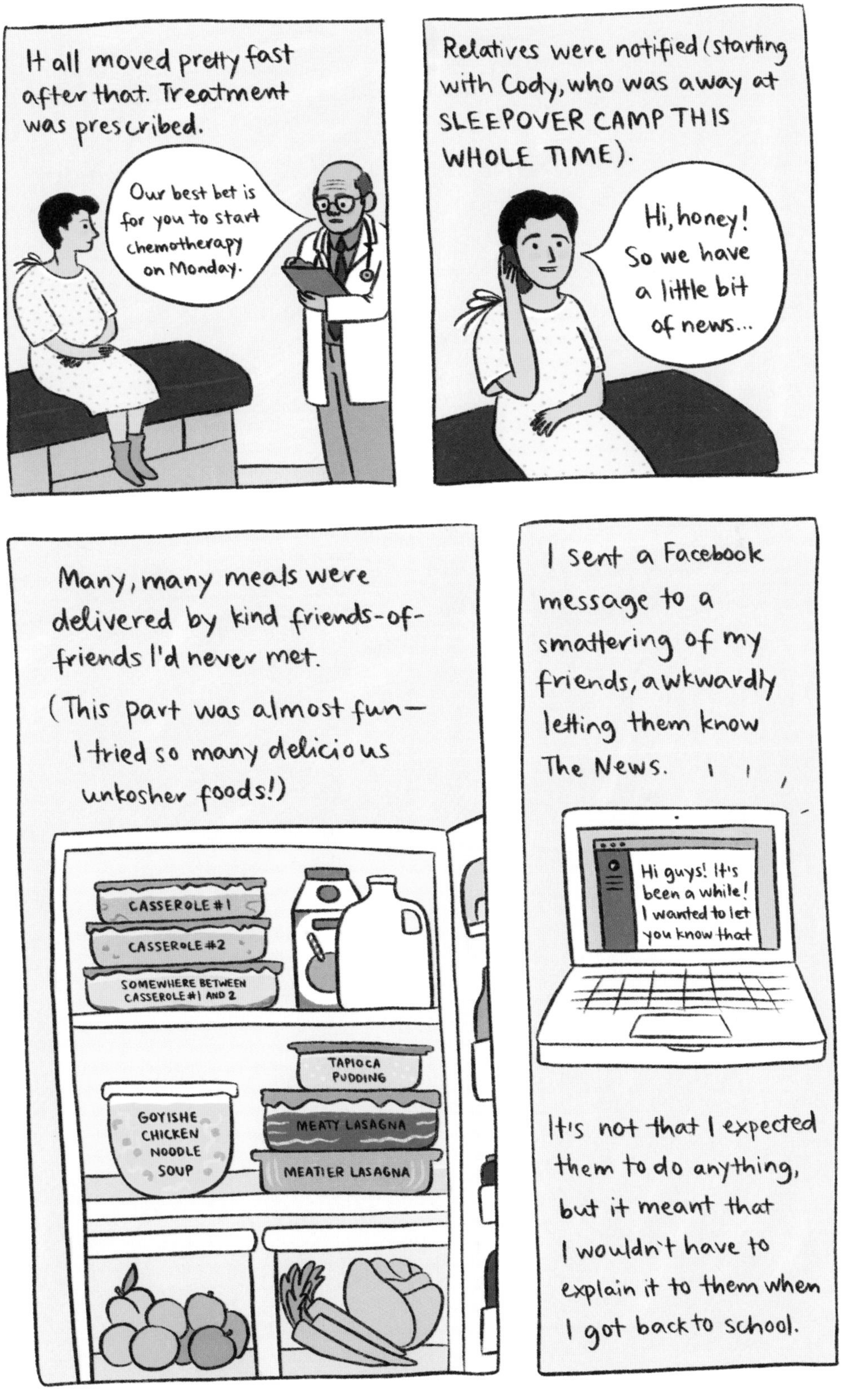
It all moved pretty fast after that. Treatment was prescribed.
Our best bet is for you to start chemotherapy on Monday.
Relatives were notified (starting with Cody, who was away at SLEEPOVER CAMP THIS WHOLE TIME).
Hi, honey! So we have a little bit of news...
Many, many meals were delivered by kind friends-of-friends I'd never met.
(This part was almost fun— I tried so many delicious unkosher foods!)
CASSEROLE #1
CASSEROLE #2
SOMEWHERE BETWEEN CASSEROLE #1 AND 2
TAPIOCA PUDDING
GOYISHE CHICKEN NOODLE SOUP
MEATY LASAGNA
MEATIER LASAGNA
I sent a Facebook message to a smattering of my friends, awkwardly letting them know The News.
Hi guys! It's been a while! I wanted to let you know that
It's not that I expected them to do anything, but it meant that I wouldn't have to explain it to them when I got back to school.

The news was so devastating to hear the first time that I was terrified I'd momentarily forget and have to re-remember.

To try to keep that from happening, I'd remind myself during every moment of quiet.

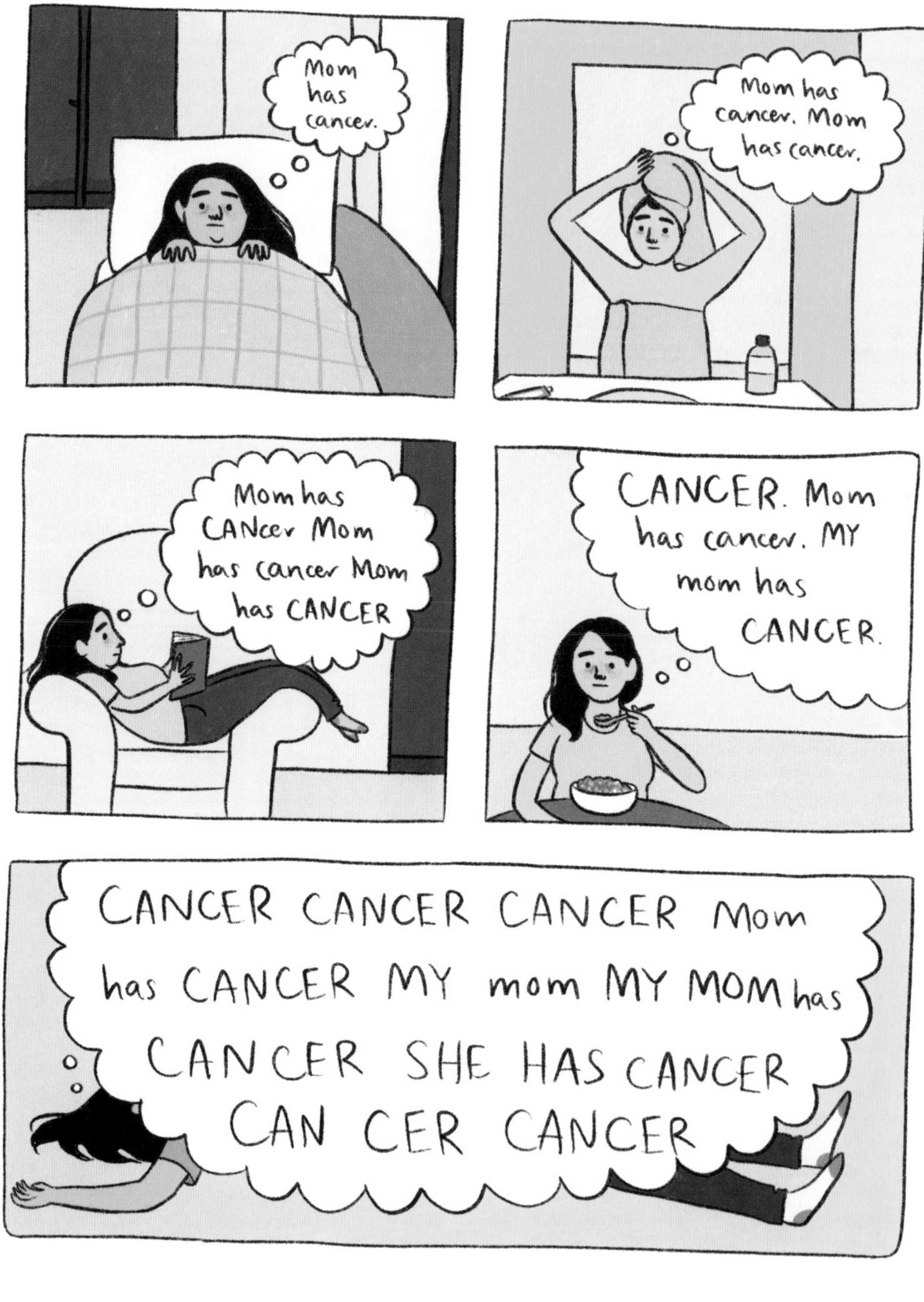
Mom has cancer.
Mom has cancer. Mom has cancer.
Mom has CANcer Mom has cancer Mom has CANCER
CANCER. Mom has cancer. MY mom has CANCER.
CANCER CANCER CANCER Mom has CANCER MY mom MY MOM has CANCER SHE HAS CANCER CAN CER CANCER

# how to make a good cry A GREAT CRY

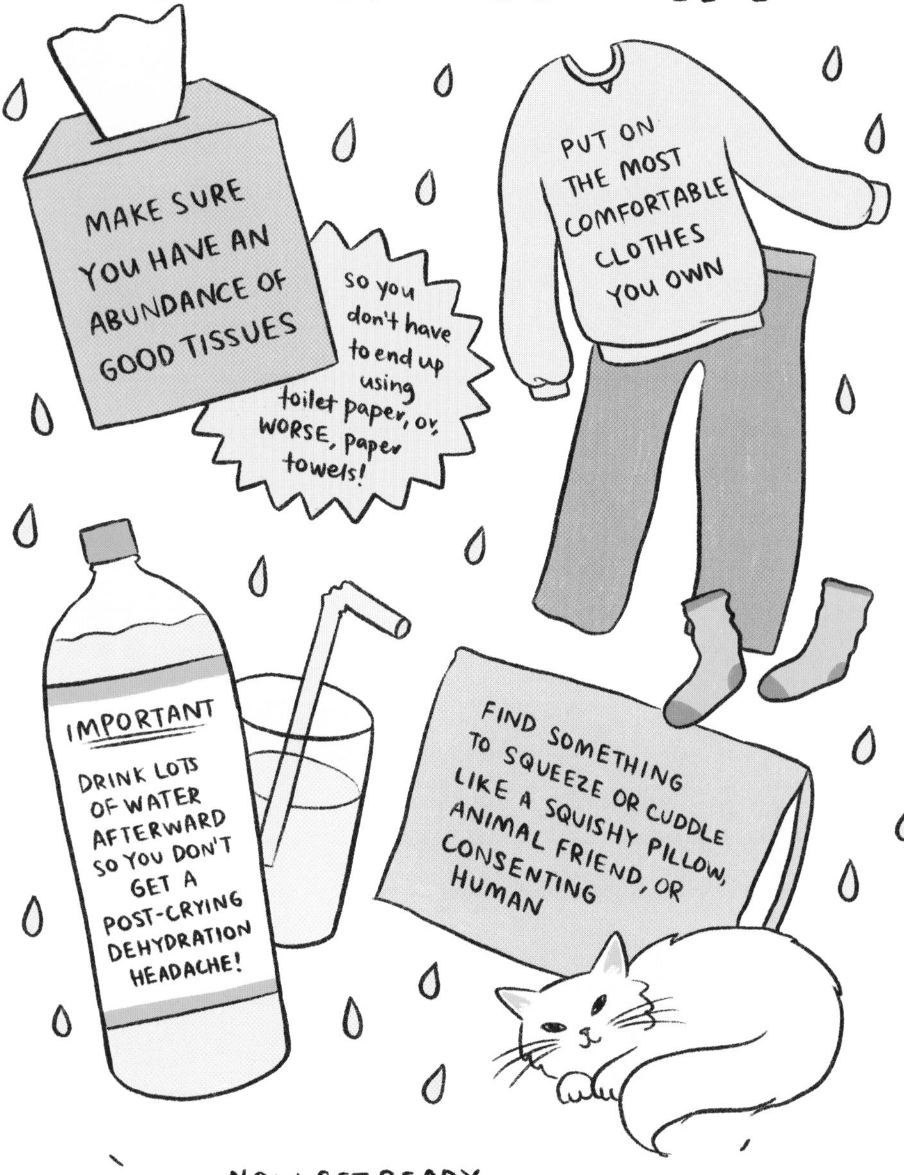
MAKE SURE YOU HAVE AN ABUNDANCE OF GOOD TISSUES
so you don't have to end up using toilet paper, or, WORSE, paper towels!
PUT ON THE MOST COMFORTABLE CLOTHES YOU OWN
IMPORTANT
DRINK LOTS OF WATER AFTERWARD SO YOU DON'T GET A POST-CRYING DEHYDRATION HEADACHE!
FIND SOMETHING TO SQUEEZE OR CUDDLE LIKE A SQUISHY PILLOW, ANIMAL FRIEND, OR CONSENTING HUMAN

NOW GET READY FOR THOSE SWEET, SWEET ENDORPHINS!

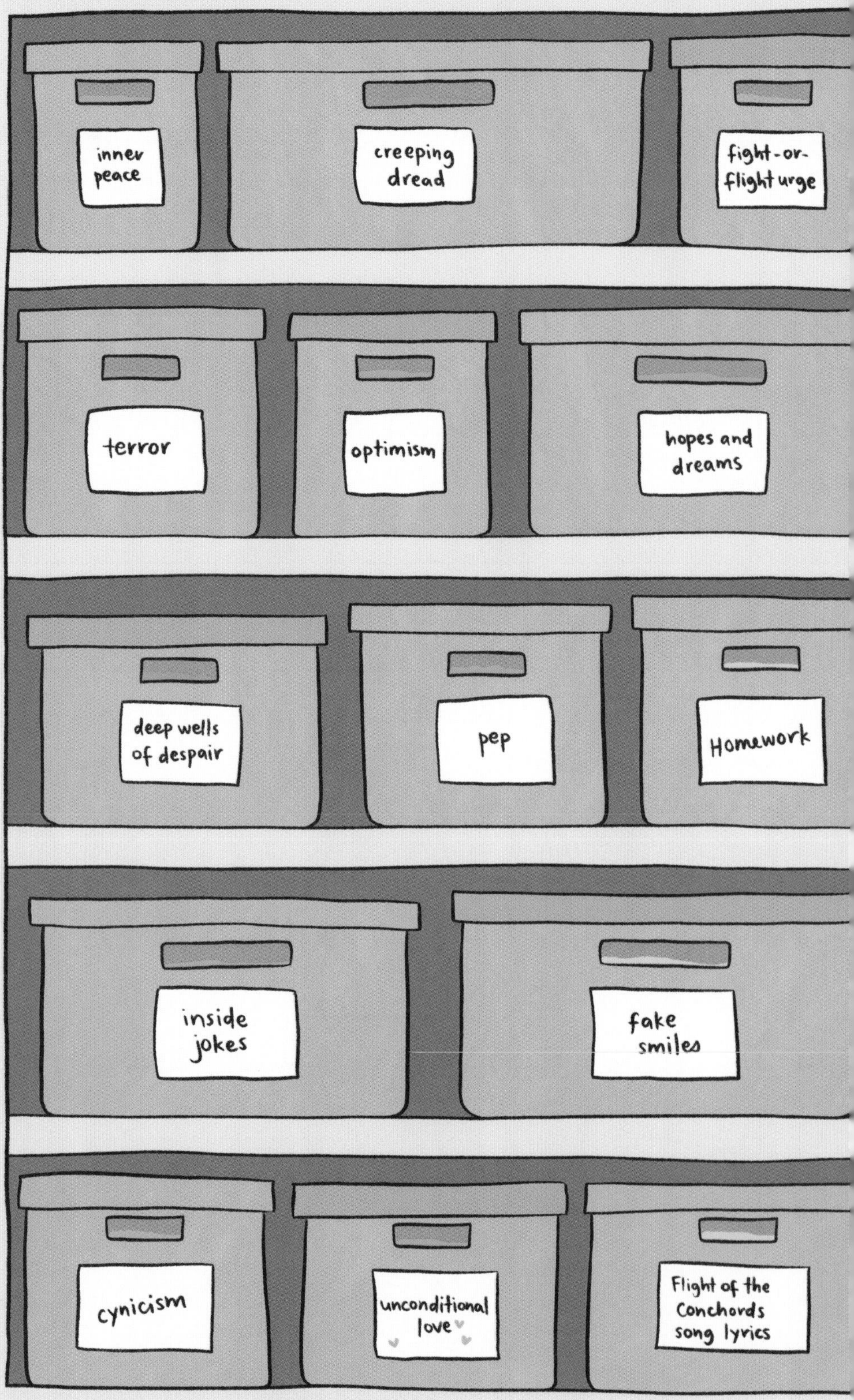
inner peace
creeping dread
fight-or-flight urge
terror
optimism
hopes and dreams
deep wells of despair
pep
Homework
inside jokes
fake smiles
cynicism
unconditional love
Flight of the Conchords song lyrics

*chapter three*

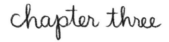

COMPARTMENTALIZATION

As a previously non-cancer family, all the trappings of cancer were completely new to us.

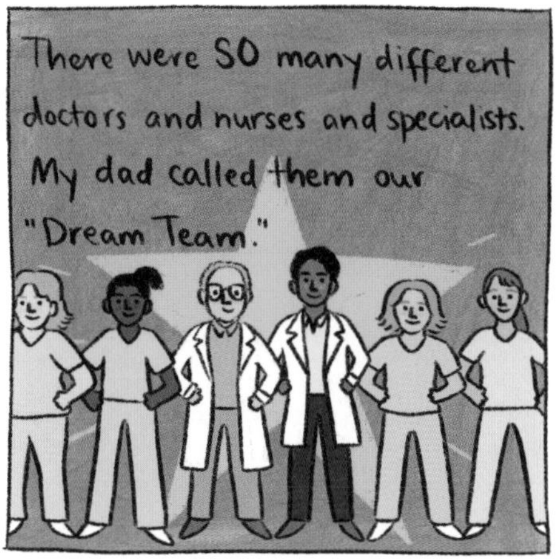
There were SO many different doctors and nurses and specialists. My dad called them our "Dream Team."

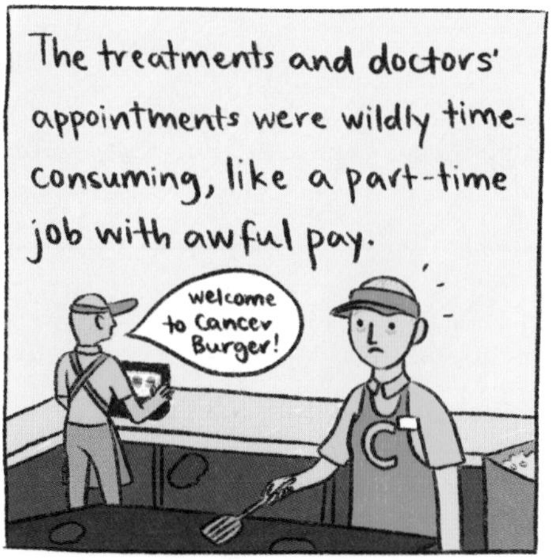
The treatments and doctors' appointments were wildly time-consuming, like a part-time job with awful pay.
welcome to Cancer Burger!

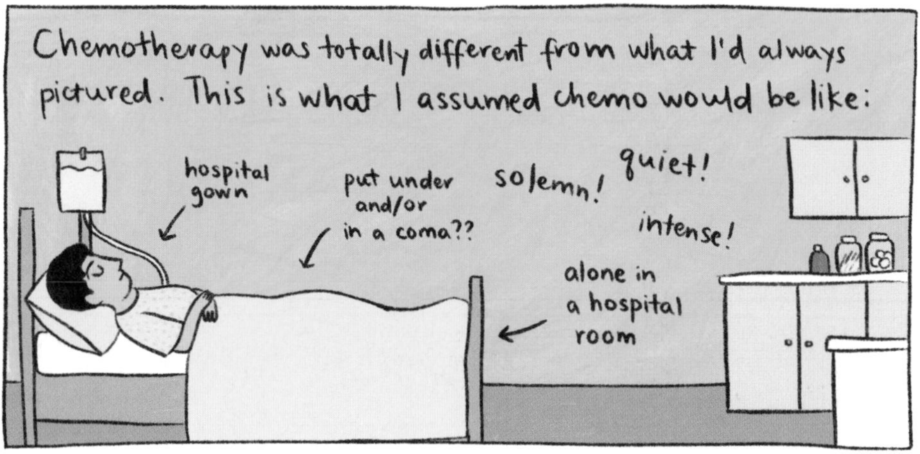
Chemotherapy was totally different from what I'd always pictured. This is what I assumed chemo would be like:
hospital gown
put under and/or in a coma??
solemn!
quiet!
intense!
alone in a hospital room

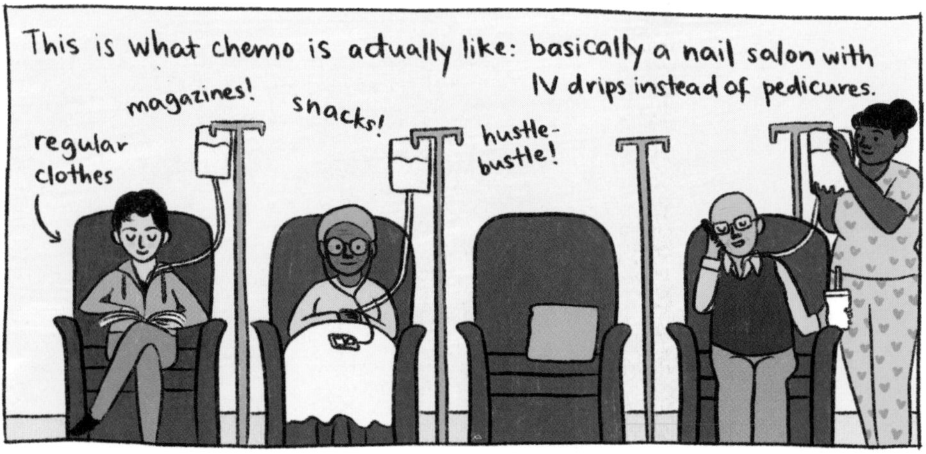
This is what chemo is actually like: basically a nail salon with IV drips instead of pedicures.
magazines!
snacks!
hustle-bustle!
regular clothes

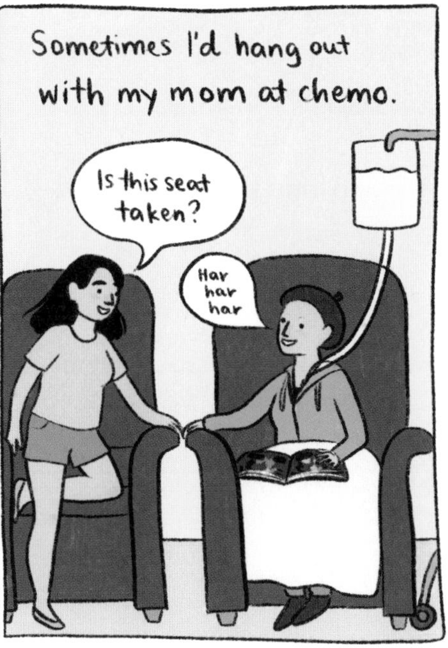
Sometimes I'd hang out with my mom at chemo.
Is this seat taken?
Har har har

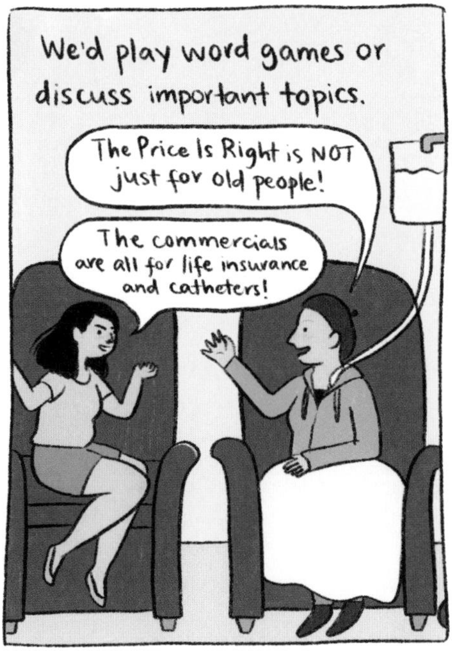
We'd play word games or discuss important topics.
The commercials are all for life insurance and catheters!
The Price Is Right is NOT just for old people!

FUN FACT!

## CHEMOTHERAPY IS POISON!

It targets and kills all fast-growing cells, the bad ones (cancer) and the good ones too (like hair). Can't get rid of the bad without also getting rid of the good (Hey! Another metaphor!).

Often, it's the side effects of the chemo, even more than the cancer itself, that make a person with cancer _feel_ sick.

My mom got so many side effects so quickly:

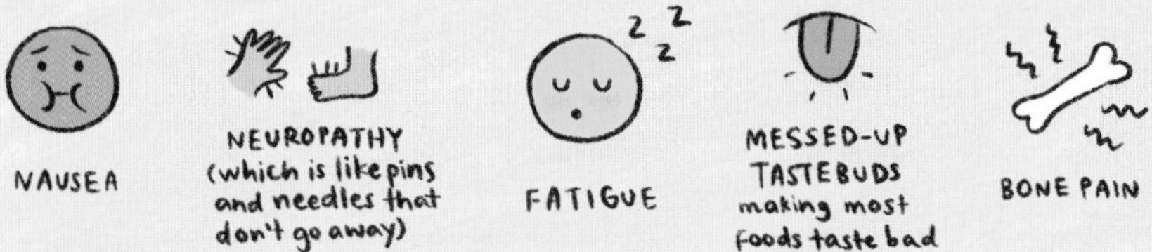
z z z

NAUSEA

NEUROPATHY (which is like pins and needles that don't go away)

FATIGUE

MESSED-UP TASTEBUDS making most foods taste bad

BONE PAIN

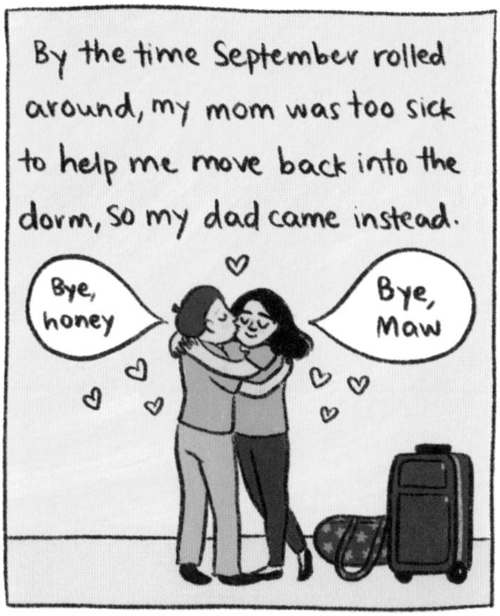
By the time September rolled around, my mom was too sick to help me move back into the dorm, so my dad came instead.
Bye, honey
Bye, Maw

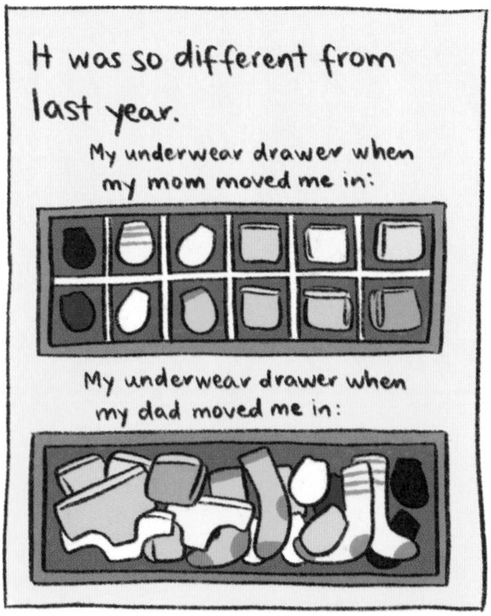
It was so different from last year.
My underwear drawer when my mom moved me in:
My underwear drawer when my dad moved me in:

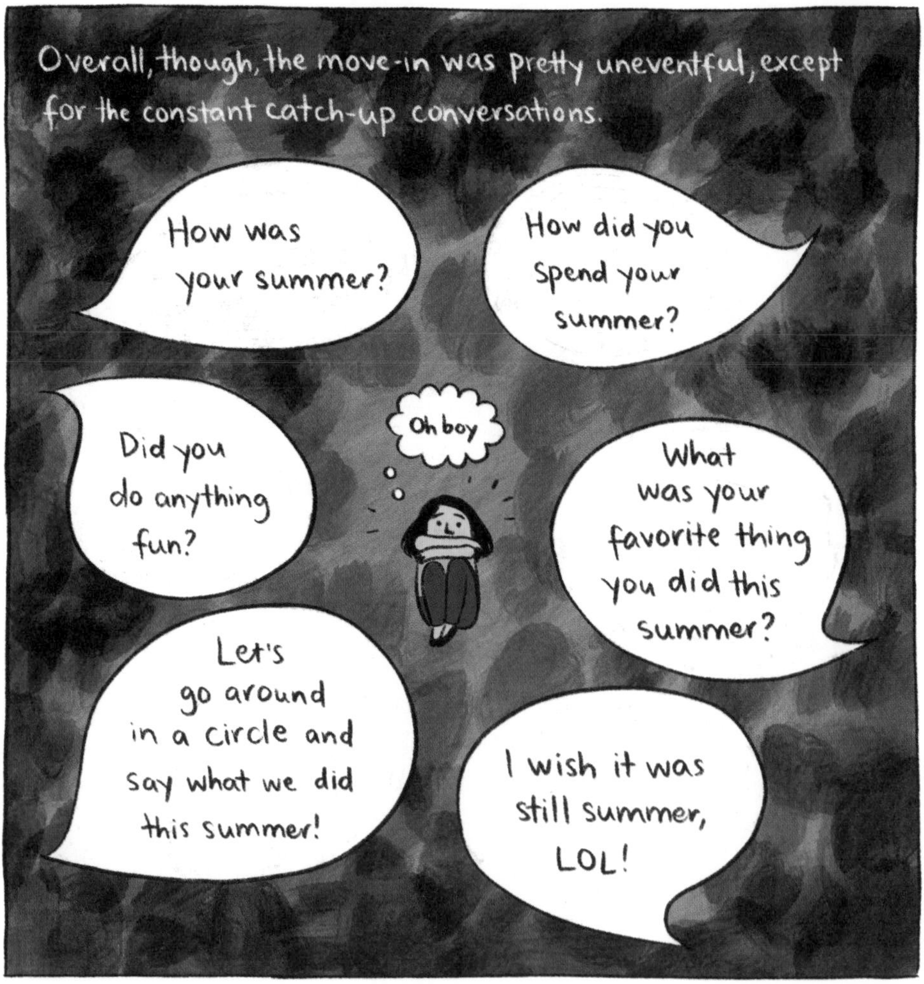
Overall, though, the move-in was pretty uneventful, except for the constant catch-up conversations.
How was your summer?
How did you spend your summer?
Did you do anything fun?
Oh boy
What was your favorite thing you did this summer?
Let's go around in a circle and say what we did this summer!
I wish it was still summer, LOL!

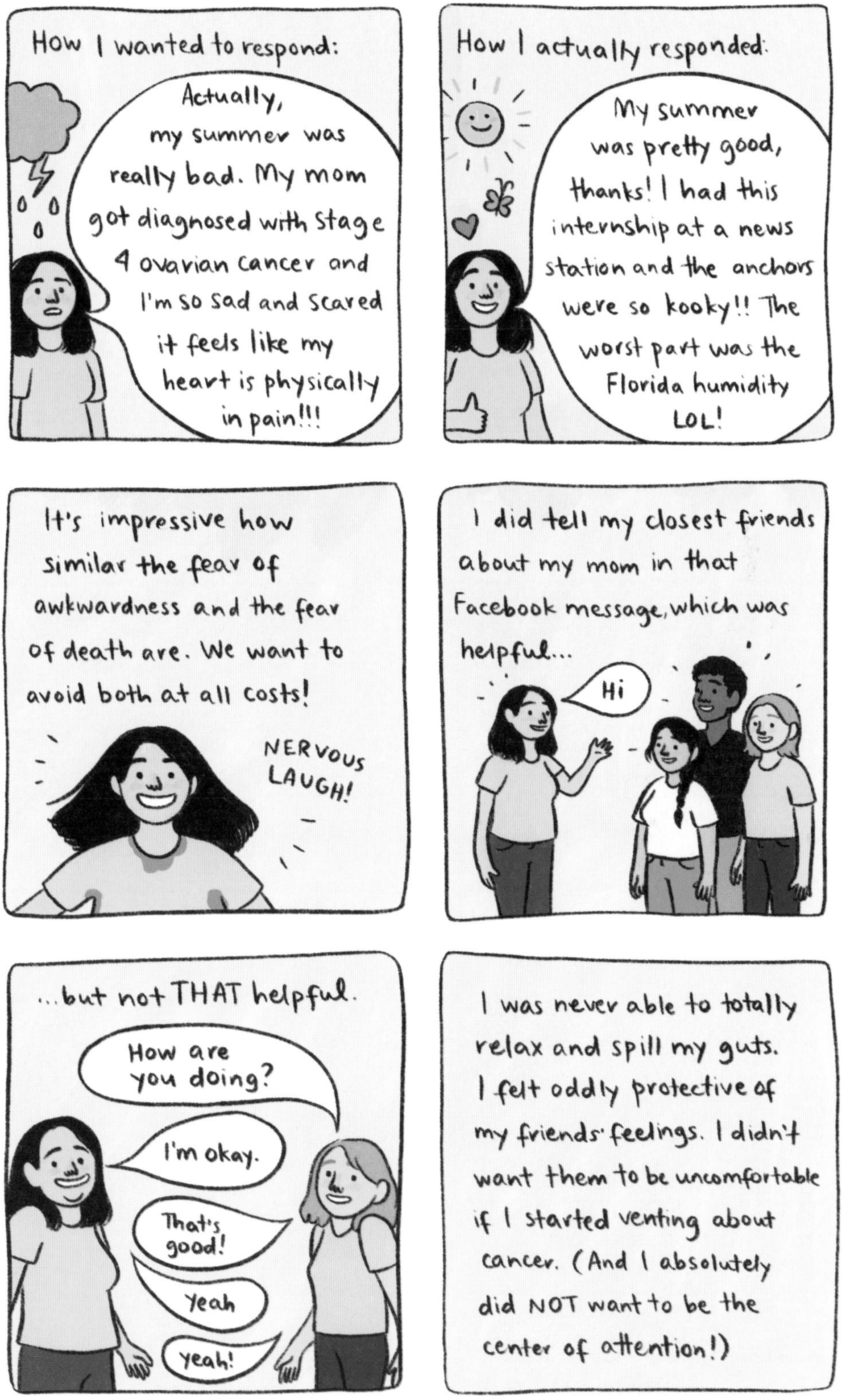
How I wanted to respond:
Actually, my summer was really bad. My mom got diagnosed with Stage 4 ovarian cancer and I'm so sad and scared it feels like my heart is physically in pain!!!
How I actually responded:
My summer was pretty good, thanks! I had this internship at a news station and the anchors were so kooky!! The worst part was the Florida humidity LOL!
It's impressive how similar the fear of awkwardness and the fear of death are. We want to avoid both at all costs!
NERVOUS LAUGH!
I did tell my closest friends about my mom in that Facebook message, which was helpful...
Hi
...but not THAT helpful.
How are you doing?
I'm okay.
That's good!
Yeah
yeah!
I was never able to totally relax and spill my guts. I felt oddly protective of my friends' feelings. I didn't want them to be uncomfortable if I started venting about cancer. (And I absolutely did NOT want to be the center of attention!)

Humans are made to adapt, though, and as the year went on, I settled into my cancer daughter/carefree college student existence.

My double life rivaled Hannah Montana's.

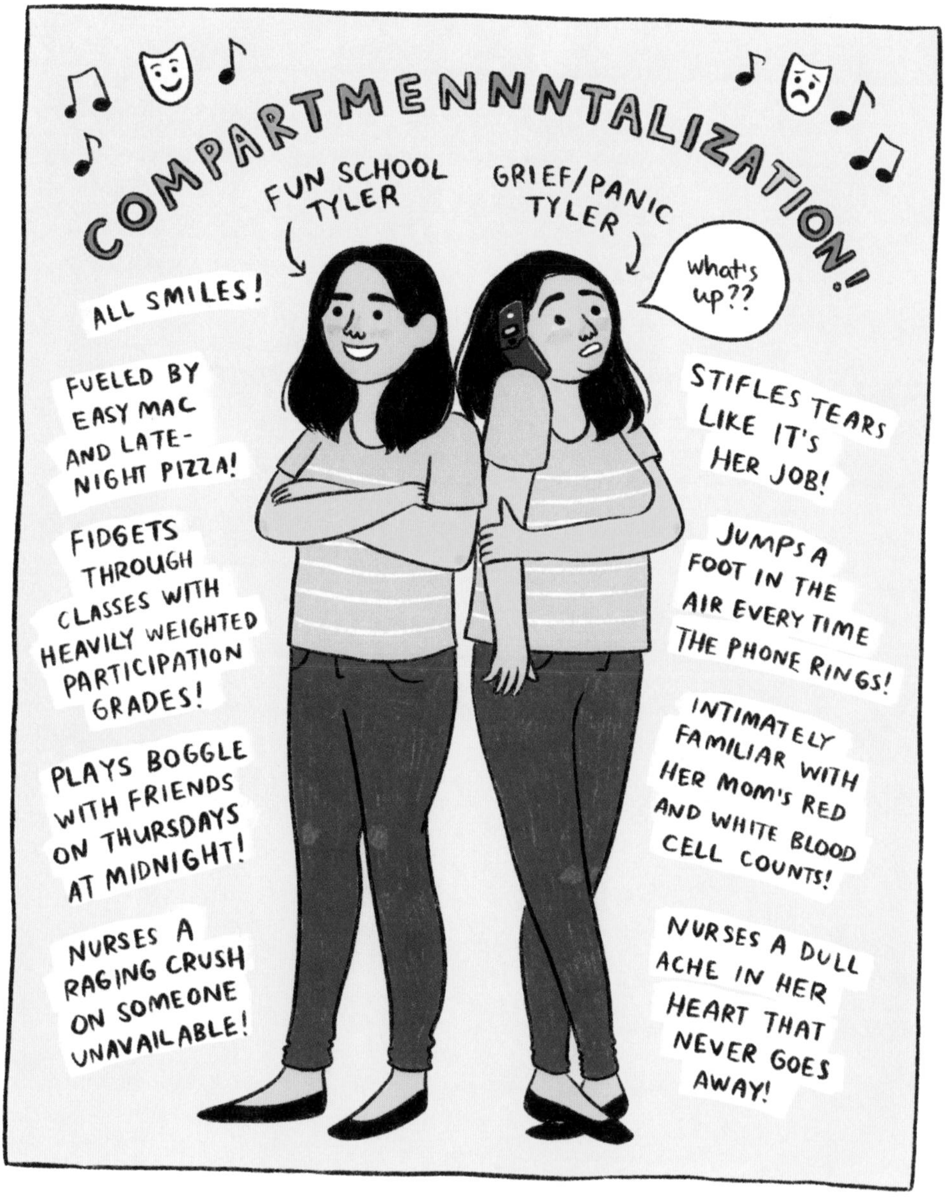
COMPARTMENNNNTALIZATION!
FUN SCHOOL TYLER
GRIEF/PANIC TYLER
what's up??
ALL SMILES!
FUELED BY EASY MAC AND LATE-NIGHT PIZZA!
FIDGETS THROUGH CLASSES WITH HEAVILY WEIGHTED PARTICIPATION GRADES!
PLAYS BOGGLE WITH FRIENDS ON THURSDAYS AT MIDNIGHT!
NURSES A RAGING CRUSH ON SOMEONE UNAVAILABLE!
STIFLES TEARS LIKE IT'S HER JOB!
JUMPS A FOOT IN THE AIR EVERY TIME THE PHONE RINGS!
INTIMATELY FAMILIAR WITH HER MOM'S RED AND WHITE BLOOD CELL COUNTS!
NURSES A DULL ACHE IN HER HEART THAT NEVER GOES AWAY!

It was the only way I knew how to cope!

# SHOULD I PICK UP THE PHONE?

(a flow chart)

**START**
**THE PHONE RINGS!**

→ **it's CODY or SPENCER**

**PICK IT UP**
You'd rather hear bad news from them anyway.

**PICK IT UP**
and get it over with.

↓ **it's SOMEONE ELSE**

**am I EXPECTING THE CALL?**

YES → **PICK IT UP** and get it over with.

NO → **LET IT GO TO VOICEMAIL**
Talking on the phone is the worst.

→ **it's DAD**

**it's A NORMAL TIME to be calling**

**PICK IT UP**
Maybe everything is okay.

**it's a WEIRD TIME OF DAY**

**am I WAITING FOR AN UPDATE?**

NO → **PICK IT UP** Maybe everything is okay.

YES → **am I MENTALLY PREPARED for VERY BAD NEWS?**

YES → **really?**

NO → **LET IT GO TO VOICEMAIL**
You can call back when you feel ready.

YES → **REALLY??**

NEVER MIND → **LET IT GO TO VOICEMAIL**

I CAN TAKE IT! → **ANSWER IT,** hold your breath, and spend the rest of the day either cheering or collapsed in despair.

Being away at school while my mom underwent her cancer treatment meant that her physical decline came at me in dramatic stages. I only saw her in person a handful of times while she was sick, and each time was worse than the last.

an artist's representation

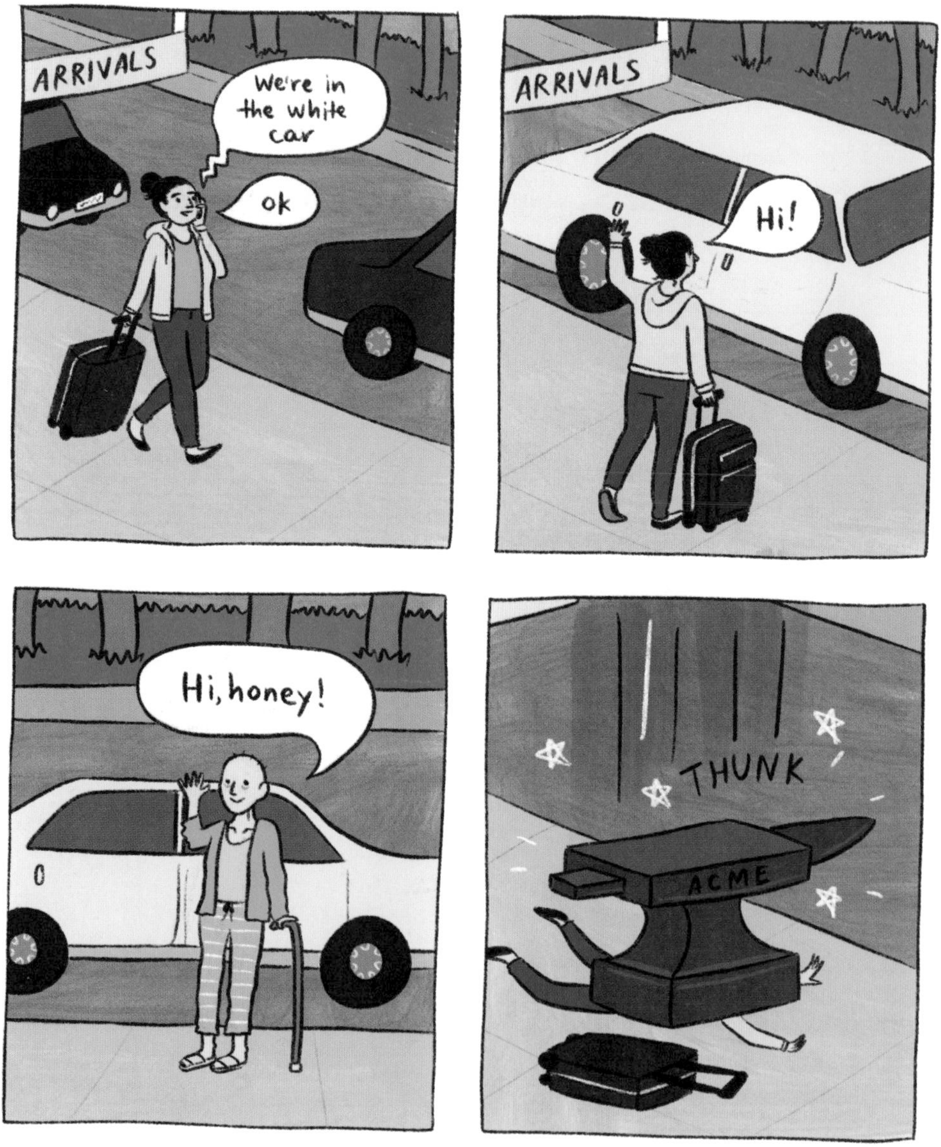

ARRIVALS
We're in the white car
ok
ARRIVALS
Hi!
Hi, honey!
THUNK
ACME

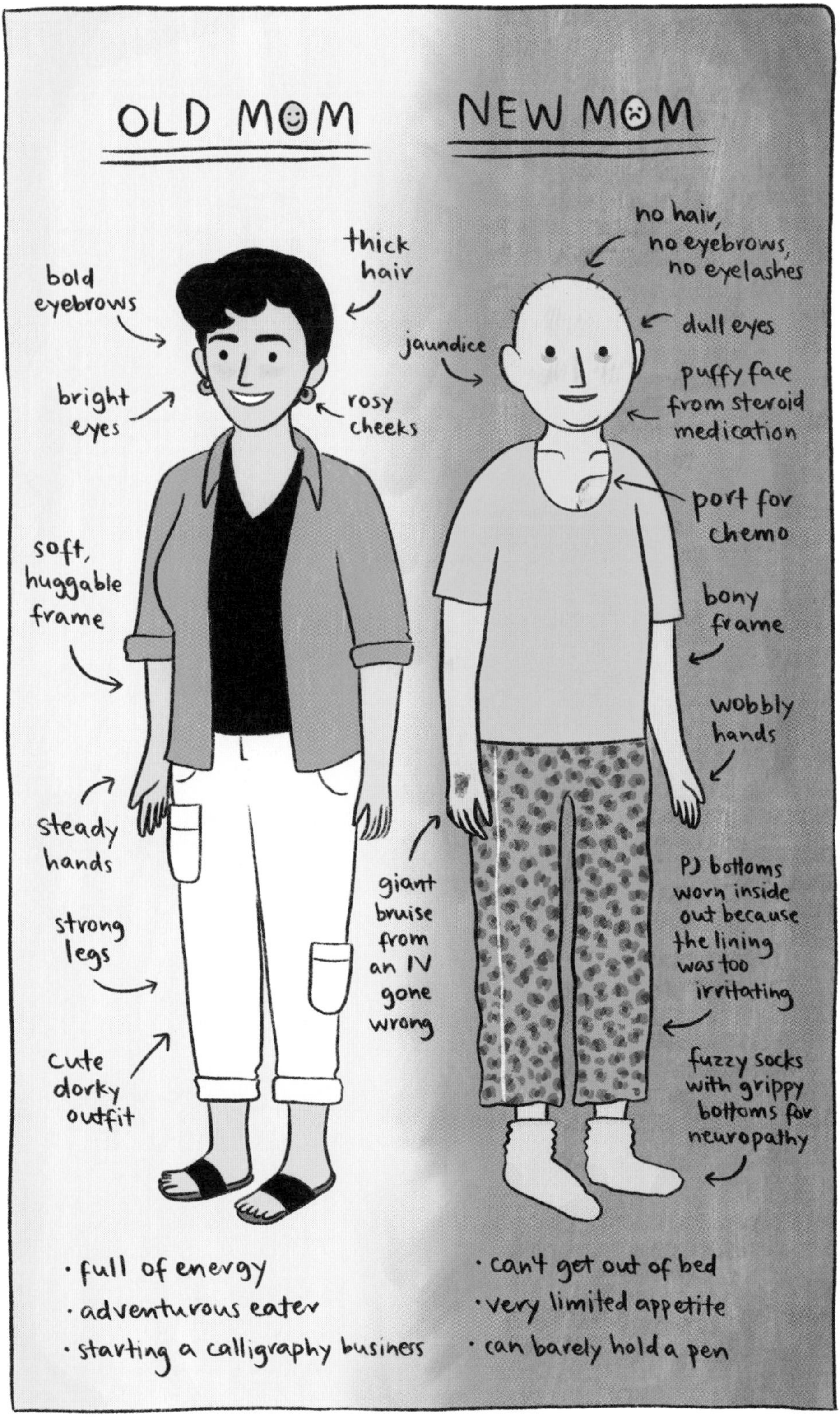
OLD MOM
NEW MOM
thick hair
bold eyebrows
bright eyes
rosy cheeks
soft, huggable frame
steady hands
strong legs
cute dorky outfit
no hair, no eyebrows, no eyelashes
dull eyes
jaundice
puffy face from steroid medication
port for chemo
bony frame
wobbly hands
giant bruise from an IV gone wrong
PJ bottoms worn inside out because the lining was too irritating
fuzzy socks with grippy bottoms for neuropathy
· full of energy
· adventurous eater
· starting a calligraphy business
· can't get out of bed
· very limited appetite
· can barely hold a pen

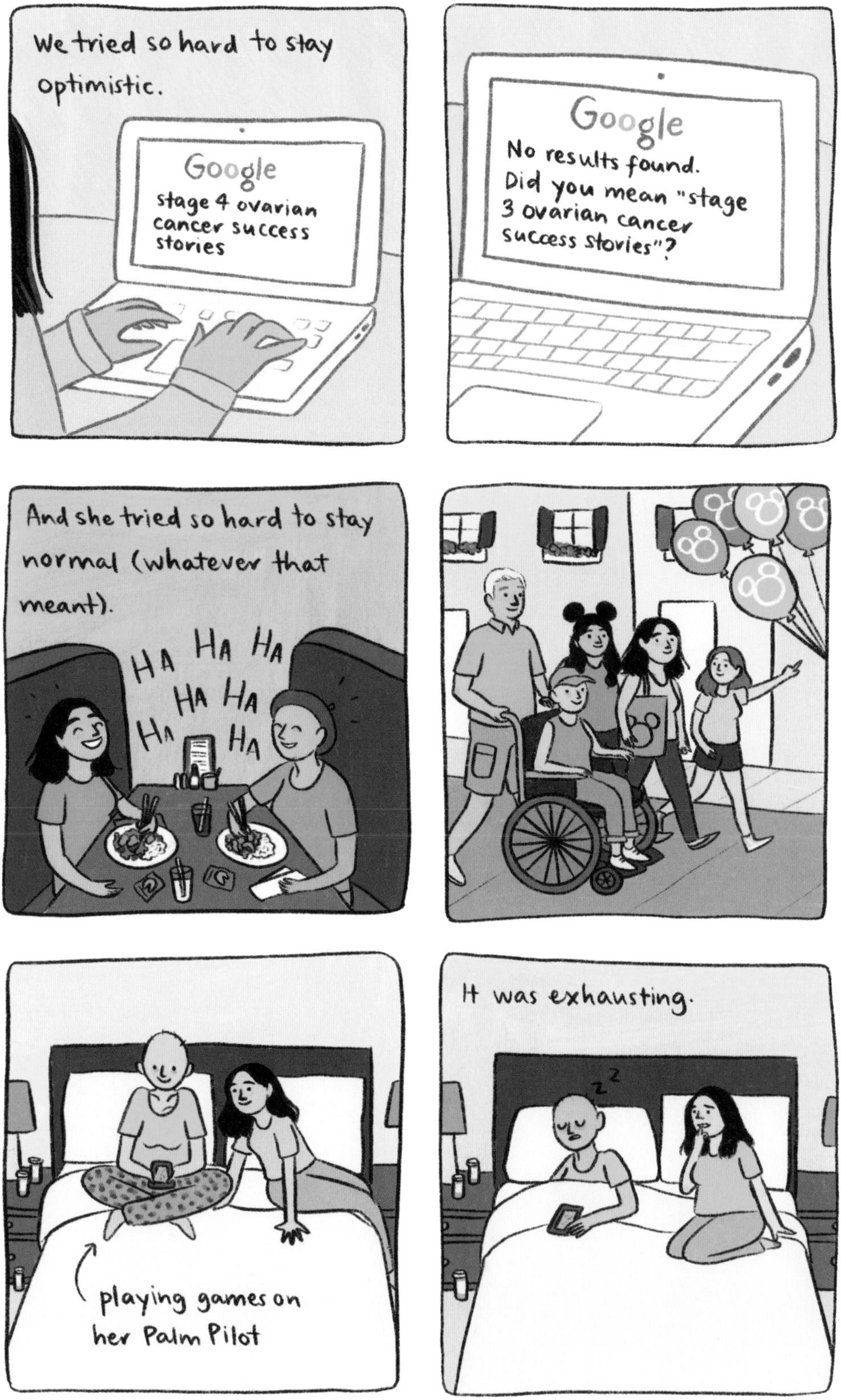

We tried so hard to stay optimistic.
Google
stage 4 ovarian cancer success stories
Google
No results found.
Did you mean "stage 3 ovarian cancer success stories"?
And she tried so hard to stay normal (whatever that meant).
HA HA HA
HA HA
HA HA
playing games on her Palm Pilot
It was exhausting.

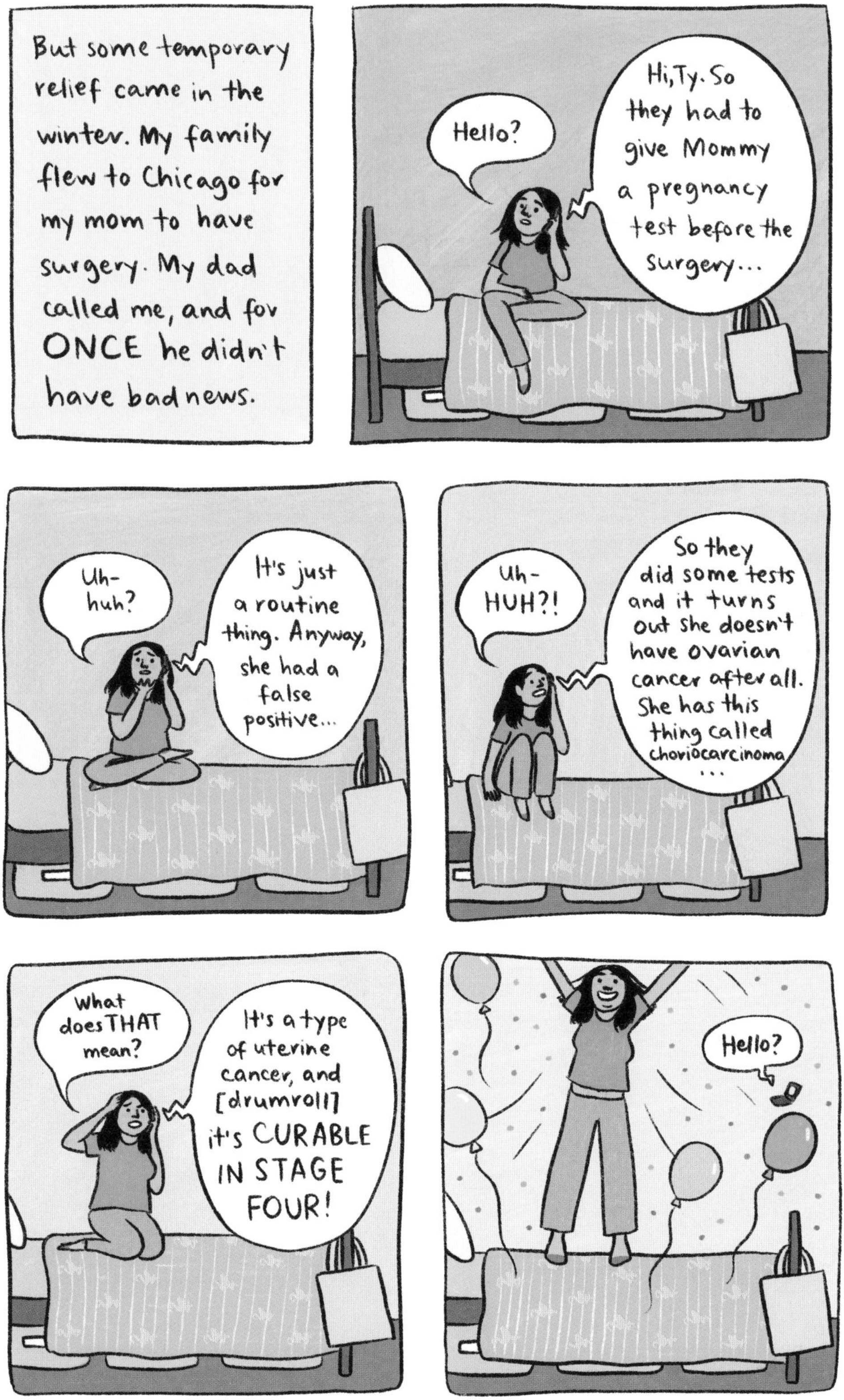
But some temporary relief came in the winter. My family flew to Chicago for my mom to have surgery. My dad called me, and for ONCE he didn't have bad news.
Hello?
Hi, Ty. So they had to give Mommy a pregnancy test before the surgery...
Uh-huh?
It's just a routine thing. Anyway, she had a false positive...
Uh-HUH?!
So they did some tests and it turns out she doesn't have ovarian cancer after all. She has this thing called choriocarcinoma...
What does THAT mean?
It's a type of uterine cancer, and [drumroll] it's CURABLE IN STAGE FOUR!
Hello?

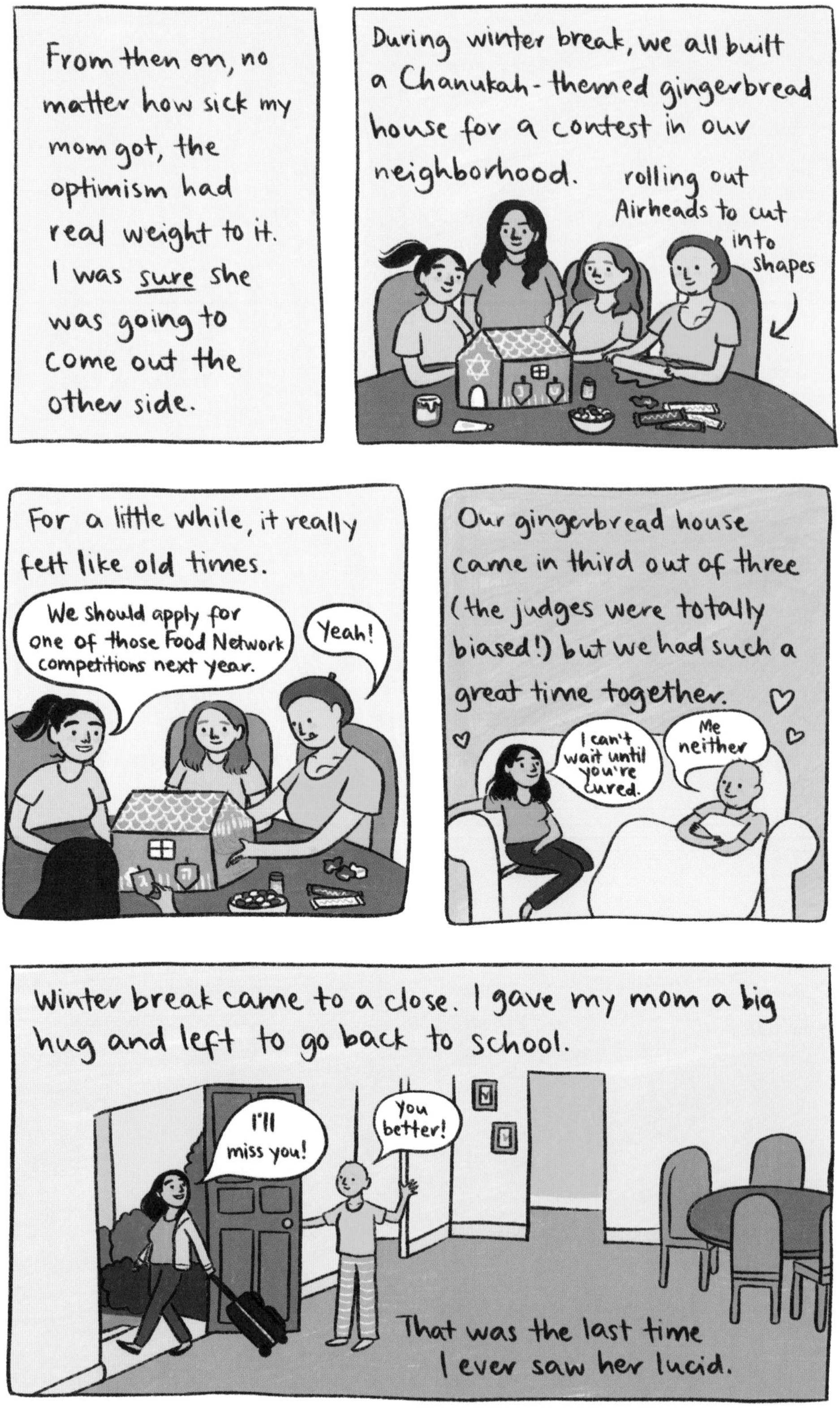
From then on, no matter how sick my mom got, the optimism had real weight to it. I was sure she was going to come out the other side.
During winter break, we all built a Chanukah-themed gingerbread house for a contest in our neighborhood.
rolling out Airheads to cut into shapes
For a little while, it really felt like old times.
We should apply for one of those Food Network competitions next year.
Yeah!
Our gingerbread house came in third out of three (the judges were totally biased!) but we had such a great time together.
I can't wait until you're cured.
Me neither
Winter break came to a close. I gave my mom a big hug and left to go back to school.
I'll miss you!
You better!
That was the last time I ever saw her lucid.

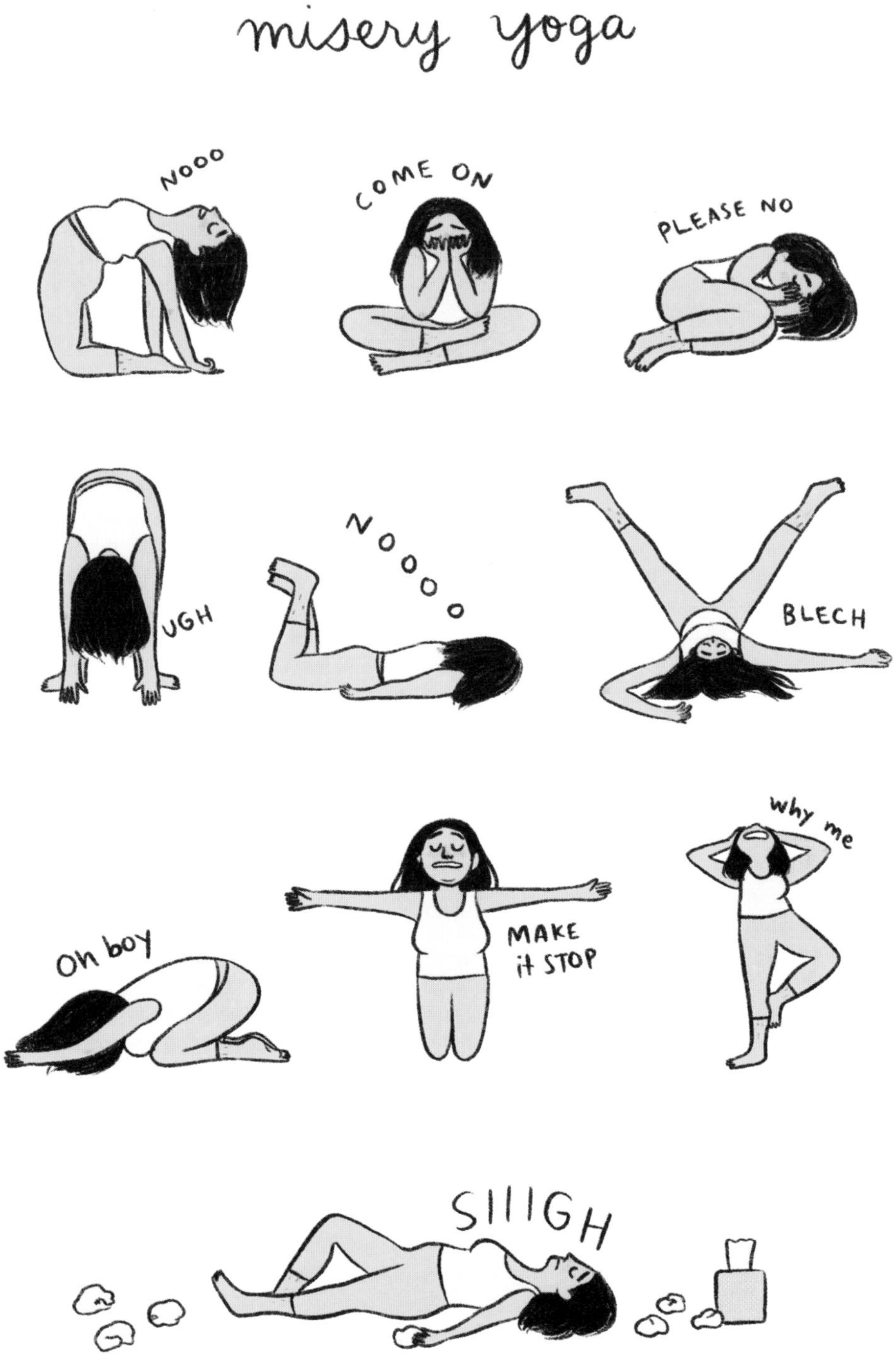
misery yoga
NOOO
COME ON
PLEASE NO
UGH
NOOOOO
BLECH
oh boy
MAKE it STOP
why me
SIIIGH

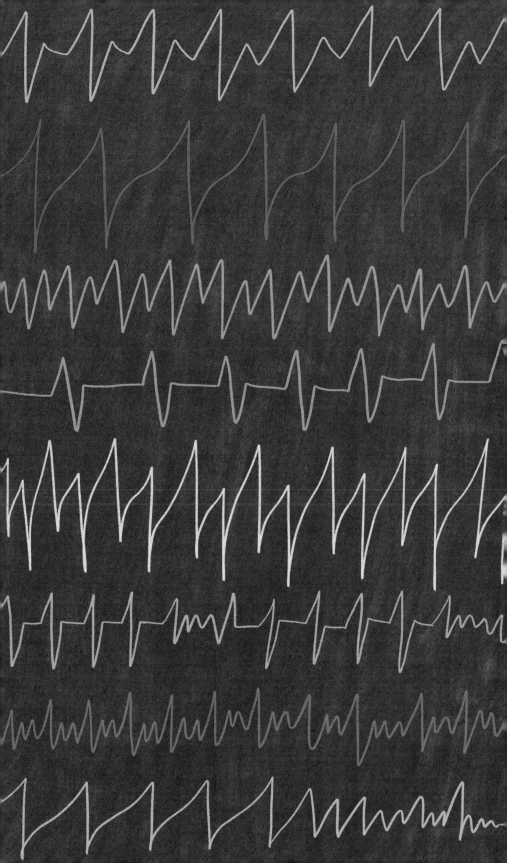

# chapter four

## the worst day

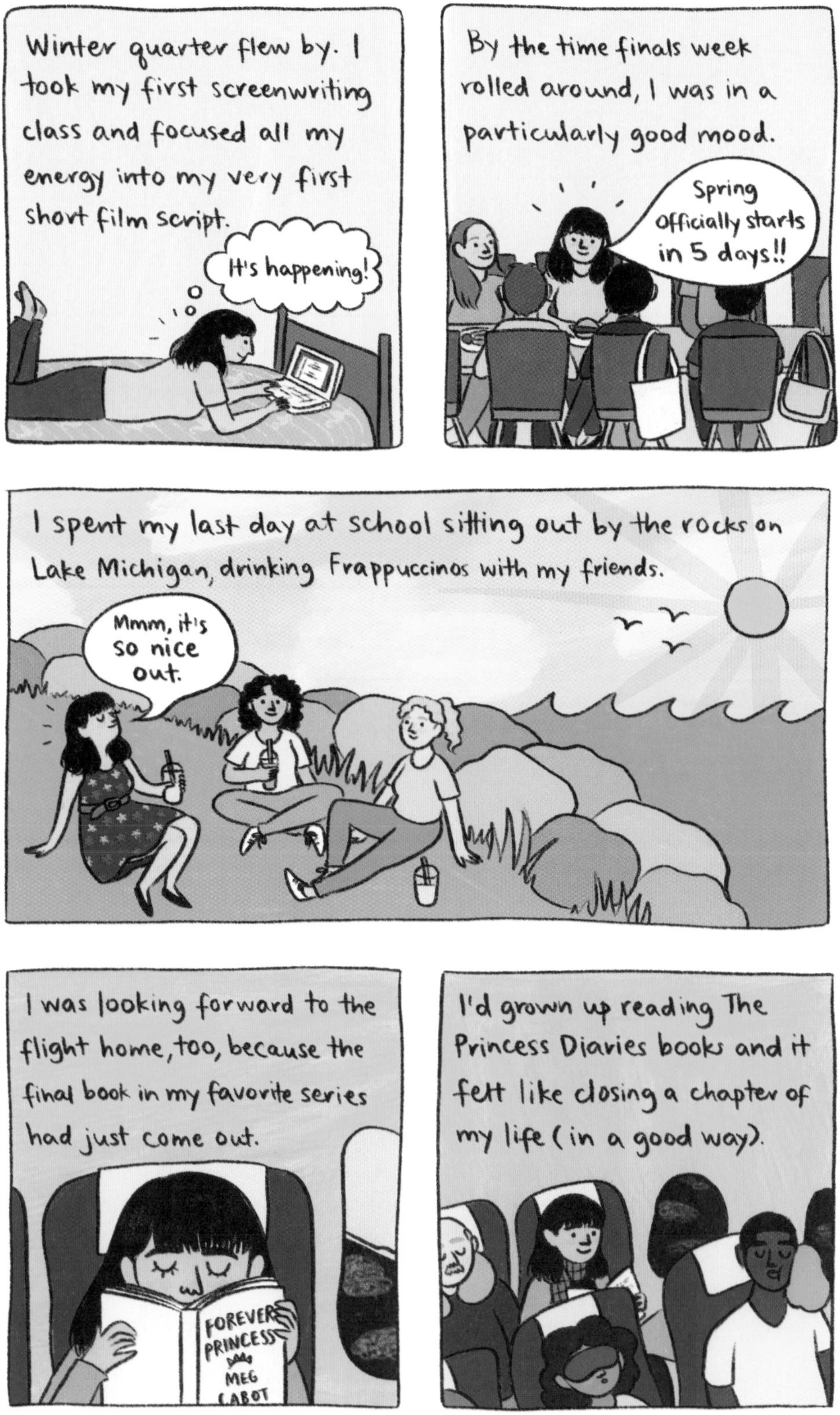
Winter quarter flew by. I took my first screenwriting class and focused all my energy into my very first short film script.
It's happening!
By the time finals week rolled around, I was in a particularly good mood.
Spring officially starts in 5 days!!
I spent my last day at school sitting out by the rocks on Lake Michigan, drinking Frappuccinos with my friends.
Mmm, it's so nice out.
I was looking forward to the flight home, too, because the final book in my favorite series had just come out.
FOREVER PRINCESS
MEG CABOT
I'd grown up reading The Princess Diaries books and it felt like closing a chapter of my life (in a good way).

I got off the plane feeling full of hope. Getting off a plane outside always feels exciting, and the night was warm and clear.

CLEARWATER
ST. PETERSBU

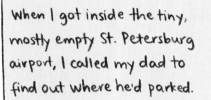

When I got inside the tiny, mostly empty St. Petersburg airport, I called my dad to find out where he'd parked.

Hi, Ty, I'll be there in about 45 minutes.

I was bummed and annoyed.

45 MINUTES?

I'm sorry, hon, it's been a busy night.

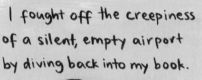

I fought off the creepiness of a silent, empty airport by diving back into my book.

When my dad finally arrived, he was oddly quiet.

Hi!

We're going to the hospital.

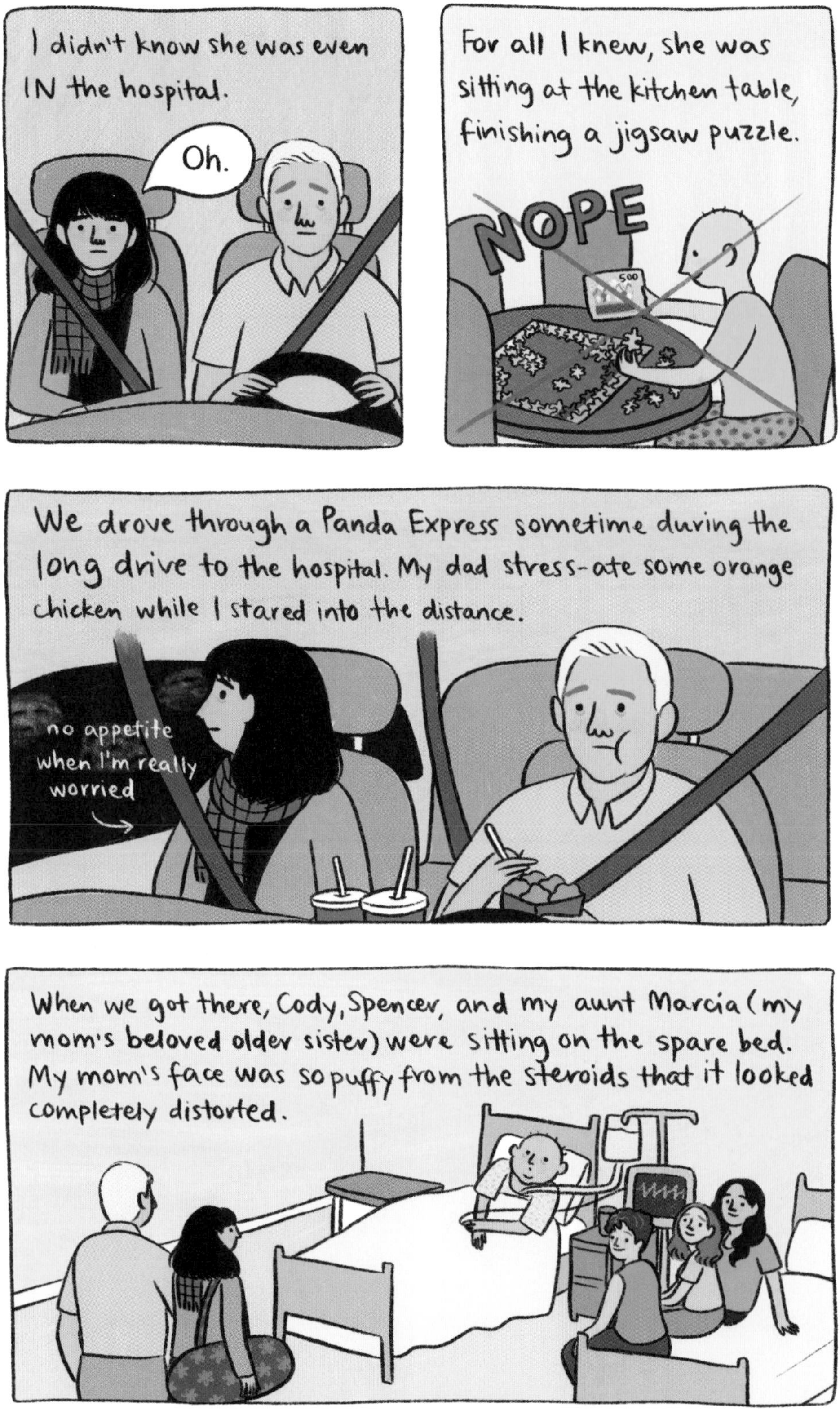
I didn't know she was even IN the hospital.
Oh.
For all I knew, she was sitting at the kitchen table, finishing a jigsaw puzzle.
NOPE
500
We drove through a Panda Express sometime during the long drive to the hospital. My dad stress-ate some orange chicken while I stared into the distance.
no appetite when I'm really worried
When we got there, Cody, Spencer, and my aunt Marcia (my mom's beloved older sister) were sitting on the spare bed. My mom's face was so puffy from the steroids that it looked completely distorted.

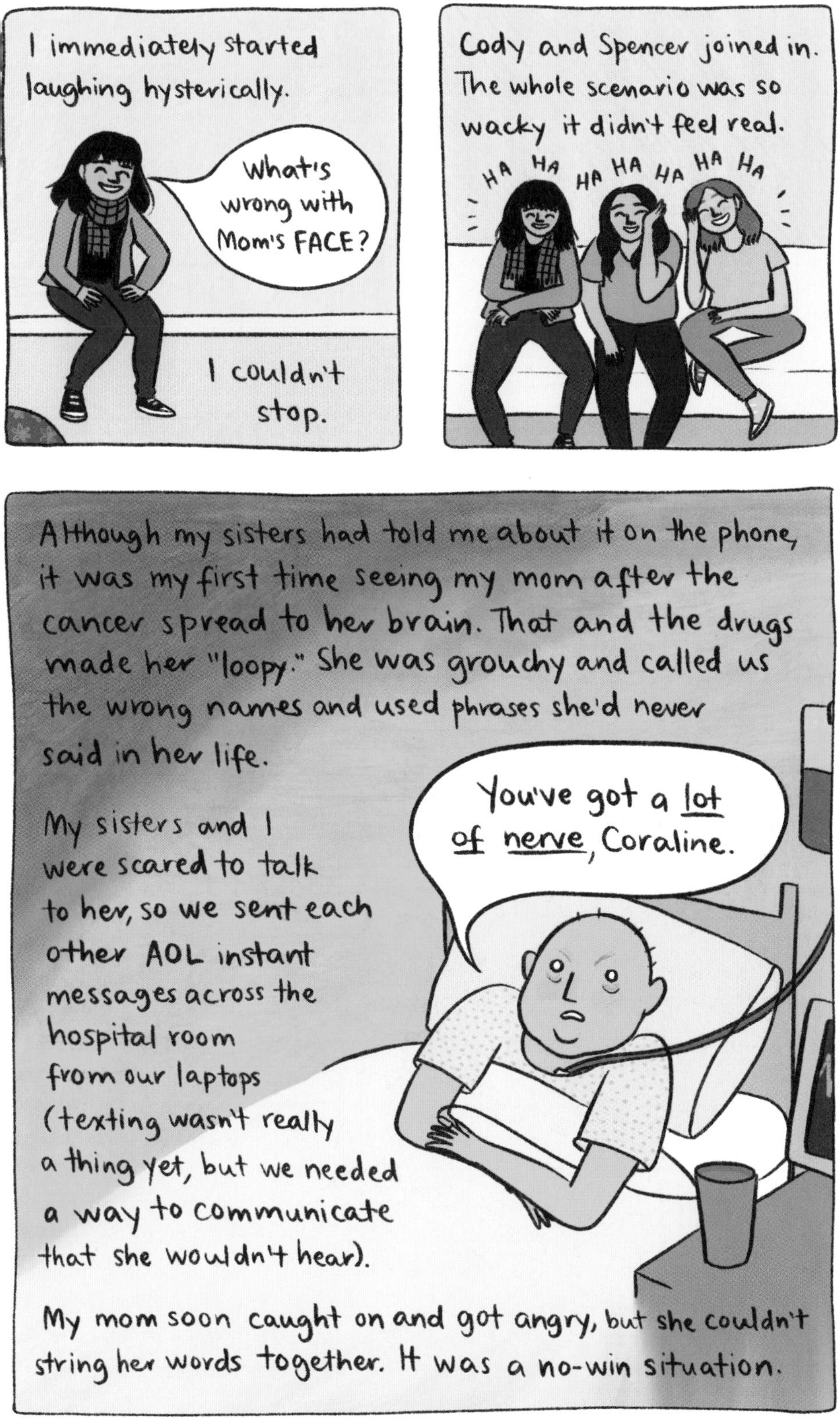
I immediately started laughing hysterically.
What's wrong with Mom's FACE?
I couldn't stop.
Cody and Spencer joined in. The whole scenario was so wacky it didn't feel real.
HA HA HA HA HA HA HA
Although my sisters had told me about it on the phone, it was my first time seeing my mom after the cancer spread to her brain. That and the drugs made her "loopy." She was grouchy and called us the wrong names and used phrases she'd never said in her life.
You've got a lot of nerve, Coraline.
My sisters and I were scared to talk to her, so we sent each other AOL instant messages across the hospital room from our laptops (texting wasn't really a thing yet, but we needed a way to communicate that she wouldn't hear).
My mom soon caught on and got angry, but she couldn't string her words together. It was a no-win situation.

At one point, my mom asked me if I would have a "sleepover" with her. I said yes, somehow thinking she meant that we'd sleep in her room at home. What it really meant was taking up residence in the spare hospital bed for the night.

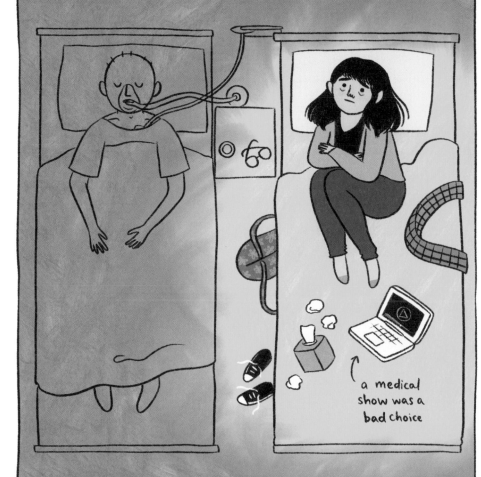

a medical
show was a
bad choice

I brushed my teeth with my finger and some of my mom's Sensodyne toothpaste and tried to fall asleep in my clothes, but the real-life nightmares kept jerking me awake.

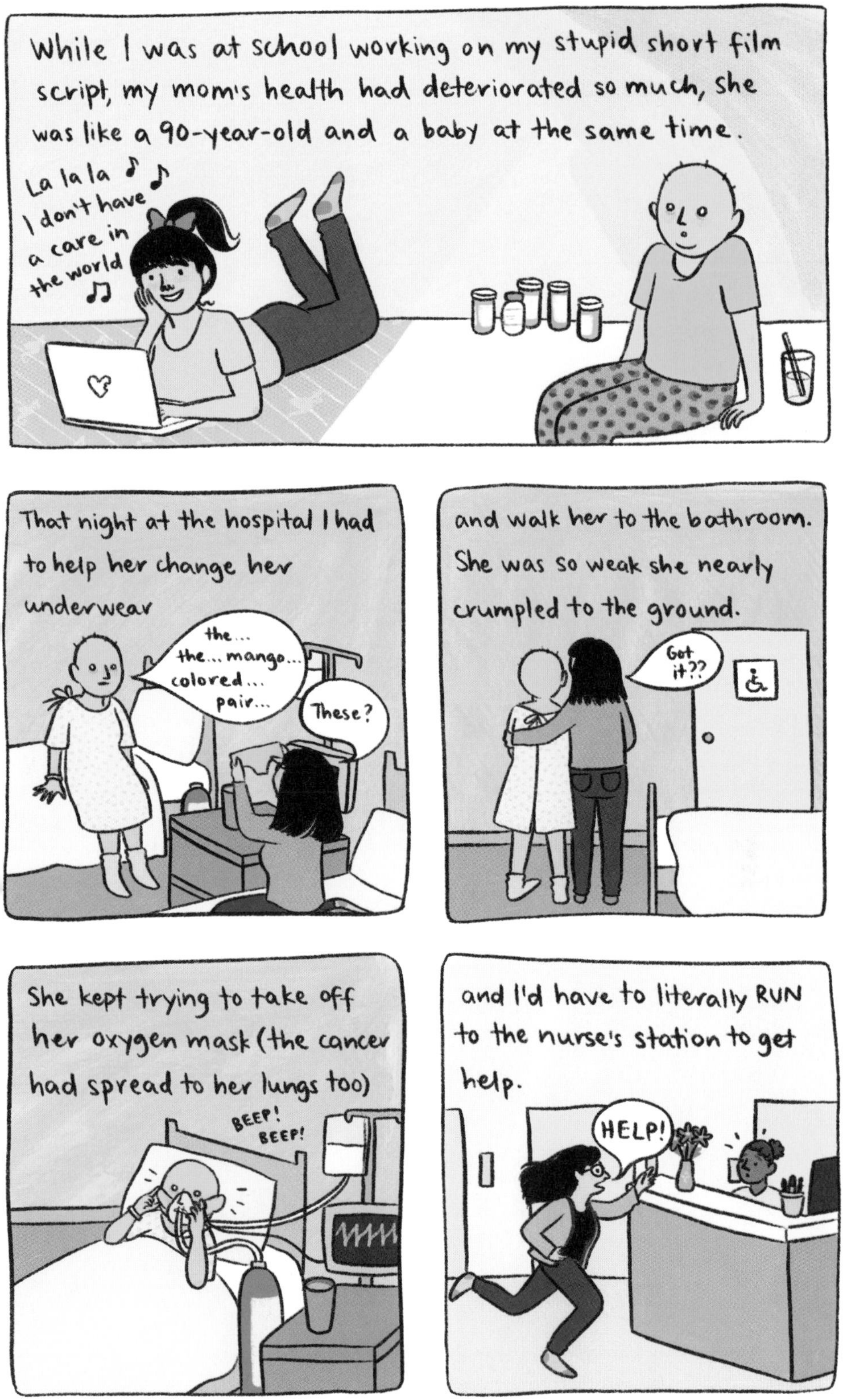
While I was at school working on my stupid short film script, my mom's health had deteriorated so much, she was like a 90-year-old and a baby at the same time.
La la la ♪ ♪ I don't have a care in the world ♫
That night at the hospital I had to help her change her underwear
the... the... mango... colored... pair...
These?
and walk her to the bathroom. She was so weak she nearly crumpled to the ground.
Got it??
She kept trying to take off her oxygen mask (the cancer had spread to her lungs too)
BEEP! BEEP!
and I'd have to literally RUN to the nurse's station to get help.
HELP!

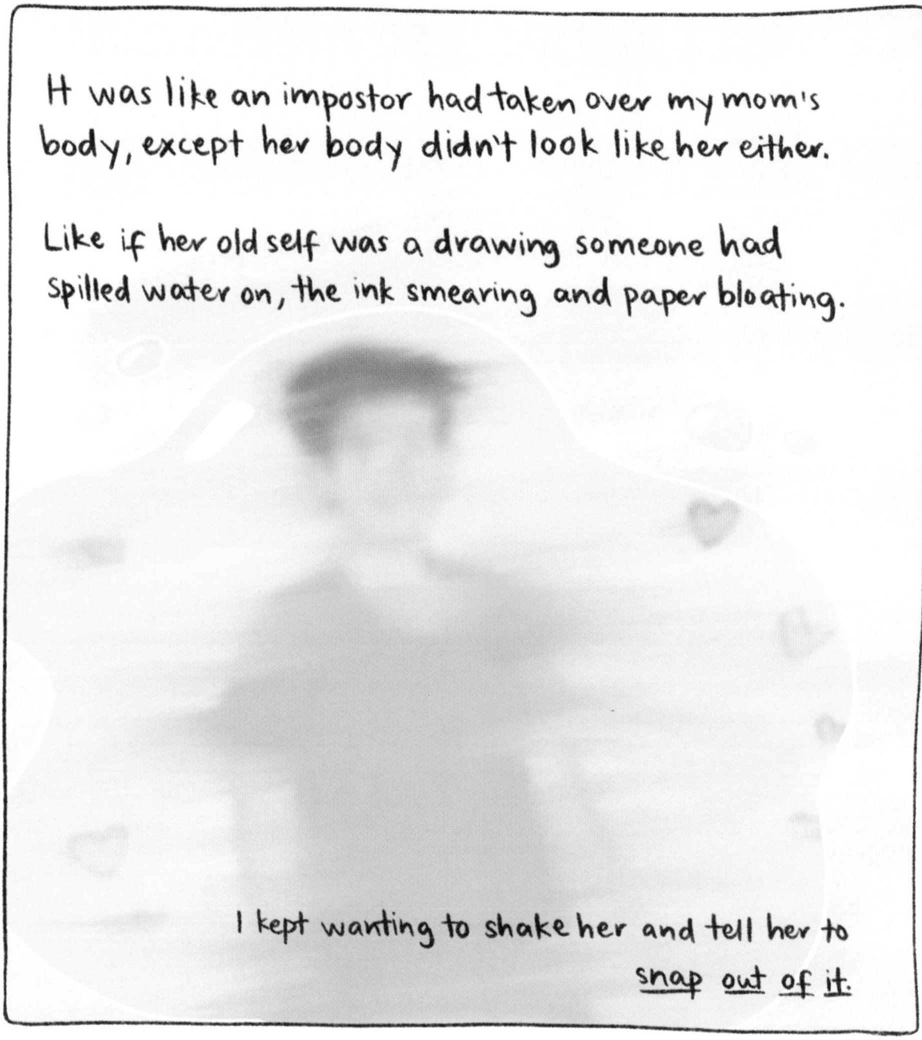
It was like an impostor had taken over my mom's body, except her body didn't look like her either.
Like if her old self was a drawing someone had spilled water on, the ink smearing and paper bloating.
I kept wanting to shake her and tell her to snap out of it.

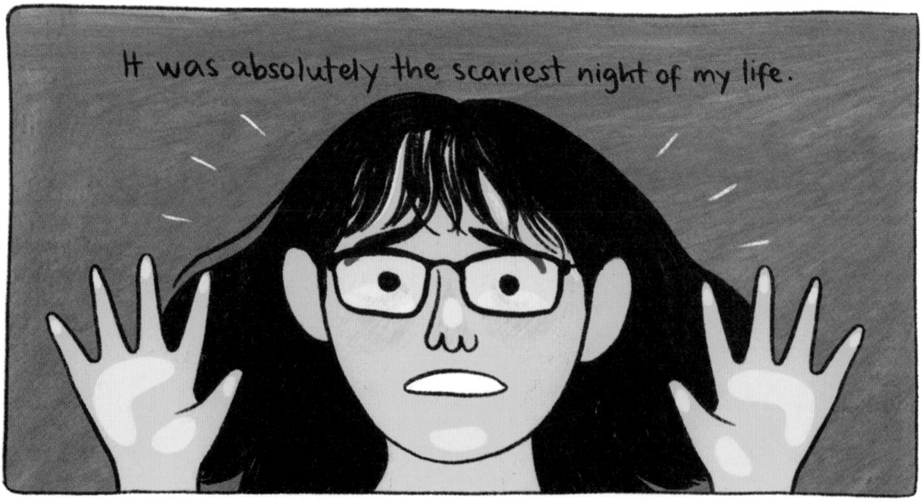
It was absolutely the scariest night of my life.

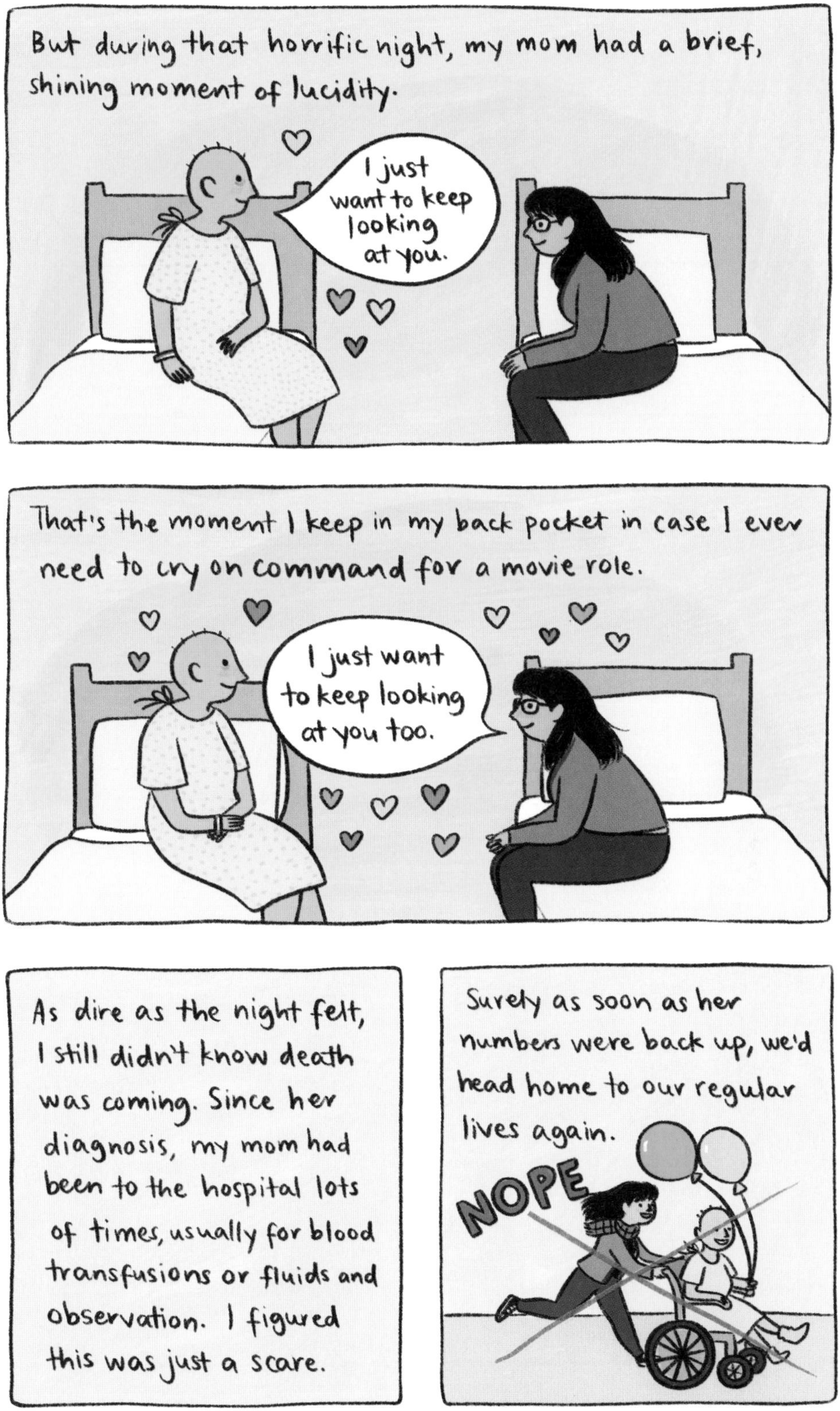
But during that horrific night, my mom had a brief, shining moment of lucidity.
I just want to keep looking at you.
That's the moment I keep in my back pocket in case I ever need to cry on command for a movie role.
I just want to keep looking at you too.
As dire as the night felt, I still didn't know death was coming. Since her diagnosis, my mom had been to the hospital lots of times, usually for blood transfusions or fluids and observation. I figured this was just a scare.
Surely as soon as her numbers were back up, we'd head home to our regular lives again.
NOPE

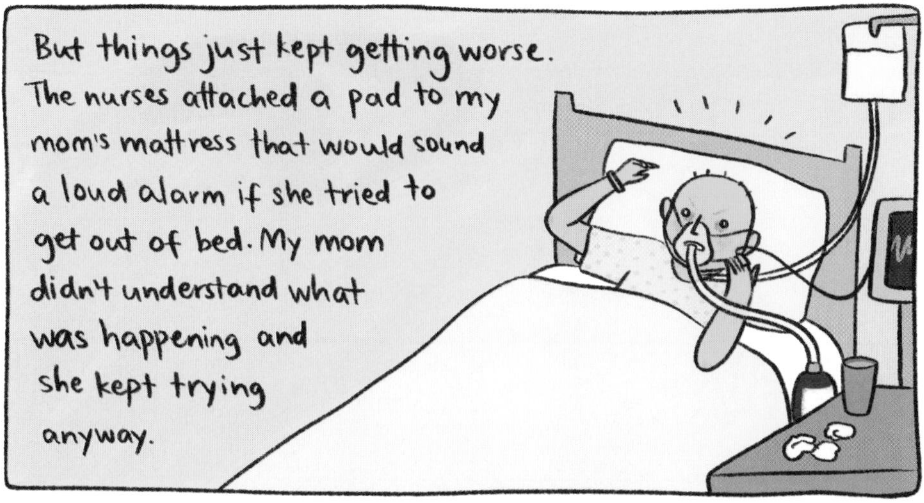
But things just kept getting worse. The nurses attached a pad to my mom's mattress that would sound a loud alarm if she tried to get out of bed. My mom didn't understand what was happening and she kept trying anyway.

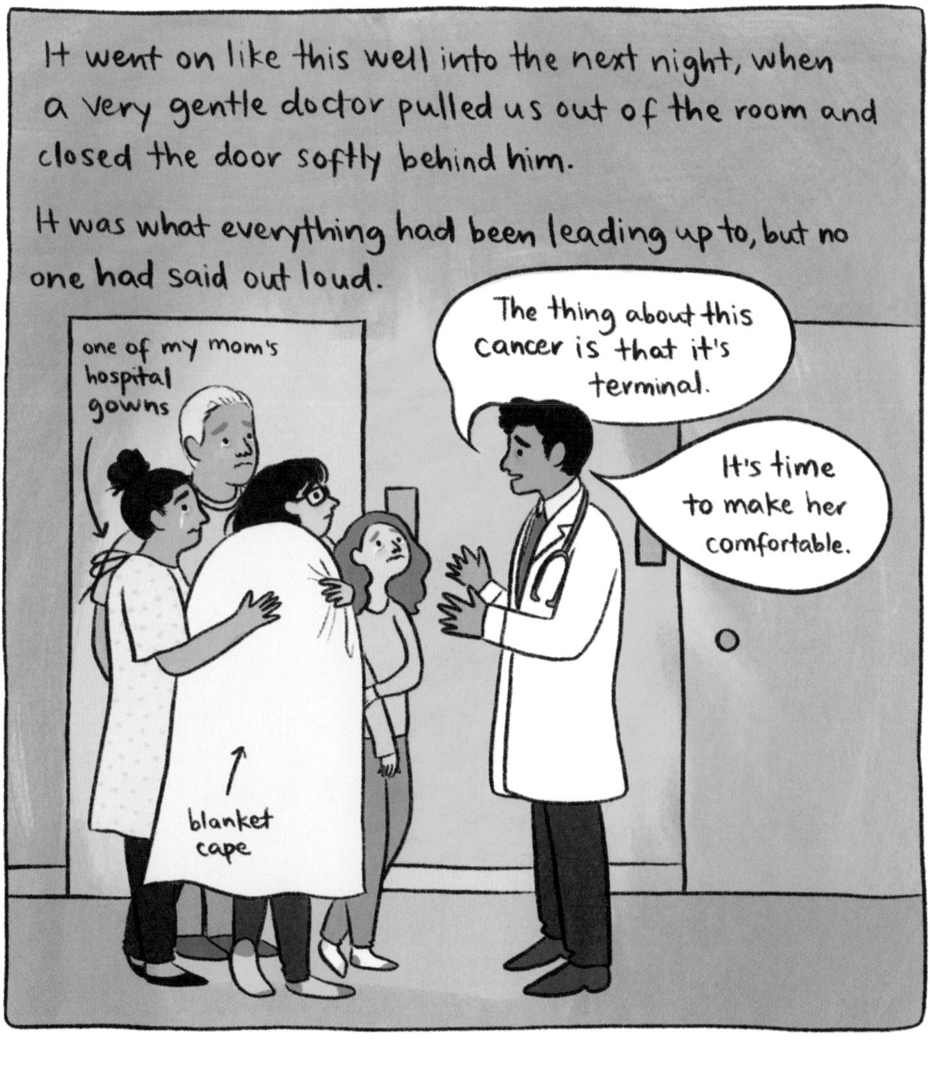
It went on like this well into the next night, when a very gentle doctor pulled us out of the room and closed the door softly behind him.
It was what everything had been leading up to, but no one had said out loud.
one of my mom's hospital gowns
blanket cape
The thing about this cancer is that it's terminal.
It's time to make her comfortable.

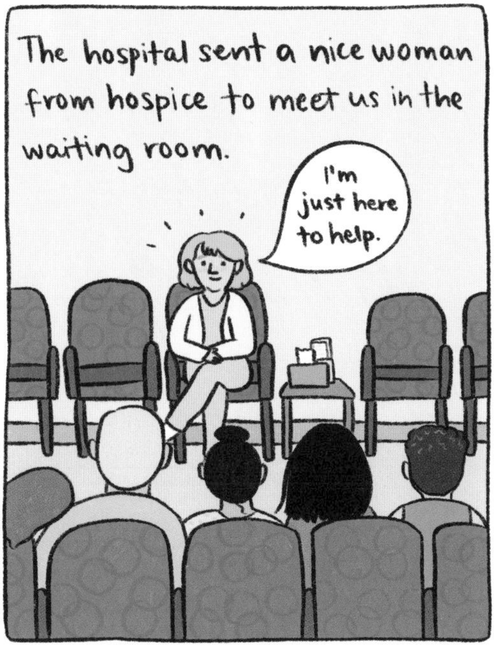
The hospital sent a nice woman from hospice to meet us in the waiting room.
I'm just here to help.

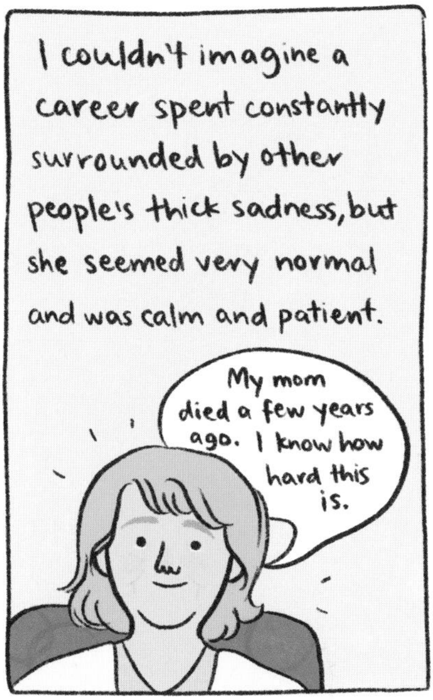
I couldn't imagine a career spent constantly surrounded by other people's thick sadness, but she seemed very normal and was calm and patient.
My mom died a few years ago. I know how hard this is.

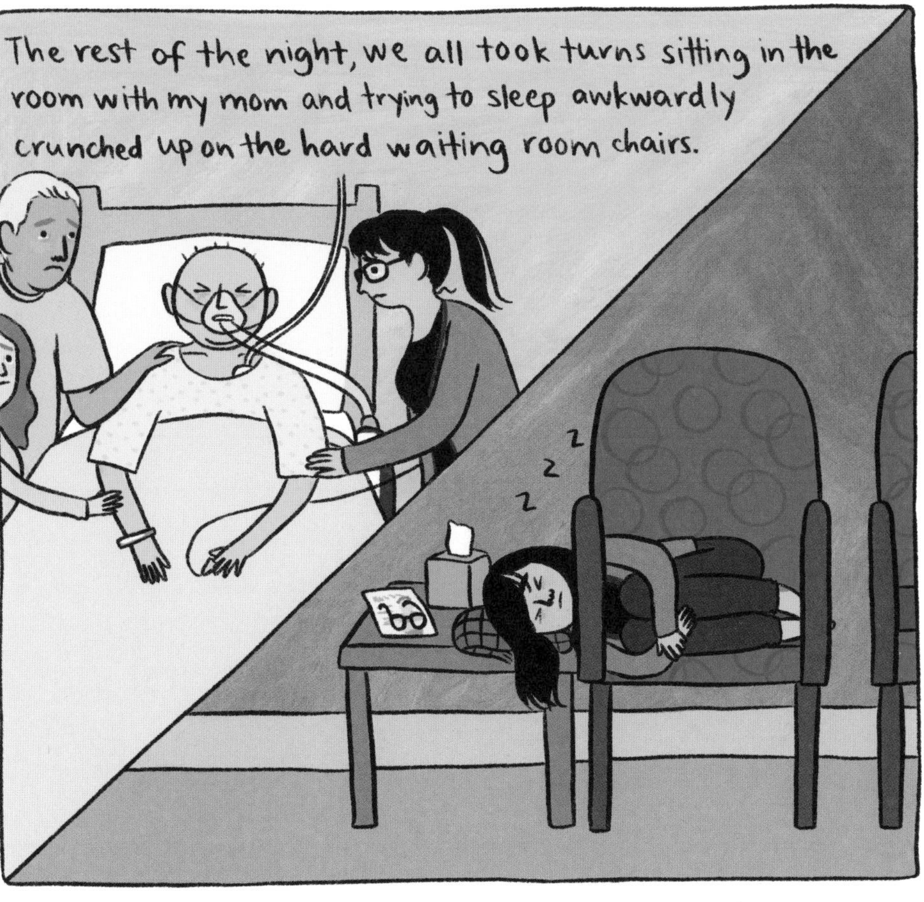
The rest of the night, we all took turns sitting in the room with my mom and trying to sleep awkwardly crunched up on the hard waiting room chairs.
Z Z Z

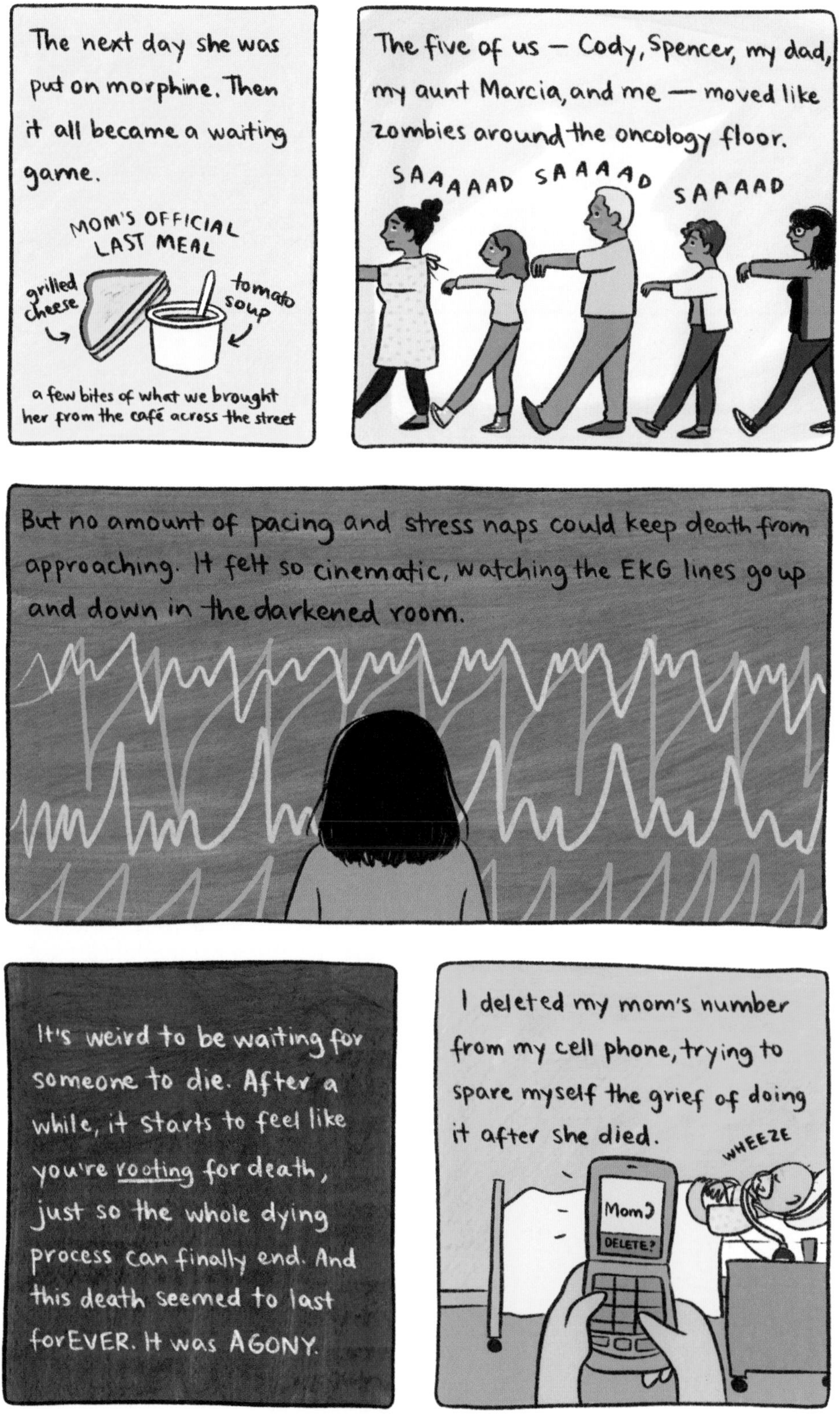
The next day she was put on morphine. Then it all became a waiting game.
MOM'S OFFICIAL LAST MEAL
grilled cheese
tomato soup
a few bites of what we brought her from the café across the street
The five of us — Cody, Spencer, my dad, my aunt Marcia, and me — moved like zombies around the oncology floor.
SAAAAAD
SAAAAD
SAAAAD
But no amount of pacing and stress naps could keep death from approaching. It felt so cinematic, watching the EKG lines go up and down in the darkened room.
It's weird to be waiting for someone to die. After a while, it starts to feel like you're rooting for death, just so the whole dying process can finally end. And this death seemed to last forEVER. It was AGONY.
I deleted my mom's number from my cell phone, trying to spare myself the grief of doing it after she died.
WHEEZE
Mom?
DELETE?

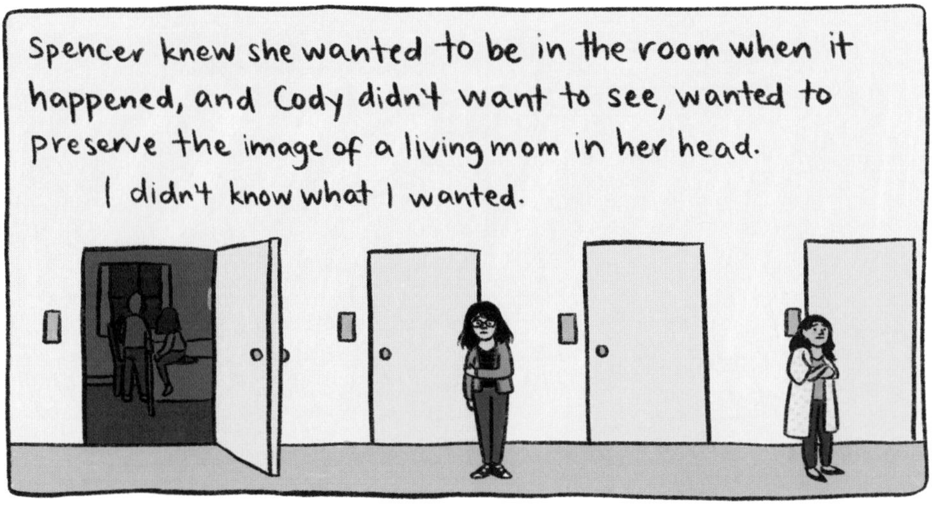
Spencer knew she wanted to be in the room when it happened, and Cody didn't want to see, wanted to preserve the image of a living mom in her head.
I didn't know what I wanted.

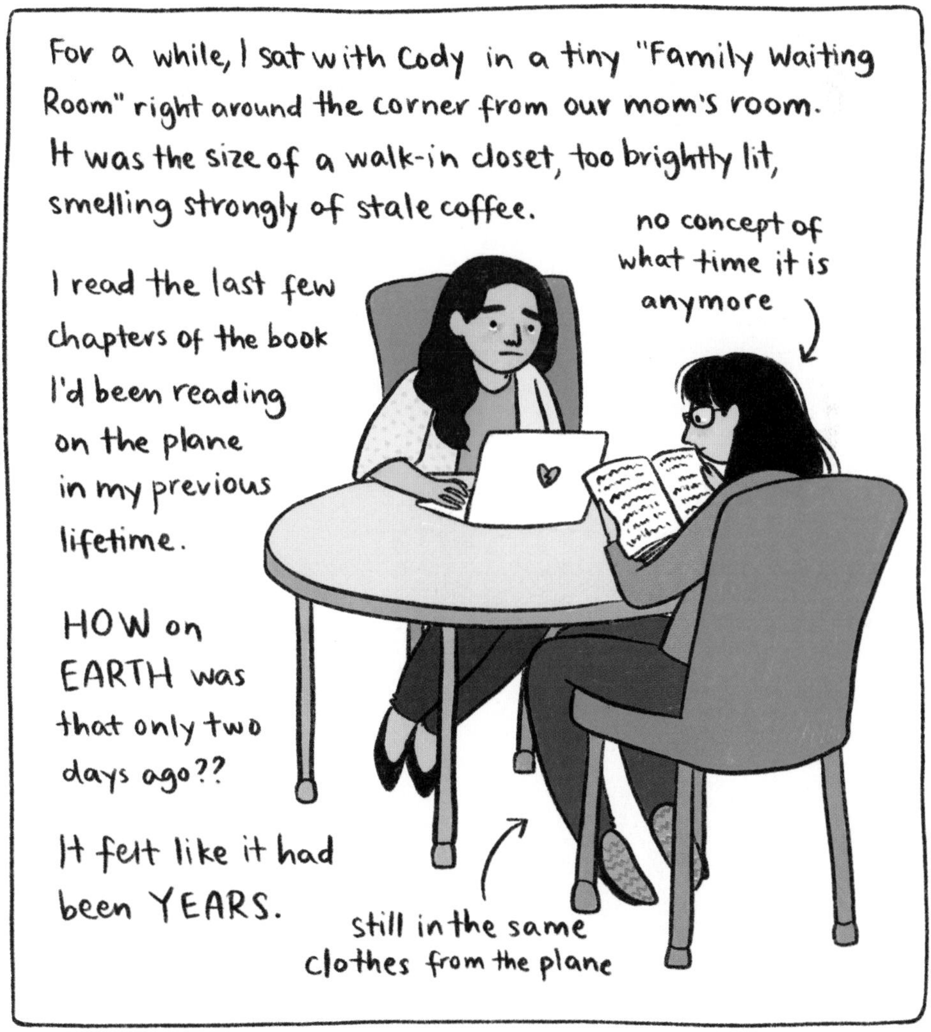
For a while, I sat with Cody in a tiny "Family Waiting Room" right around the corner from our mom's room. It was the size of a walk-in closet, too brightly lit, smelling strongly of stale coffee.
no concept of what time it is anymore
I read the last few chapters of the book I'd been reading on the plane in my previous lifetime.
HOW on EARTH was that only two days ago??
It felt like it had been YEARS.
still in the same clothes from the plane

As I read the last sentence, that familiar finishing-a-book sense of closure washed over me.

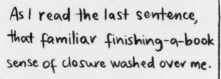

FOREVER PRINCESS

MEG CABOT

It was warm and comforting. For a second, I forgot what was actually going on.

I'm ready for <u>MY</u> happy ending!

But only for a second.

OMG MY MOM'S ABOUT TO DIE!!!!

I reached for my laptop, but, like my mom, it didn't have much battery left.

My charger cord was still in my bag in my mom's room.

I'll be right back

FAMILY WAITING ROOM

Schrödinger's mom awaits

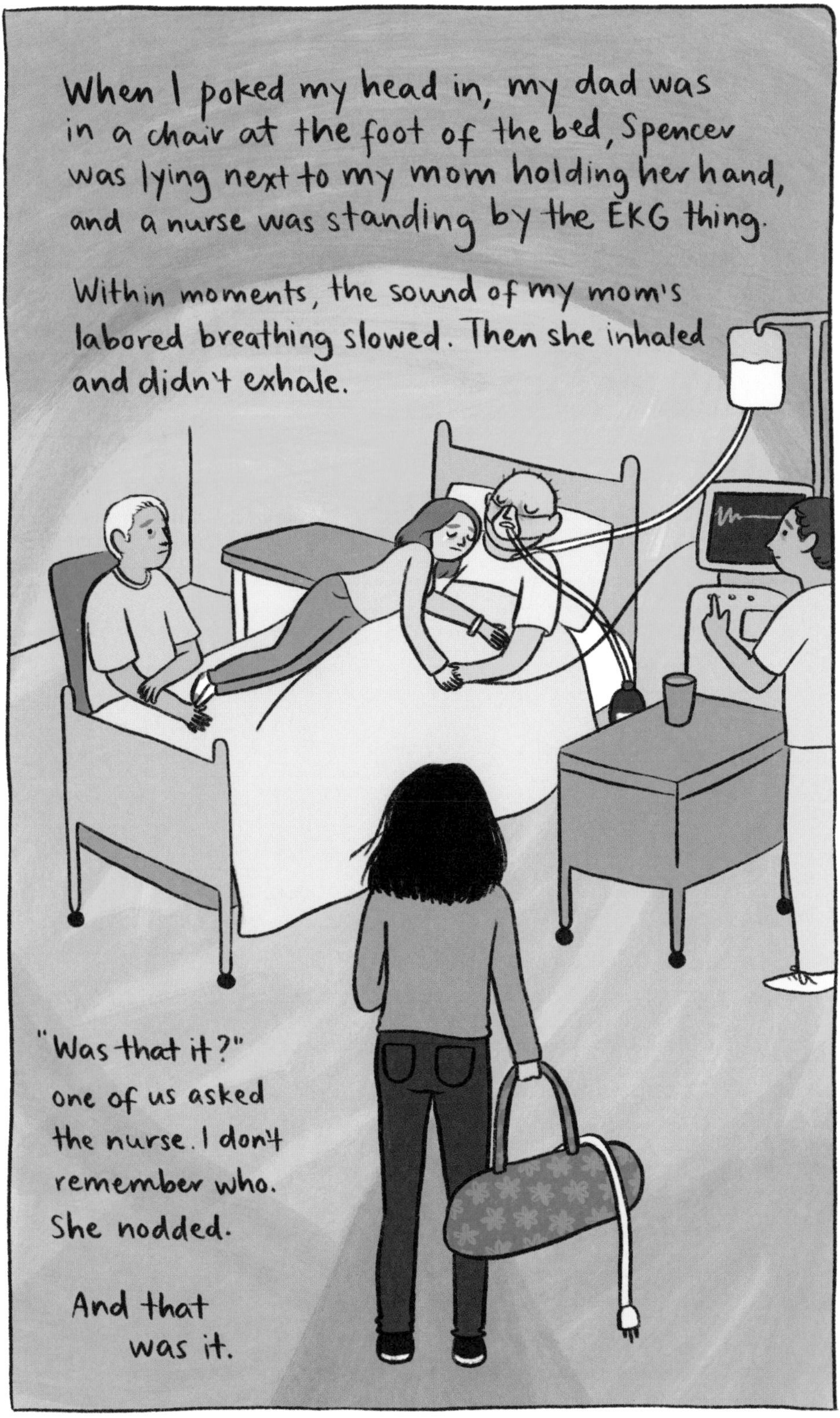
When I poked my head in, my dad was in a chair at the foot of the bed, Spencer was lying next to my mom holding her hand, and a nurse was standing by the EKG thing.
Within moments, the sound of my mom's labored breathing slowed. Then she inhaled and didn't exhale.
"Was that it?" one of us asked the nurse. I don't remember who. She nodded.
And that was it.

# things that died with my mom

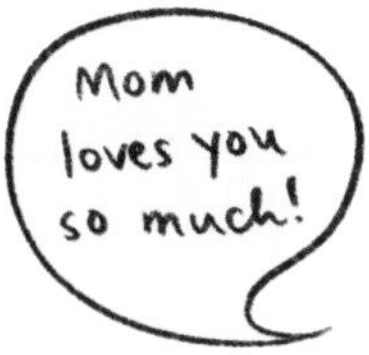
Mom loves you so much!

talking about her in the present tense

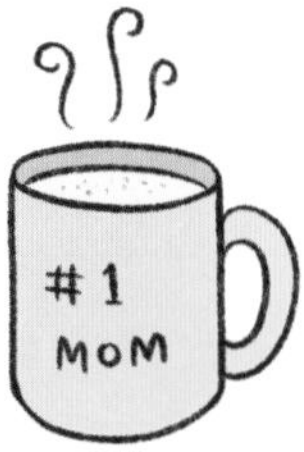
#1 MOM

her recipe for the warm vanilla milk she'd make when we were little

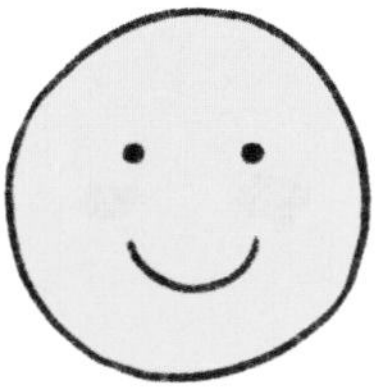

feeling "normal"

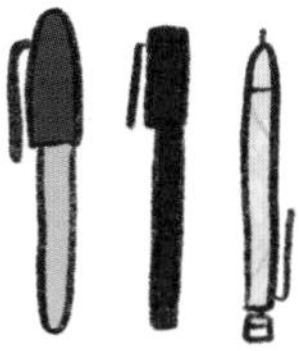

her handwriting

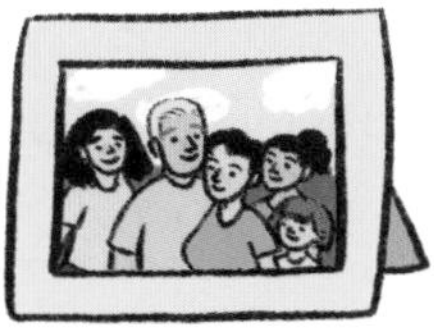

feeling like our family was WHOLE

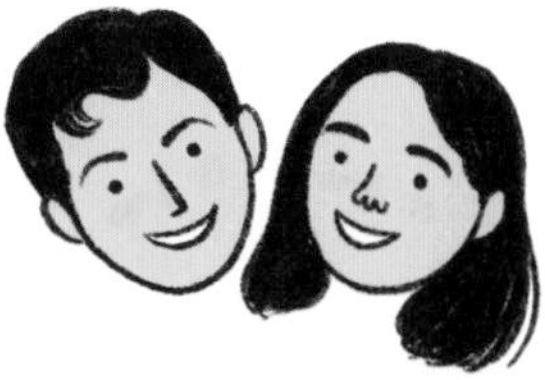

having someone in my family who was so much like me and still turned out OK

PLUS: all her stories and memories and opinions and secrets and the weirdly specific things she knew off the top of her head

## THE ELISABETH KÜBLER-ROSS STAGES of GRIEF

(which were actually meant to describe the emotional progression of patients diagnosed with terminal illnesses, not people coping with loss)
(but anyway)

1. DENIAL
2. ANGER
3. BARGAINING
4. DEPRESSION
5. ACCEPTANCE

## THE STAGES OF GRIEF I HAVE PERSONALLY EXPERIENCED

emotional eating
depression
insomnia
dramatic sighing
wild laughter
impossible bargaining
annoyance
inappropriate jokes
fury
sleepiness
obsessive research
wanting to be alone
neediness
screaming
nail biting
stress dancing

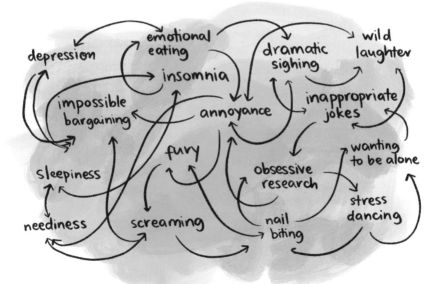

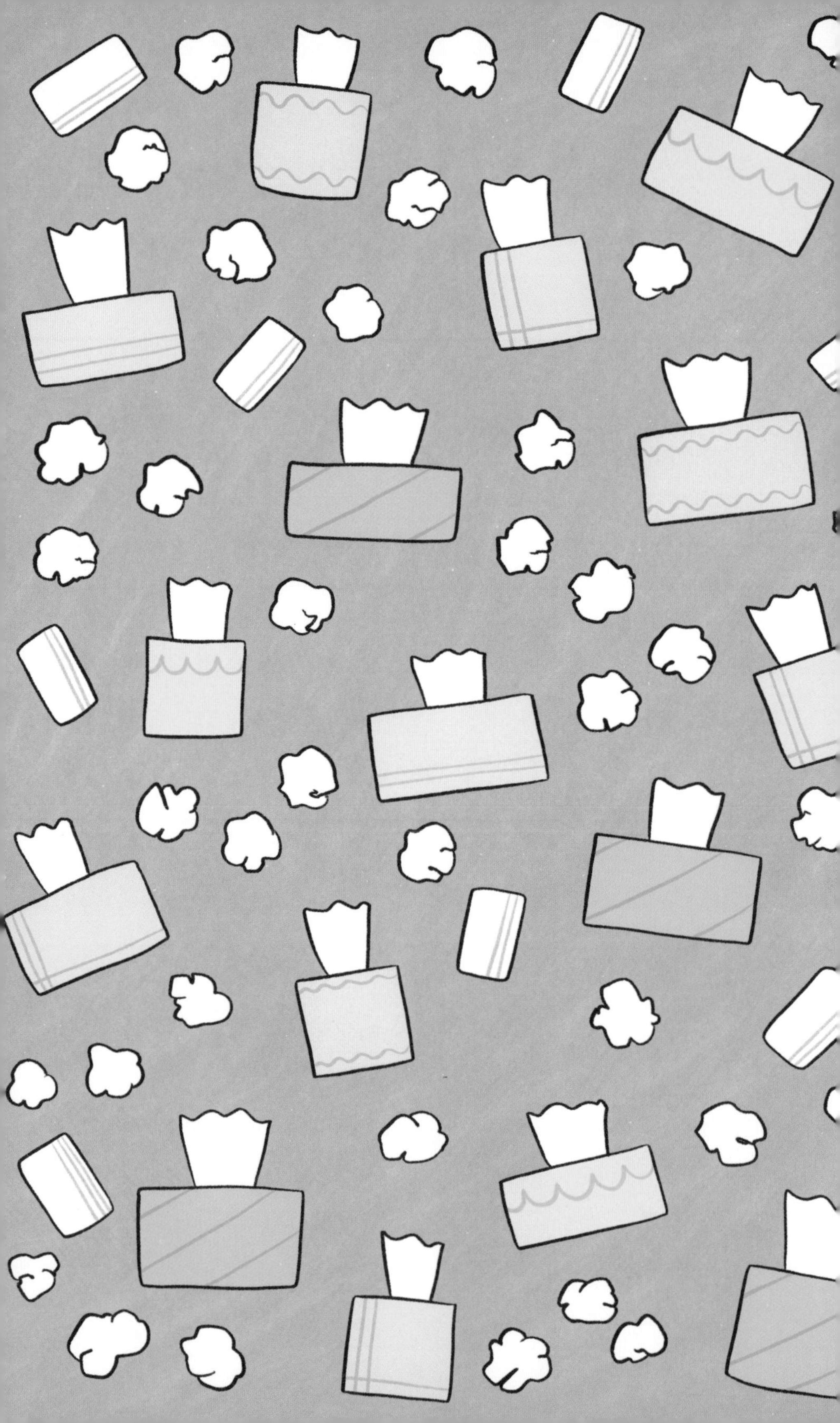

# chapter five

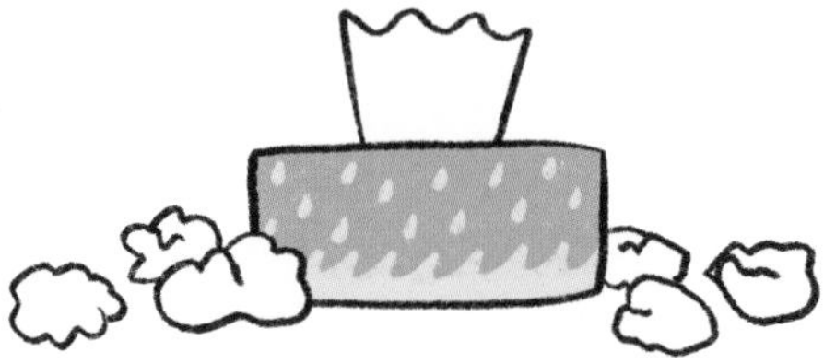

## Making Arrangements

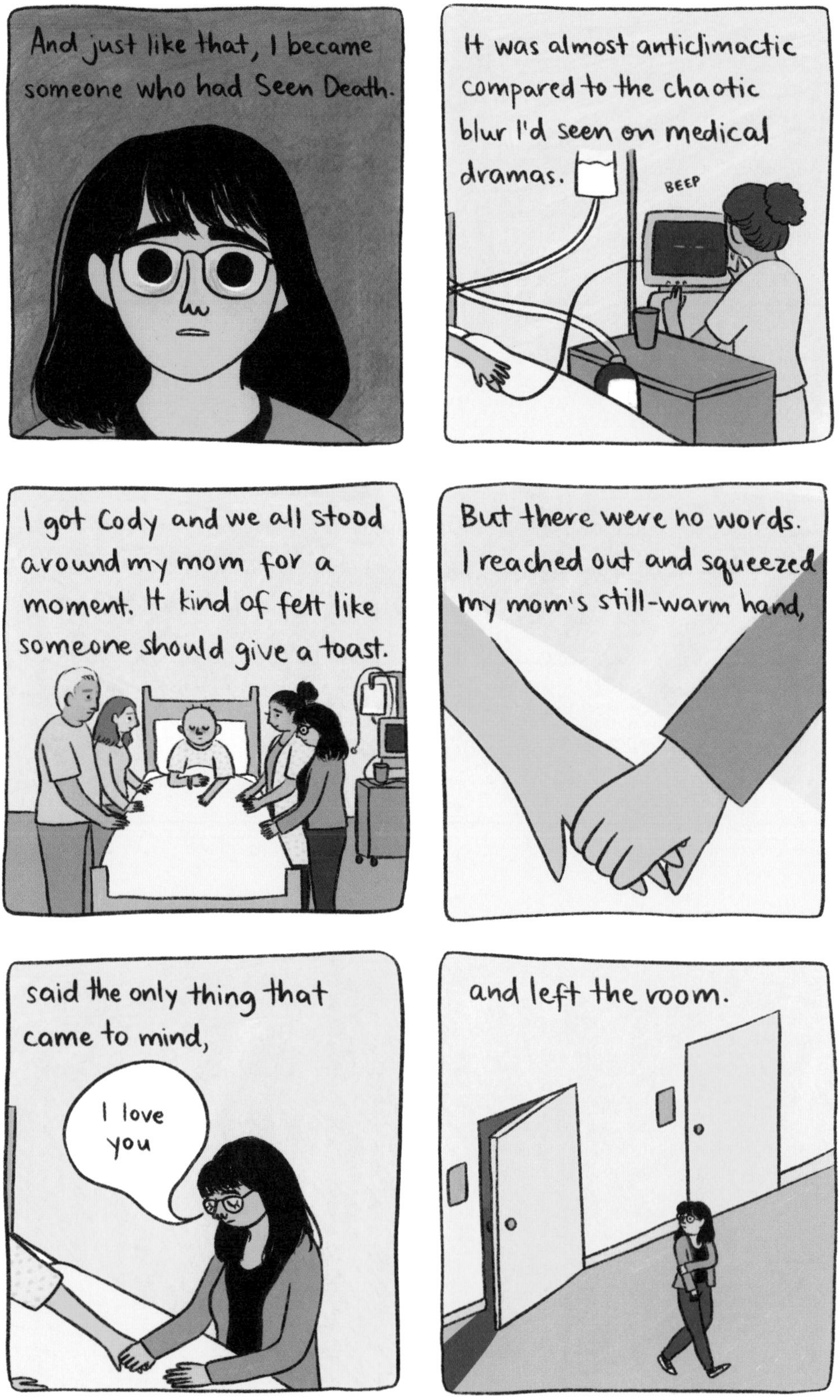
And just like that, I became someone who had Seen Death.
It was almost anticlimactic compared to the chaotic blur I'd seen on medical dramas.
BEEP
I got Cody and we all stood around my mom for a moment. It kind of felt like someone should give a toast.
But there were no words. I reached out and squeezed my mom's still-warm hand,
said the only thing that came to mind,
I love you
and left the room.

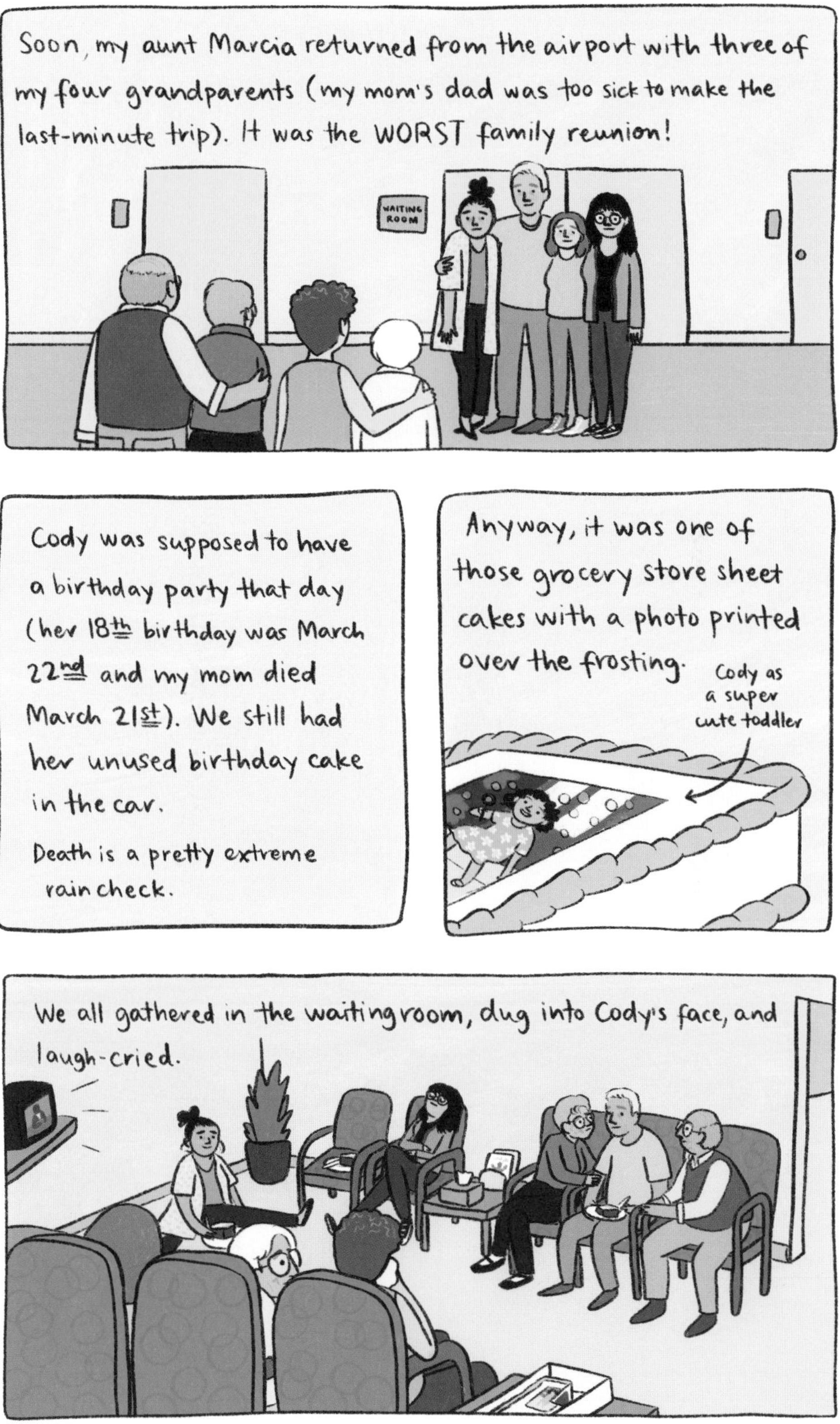
Soon, my aunt Marcia returned from the airport with three of my four grandparents (my mom's dad was too sick to make the last-minute trip). It was the WORST family reunion!
WAITING ROOM
Cody was supposed to have a birthday party that day (her 18th birthday was March 22nd and my mom died March 21st). We still had her unused birthday cake in the car.
Death is a pretty extreme rain check.
Anyway, it was one of those grocery store sheet cakes with a photo printed over the frosting.
Cody as a super cute toddler
We all gathered in the waiting room, dug into Cody's face, and laugh-cried.

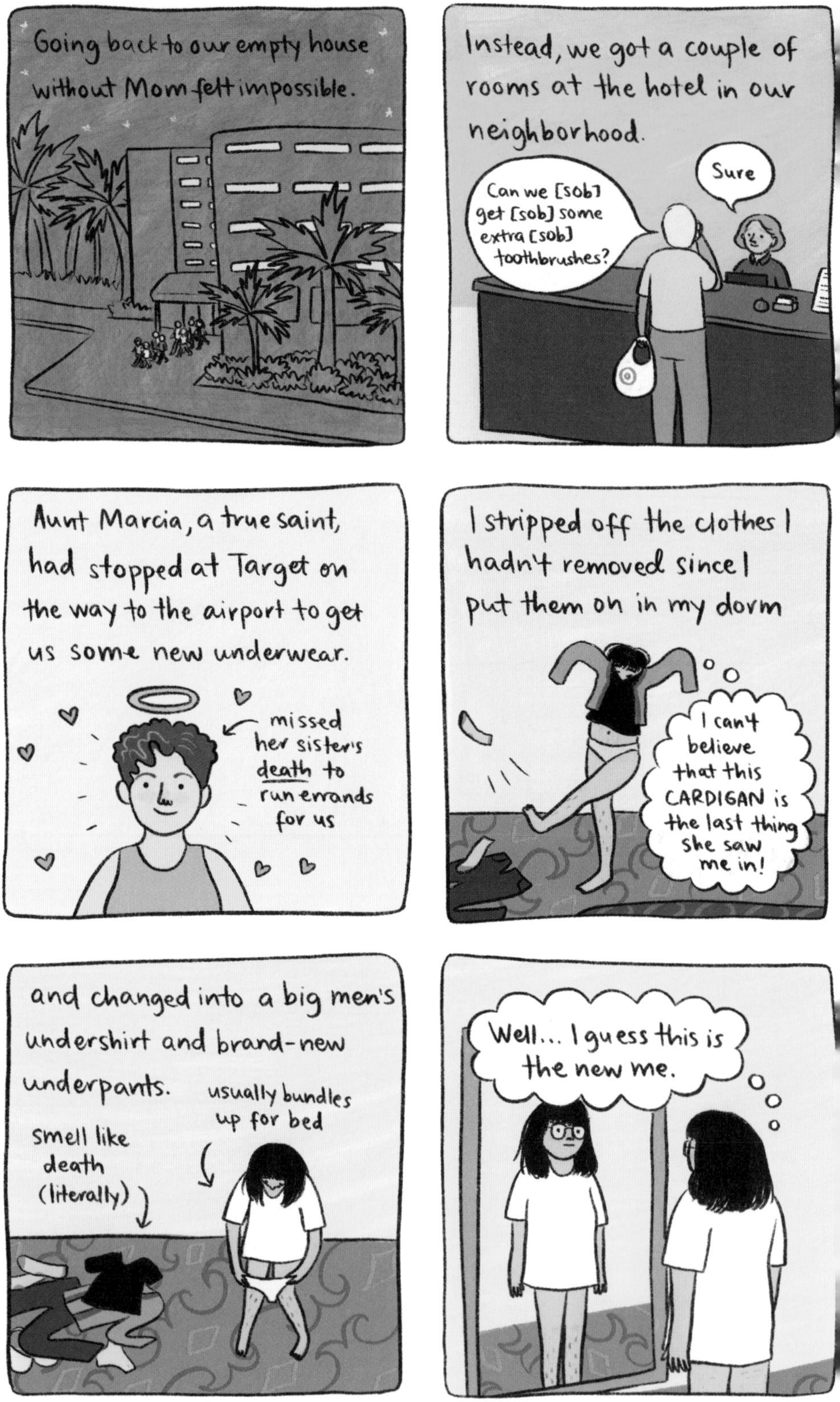
Going back to our empty house without Mom felt impossible.
Instead, we got a couple of rooms at the hotel in our neighborhood.
Can we [sob] get [sob] some extra [sob] toothbrushes?
Sure
Aunt Marcia, a true saint, had stopped at Target on the way to the airport to get us some new underwear.
missed her sister's death to run errands for us
I stripped off the clothes I hadn't removed since I put them on in my dorm
I can't believe that this CARDIGAN is the last thing she saw me in!
and changed into a big men's undershirt and brand-new underpants.
usually bundles up for bed
smell like death (literally)
Well... I guess this is the new me.

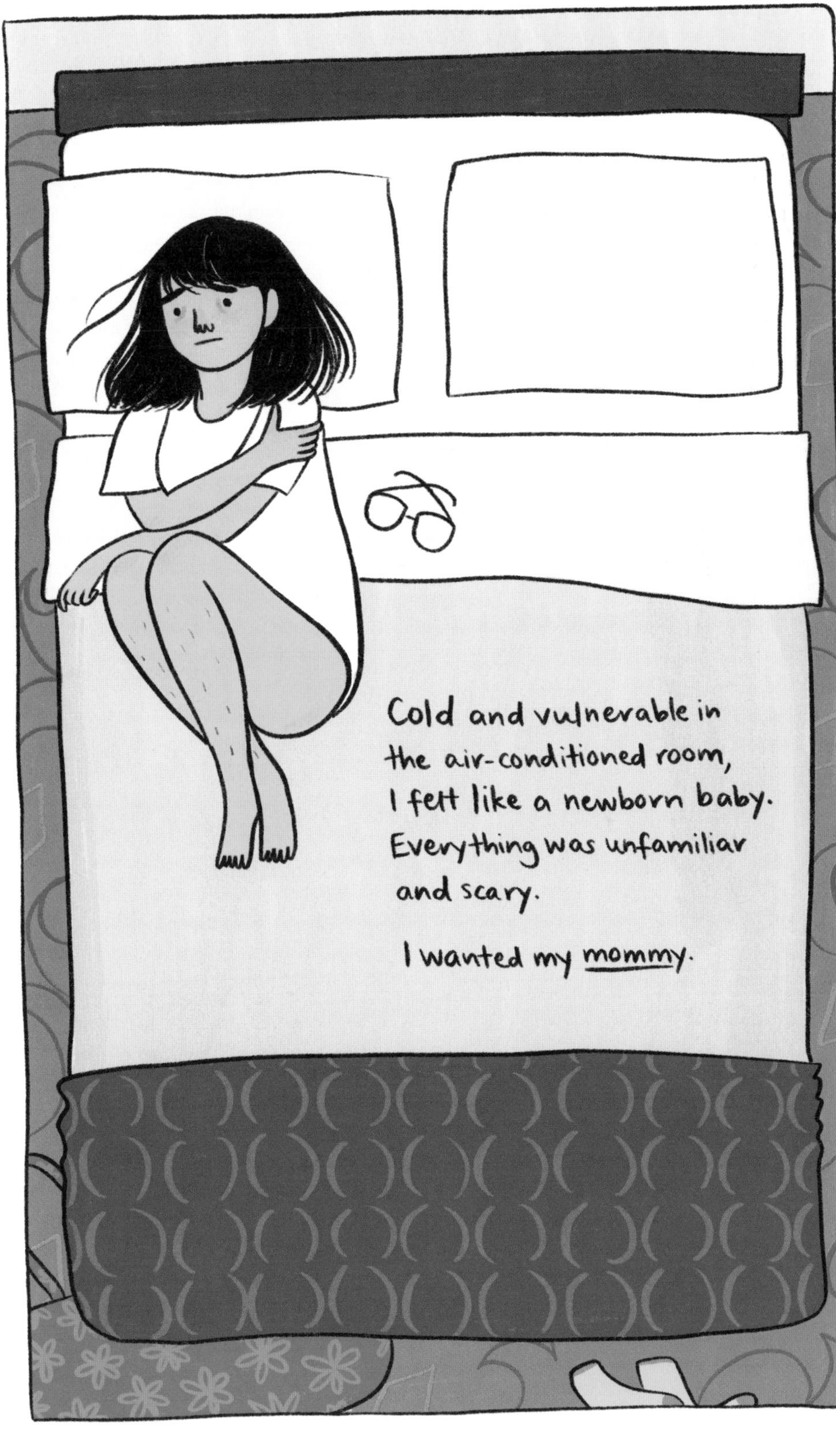
Cold and vulnerable in the air-conditioned room, I felt like a newborn baby. Everything was unfamiliar and scary.
I wanted my mommy.

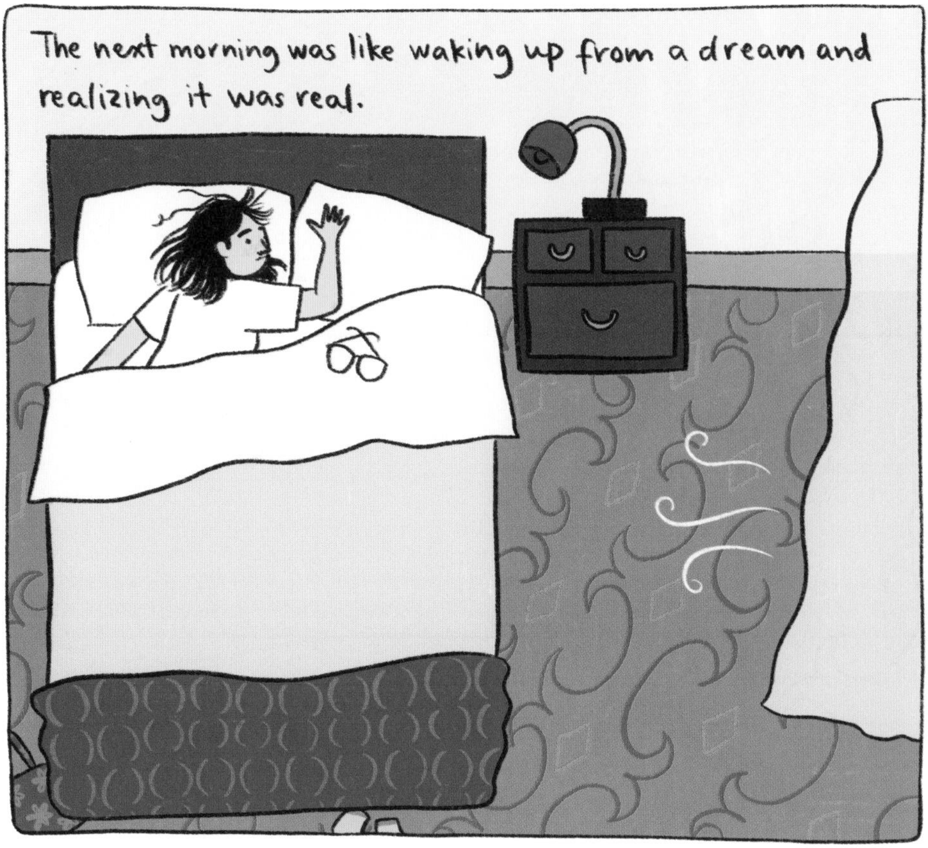
The next morning was like waking up from a dream and realizing it was real.

I couldn't believe I'd watched my mom DIE! She was DEAD. That doesn't sound like a thing that can just happen to anyone!!

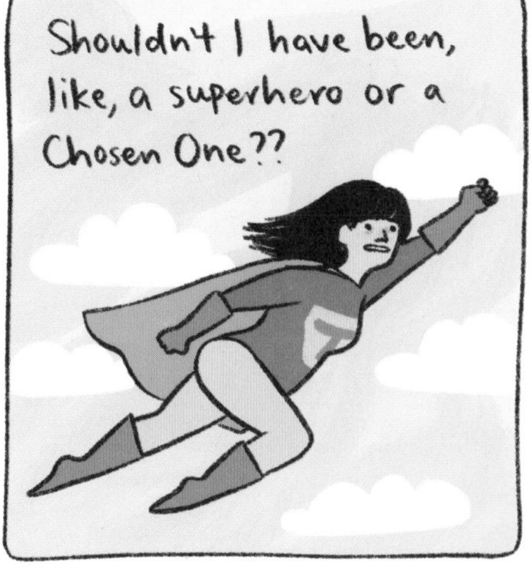
Shouldn't I have been, like, a superhero or a Chosen One??

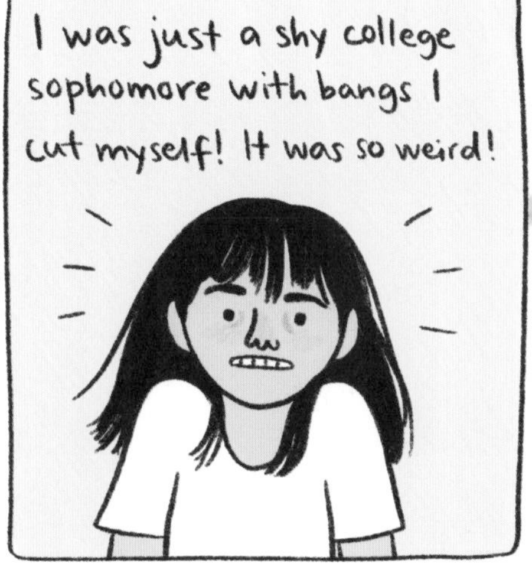
I was just a shy college sophomore with bangs I cut myself! It was so weird!

And yet, there was the teensiest bit of relief.

The nice (?) part of having a parent die of cancer is that, once they're dead, they can never die again. The pain of losing my mom would never go away, but the pain of seeing her sick was OVER.

No more hearing secondhand that she needs a walker now or watching the light go out of her eyes in stages.

PLOP

No more phone calls with "a little bit of news."

EXHALE

No more wondering.

The certainty of loss was cold and steady under my feet.

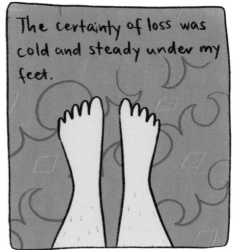

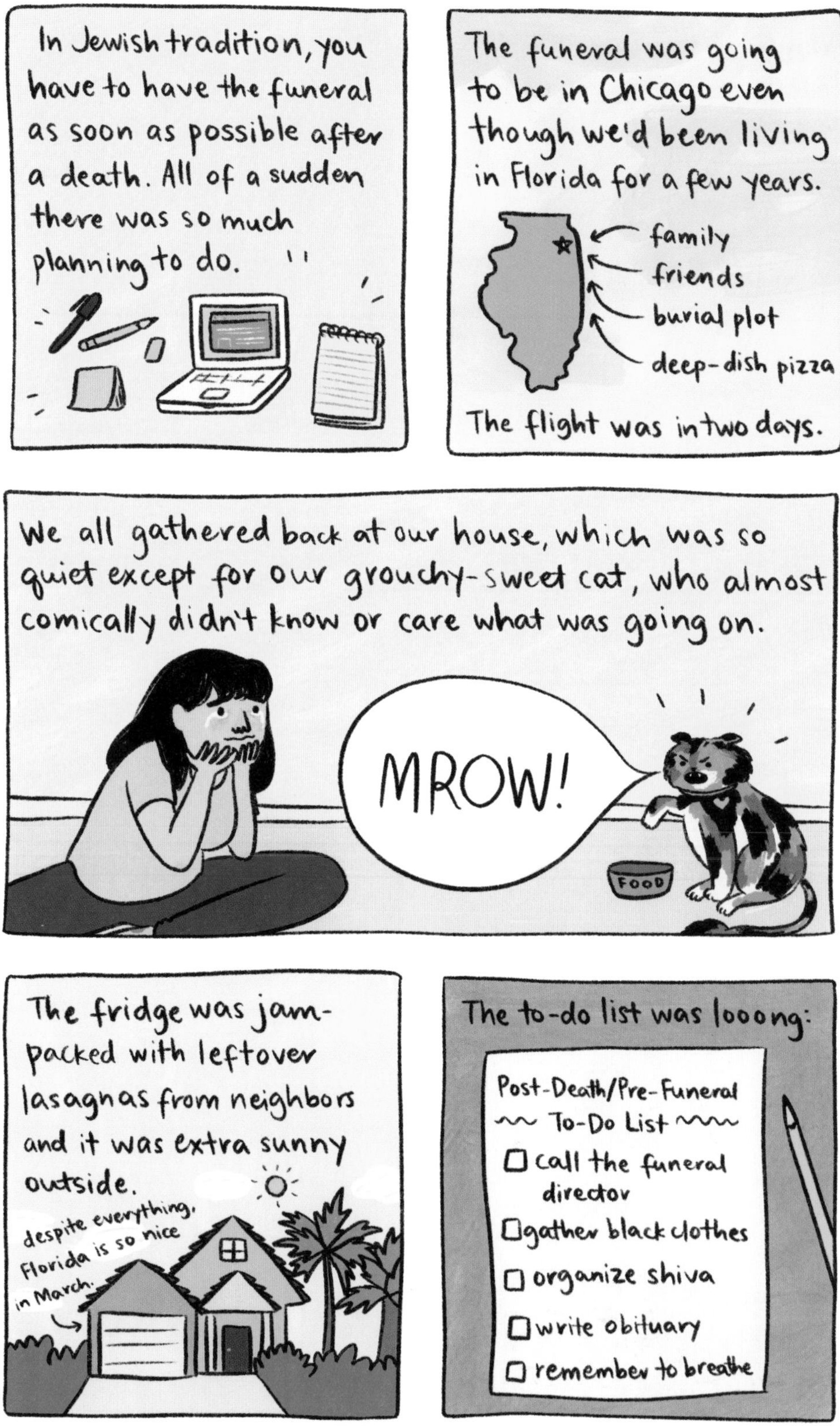
In Jewish tradition, you have to have the funeral as soon as possible after a death. All of a sudden there was so much planning to do.
The funeral was going to be in Chicago even though we'd been living in Florida for a few years.
family
friends
burial plot
deep-dish pizza
The flight was in two days.
We all gathered back at our house, which was so quiet except for our grouchy-sweet cat, who almost comically didn't know or care what was going on.
MROW!
FOOD
The fridge was jam-packed with leftover lasagnas from neighbors and it was extra sunny outside.
despite everything, Florida is so nice in March.
The to-do list was looong:
Post-Death/Pre-Funeral
To-Do List
call the funeral director
gather black clothes
organize shiva
write obituary
remember to breathe

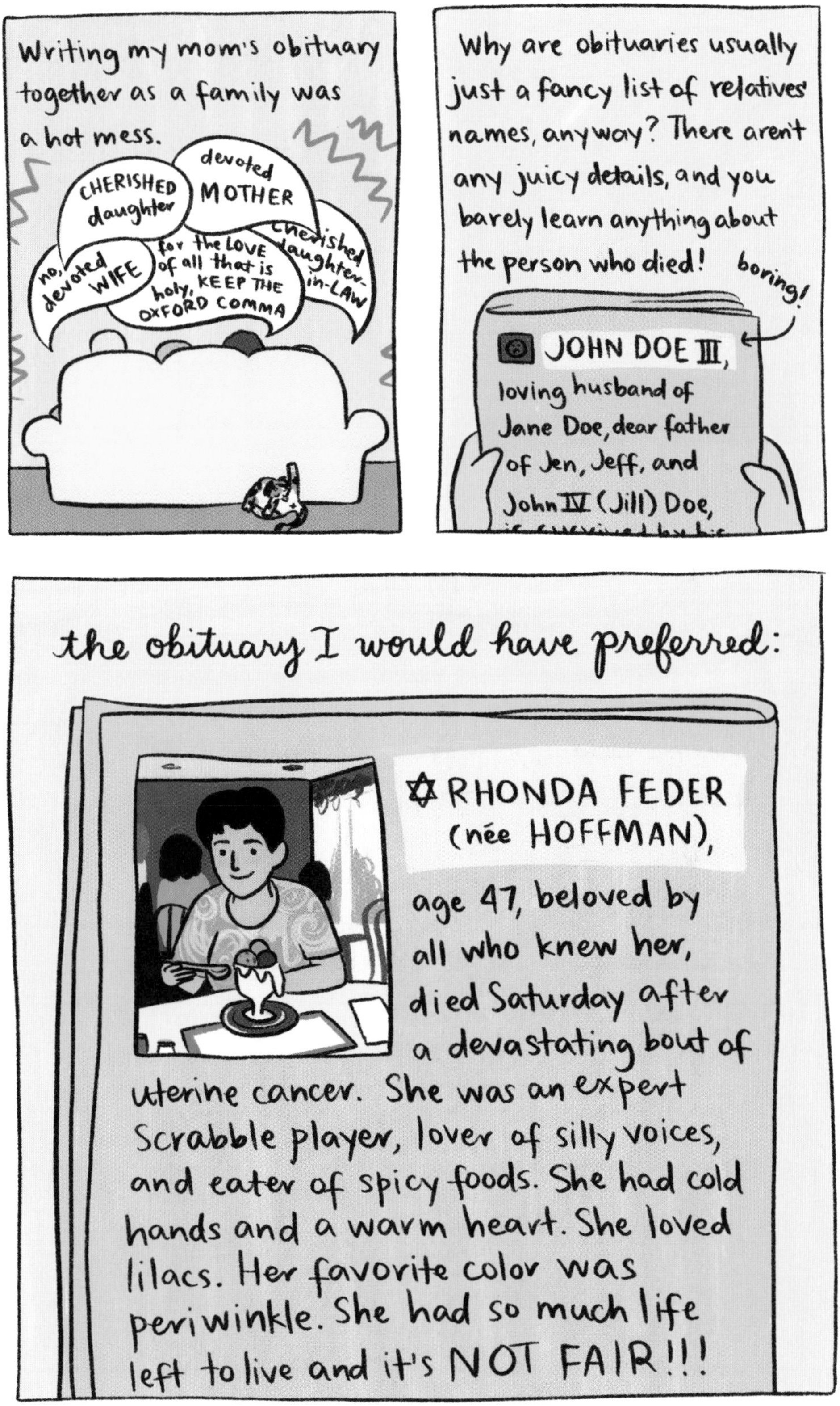
Writing my mom's obituary together as a family was a hot mess.
CHERISHED daughter
devoted MOTHER
cherished daughter-in-LAW
no, devoted WIFE
for the LOVE of all that is holy, KEEP THE OXFORD COMMA
Why are obituaries usually just a fancy list of relatives' names, anyway? There aren't any juicy details, and you barely learn anything about the person who died!
boring!
JOHN DOE III,
loving husband of Jane Doe, dear father of Jen, Jeff, and John IV (Jill) Doe,
the obituary I would have preferred:
✡ RHONDA FEDER (née HOFFMAN),
age 47, beloved by all who knew her, died Saturday after a devastating bout of uterine cancer. She was an expert Scrabble player, lover of silly voices, and eater of spicy foods. She had cold hands and a warm heart. She loved lilacs. Her favorite color was periwinkle. She had so much life left to live and it's NOT FAIR!!!

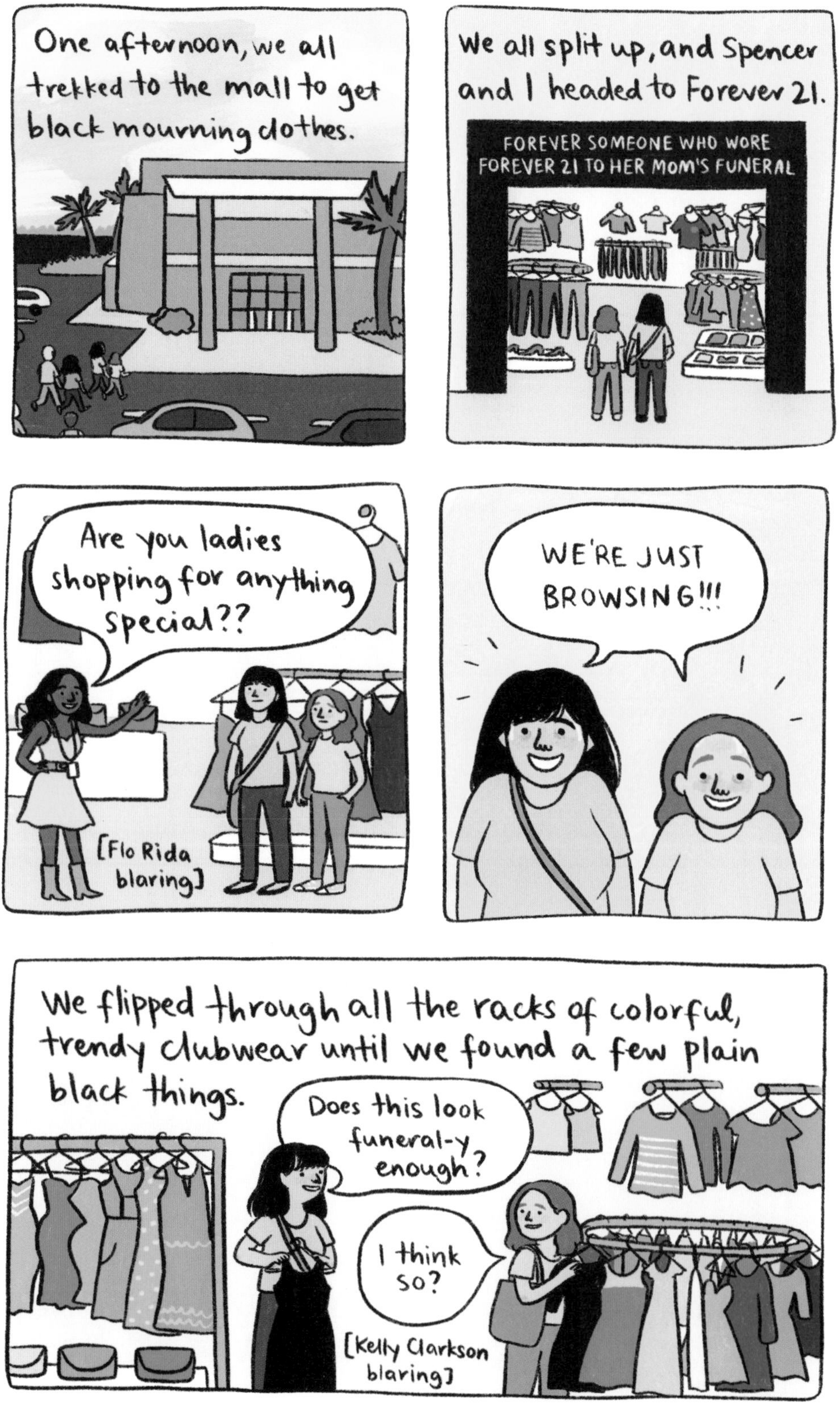

One afternoon, we all trekked to the mall to get black mourning clothes.
We all split up, and Spencer and I headed to Forever 21.
FOREVER SOMEONE WHO WORE FOREVER 21 TO HER MOM'S FUNERAL
Are you ladies shopping for anything special??
[Flo Rida blaring]
WE'RE JUST BROWSING!!!
We flipped through all the racks of colorful, trendy clubwear until we found a few plain black things.
Does this look funeral-y enough?
I think so?
[Kelly Clarkson blaring]

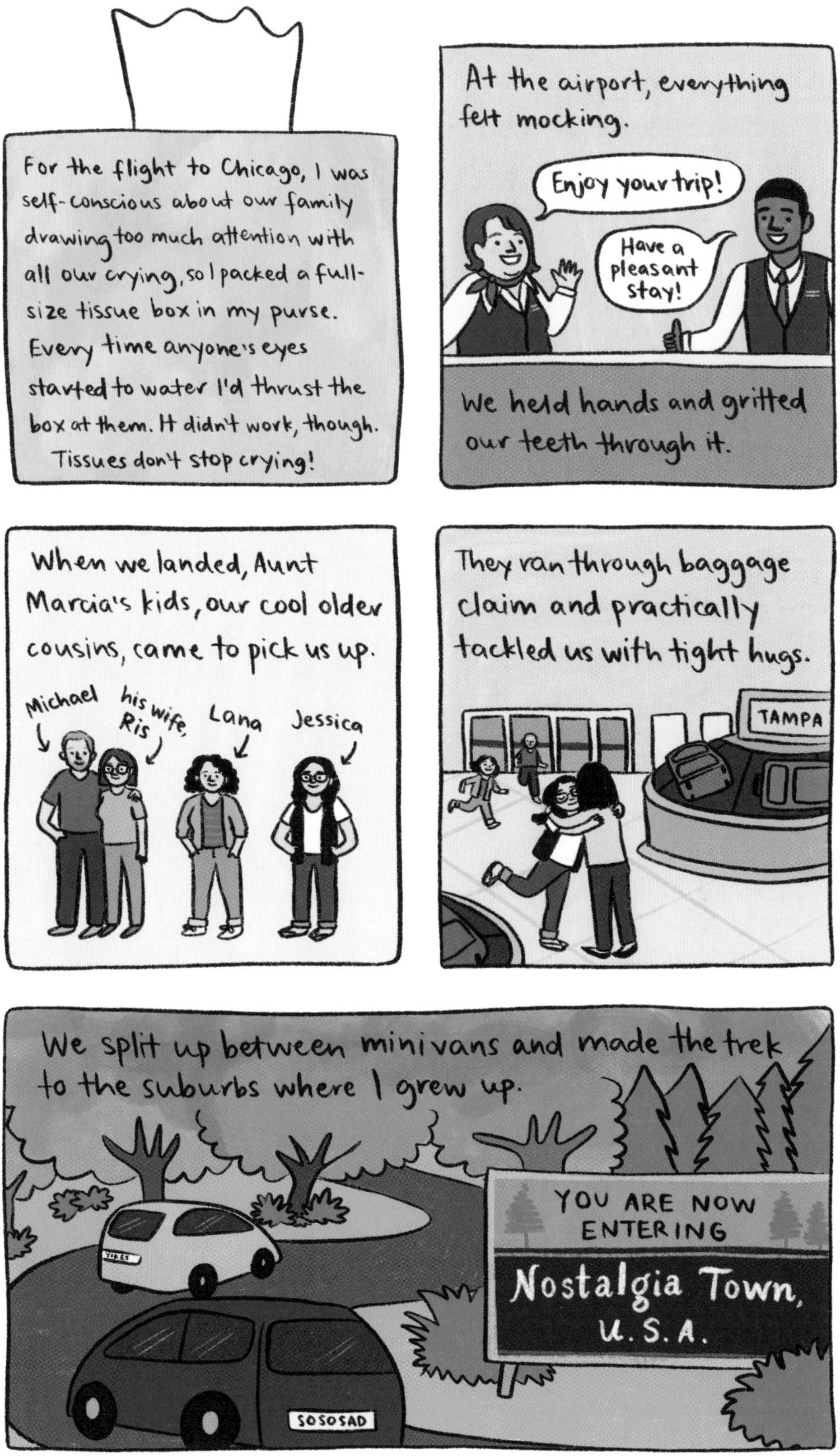
For the flight to Chicago, I was self-conscious about our family drawing too much attention with all our crying, so I packed a full-size tissue box in my purse. Every time anyone's eyes started to water I'd thrust the box at them. It didn't work, though.
Tissues don't stop crying!
At the airport, everything felt mocking.
Enjoy your trip!
Have a pleasant stay!
We held hands and gritted our teeth through it.
When we landed, Aunt Marcia's kids, our cool older cousins, came to pick us up.
Michael
his wife, Ris
Lana
Jessica
They ran through baggage claim and practically tackled us with tight hugs.
TAMPA
We split up between minivans and made the trek to the suburbs where I grew up.
YOU ARE NOW ENTERING
Nostalgia Town, U.S.A.
SOSOSAD

Jewish mourning rituals usually take place at the home of the deceased, but since we didn't live in Chicago anymore, we had ours at Aunt Marcia's.

With my dad, my sisters, and me, PLUS Mike, Ris, Lana, and Jessica all staying there, it was a __full__ house.

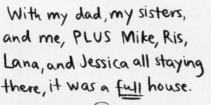

It was loud and busy, everyone joking and interrupting each other.

The chaos of all of us living in one house was comforting and familiar.

Like a damp cloth on the forehead when you have a headache, the relief was immense, if temporary.

Mmm

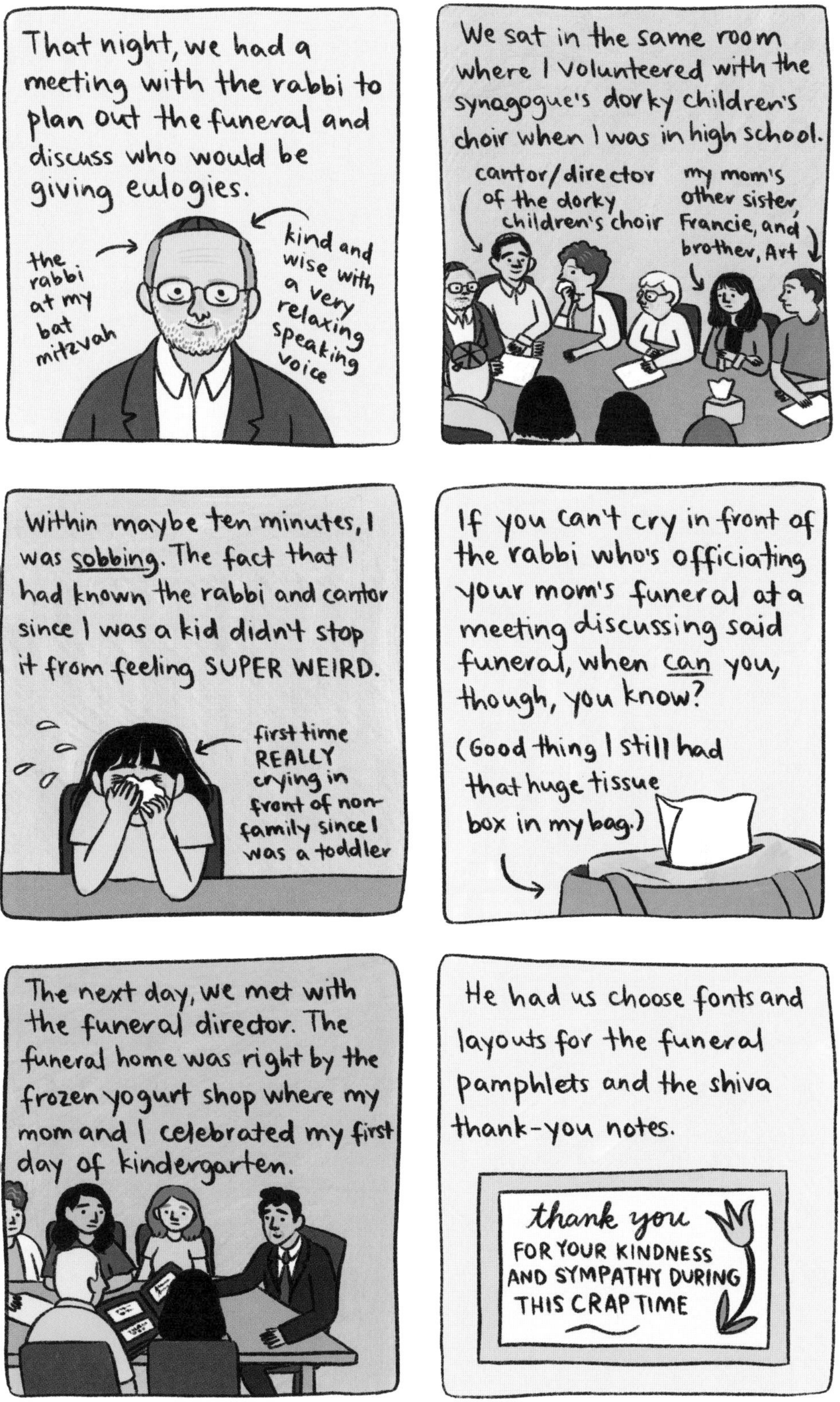
That night, we had a meeting with the rabbi to plan out the funeral and discuss who would be giving eulogies.
the rabbi at my bat mitzvah
kind and wise with a very relaxing speaking voice
We sat in the same room where I volunteered with the synagogue's dorky children's choir when I was in high school.
cantor/director of the dorky children's choir
my mom's other sister, Francie, and brother, Art
Within maybe ten minutes, I was sobbing. The fact that I had known the rabbi and cantor since I was a kid didn't stop it from feeling SUPER WEIRD.
first time REALLY crying in front of non-family since I was a toddler
If you can't cry in front of the rabbi who's officiating your mom's funeral at a meeting discussing said funeral, when can you, though, you know?
(Good thing I still had that huge tissue box in my bag.)
The next day, we met with the funeral director. The funeral home was right by the frozen yogurt shop where my mom and I celebrated my first day of kindergarten.
He had us choose fonts and layouts for the funeral pamphlets and the shiva thank-you notes.
thank you
FOR YOUR KINDNESS AND SYMPATHY DURING THIS CRAP TIME

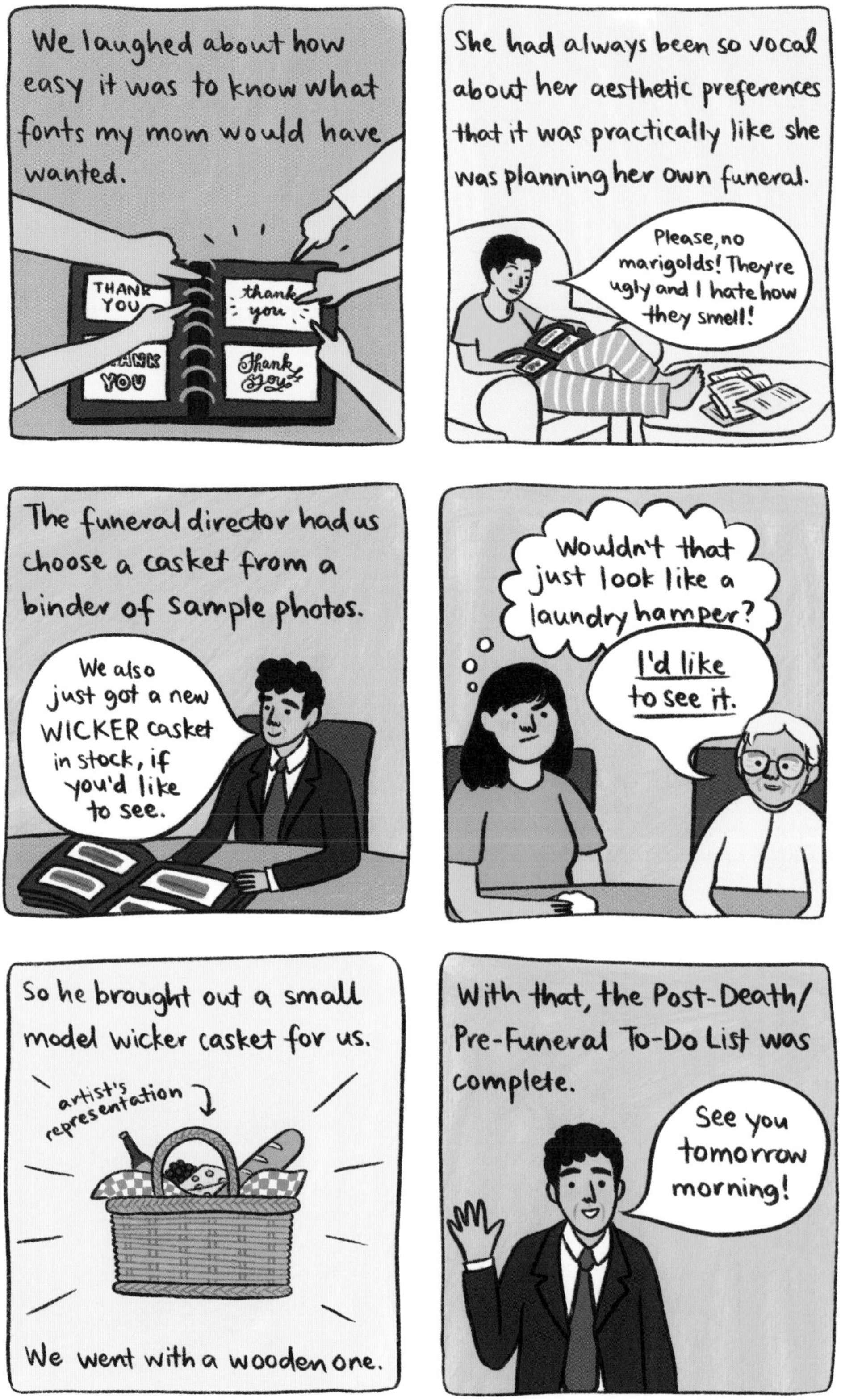
We laughed about how easy it was to know what fonts my mom would have wanted.
THANK YOU
thank you
THANK YOU
Thank You
She had always been so vocal about her aesthetic preferences that it was practically like she was planning her own funeral.
Please, no marigolds! They're ugly and I hate how they smell!
The funeral director had us choose a casket from a binder of sample photos.
We also just got a new WICKER casket in stock, if you'd like to see.
Wouldn't that just look like a laundry hamper?
I'd like to see it.
So he brought out a small model wicker casket for us.
artist's representation
We went with a wooden one.
With that, the Post-Death/ Pre-Funeral To-Do List was complete.
See you tomorrow morning!

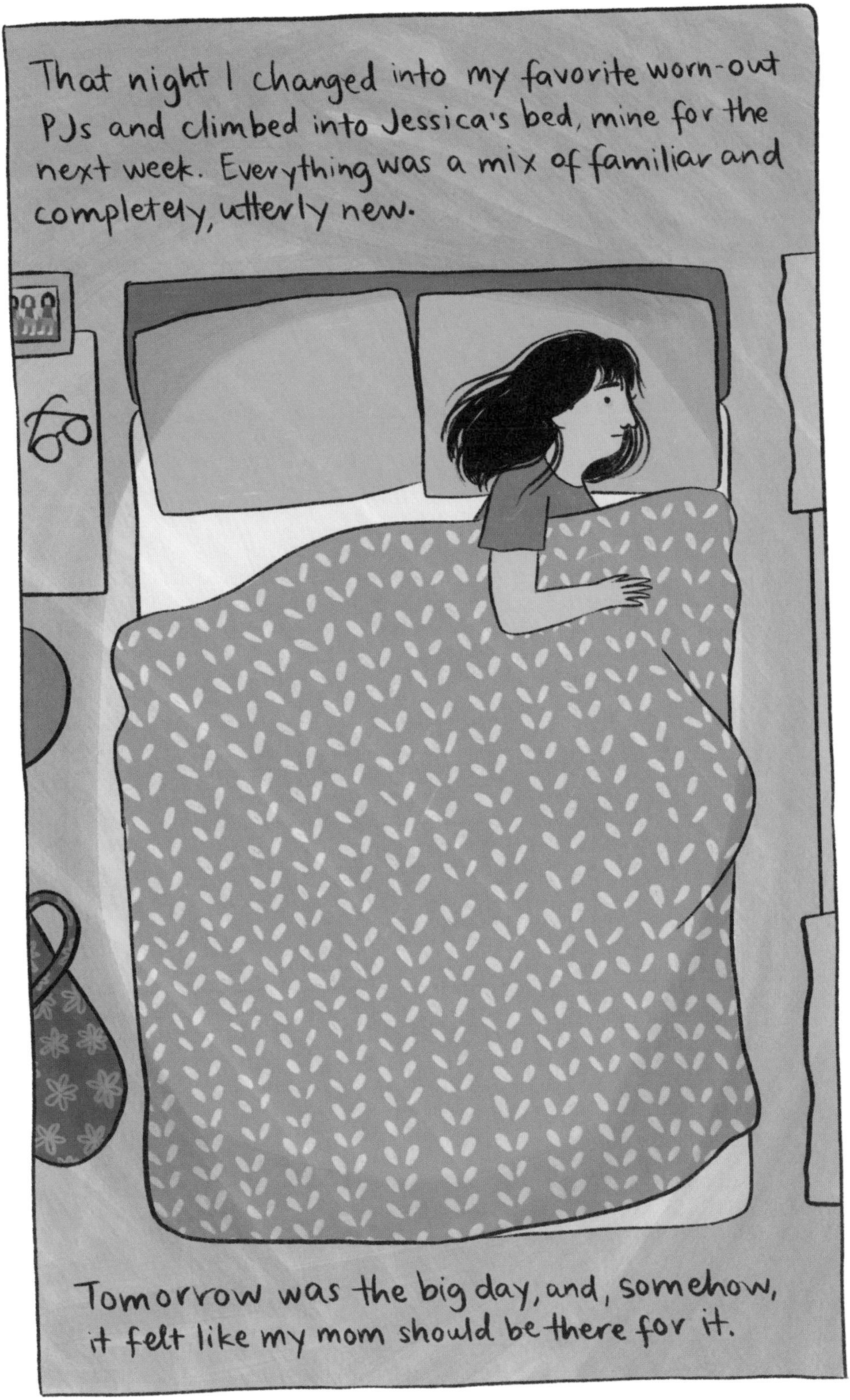
That night I changed into my favorite worn-out PJs and climbed into Jessica's bed, mine for the next week. Everything was a mix of familiar and completely, utterly new.
Tomorrow was the big day, and, somehow, it felt like my mom should be there for it.

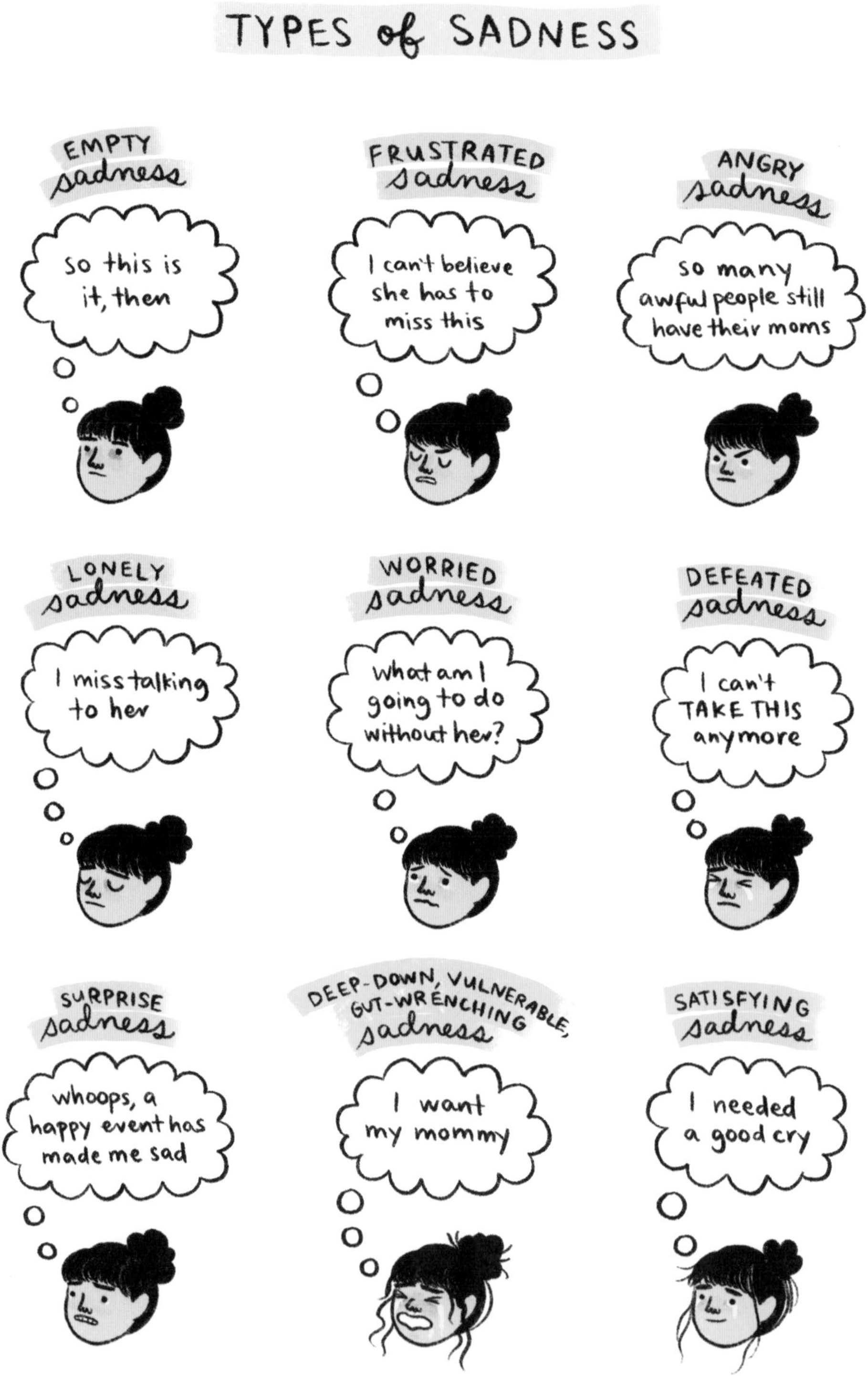
TYPES of SADNESS
EMPTY sadness
so this is it, then
FRUSTRATED sadness
I can't believe she has to miss this
ANGRY sadness
so many awful people still have their moms
LONELY sadness
I miss talking to her
WORRIED sadness
what am I going to do without her?
DEFEATED sadness
I can't TAKE THIS anymore
SURPRISE sadness
whoops, a happy event has made me sad
DEEP-DOWN, VULNERABLE, GUT-WRENCHING sadness
I want my mommy
SATISFYING sadness
I needed a good cry

*chapter six*

## THE DEATH CIRCUS
### part 1

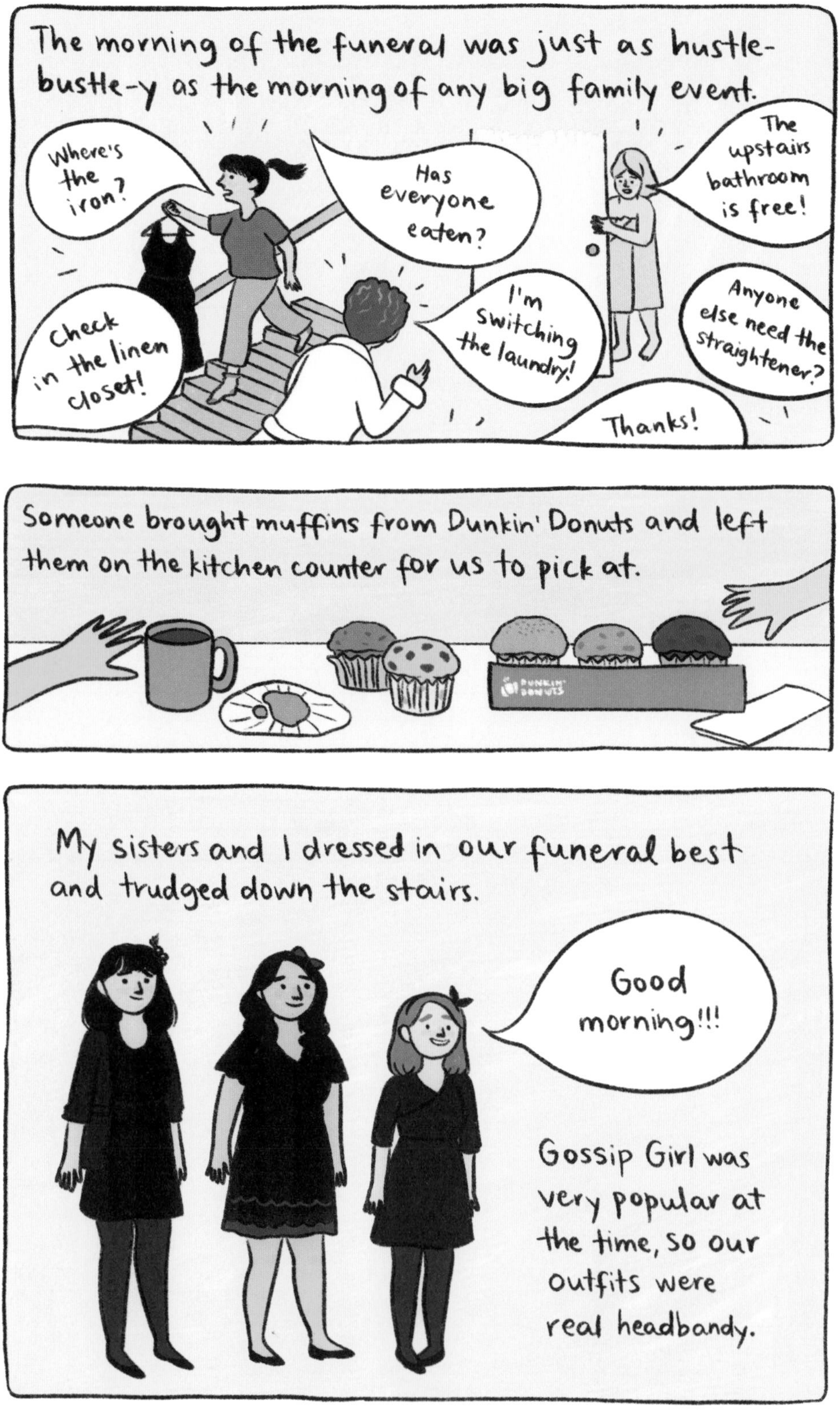
The morning of the funeral was just as hustle-bustle-y as the morning of any big family event.
Where's the iron?
Check in the linen closet!
Has everyone eaten?
I'm switching the laundry!
The upstairs bathroom is free!
Anyone else need the straightener?
Thanks!
Someone brought muffins from Dunkin' Donuts and left them on the kitchen counter for us to pick at.
DUNKIN' DONUTS
My sisters and I dressed in our funeral best and trudged down the stairs.
Good morning!!!
Gossip Girl was very popular at the time, so our outfits were real headbandy.

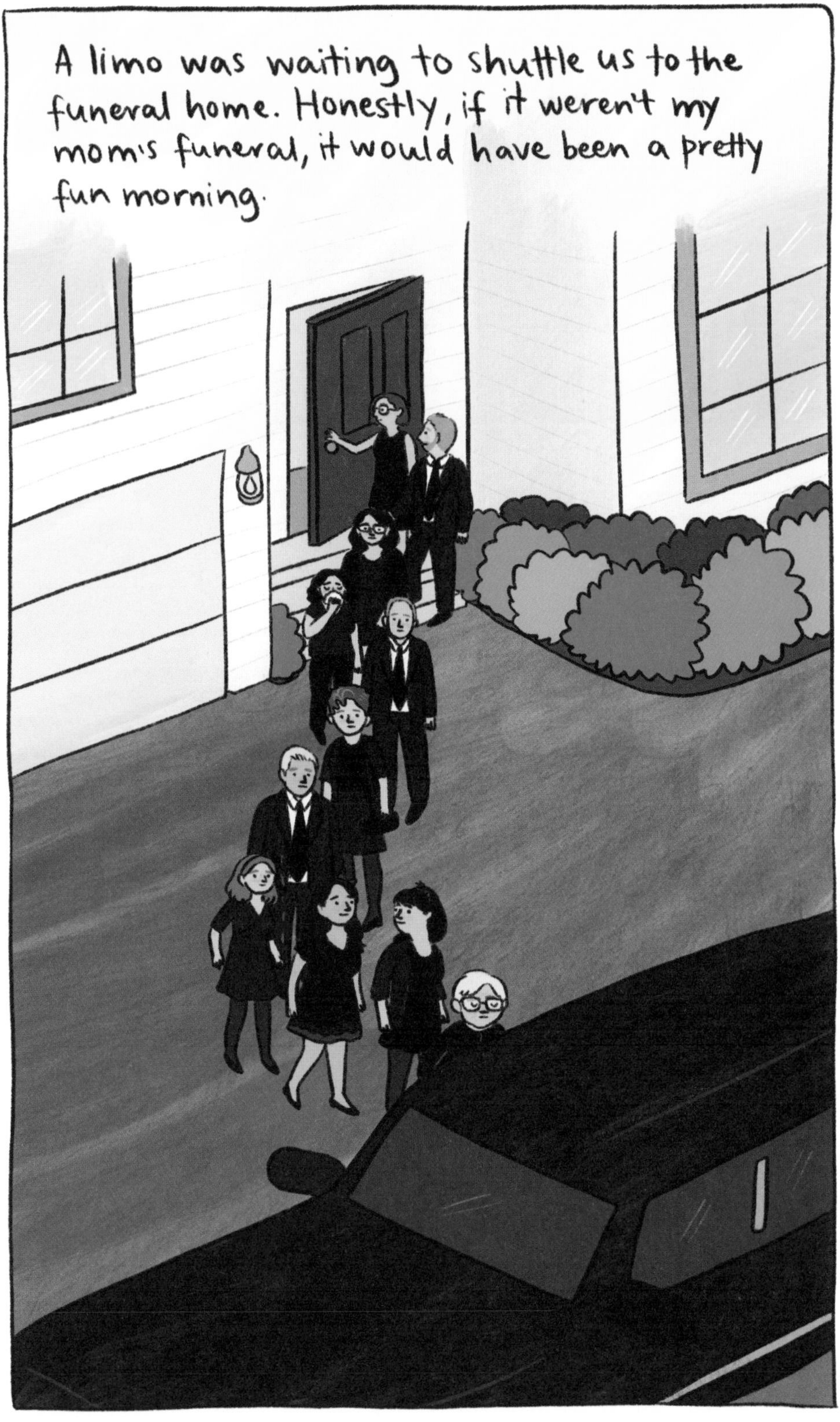
A limo was waiting to shuttle us to the funeral home. Honestly, if it weren't my mom's funeral, it would have been a pretty fun morning.

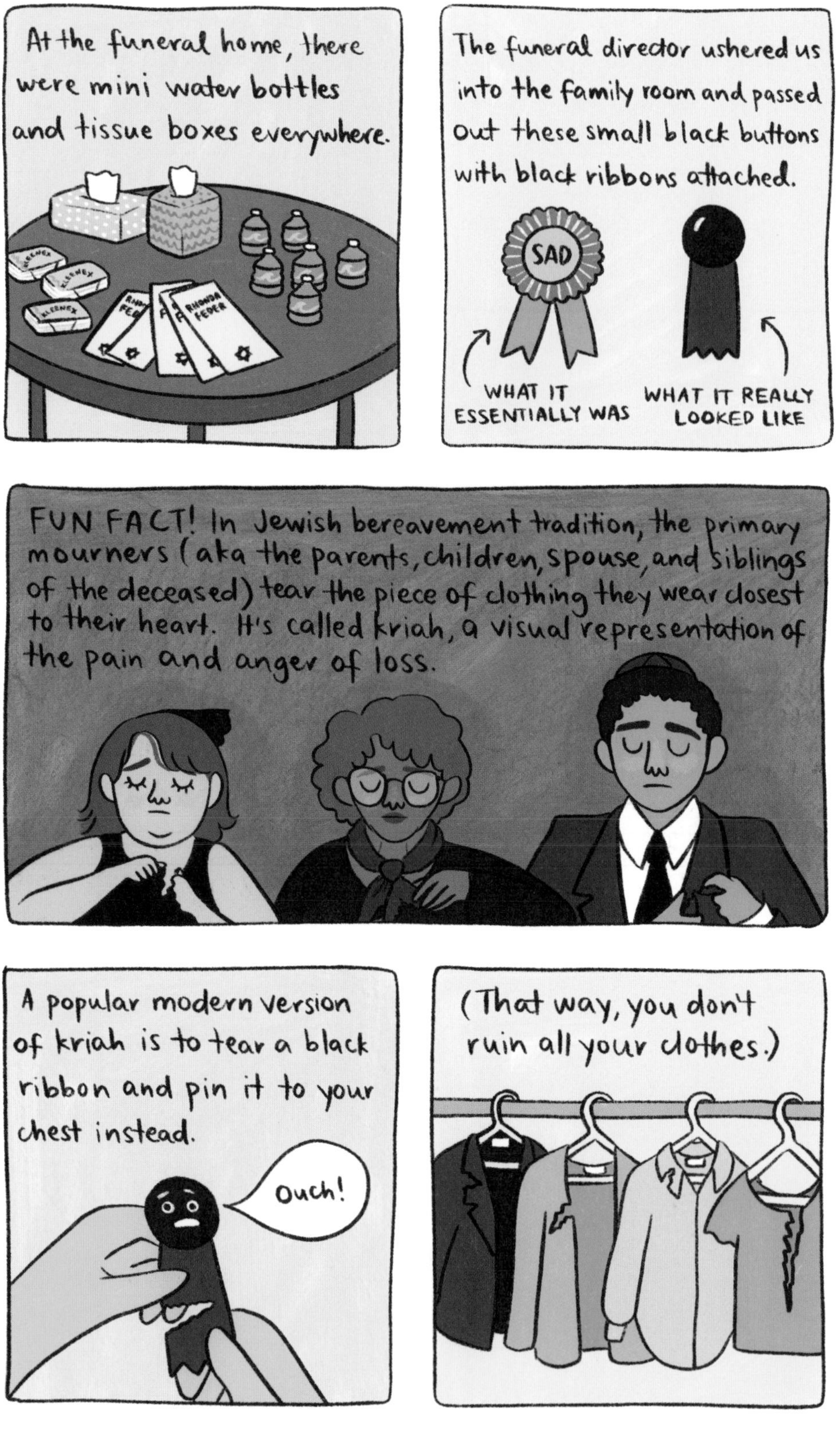
At the funeral home, there were mini water bottles and tissue boxes everywhere.
KLEENEX
KLEENEX
KLEENEX
RHONDA FEDER
The funeral director ushered us into the family room and passed out these small black buttons with black ribbons attached.
SAD
WHAT IT ESSENTIALLY WAS
WHAT IT REALLY LOOKED LIKE
FUN FACT! In Jewish bereavement tradition, the primary mourners (aka the parents, children, spouse, and siblings of the deceased) tear the piece of clothing they wear closest to their heart. It's called kriah, a visual representation of the pain and anger of loss.
A popular modern version of kriah is to tear a black ribbon and pin it to your chest instead.
Ouch!
(That way, you don't ruin all your clothes.)

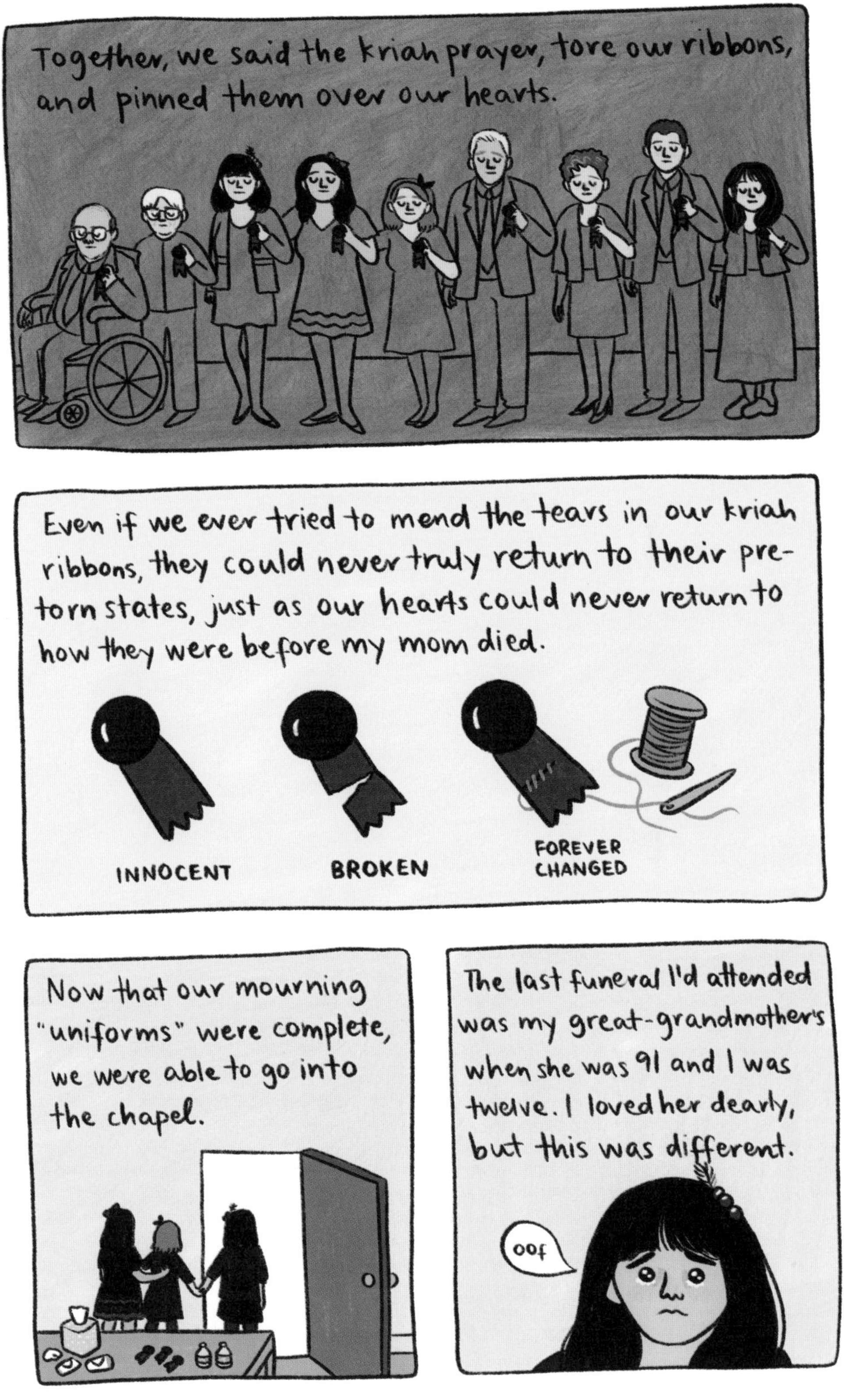
Together, we said the kriah prayer, tore our ribbons, and pinned them over our hearts.
Even if we ever tried to mend the tears in our kriah ribbons, they could never truly return to their pre-torn states, just as our hearts could never return to how they were before my mom died.
INNOCENT
BROKEN
FOREVER CHANGED
Now that our mourning "uniforms" were complete, we were able to go into the chapel.
The last funeral I'd attended was my great-grandmother's when she was 91 and I was twelve. I loved her dearly, but this was different.
oof

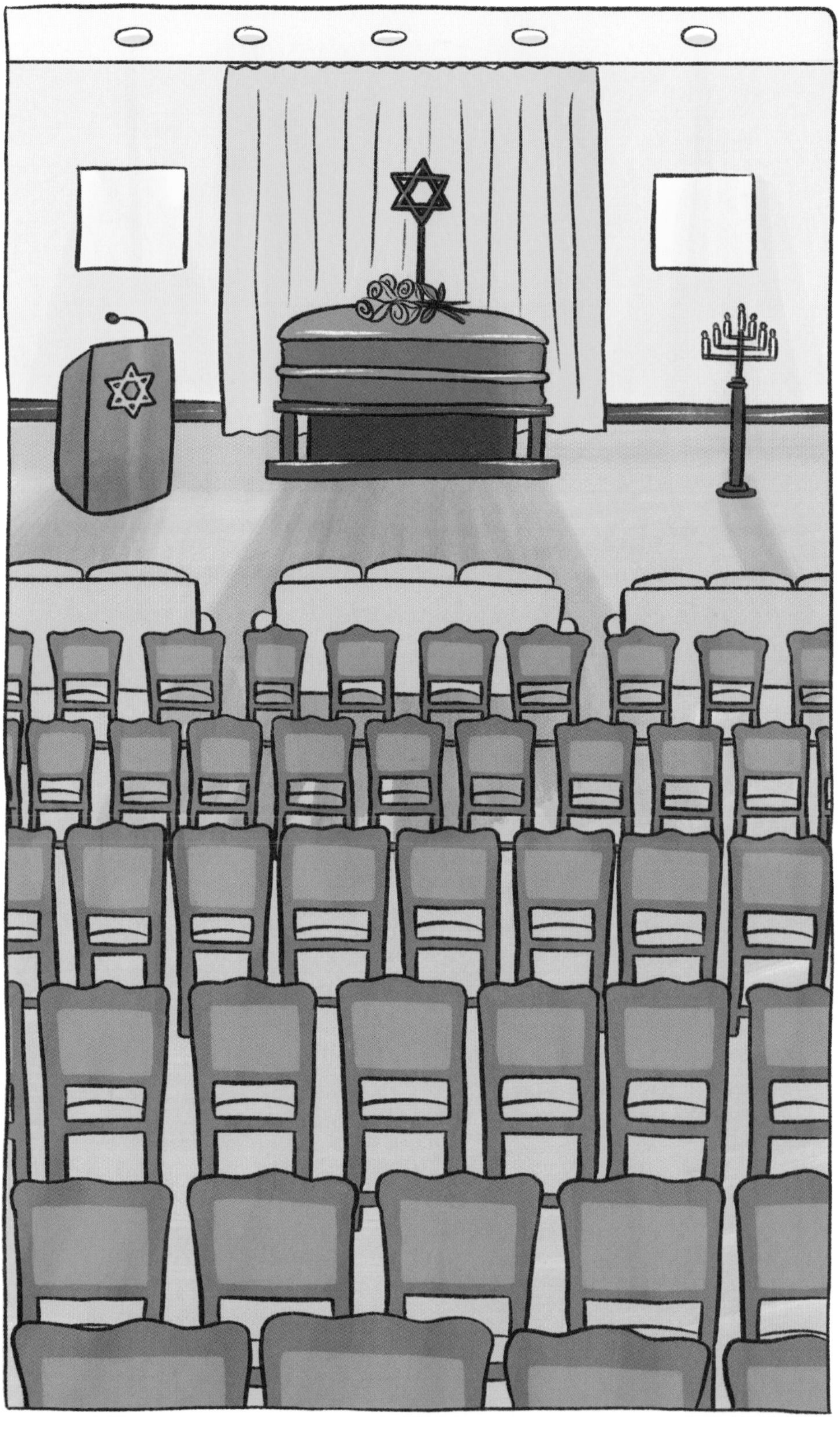

It was so <u>real</u>.

My mom's casket was shiny and surprisingly grand, propped up in the front of the room with a small pile of peach-colored roses draped on top. My whole life, my dad almost exclusively called my mom Peach. He always said that the nickname came from her peaches-and-cream complexion, but I secretly wondered if he got it from the pale layer of peach fuzz on her cheeks that I loved and she would be so mad that I'm mentioning here.

The rest of the room was filled with cushioned chairs, not unlike a synagogue or church, but the first row was instead made up of worn, velvety couches dotted with tissue boxes. Early morning sunlight was streaming through the small square windows so you could see tiny particles of dust lazily floating through the air.

It was a little stuffy and formal, but mostly comfortable and peaceful, a room that would look just right with a cat snoozing in a patch of warmth on the carpet.

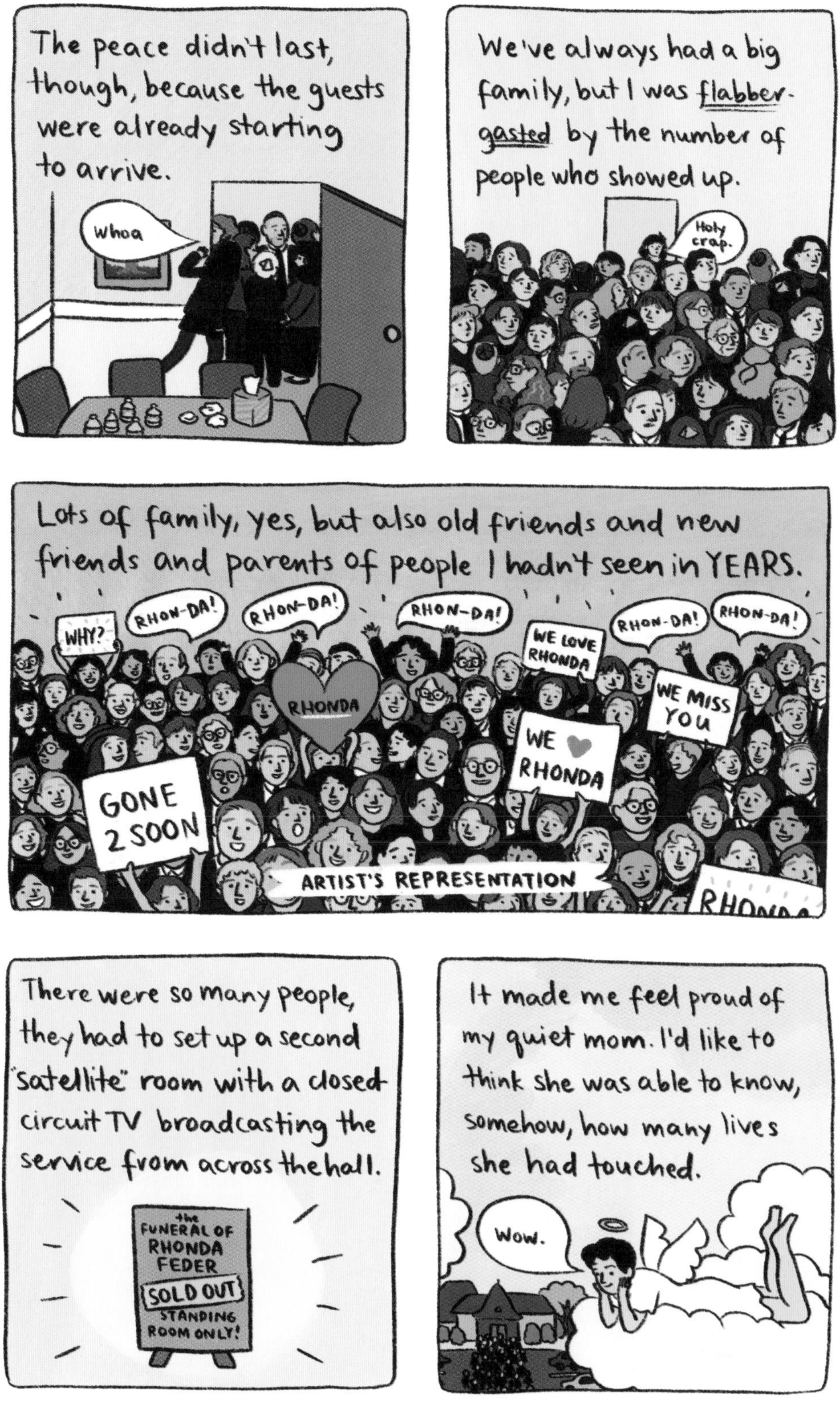
The peace didn't last, though, because the guests were already starting to arrive.
Whoa
We've always had a big family, but I was flabbergasted by the number of people who showed up.
Holy crap.
Lots of family, yes, but also old friends and new friends and parents of people I hadn't seen in YEARS.
WHY?
RHON-DA!
RHON-DA!
RHON-DA!
WE LOVE RHONDA
RHON-DA!
RHON-DA!
RHONDA
WE MISS YOU
WE ♥ RHONDA
GONE 2 SOON
ARTIST'S REPRESENTATION
There were so many people, they had to set up a second "satellite" room with a closed circuit TV broadcasting the service from across the hall.
the FUNERAL OF RHONDA FEDER
SOLD OUT
STANDING ROOM ONLY!
It made me feel proud of my quiet mom. I'd like to think she was able to know, somehow, how many lives she had touched.
Wow.

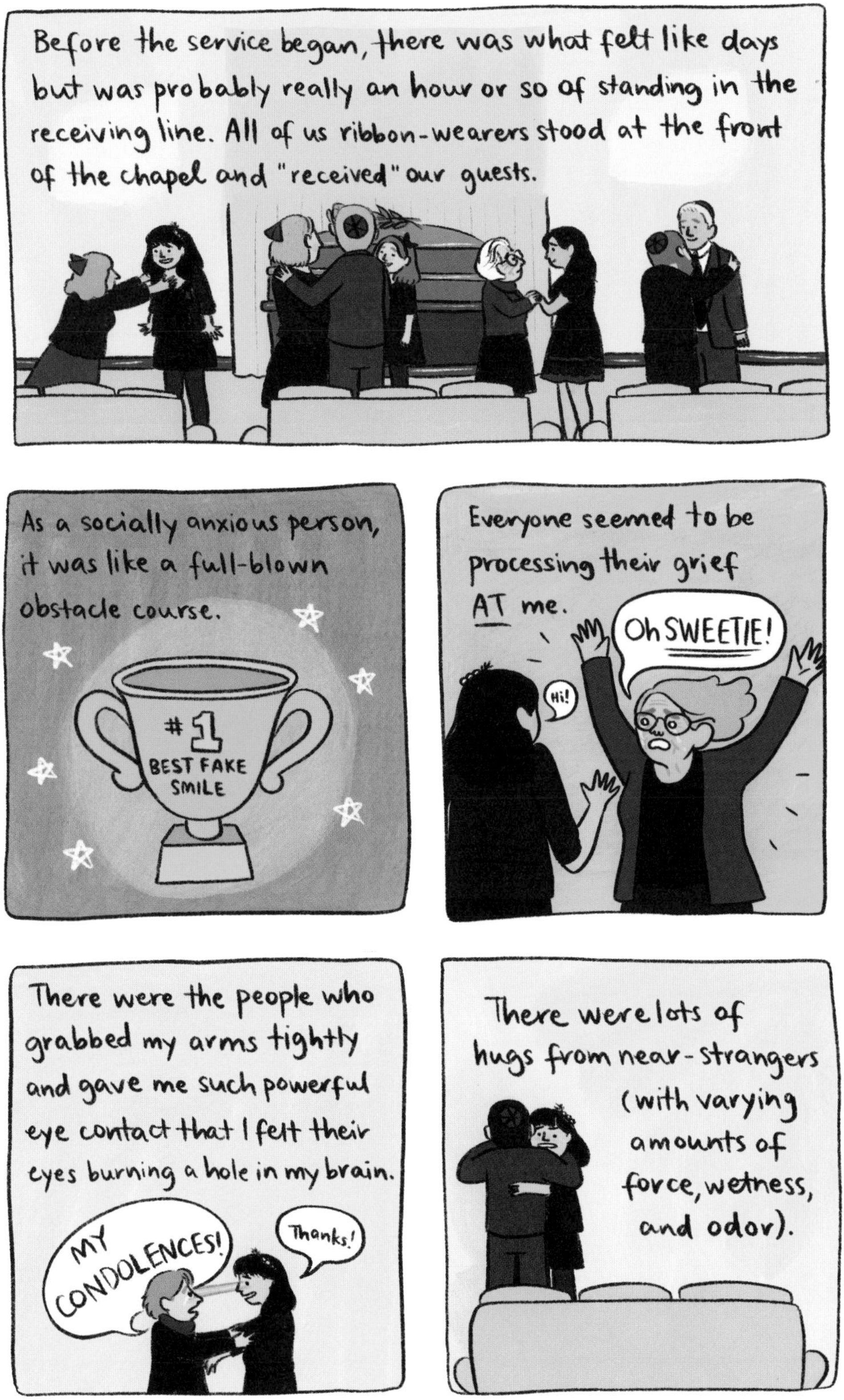
Before the service began, there was what felt like days but was probably really an hour or so of standing in the receiving line. All of us ribbon-wearers stood at the front of the chapel and "received" our guests.
As a socially anxious person, it was like a full-blown obstacle course.
#1
BEST FAKE SMILE
Everyone seemed to be processing their grief AT me.
Oh SWEETIE!
Hi!
There were the people who grabbed my arms tightly and gave me such powerful eye contact that I felt their eyes burning a hole in my brain.
MY CONDOLENCES!
Thanks!
There were lots of hugs from near-strangers (with varying amounts of force, wetness, and odor).

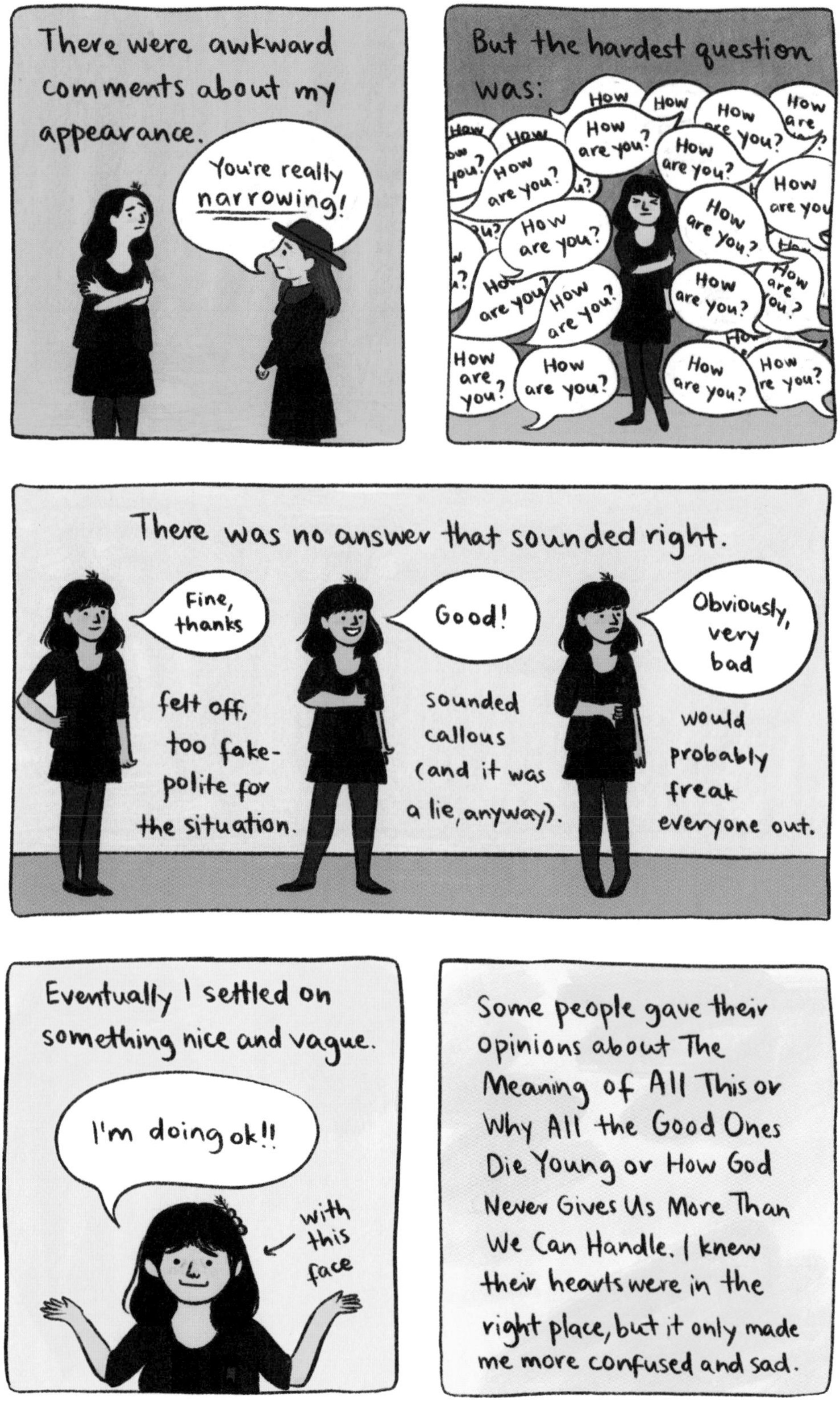
There were awkward comments about my appearance.
You're really narrowing!
But the hardest question was:
How are you?
How are you?
How are you?
How are you?
How are you?
How are you?
How are you?
How are you?
How are you?
How are you?
How are you?
How are you?
How are you?
How are you?
How are you?
How are you?
There was no answer that sounded right.
Fine, thanks
felt off, too fake-polite for the situation.
Good!
sounded callous (and it was a lie, anyway).
Obviously, very bad
would probably freak everyone out.
Eventually I settled on something nice and vague.
I'm doing ok!!
with this face
Some people gave their opinions about The Meaning of All This or Why All the Good Ones Die Young or How God Never Gives Us More Than We Can Handle. I knew their hearts were in the right place, but it only made me more confused and sad.

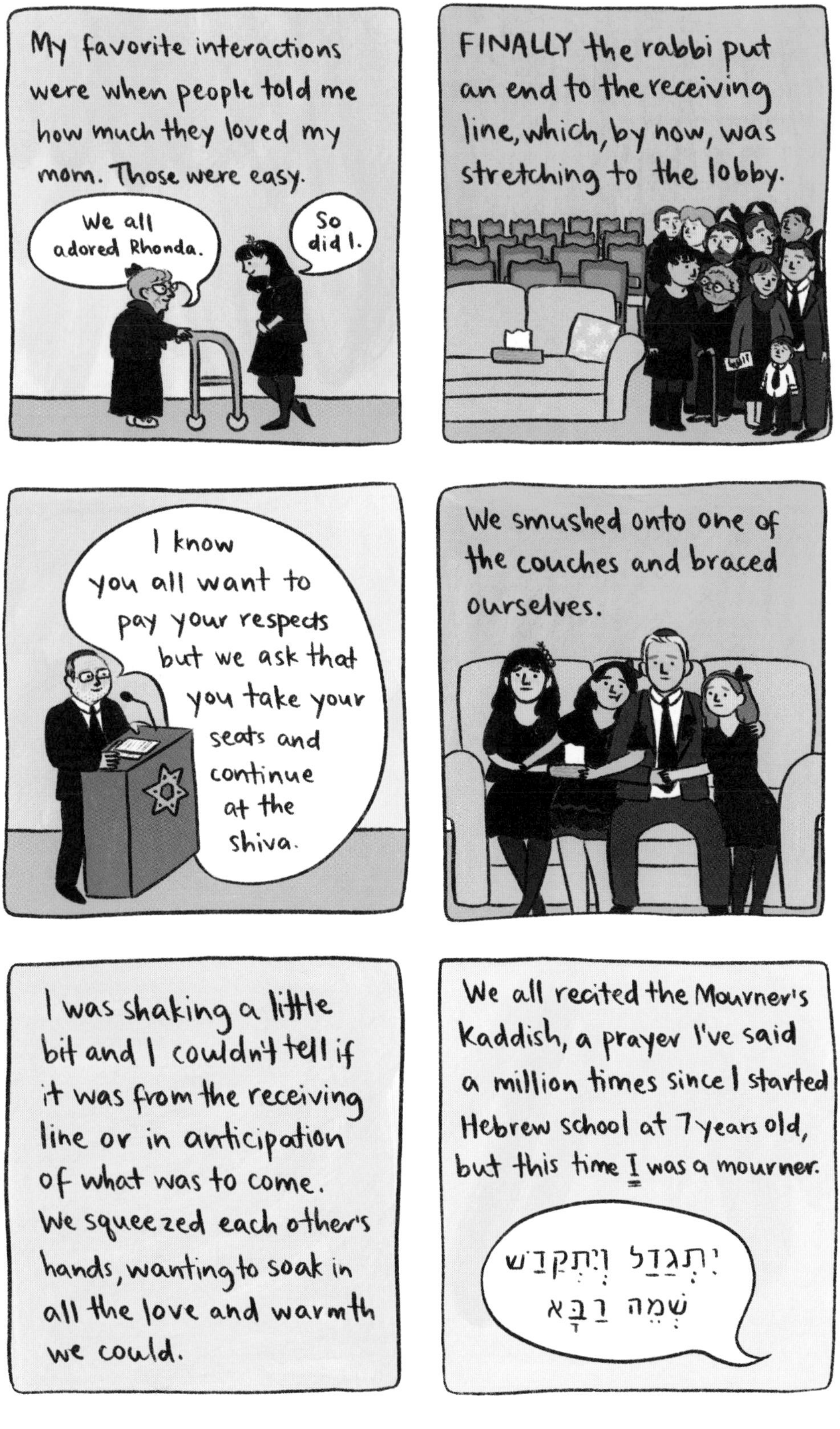
My favorite interactions were when people told me how much they loved my mom. Those were easy.
We all adored Rhonda.
So did I.
FINALLY the rabbi put an end to the receiving line, which, by now, was stretching to the lobby.
I know you all want to pay your respects but we ask that you take your seats and continue at the shiva.
We smushed onto one of the couches and braced ourselves.
I was shaking a little bit and I couldn't tell if it was from the receiving line or in anticipation of what was to come. We squeezed each other's hands, wanting to soak in all the love and warmth we could.
We all recited the Mourner's Kaddish, a prayer I've said a million times since I started Hebrew school at 7 years old, but this time I was a mourner.
יִתְגַּדַּל וְיִתְקַדַּשׁ
שְׁמֵהּ רַבָּא

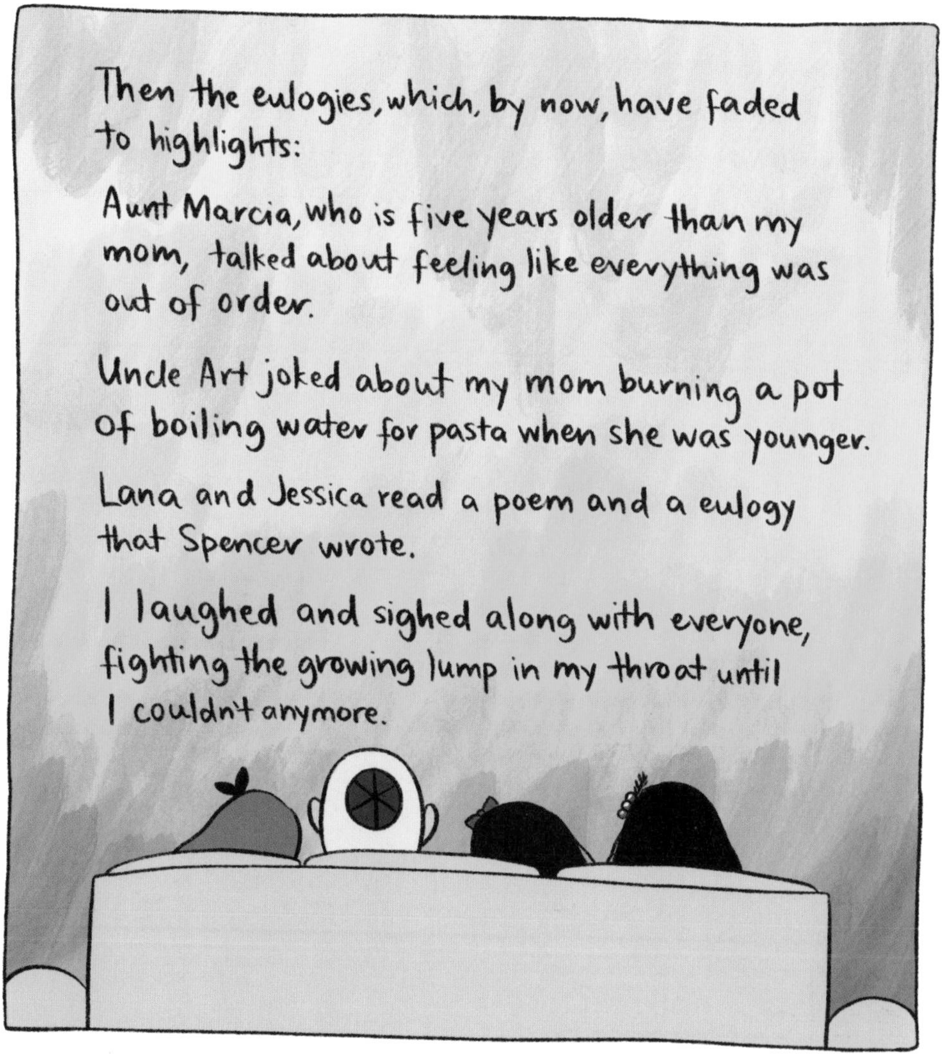
Then the eulogies, which, by now, have faded to highlights:
Aunt Marcia, who is five years older than my mom, talked about feeling like everything was out of order.
Uncle Art joked about my mom burning a pot of boiling water for pasta when she was younger.
Lana and Jessica read a poem and a eulogy that Spencer wrote.
I laughed and sighed along with everyone, fighting the growing lump in my throat until I couldn't anymore.

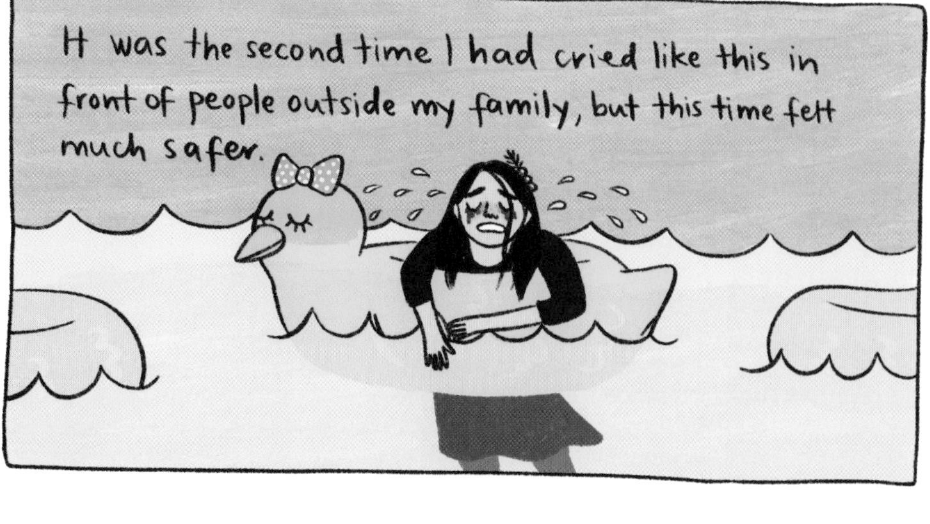
It was the second time I had cried like this in front of people outside my family, but this time felt much safer.

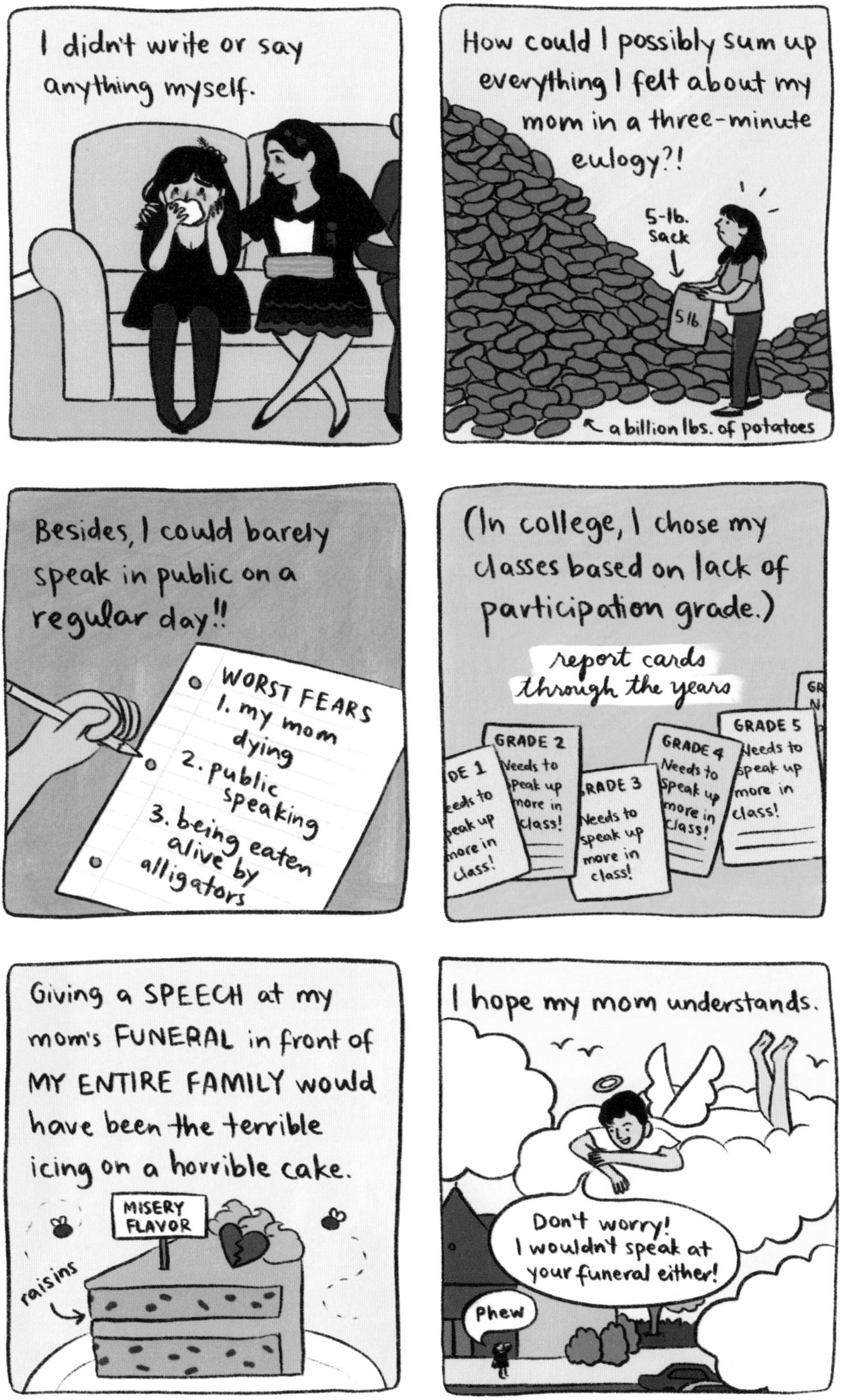
I didn't write or say anything myself.
How could I possibly sum up everything I felt about my mom in a three-minute eulogy?!
5-lb. sack
5 lb.
a billion lbs. of potatoes
Besides, I could barely speak in public on a regular day!!
WORST FEARS
1. my mom dying
2. public speaking
3. being eaten alive by alligators
(In college, I chose my classes based on lack of participation grade.)
report cards through the years
GRADE 2
Needs to speak up more in class!
GRADE 4
Needs to speak up more in class!
GRADE 5
Needs to speak up more in class!
Needs to speak up more in class!
Giving a SPEECH at my mom's FUNERAL in front of MY ENTIRE FAMILY would have been the terrible icing on a horrible cake.
MISERY FLAVOR
raisins
I hope my mom understands.
Don't worry! I wouldn't speak at your funeral either!
Phew

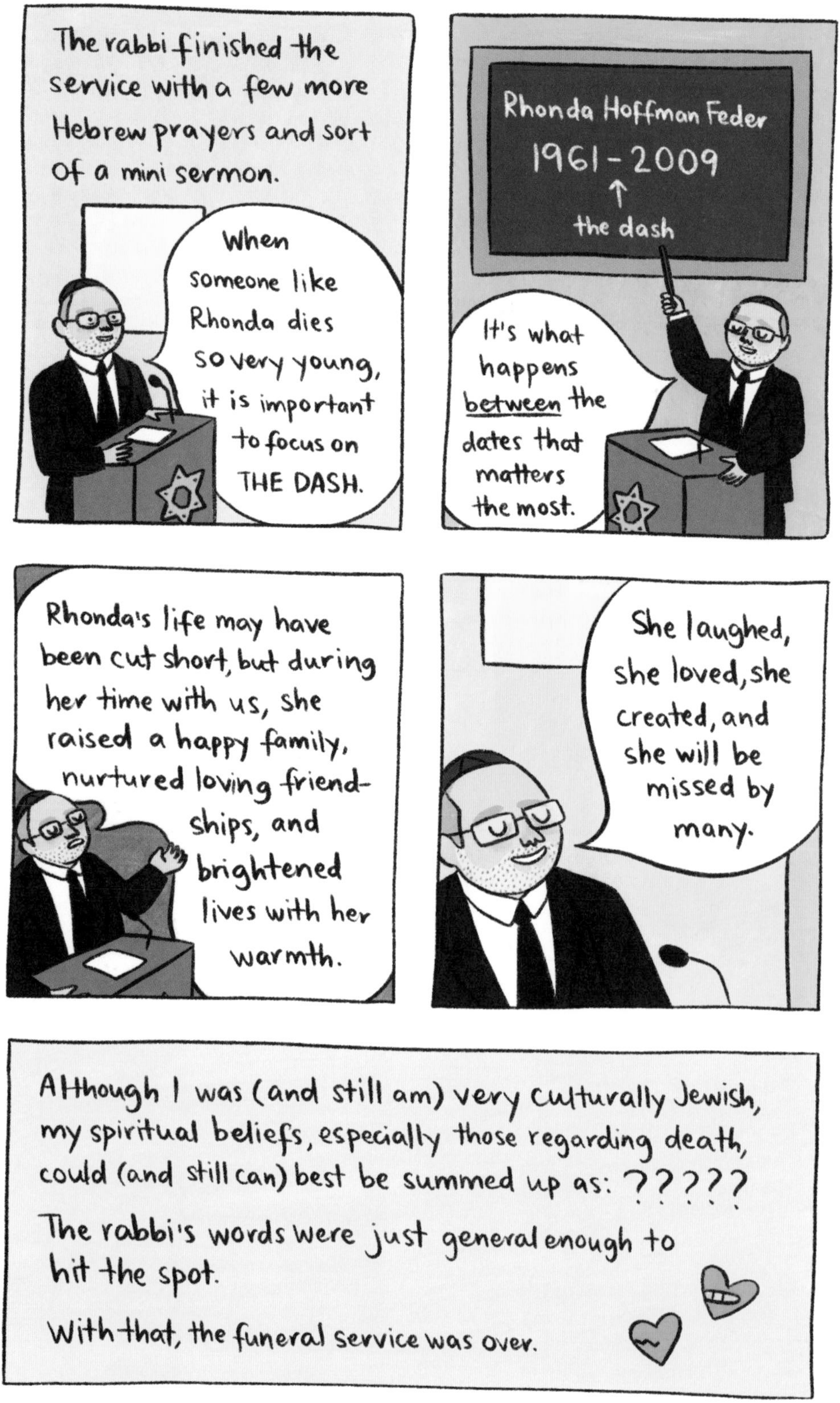

The rabbi finished the service with a few more Hebrew prayers and sort of a mini sermon.
When someone like Rhonda dies so very young, it is important to focus on THE DASH.
Rhonda Hoffman Feder
1961 - 2009
the dash
It's what happens between the dates that matters the most.
Rhonda's life may have been cut short, but during her time with us, she raised a happy family, nurtured loving friendships, and brightened lives with her warmth.
She laughed, she loved, she created, and she will be missed by many.
Although I was (and still am) very culturally Jewish, my spiritual beliefs, especially those regarding death, could (and still can) best be summed up as: ?????
The rabbi's words were just general enough to hit the spot.
With that, the funeral service was over.

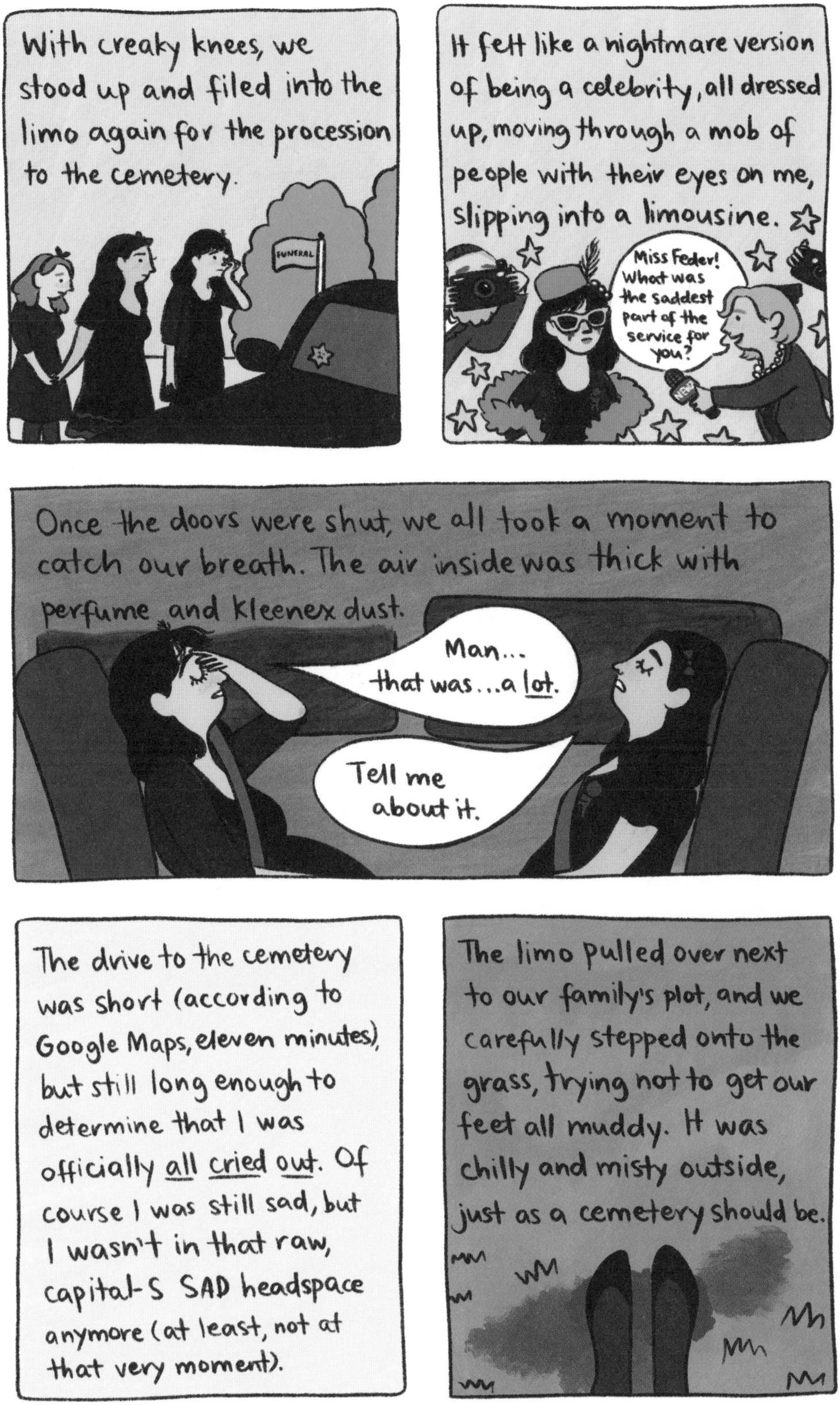
With creaky knees, we stood up and filed into the limo again for the procession to the cemetery.
FUNERAL
It felt like a nightmare version of being a celebrity, all dressed up, moving through a mob of people with their eyes on me, slipping into a limousine.
Miss Feder! What was the saddest part of the service for you?
NEWS
Once the doors were shut, we all took a moment to catch our breath. The air inside was thick with perfume and kleenex dust.
Man... that was...a lot.
Tell me about it.
The drive to the cemetery was short (according to Google Maps, eleven minutes), but still long enough to determine that I was officially all cried out. Of course I was still sad, but I wasn't in that raw, capital-S SAD headspace anymore (at least, not at that very moment).
The limo pulled over next to our family's plot, and we carefully stepped onto the grass, trying not to get our feet all muddy. It was chilly and misty outside, just as a cemetery should be.

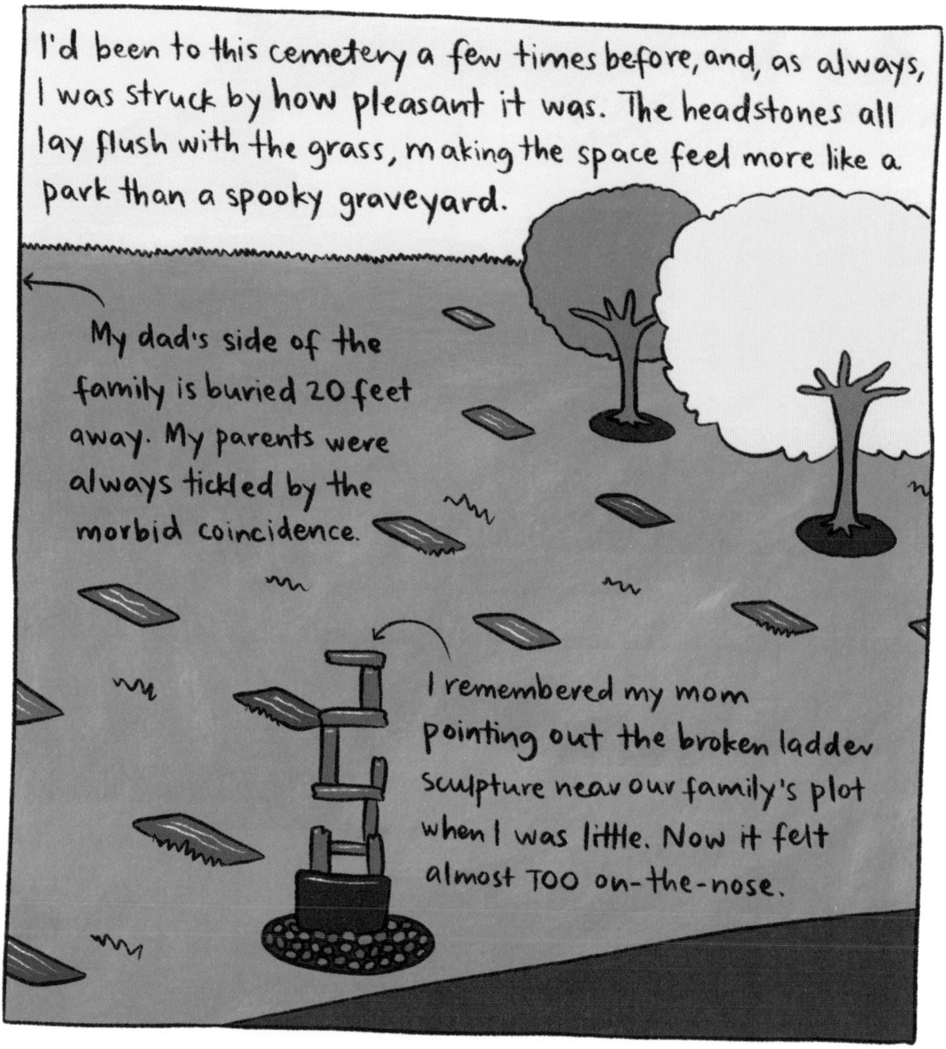
I'd been to this cemetery a few times before, and, as always, I was struck by how pleasant it was. The headstones all lay flush with the grass, making the space feel more like a park than a spooky graveyard.
My dad's side of the family is buried 20 feet away. My parents were always tickled by the morbid coincidence.
I remembered my mom pointing out the broken ladder sculpture near our family's plot when I was little. Now it felt almost TOO on-the-nose.

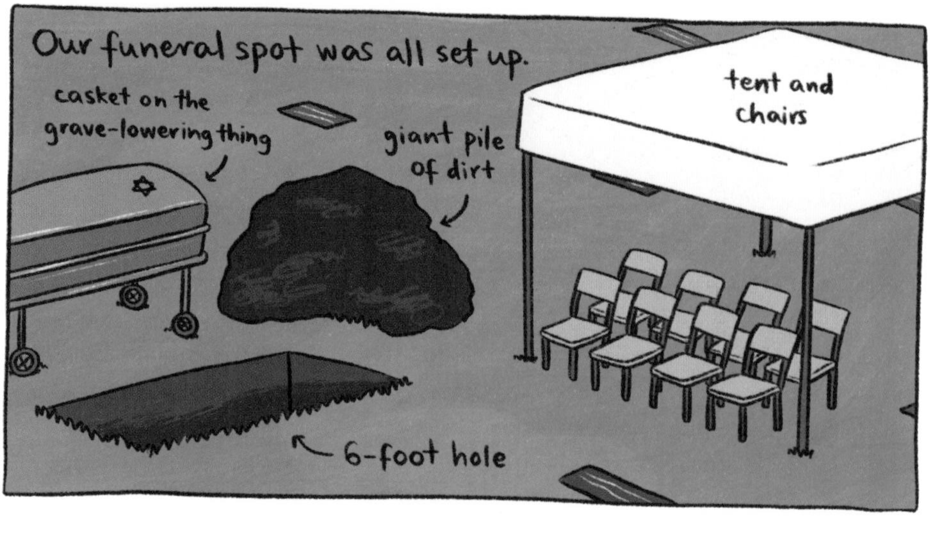
Our funeral spot was all set up.
casket on the grave-lowering thing
giant pile of dirt
tent and chairs
6-foot hole

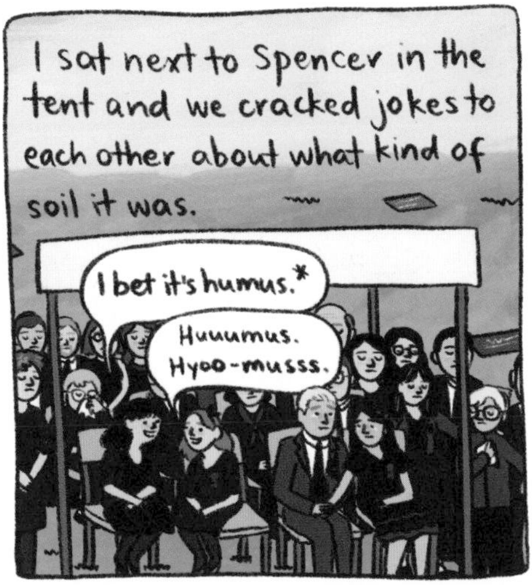
I sat next to Spencer in the tent and we cracked jokes to each other about what kind of soil it was.
I bet it's humus.*
Huuumus. Hyoo-musss.

* In high school, I had taken an environmental science class with a whole unit about soil. We learned that the three main components were sand, silt, and clay and that humus was the PERFECT combo of the three. My sisters and I got a huge kick out of how PERRRFECT humus was. (It's way less funny explaining it now, so you'll have to trust me.)

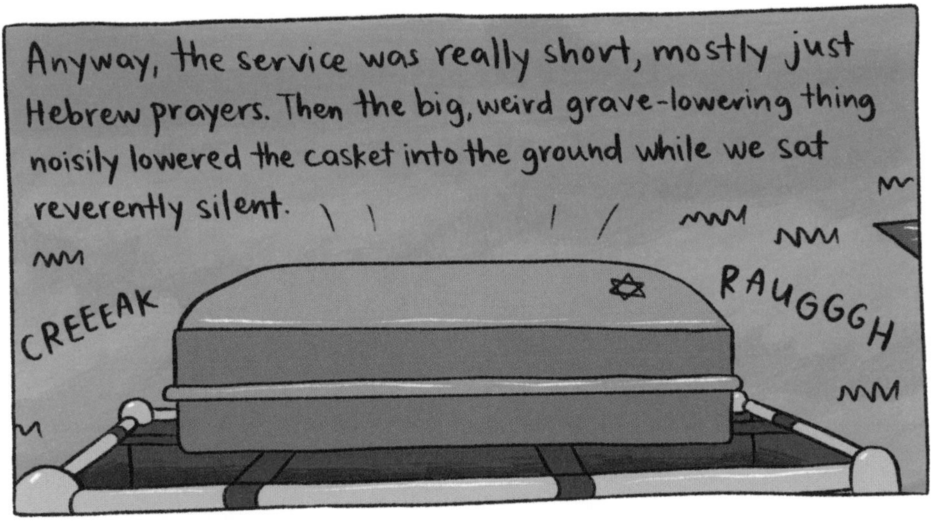
Anyway, the service was really short, mostly just Hebrew prayers. Then the big, weird grave-lowering thing noisily lowered the casket into the ground while we sat reverently silent.
CREEEAK
RAUGGGH

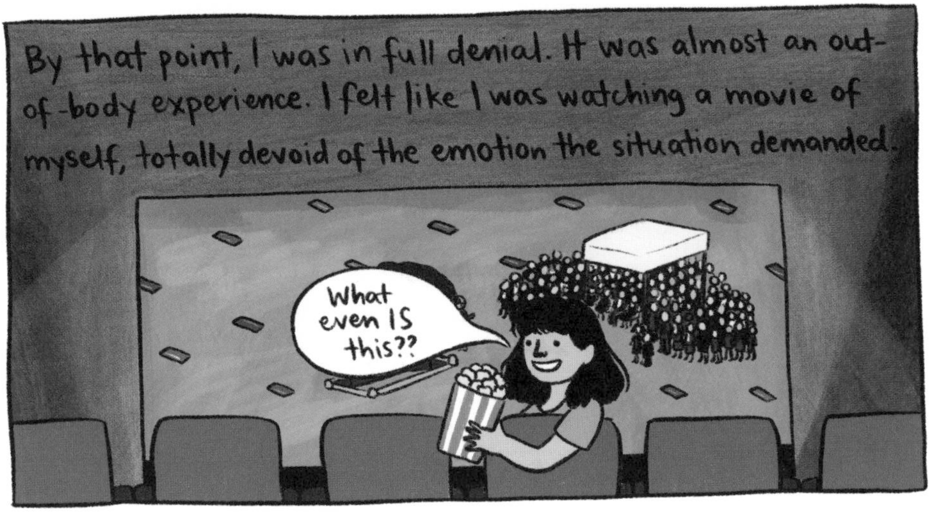
By that point, I was in full denial. It was almost an out-of-body experience. I felt like I was watching a movie of myself, totally devoid of the emotion the situation demanded.
What even IS this??

Everyone took turns filling the grave with dirt (humus?).

The casket in the ground felt completely unrelated to my mom. This was a physical task and nothing more.

I took my place, lifted the surprisingly heavy shovel, and jammed it into the pile of dirt.

The casket's only decoration was a palm-size star of David toward one end, like where the title would be on a book cover. I carefully tipped my shovelful of dirt right on top of it.

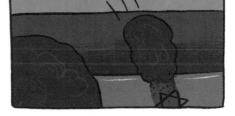

There. The tiniest tribute to my mom's precision. I set the shovel down for the next person in line and went back to my seat.

It went on like this for a while, until everyone in line had done their ceremonial shoveling. My uncles filled it the rest of the way themselves.

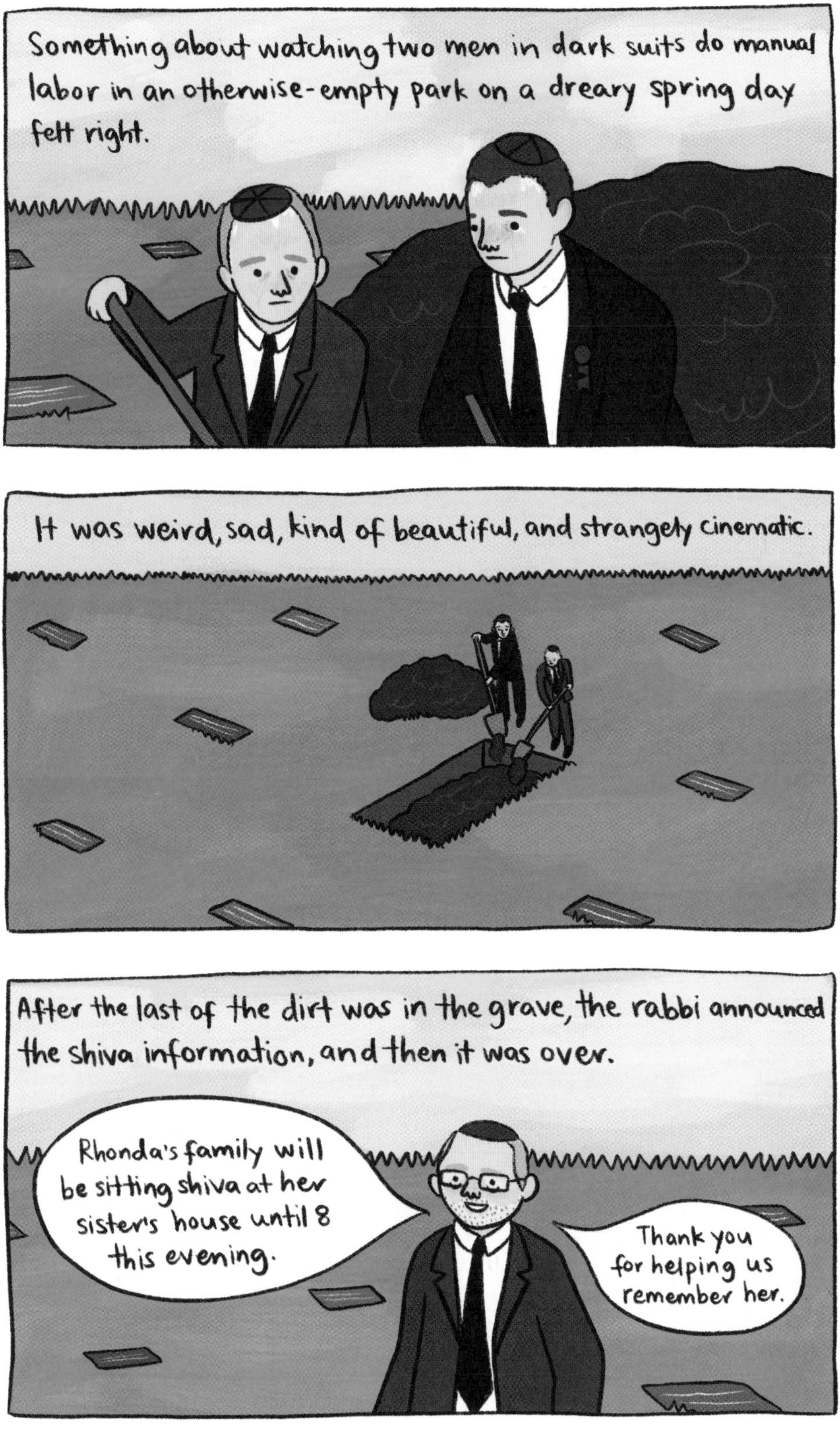
Something about watching two men in dark suits do manual labor in an otherwise-empty park on a dreary spring day felt right.
It was weird, sad, kind of beautiful, and strangely cinematic.
After the last of the dirt was in the grave, the rabbi announced the shiva information, and then it was over.
Rhonda's family will be sitting shiva at her sister's house until 8 this evening.
Thank you for helping us remember her.

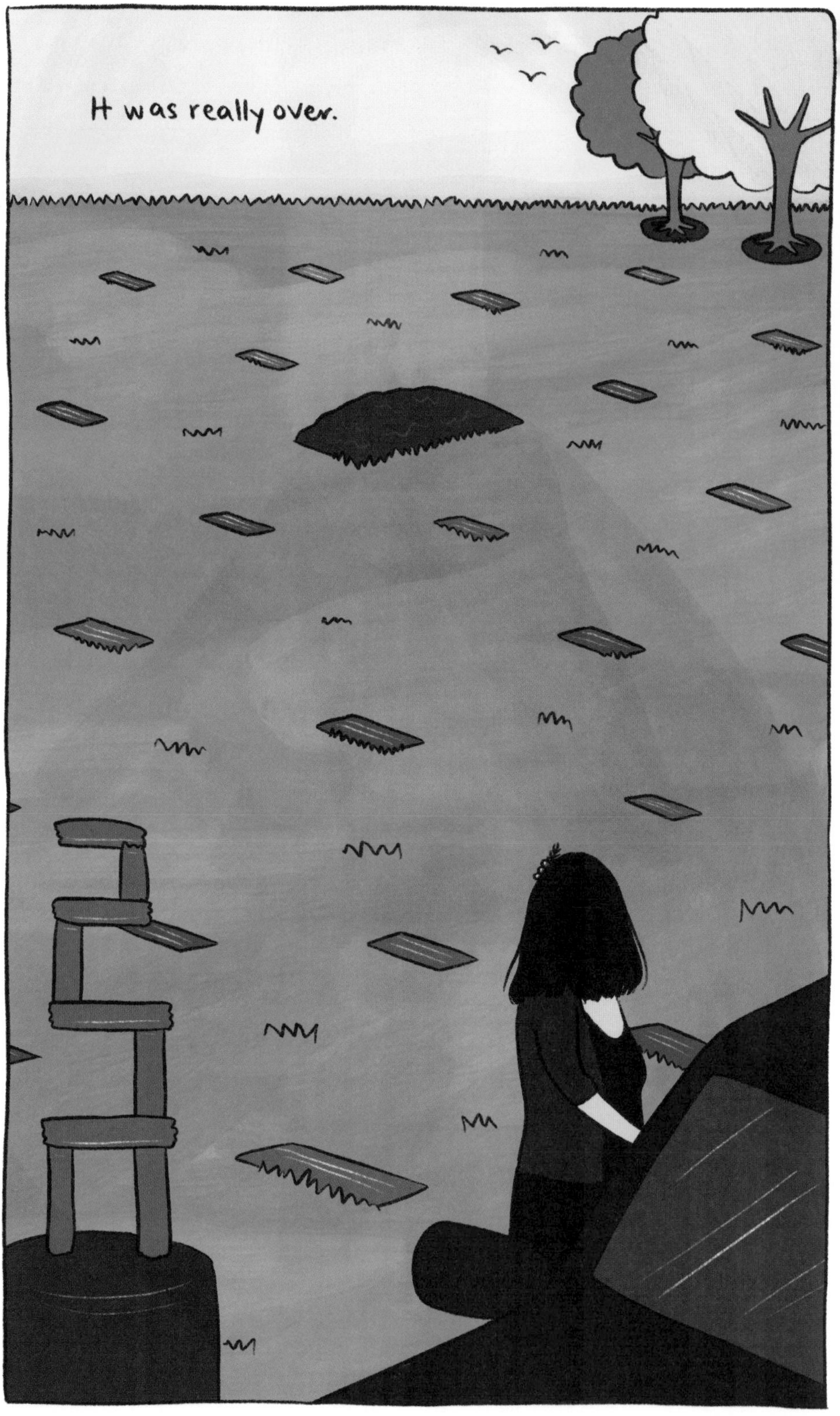
It was really over.

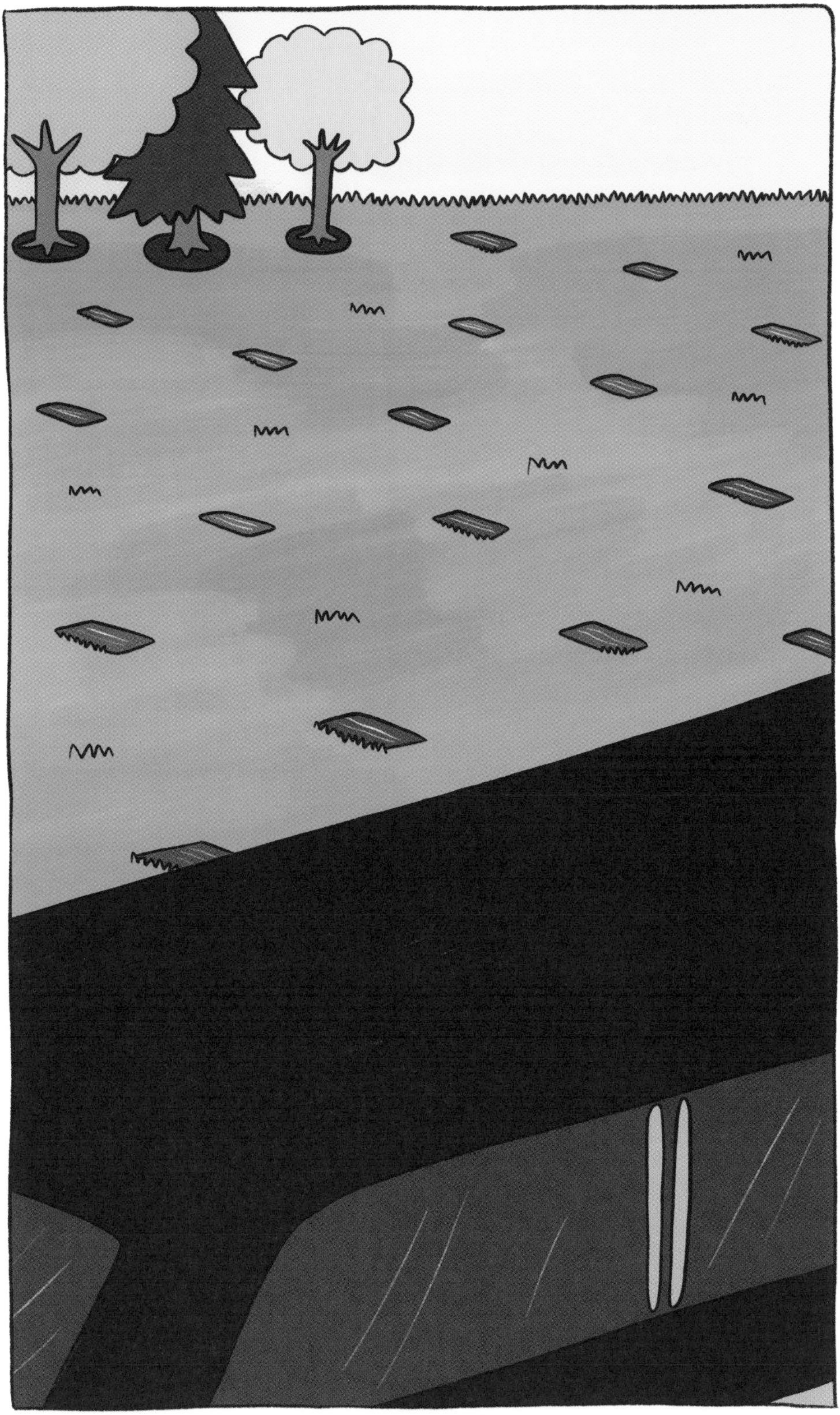

# DOs and DON'Ts
## for dealing with a grieving person

- DO ask them questions about their loved one! They're probably itching to talk about them!

- DO laugh and smile if they are!

- DO tell them stories about their loved one if you have them! (Happy stories, obv)

- DO reach out a few months later after all the fuss dies down

- DO make note of important birthdays/deathiversaries and reach out then

- DO acknowledge how crappy the situation is! "I can't imagine how hard this is" is so refreshing amid the sugar coating!

- DO bring cookies! ☺

- DON'T presume you know how they feel

- DON'T one-up them with your own story

- DON'T try to comfort them with religious thoughts they don't share

- DON'T compare their loss to yours unless the situations are EXTREMELY similar

- DON'T try to tie everything up in a bow

- DON'T stop reaching out after a week

- DON'T pretend their loved one never existed

- DON'T ask what you can do to help! (Just help!) (Don't make them awkwardly give orders while they're sad!)

# chapter seven

## THE DEATH CIRCUS
### part 2

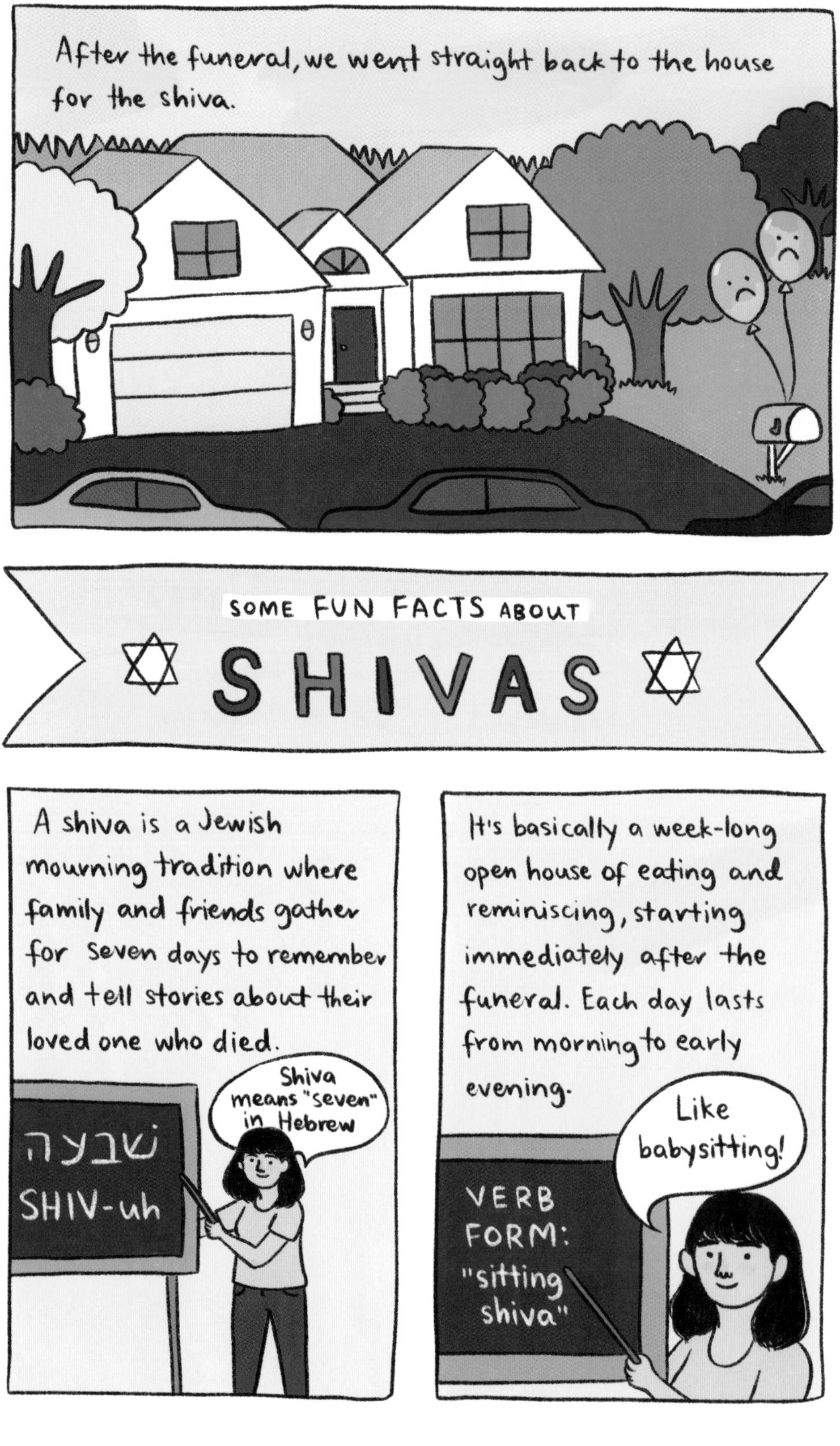
After the funeral, we went straight back to the house for the shiva.
SOME FUN FACTS ABOUT
SHIVAS
A shiva is a Jewish mourning tradition where family and friends gather for seven days to remember and tell stories about their loved one who died.
Shiva means "seven" in Hebrew
שבעה
SHIV-uh
It's basically a week-long open house of eating and reminiscing, starting immediately after the funeral. Each day lasts from morning to early evening.
Like babysitting!
VERB FORM: "sitting shiva"

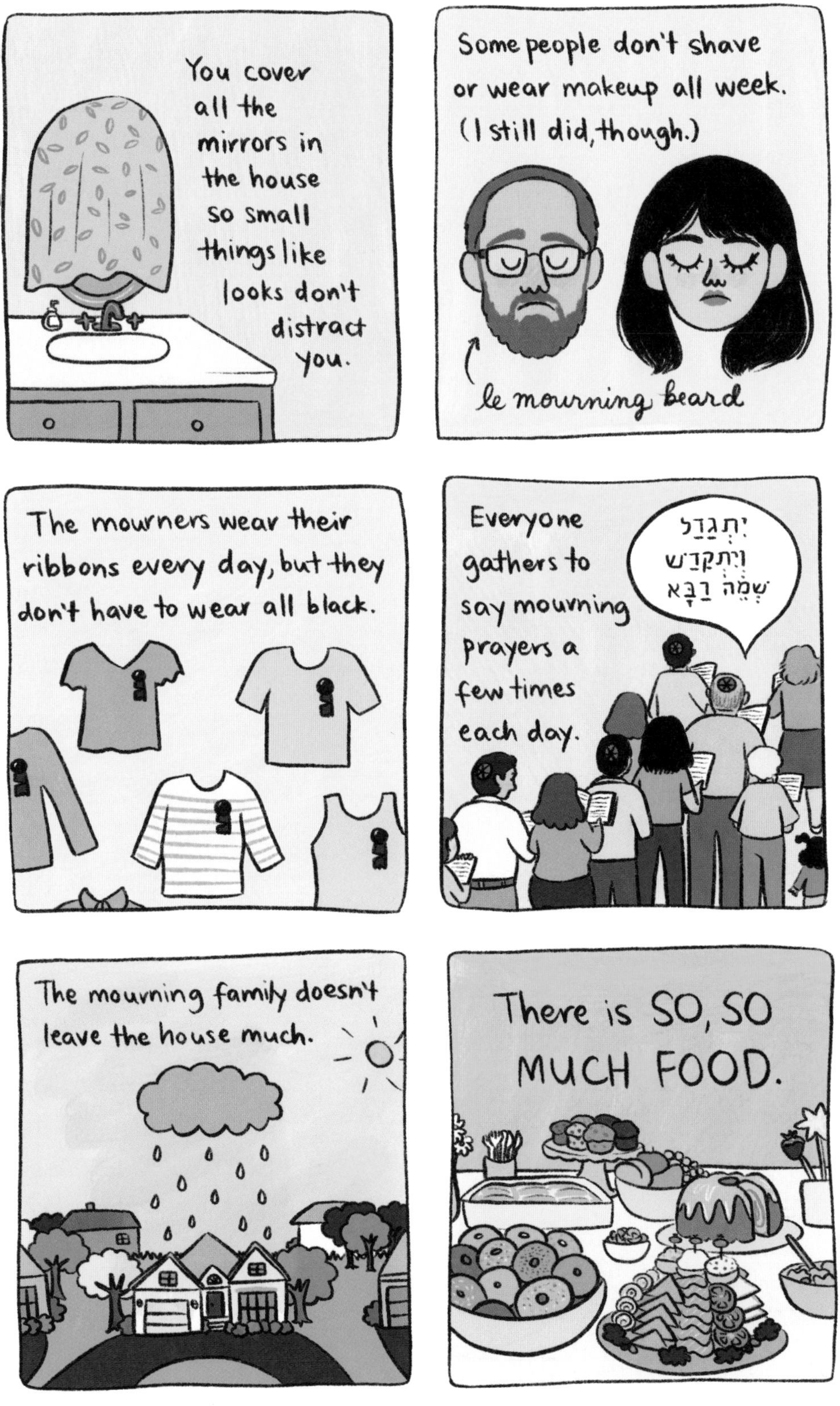
You cover all the mirrors in the house so small things like looks don't distract you.
Some people don't shave or wear makeup all week. (I still did, though.)
le mourning beard
The mourners wear their ribbons every day, but they don't have to wear all black.
Everyone gathers to say mourning prayers a few times each day.
יִתְגַּדַּל
וְיִתְקַדַּשׁ
שְׁמֵהּ רַבָּא
The mourning family doesn't leave the house much.
There is SO, SO MUCH FOOD.

I love food, but I'm one of those people who loses their appetite completely in times of extreme misery. When my mom was first diagnosed, even a saltine sounded nauseating.

So when we got to the shiva and the lox and bagels called to me, I knew I was going to be okay.

The house smelled delicious and familiar in that specific Jewish way.

PICKLES

SMOKED FISH

ENTENMANN'S DANISHES

I kicked off my shoes and maneuvered toward the deli platter

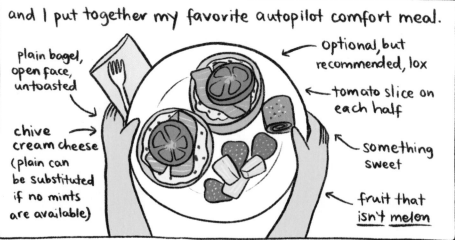

and I put together my favorite autopilot comfort meal.

plain bagel, open face, untoasted

chive cream cheese (plain can be substituted if no mints are available)

optional, but recommended, lox

tomato slice on each half

something sweet

fruit that isn't melon

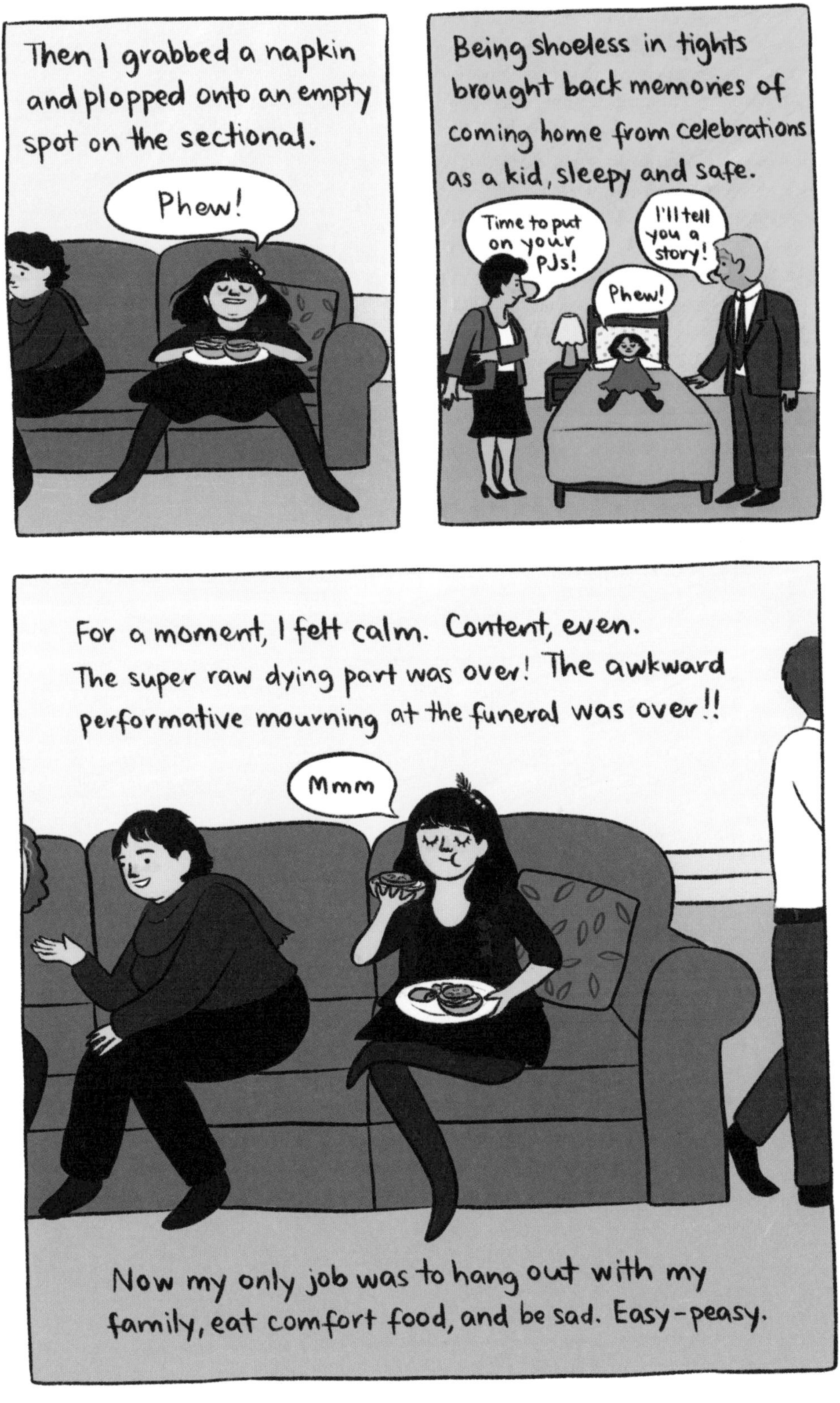
Then I grabbed a napkin and plopped onto an empty spot on the sectional.
Phew!
Being shoeless in tights brought back memories of coming home from celebrations as a kid, sleepy and safe.
Time to put on your PJs!
I'll tell you a story!
Phew!
For a moment, I felt calm. Content, even. The super raw dying part was over! The awkward performative mourning at the funeral was over!!
Mmm
Now my only job was to hang out with my family, eat comfort food, and be sad. Easy-peasy.

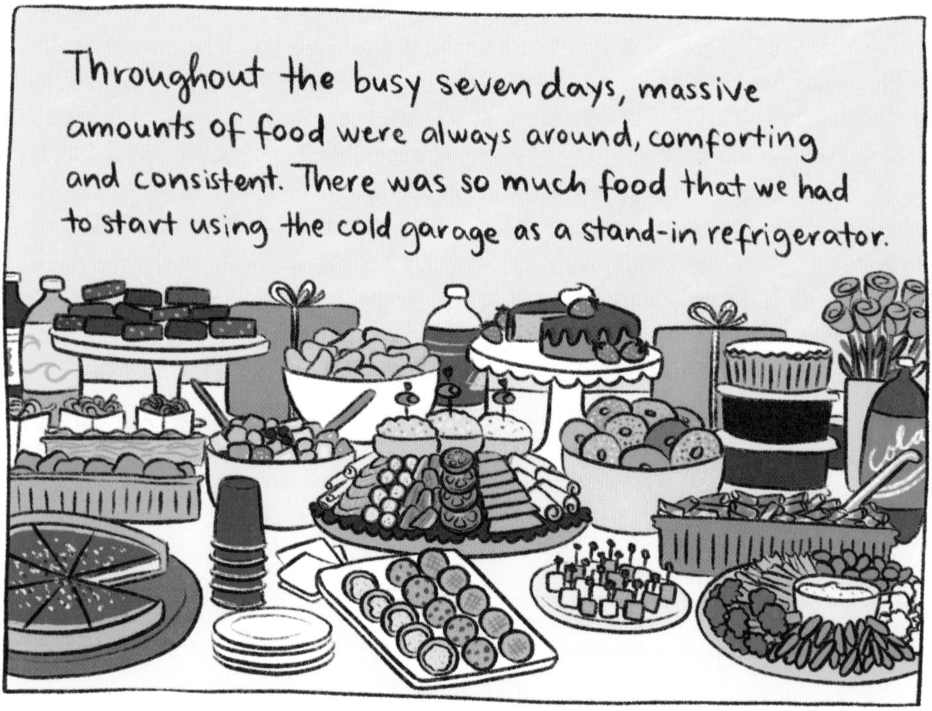
Throughout the busy seven days, massive amounts of food were always around, comforting and consistent. There was so much food that we had to start using the cold garage as a stand-in refrigerator.
Cola

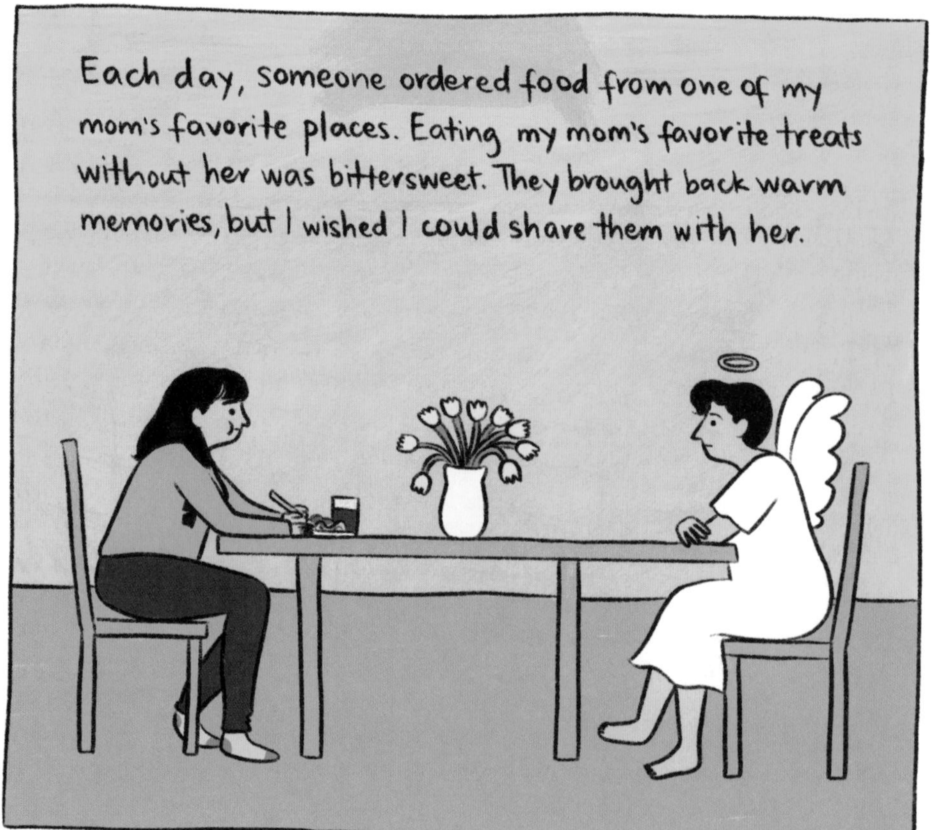
Each day, someone ordered food from one of my mom's favorite places. Eating my mom's favorite treats without her was bittersweet. They brought back warm memories, but I wished I could share them with her.

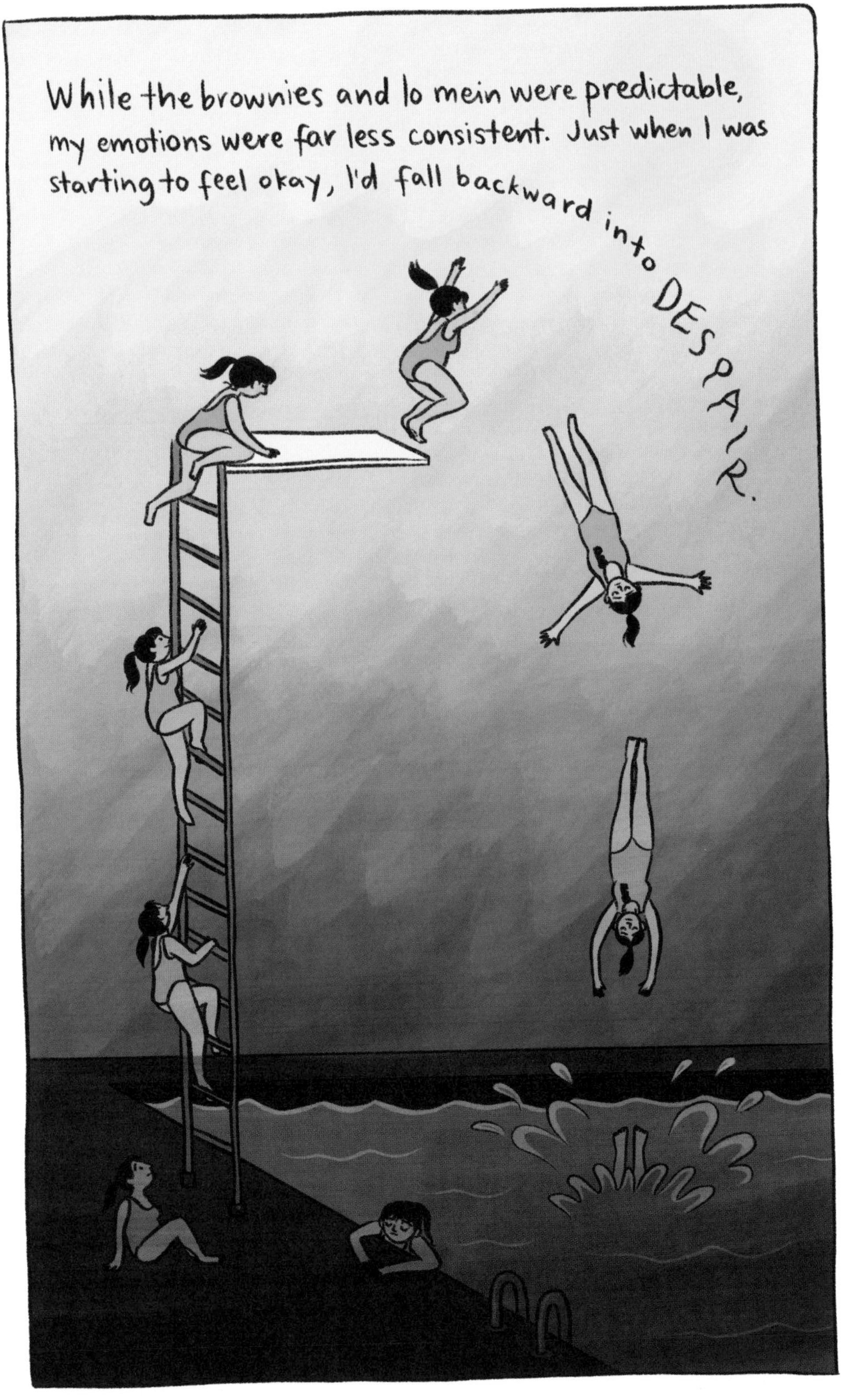
While the brownies and lo mein were predictable, my emotions were far less consistent. Just when I was starting to feel okay, I'd fall backward into DESPAIR.

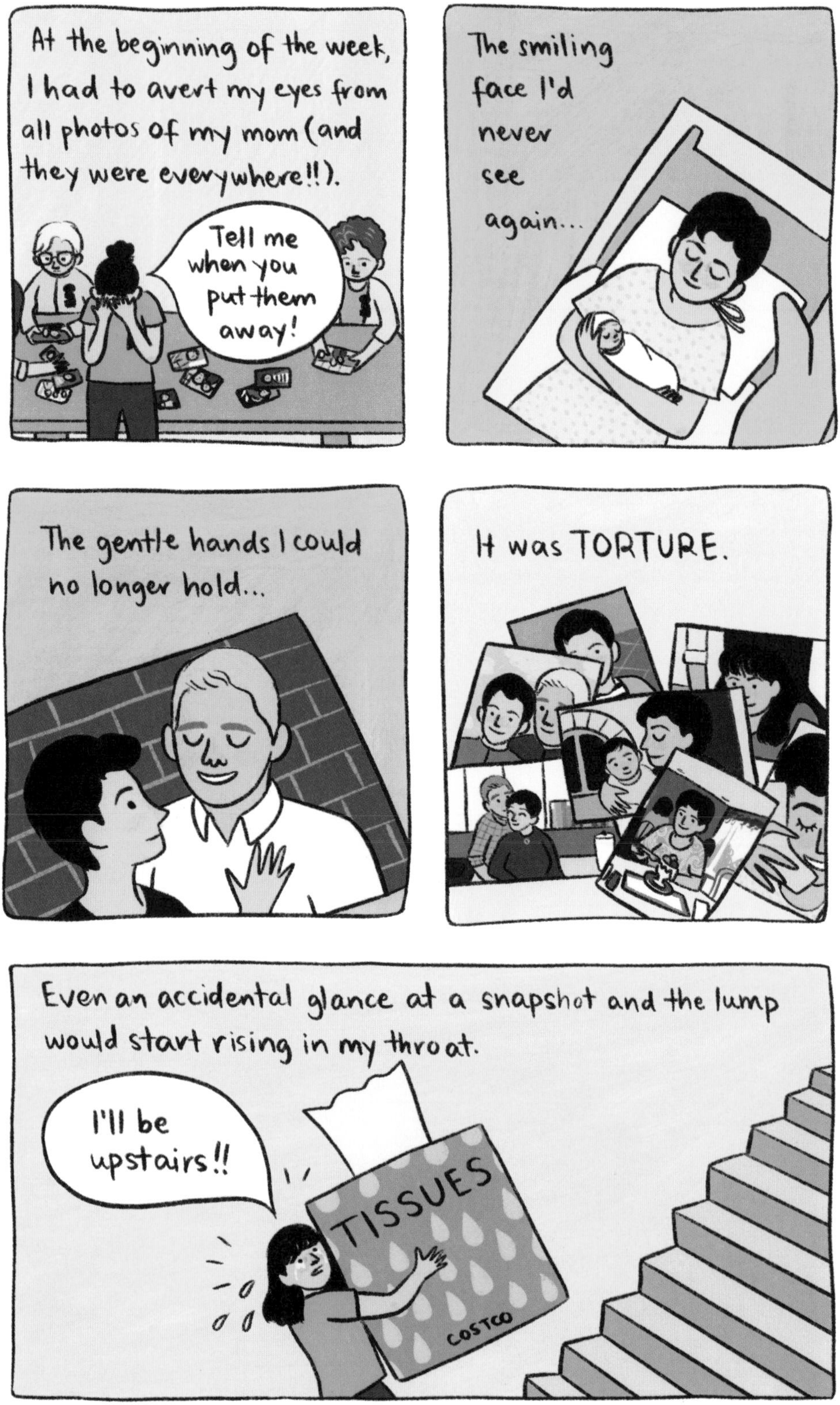
At the beginning of the week, I had to avert my eyes from all photos of my mom (and they were everywhere!!).
Tell me when you put them away!
The smiling face I'd never see again...
The gentle hands I could no longer hold...
It was TORTURE.
Even an accidental glance at a snapshot and the lump would start rising in my throat.
I'll be upstairs!!
TISSUES
COSTCO

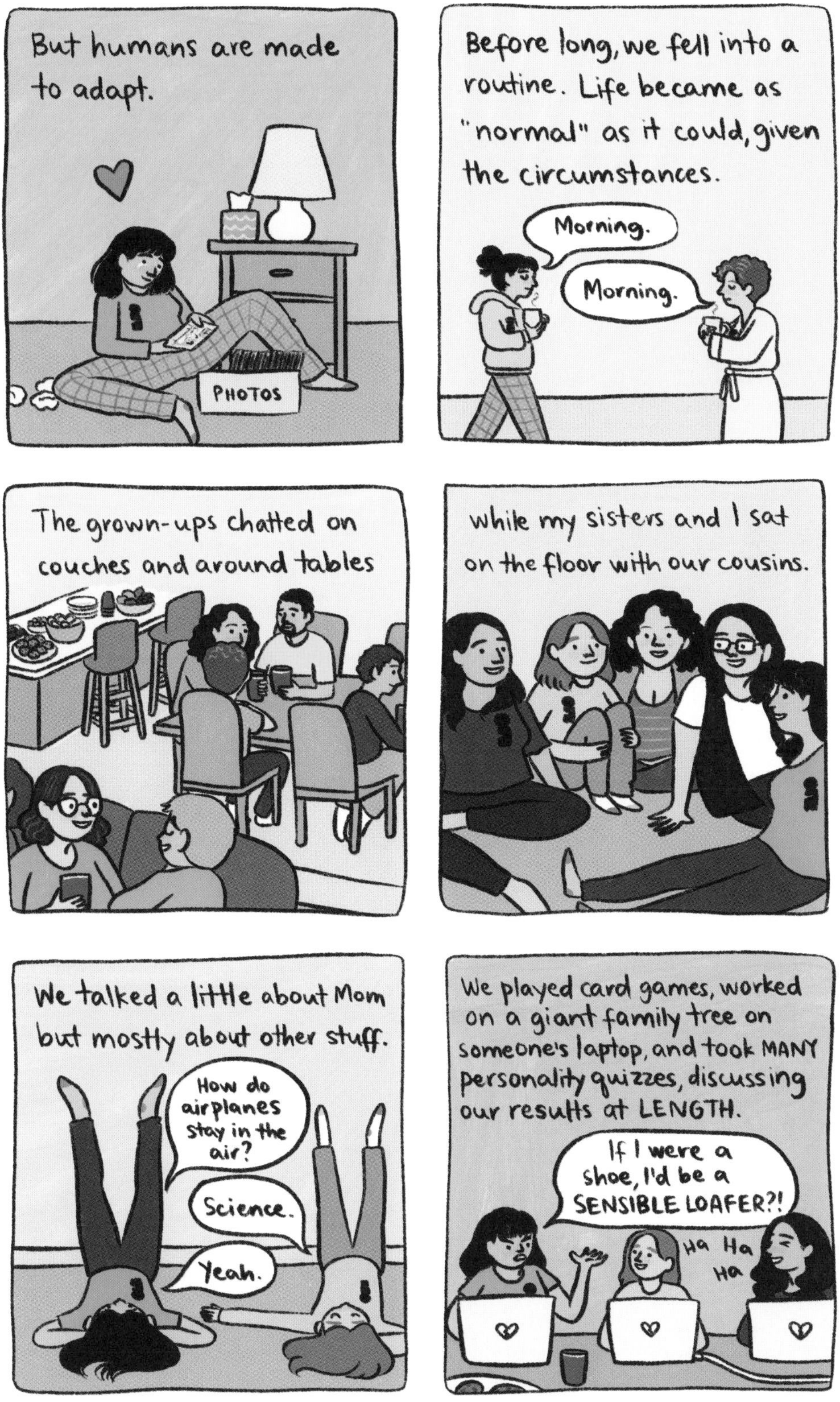
But humans are made to adapt.
PHOTOS
Before long, we fell into a routine. Life became as "normal" as it could, given the circumstances.
Morning.
Morning.
The grown-ups chatted on couches and around tables
while my sisters and I sat on the floor with our cousins.
We talked a little about Mom but mostly about other stuff.
How do airplanes stay in the air?
Science.
Yeah.
We played card games, worked on a giant family tree on someone's laptop, and took MANY personality quizzes, discussing our results at LENGTH.
If I were a shoe, I'd be a SENSIBLE LOAFER?!
Ha Ha Ha

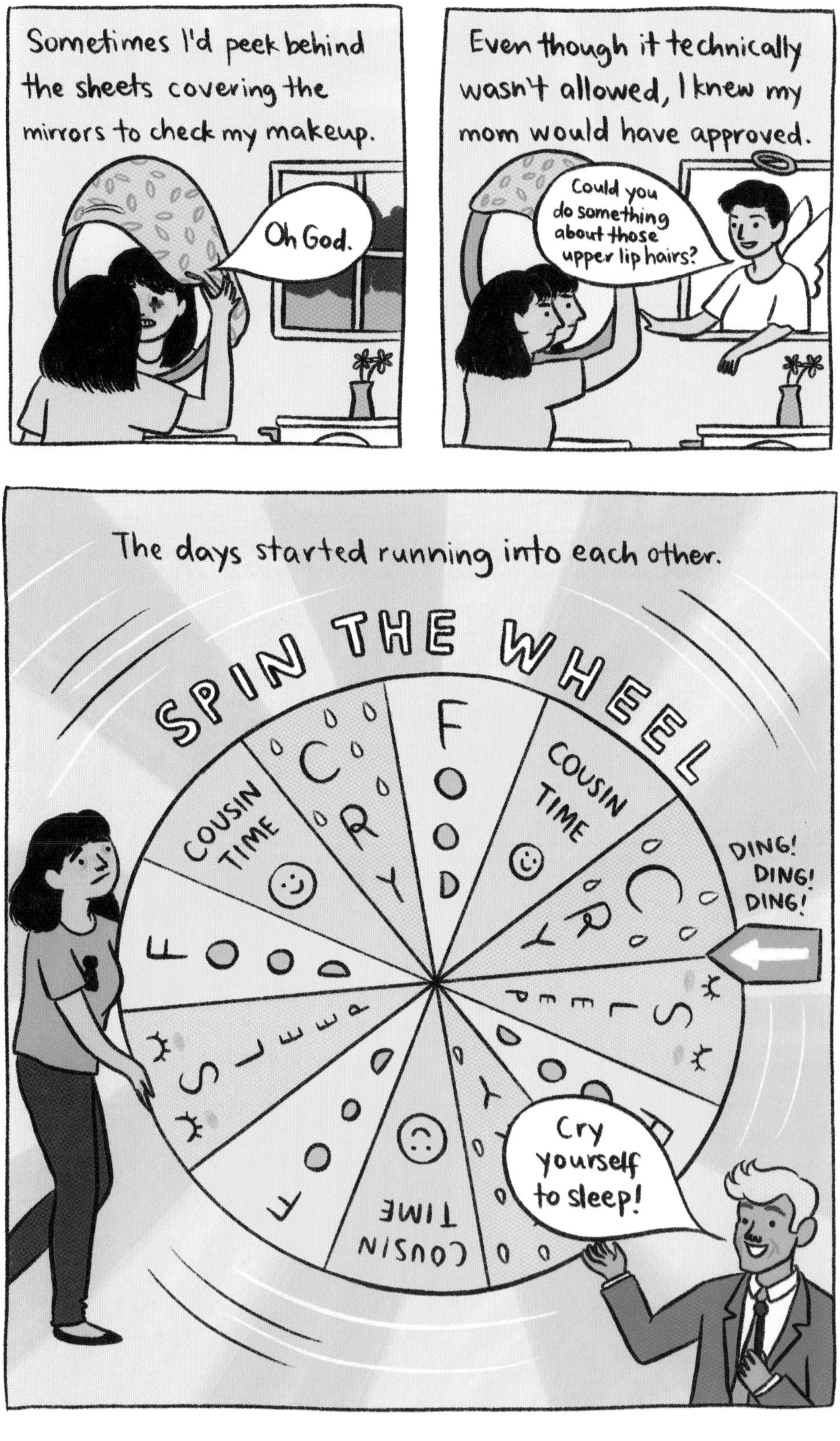
Sometimes I'd peek behind the sheets covering the mirrors to check my makeup.
Oh God.
Even though it technically wasn't allowed, I knew my mom would have approved.
Could you do something about those upper lip hairs?
The days started running into each other.
SPIN THE WHEEL
COUSIN TIME
CRY
FOOD
COUSIN TIME
CRY
SLEEP
FOOD
CRY
FOOD
COUSIN TIME
FOOD
SLEEP
FOOD
DING! DING! DING!
Cry yourself to sleep!

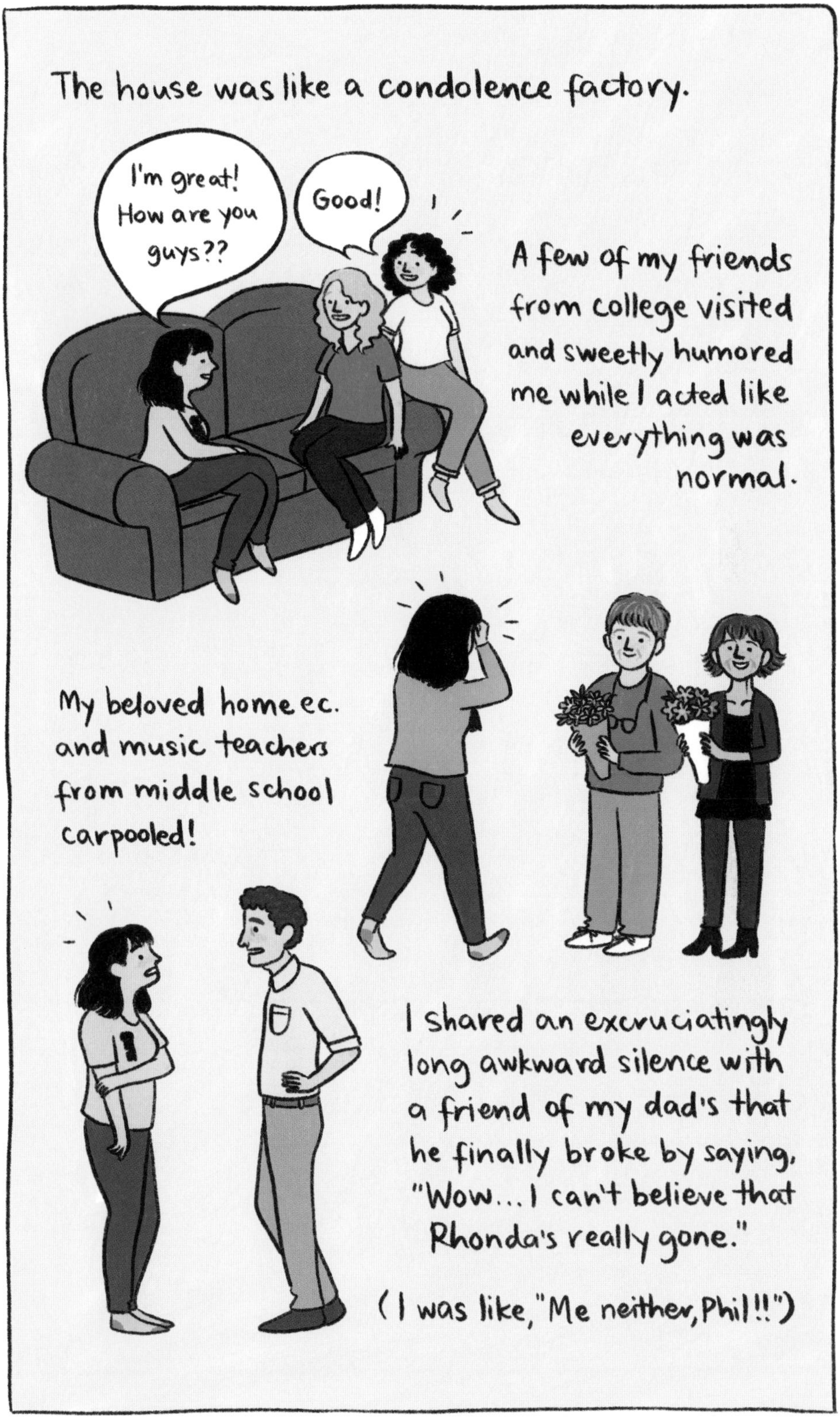
The house was like a condolence factory.
I'm great! How are you guys??
Good!
A few of my friends from college visited and sweetly humored me while I acted like everything was normal.
My beloved home ec. and music teachers from middle school carpooled!
I shared an excruciatingly long awkward silence with a friend of my dad's that he finally broke by saying, "Wow... I can't believe that Rhonda's really gone."
(I was like, "Me neither, Phil!!")

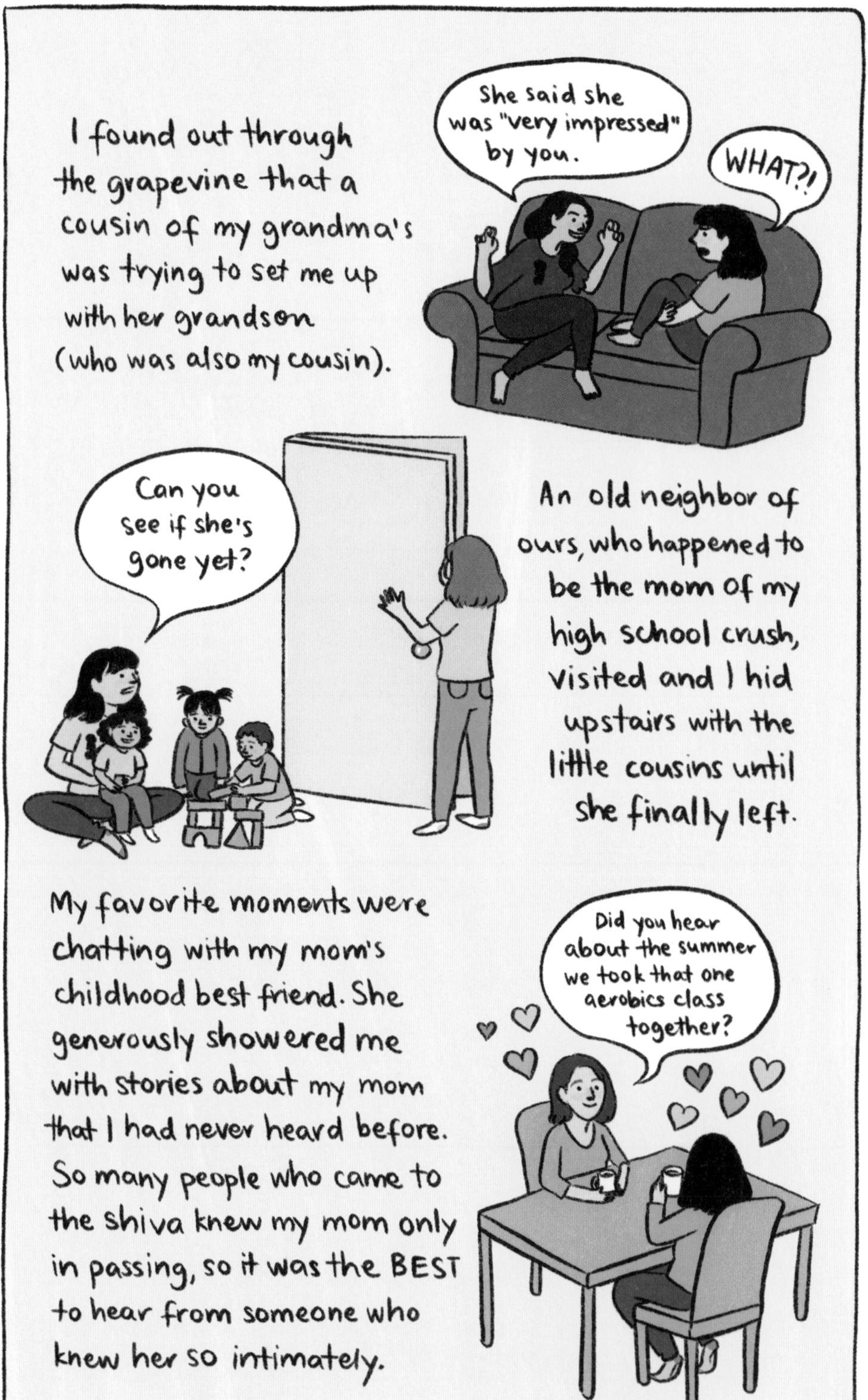
I found out through the grapevine that a cousin of my grandma's was trying to set me up with her grandson (who was also my cousin).
She said she was "very impressed" by you.
WHAT?!
An old neighbor of ours, who happened to be the mom of my high school crush, visited and I hid upstairs with the little cousins until she finally left.
Can you see if she's gone yet?
My favorite moments were chatting with my mom's childhood best friend. She generously showered me with stories about my mom that I had never heard before. So many people who came to the shiva knew my mom only in passing, so it was the BEST to hear from someone who knew her so intimately.
Did you hear about the summer we took that one aerobics class together?

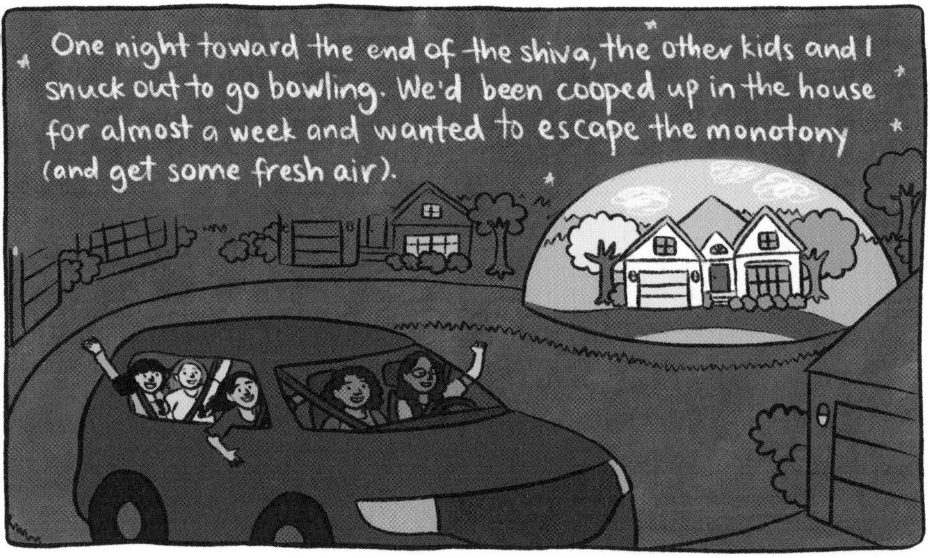
One night toward the end of the shiva, the other kids and I snuck out to go bowling. We'd been cooped up in the house for almost a week and wanted to escape the monotony (and get some fresh air).

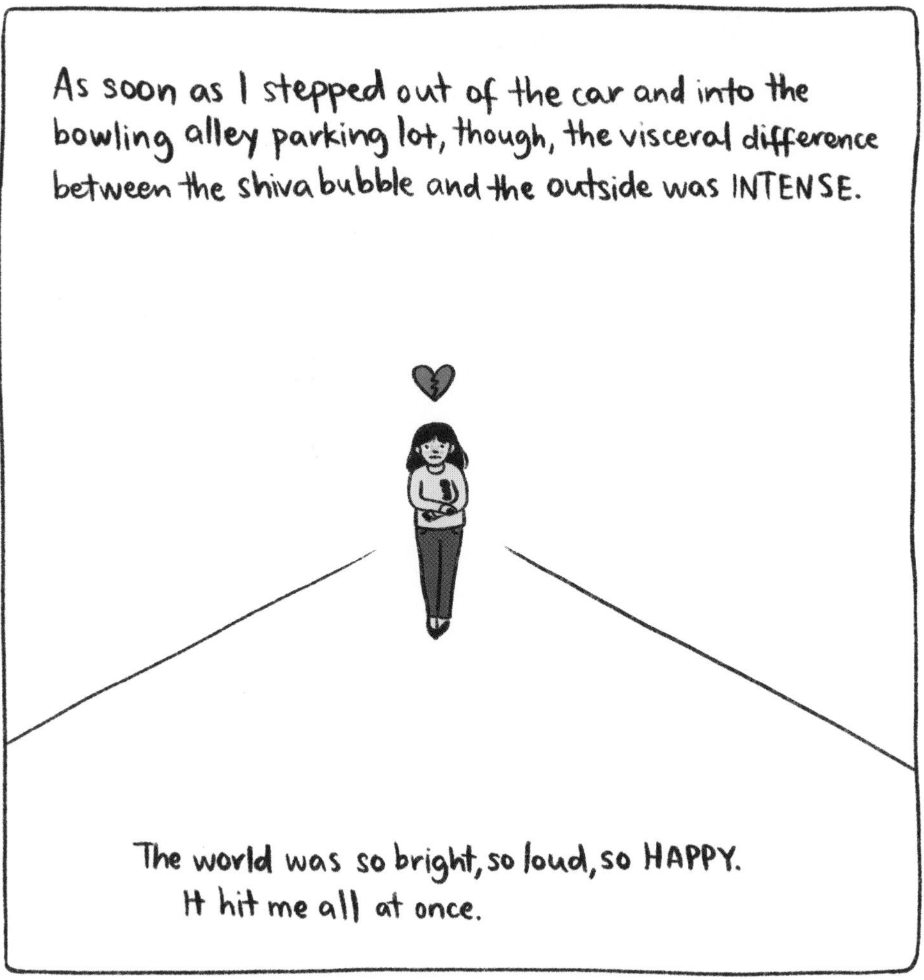
As soon as I stepped out of the car and into the bowling alley parking lot, though, the visceral difference between the shiva bubble and the outside was INTENSE.
The world was so bright, so loud, so HAPPY.
It hit me all at once.

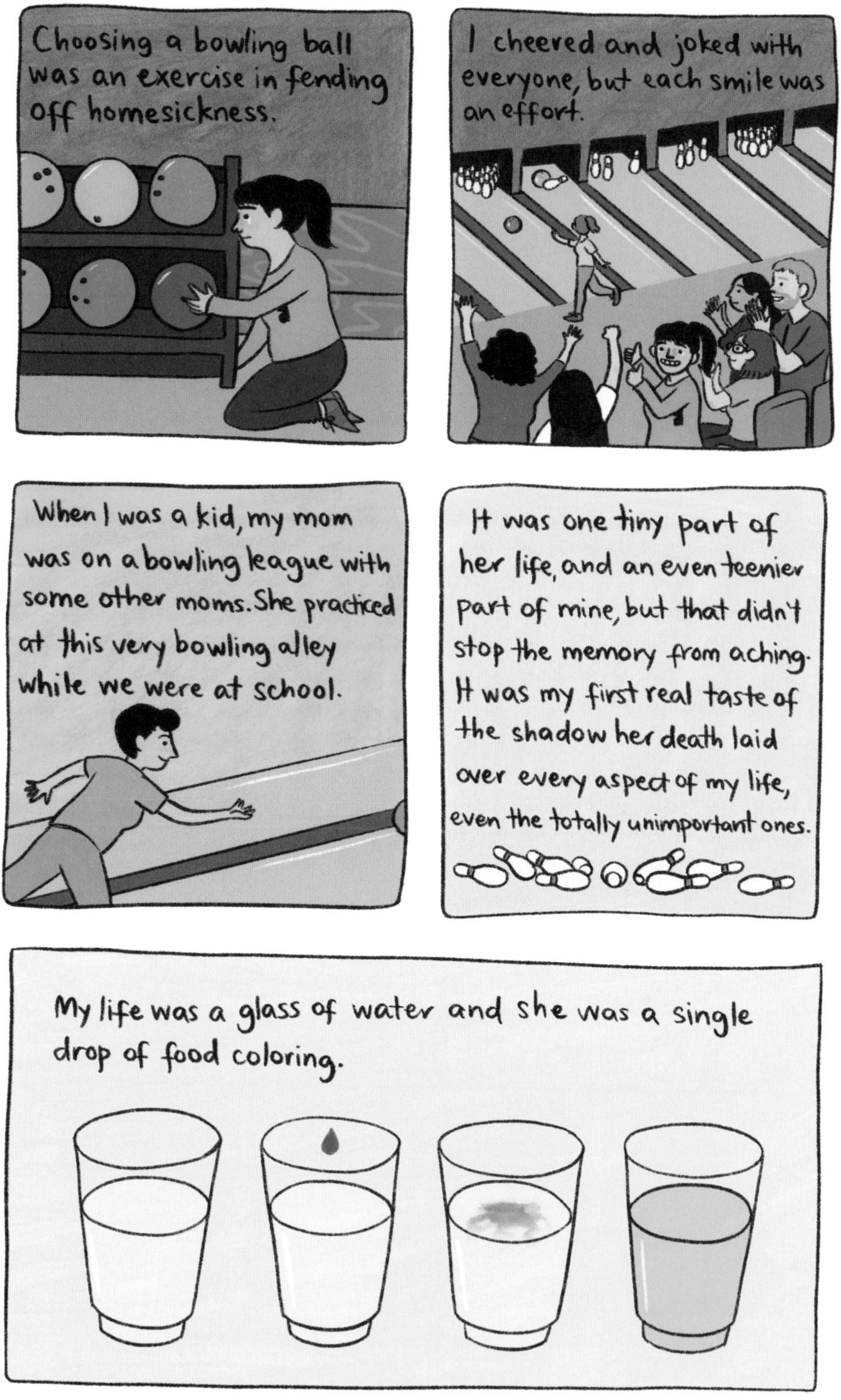
Choosing a bowling ball was an exercise in fending off homesickness.
I cheered and joked with everyone, but each smile was an effort.
When I was a kid, my mom was on a bowling league with some other moms. She practiced at this very bowling alley while we were at school.
It was one tiny part of her life, and an even teenier part of mine, but that didn't stop the memory from aching. It was my first real taste of the shadow her death laid over every aspect of my life, even the totally unimportant ones.
My life was a glass of water and she was a single drop of food coloring.

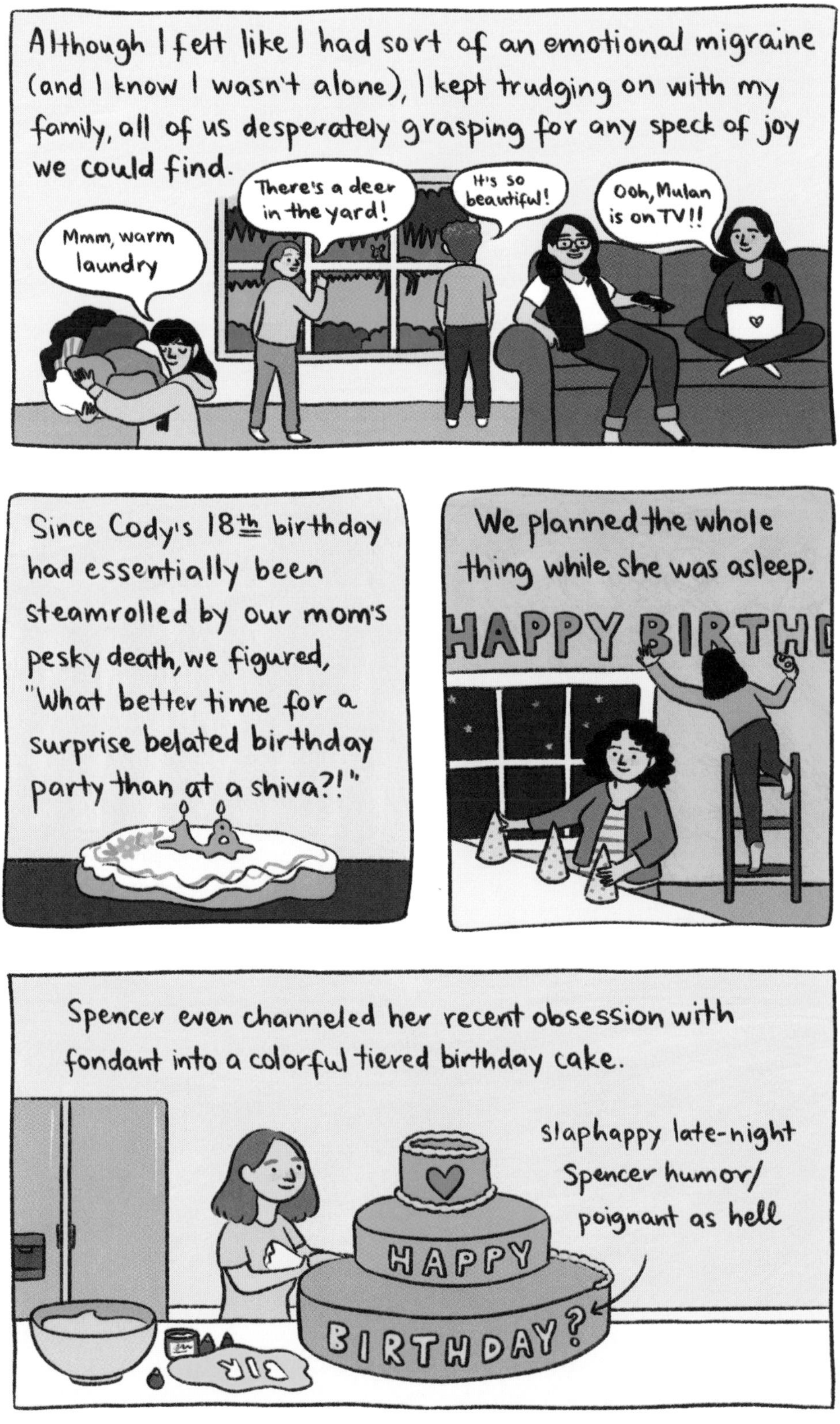
Although I felt like I had sort of an emotional migraine (and I know I wasn't alone), I kept trudging on with my family, all of us desperately grasping for any speck of joy we could find.
Mmm, warm laundry
There's a deer in the yard!
It's so beautiful!
Ooh, Mulan is on TV!!
Since Cody's 18th birthday had essentially been steamrolled by our mom's pesky death, we figured, "What better time for a surprise belated birthday party than at a shiva?!"
We planned the whole thing while she was asleep.
HAPPY BIRTH
Spencer even channeled her recent obsession with fondant into a colorful tiered birthday cake.
slaphappy late-night Spencer humor/ poignant as hell
HAPPY
BIRTHDAY?

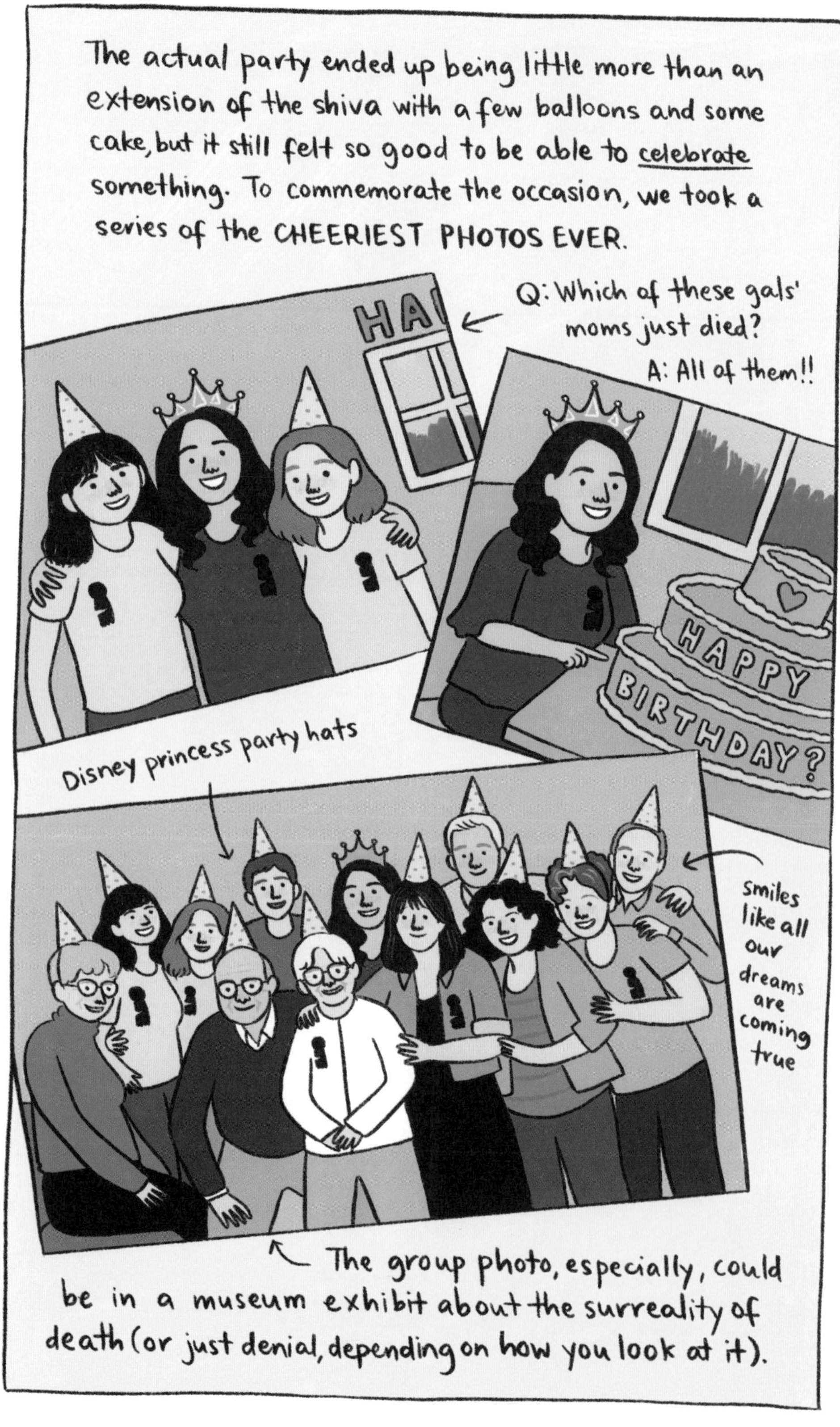
The actual party ended up being little more than an extension of the shiva with a few balloons and some cake, but it still felt so good to be able to celebrate something. To commemorate the occasion, we took a series of the CHEERIEST PHOTOS EVER.
HA
Q: Which of these gals' moms just died?
A: All of them!!
HAPPY BIRTHDAY?
Disney princess party hats
smiles like all our dreams are coming true
The group photo, especially, could be in a museum exhibit about the surreality of death (or just denial, depending on how you look at it).

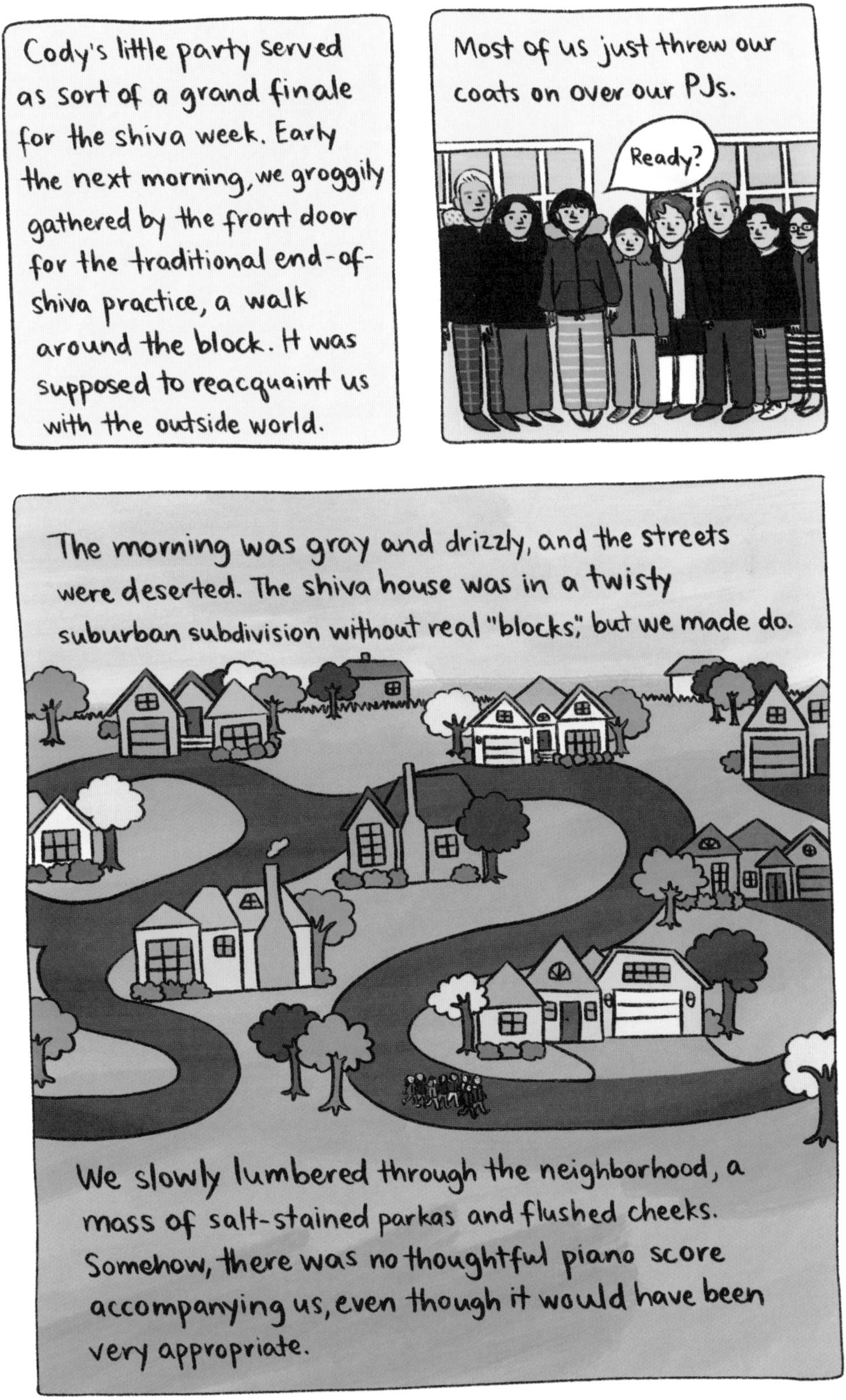
Cody's little party served as sort of a grand finale for the shiva week. Early the next morning, we groggily gathered by the front door for the traditional end-of-shiva practice, a walk around the block. It was supposed to reacquaint us with the outside world.
Most of us just threw our coats on over our PJs.
Ready?
The morning was gray and drizzly, and the streets were deserted. The shiva house was in a twisty suburban subdivision without real "blocks," but we made do.
We slowly lumbered through the neighborhood, a mass of salt-stained parkas and flushed cheeks. Somehow, there was no thoughtful piano score accompanying us, even though it would have been very appropriate.

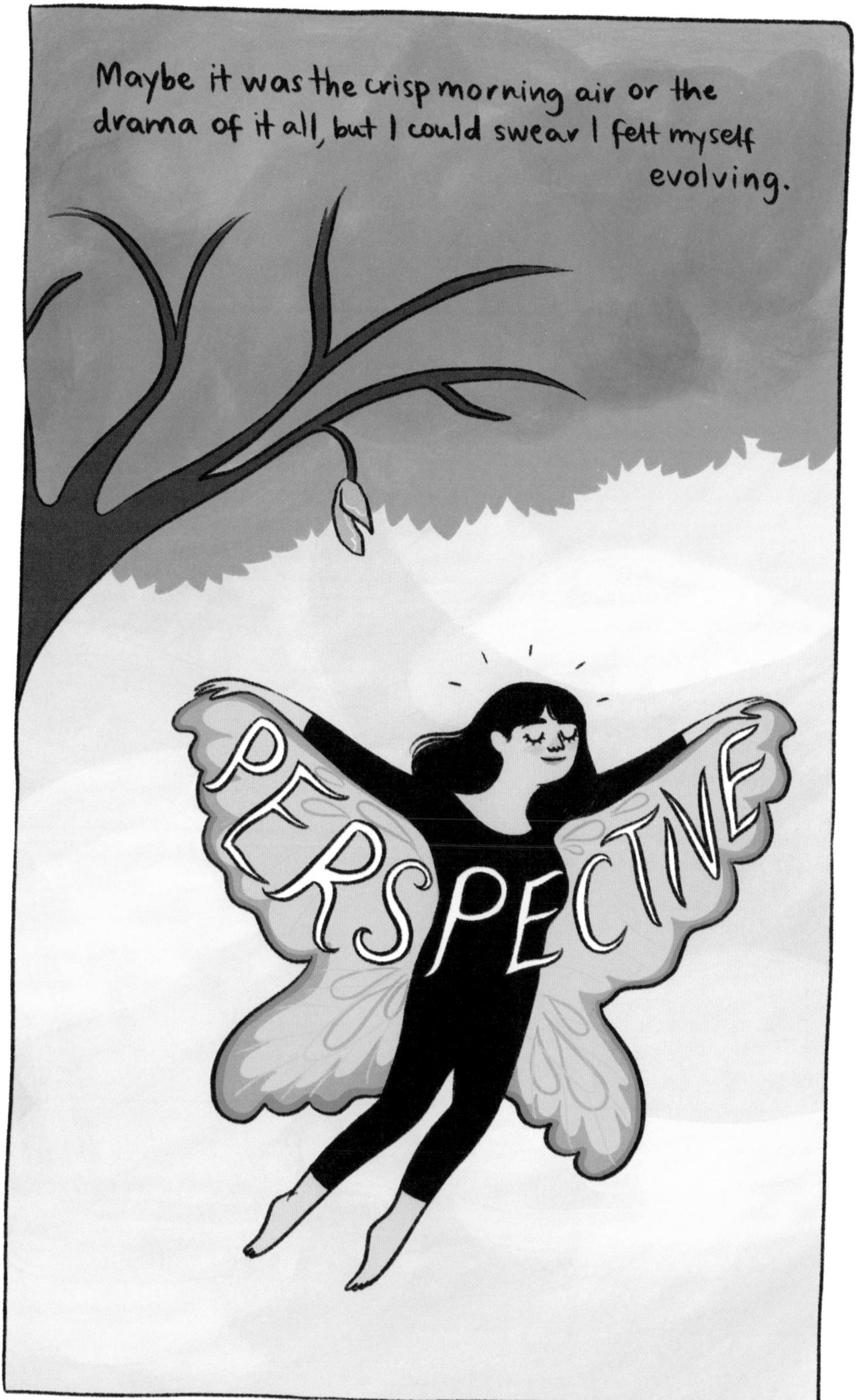
Maybe it was the crisp morning air or the drama of it all, but I could swear I felt myself evolving.
PERSPECTIVE

# "my mom died young" reaction

# BING ☹

| "God never gives us more than we can handle" | "My mom had a cancer scare once" | "Only the good die young" | "She's not suffering anymore" | [changes the subject] |
|---|---|---|---|---|
| "I'll be hugging my mom a little tighter tonight" | tight hug (pleasant) | "I know how you feel because my parents got divorced" | [is comforting for one week max and then acts like it never happened] | any reaction that starts with "at least" |
| "God just needed another angel" | [one-ups your tragedy with their own tragedy] | FREE SPACE "thoughts and prayers" | (becomes very formal all of a sudden) | "I know how you feel because my dog died" |
| "I'm praying for you" | "My condolences to your family" | [radio silence] | "She's in a better place" | "I'm sorry for your loss" |
| Pity Face ™ | "I know how you feel because my mom died at the young age of 86" | tight hug (unpleasant) | "How did she die?" | "May her memory be a blessing" |

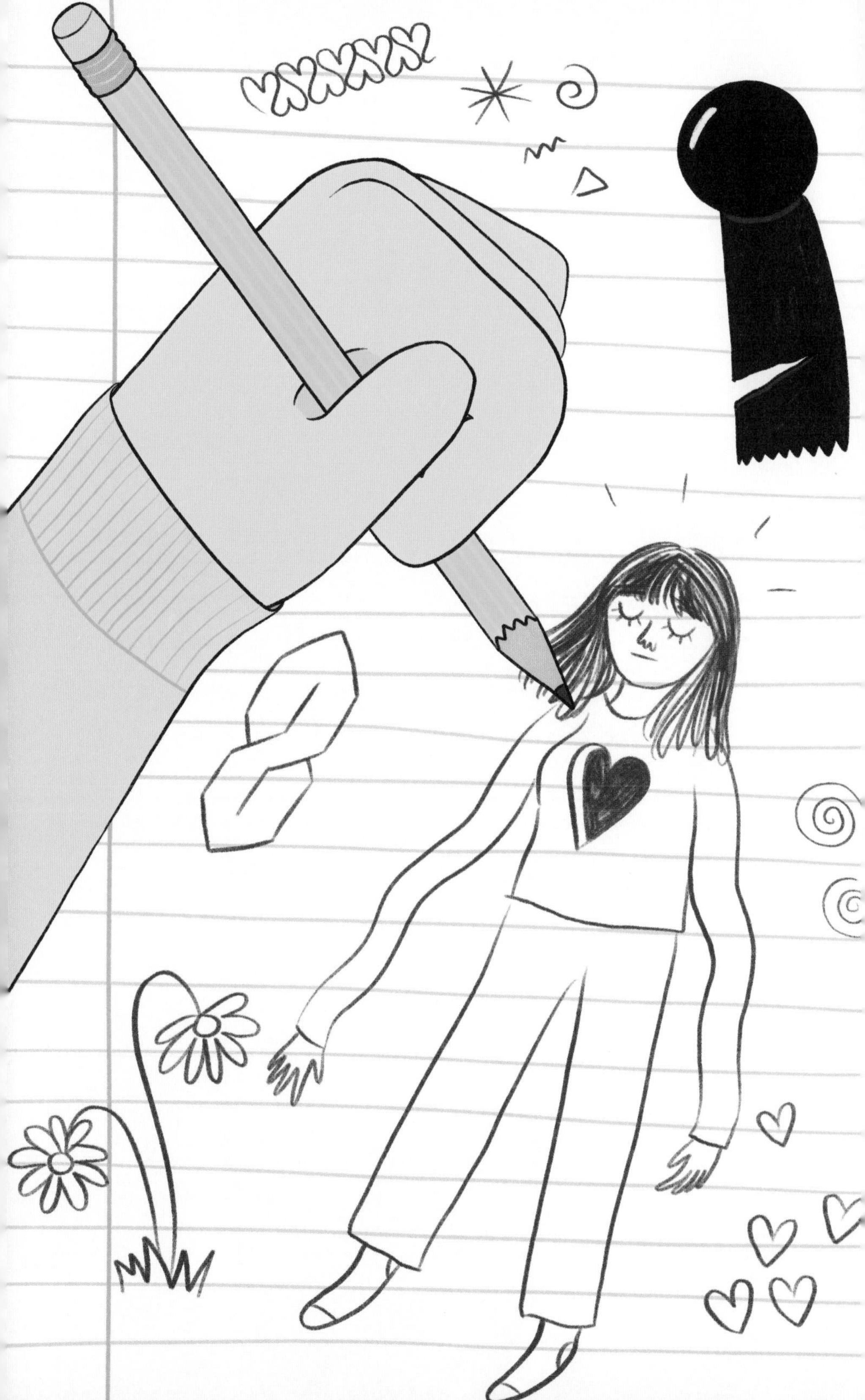

# chapter eight

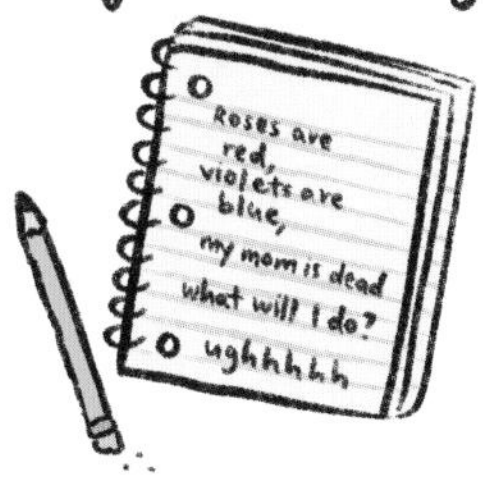

Roses are
red,
violets are
blue,
my mom is dead
what will I do?
ughhhhh

# THE NEW NORMAL

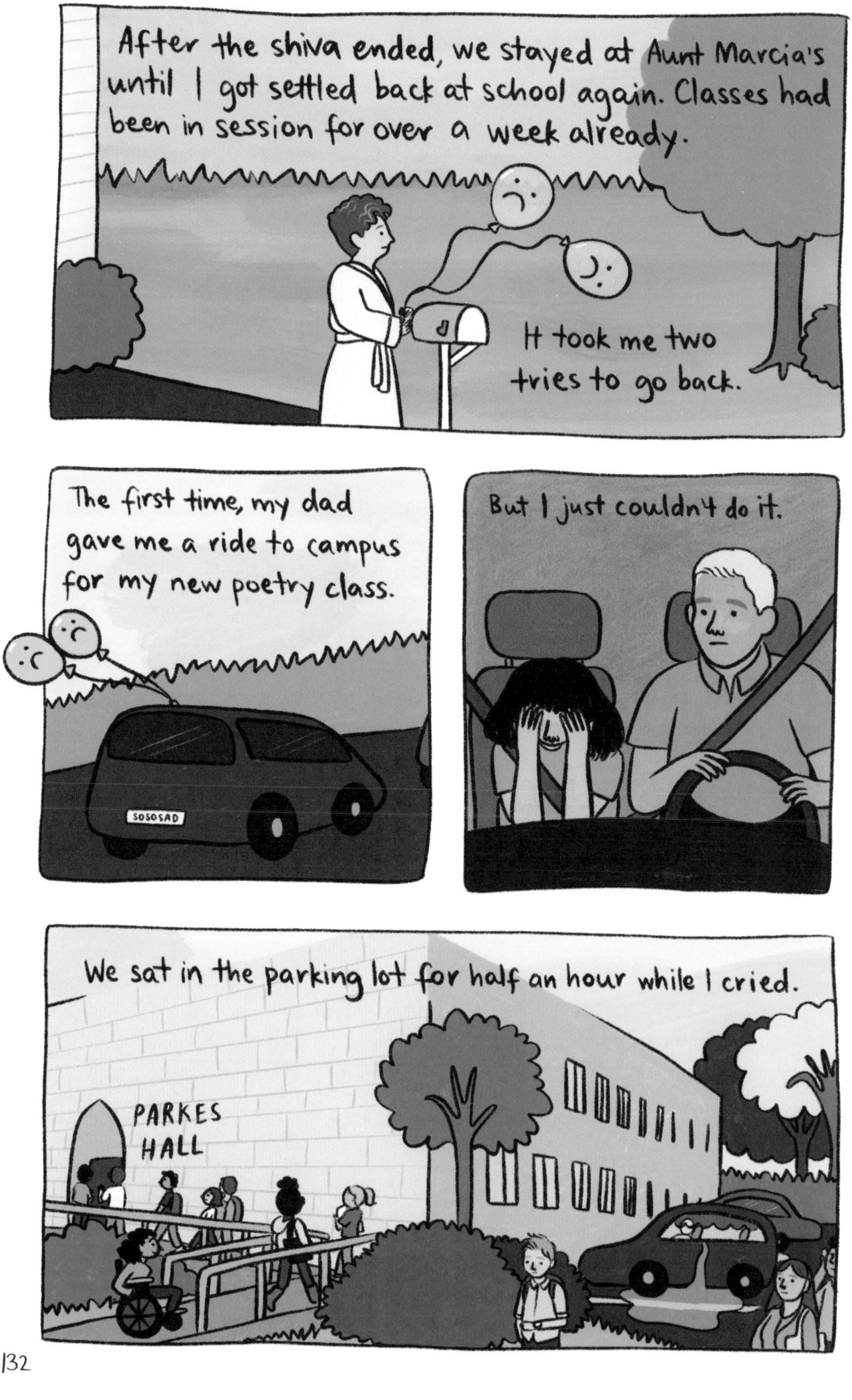
After the shiva ended, we stayed at Aunt Marcia's until I got settled back at school again. Classes had been in session for over a week already.
It took me two tries to go back.
The first time, my dad gave me a ride to campus for my new poetry class.
SOSOSAD
But I just couldn't do it.
We sat in the parking lot for half an hour while I cried.
PARKES HALL

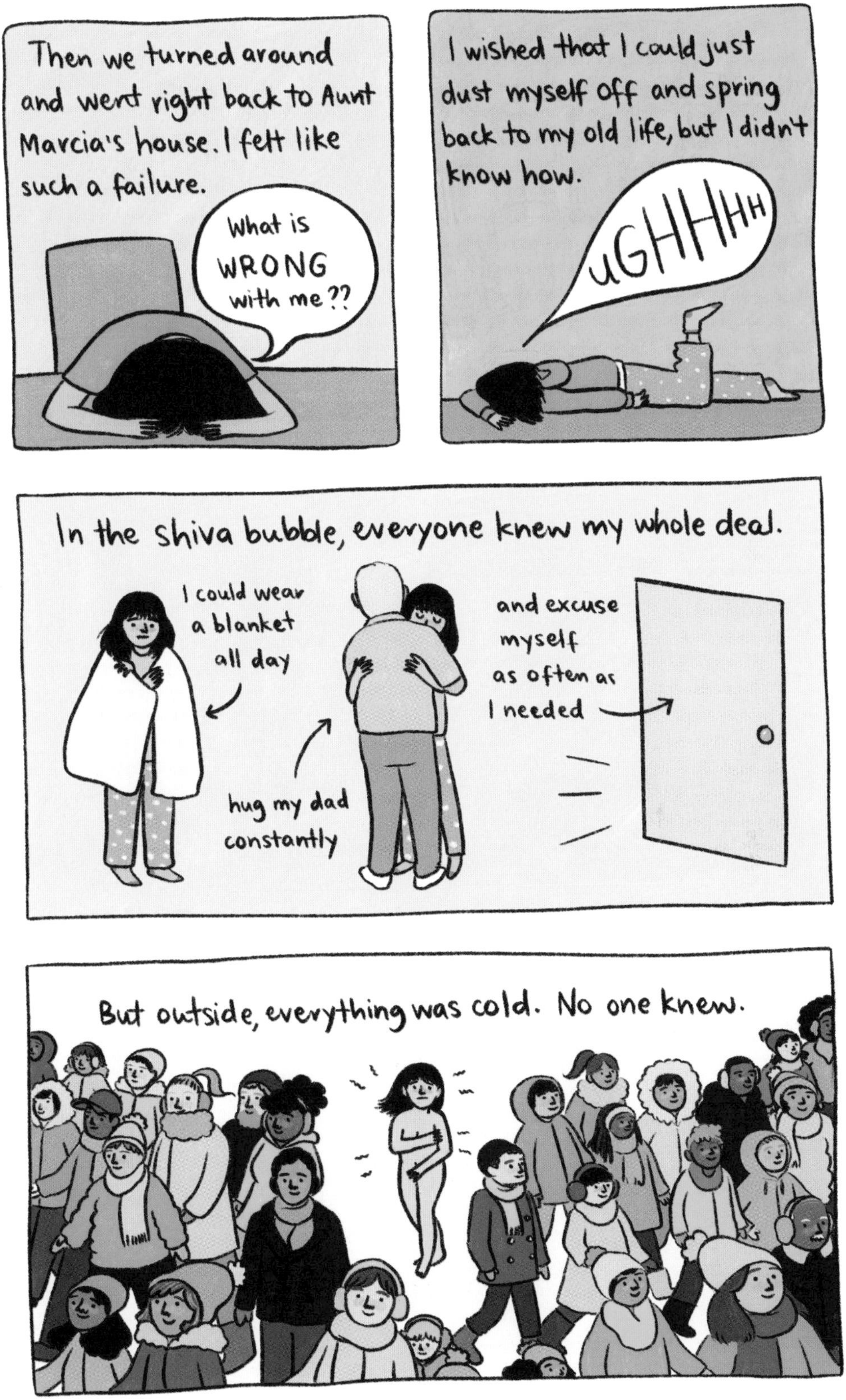
Then we turned around and went right back to Aunt Marcia's house. I felt like such a failure.
What is WRONG with me??
I wished that I could just dust myself off and spring back to my old life, but I didn't know how.
uGHHHHH
In the shiva bubble, everyone knew my whole deal.
I could wear a blanket all day
hug my dad constantly
and excuse myself as often as I needed
But outside, everything was cold. No one knew.

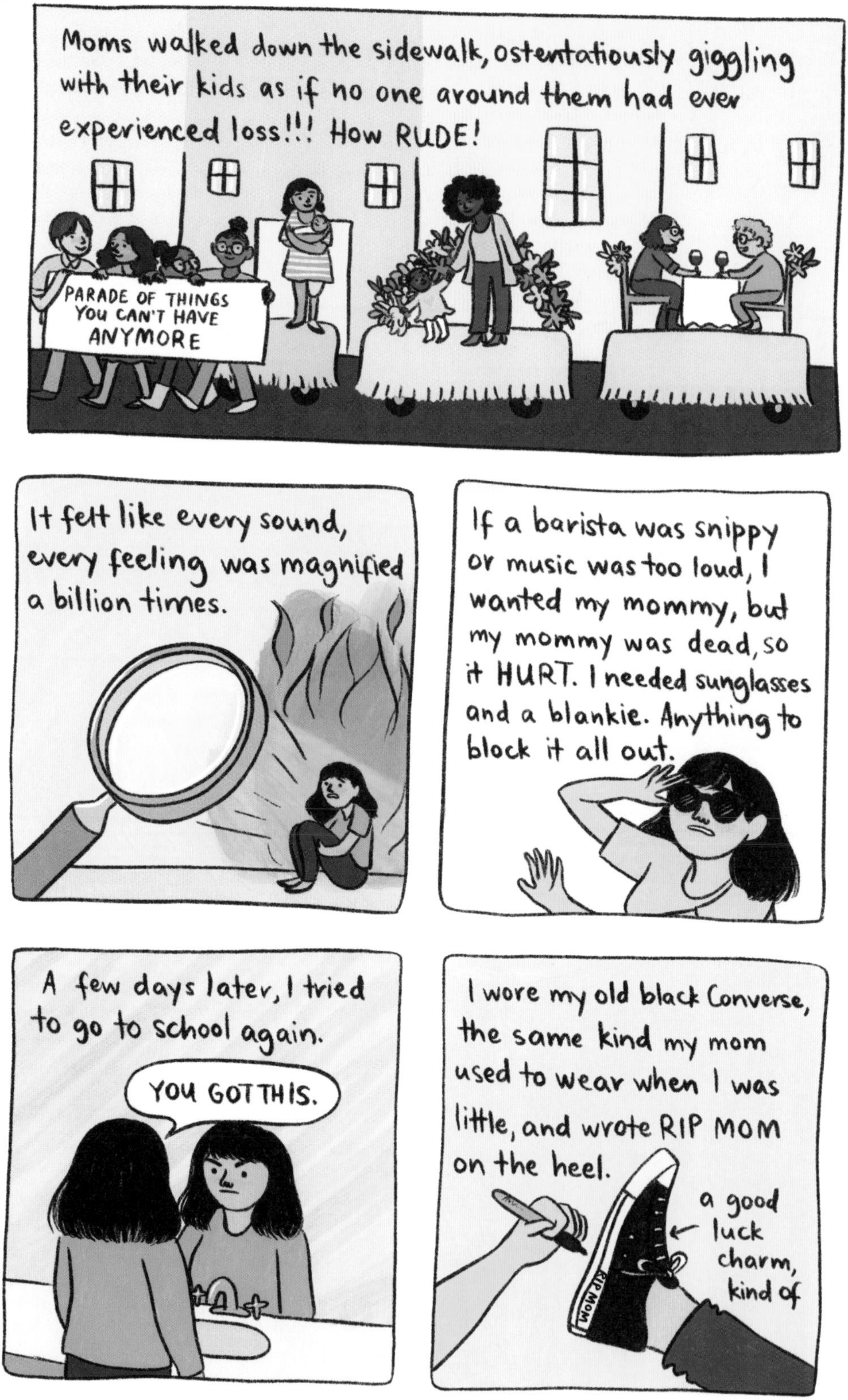
Moms walked down the sidewalk, ostentatiously giggling with their kids as if no one around them had ever experienced loss!!! How RUDE!
PARADE OF THINGS YOU CAN'T HAVE ANYMORE
It felt like every sound, every feeling was magnified a billion times.
If a barista was snippy or music was too loud, I wanted my mommy, but my mommy was dead, so it HURT. I needed sunglasses and a blankie. Anything to block it all out.
A few days later, I tried to go to school again.
YOU GOT THIS.
I wore my old black Converse, the same kind my mom used to wear when I was little, and wrote RIP MOM on the heel.
a good luck charm, kind of
RIP MOM

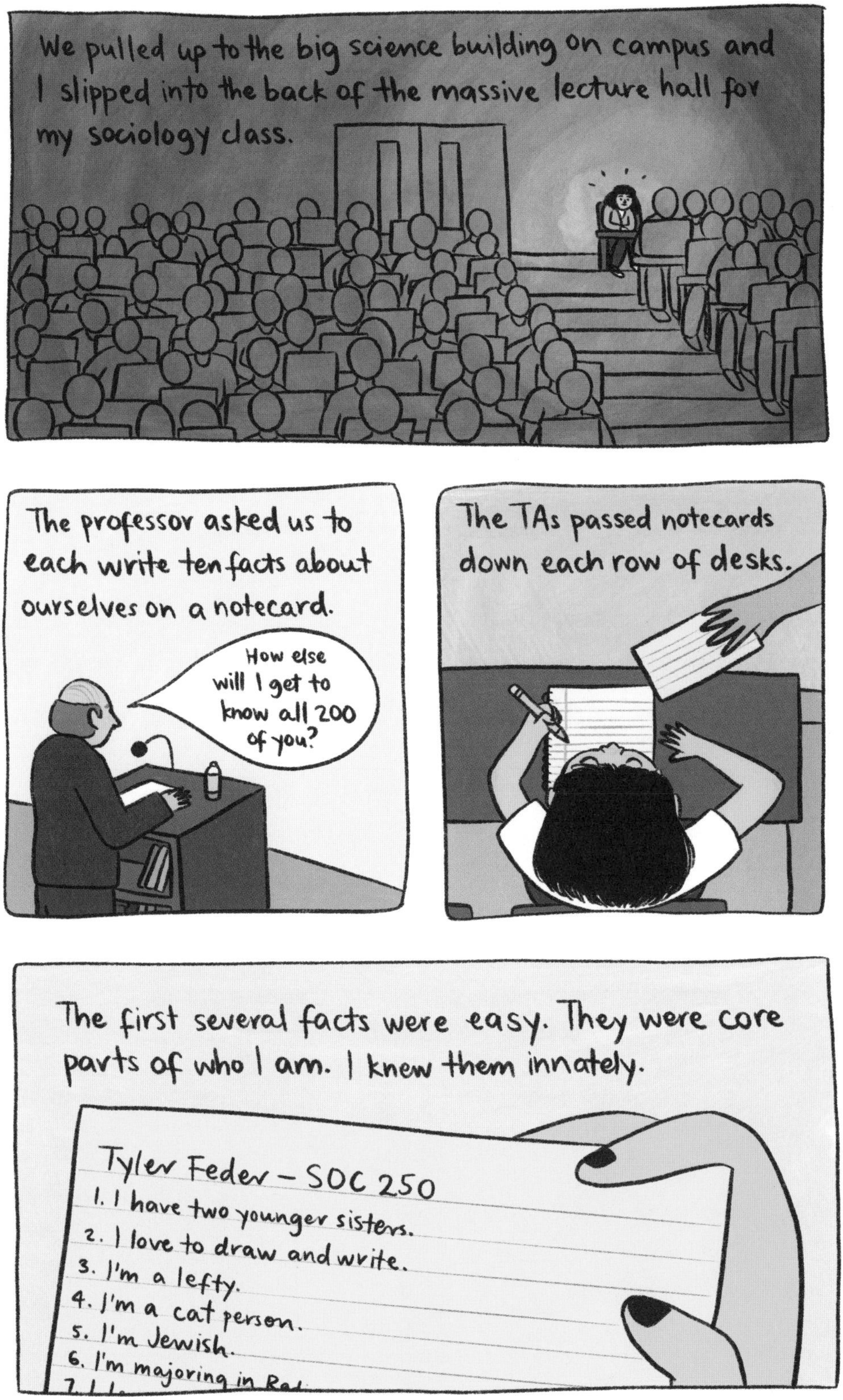
We pulled up to the big science building on campus and I slipped into the back of the massive lecture hall for my sociology class.
The professor asked us to each write ten facts about ourselves on a notecard.
How else will I get to know all 200 of you?
The TAs passed notecards down each row of desks.
The first several facts were easy. They were core parts of who I am. I knew them innately.
Tyler Feder – SOC 250
1. I have two younger sisters.
2. I love to draw and write.
3. I'm a lefty.
4. I'm a cat person.
5. I'm Jewish.
6. I'm majoring in

The TA came back to collect the cards and I scribbled down my last fact.

Tyler Fed...

10. My mom died when I was young.

Since the class was a giant lecture and I am very much not a hand-raiser, I never got to directly interact with the professor (about the note-card or anything else) but that didn't matter. Writing it down made it real.

How strange to gain a new core part of my identity.

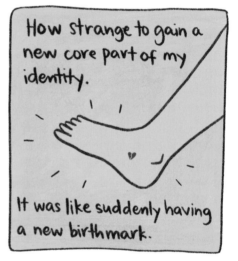

It was like suddenly having a new birthmark.

Moving back into the dorm was awkward, the unspoken knowledge of my mom's death hanging in the air.

DEAD MOM

Hi, guys!

How...have you...been??

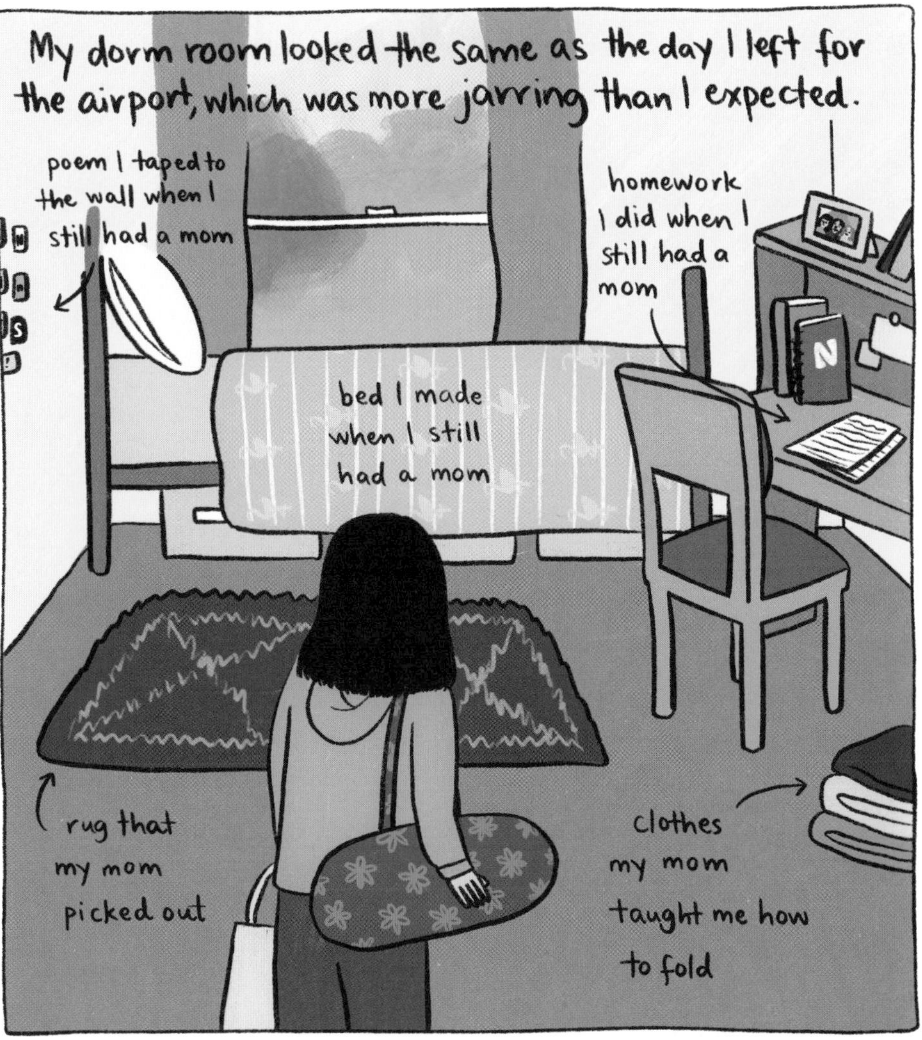
My dorm room looked the same as the day I left for the airport, which was more jarring than I expected.
poem I taped to the wall when I still had a mom
homework I did when I still had a mom
bed I made when I still had a mom
rug that my mom picked out
clothes my mom taught me how to fold

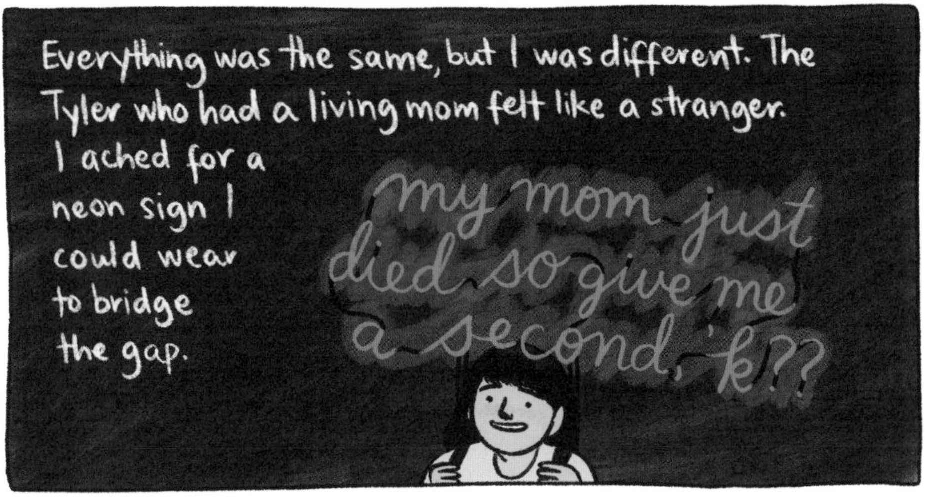
Everything was the same, but I was different. The Tyler who had a living mom felt like a stranger.
I ached for a neon sign I could wear to bridge the gap.
my mom just died so give me a second, 'k??

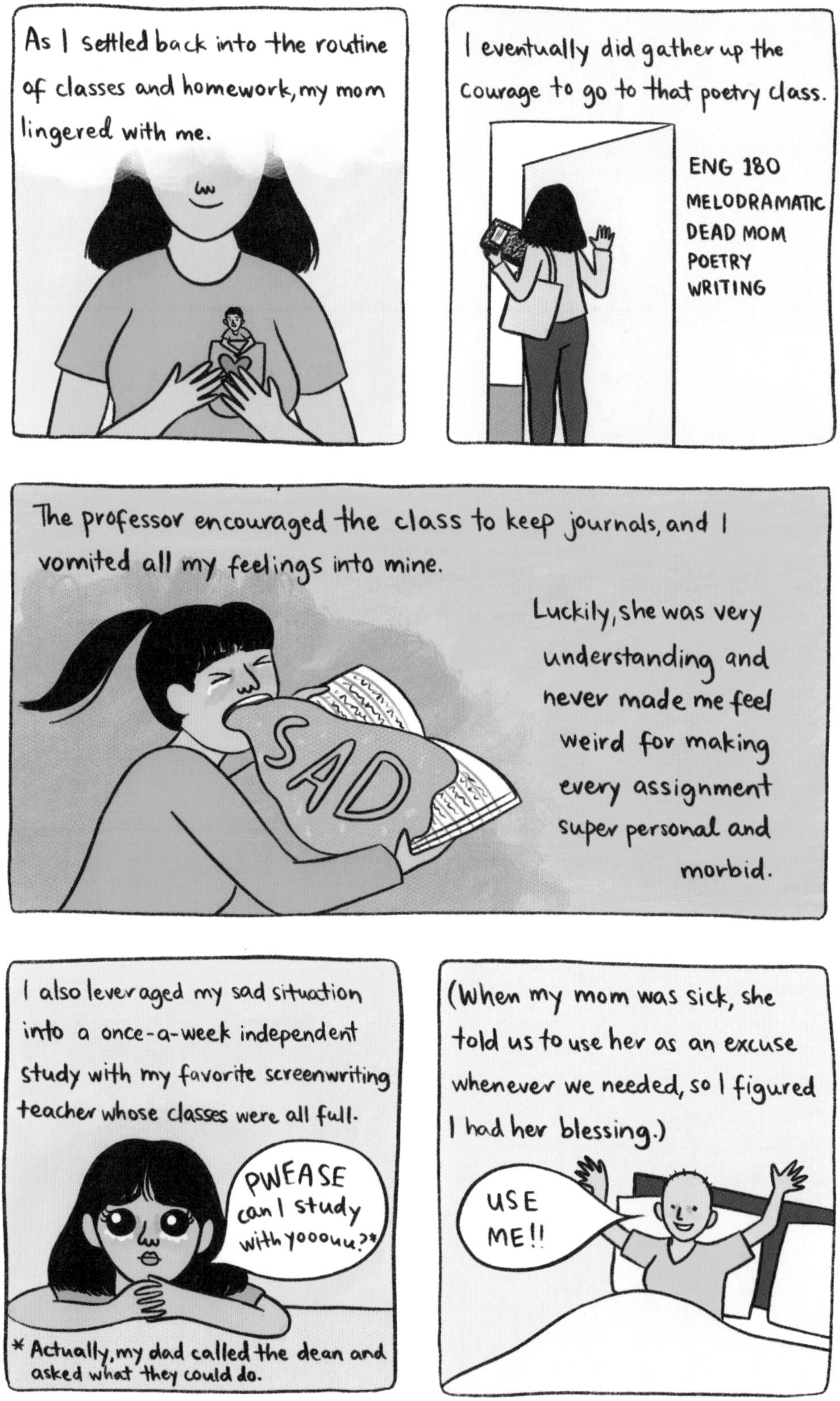

As I settled back into the routine of classes and homework, my mom lingered with me.
I eventually did gather up the courage to go to that poetry class.
ENG 180
MELODRAMATIC
DEAD MOM
POETRY
WRITING
The professor encouraged the class to keep journals, and I vomited all my feelings into mine.
SAD
Luckily, she was very understanding and never made me feel weird for making every assignment super personal and morbid.
I also leveraged my sad situation into a once-a-week independent study with my favorite screenwriting teacher whose classes were all full.
PWEASE can I study with yooouu?*
* Actually, my dad called the dean and asked what they could do.
(When my mom was sick, she told us to use her as an excuse whenever we needed, so I figured I had her blessing.)
USE ME!!

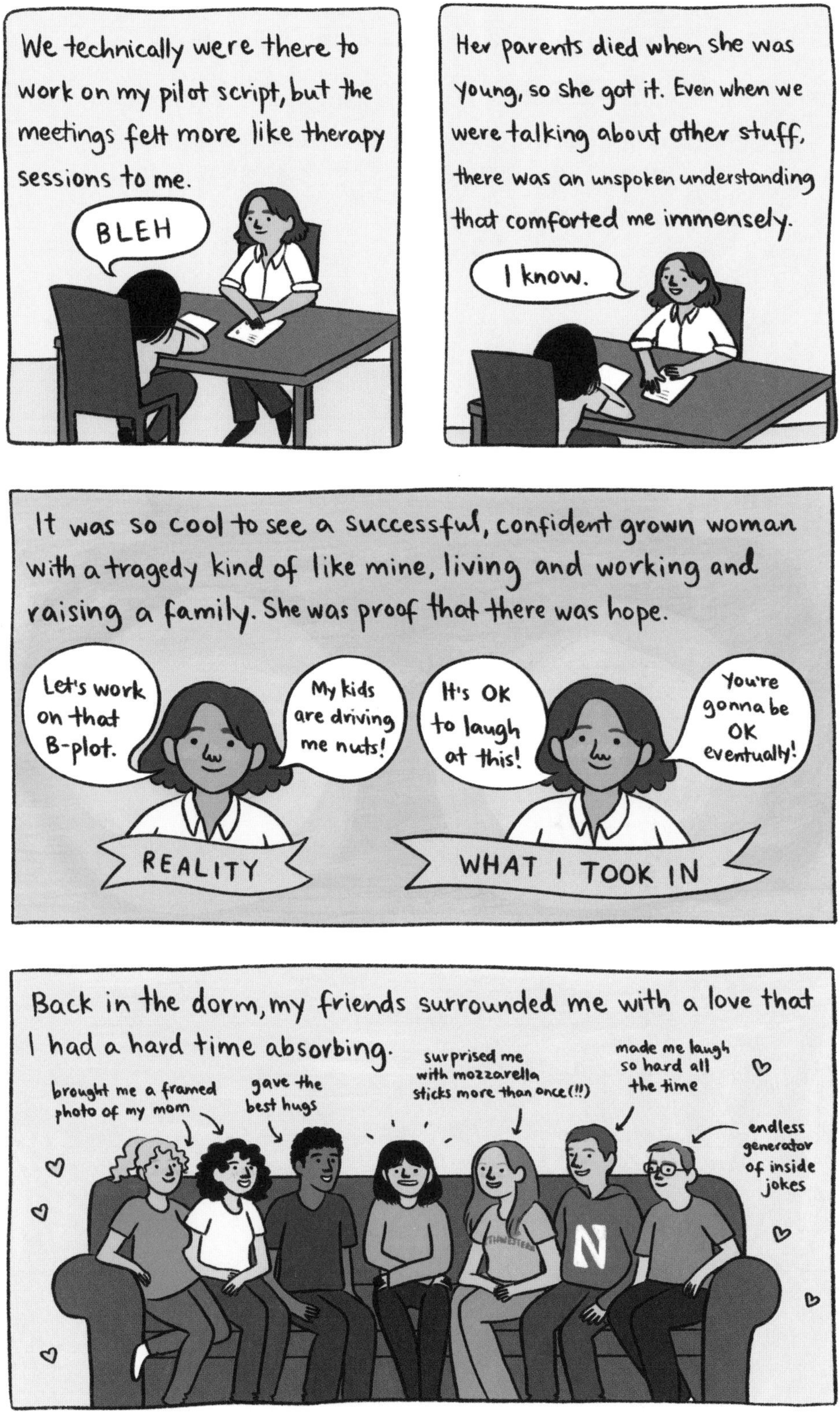

We technically were there to work on my pilot script, but the meetings felt more like therapy sessions to me.
BLEH
Her parents died when she was young, so she got it. Even when we were talking about other stuff, there was an unspoken understanding that comforted me immensely.
I know.
It was so cool to see a successful, confident grown woman with a tragedy kind of like mine, living and working and raising a family. She was proof that there was hope.
Let's work on that B-plot.
My kids are driving me nuts!
REALITY
It's OK to laugh at this!
You're gonna be OK eventually!
WHAT I TOOK IN
Back in the dorm, my friends surrounded me with a love that I had a hard time absorbing.
brought me a framed photo of my mom
gave the best hugs
surprised me with mozzarella sticks more than once (!!)
made me laugh so hard all the time
endless generator of inside jokes
N

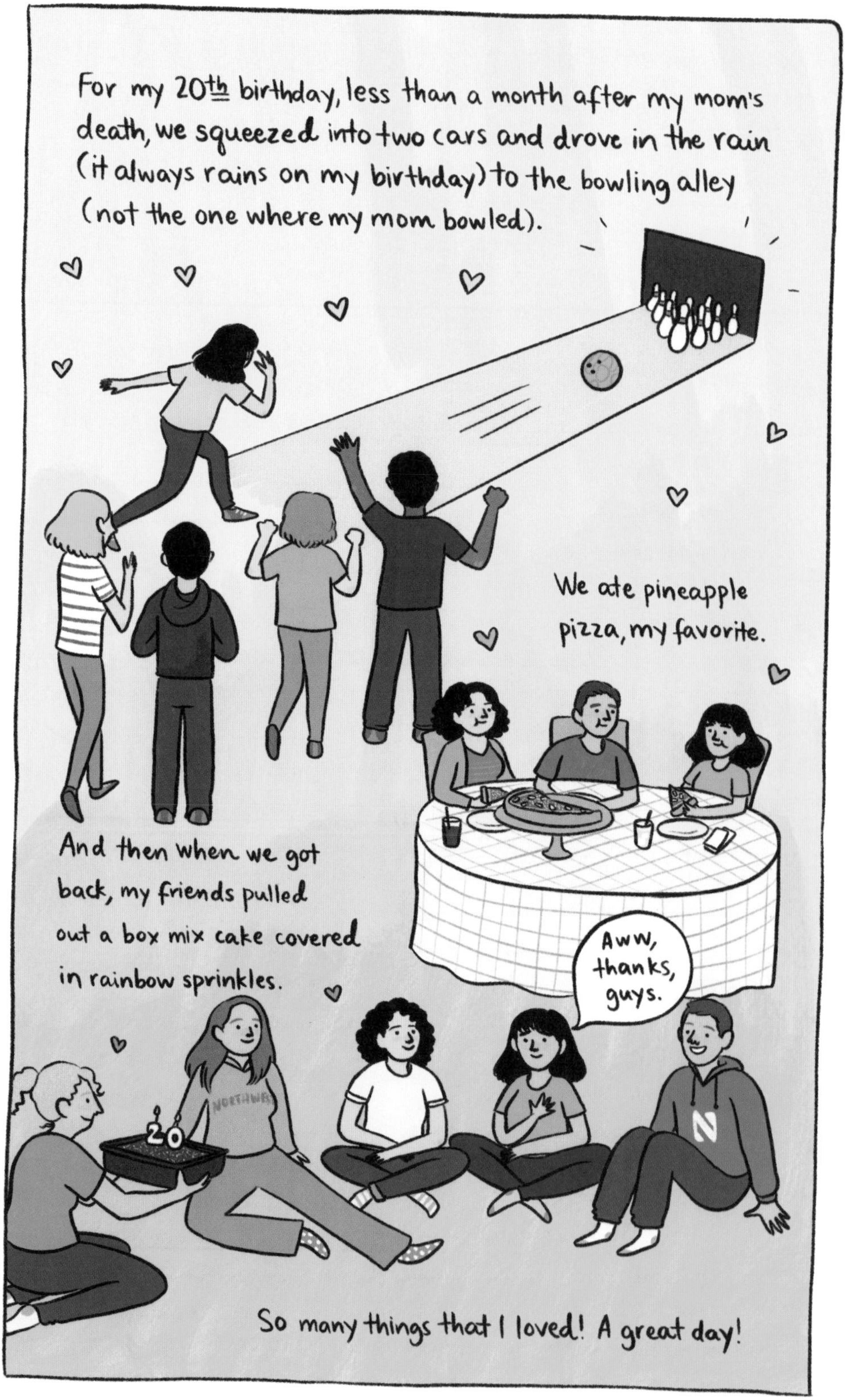
For my 20th birthday, less than a month after my mom's death, we squeezed into two cars and drove in the rain (it always rains on my birthday) to the bowling alley (not the one where my mom bowled).
We ate pineapple pizza, my favorite.
And then when we got back, my friends pulled out a box mix cake covered in rainbow sprinkles.
Aww, thanks, guys.
20
So many things that I loved! A great day!

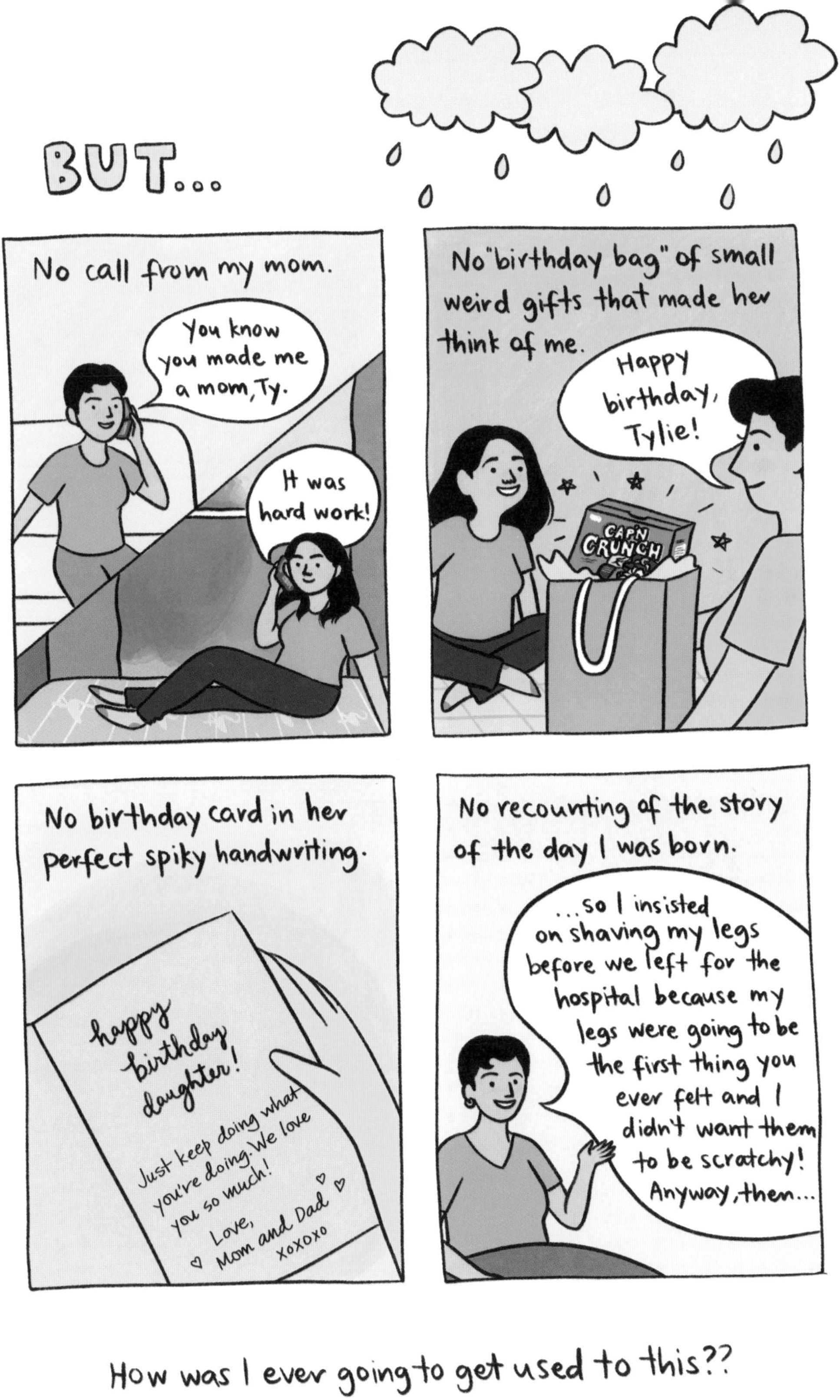
BUT...
No call from my mom.
You know you made me a mom, Ty.
It was hard work!
No "birthday bag" of small weird gifts that made her think of me.
Happy birthday, Tylie!
CAP'N CRUNCH
No birthday card in her perfect spiky handwriting.
happy birthday daughter!
Just keep doing what you're doing. We love you so much!
Love, Mom and Dad
XOXOXO
No recounting of the story of the day I was born.
...so I insisted on shaving my legs before we left for the hospital because my legs were going to be the first thing you ever felt and I didn't want them to be scratchy! Anyway, then...
How was I ever going to get used to this??

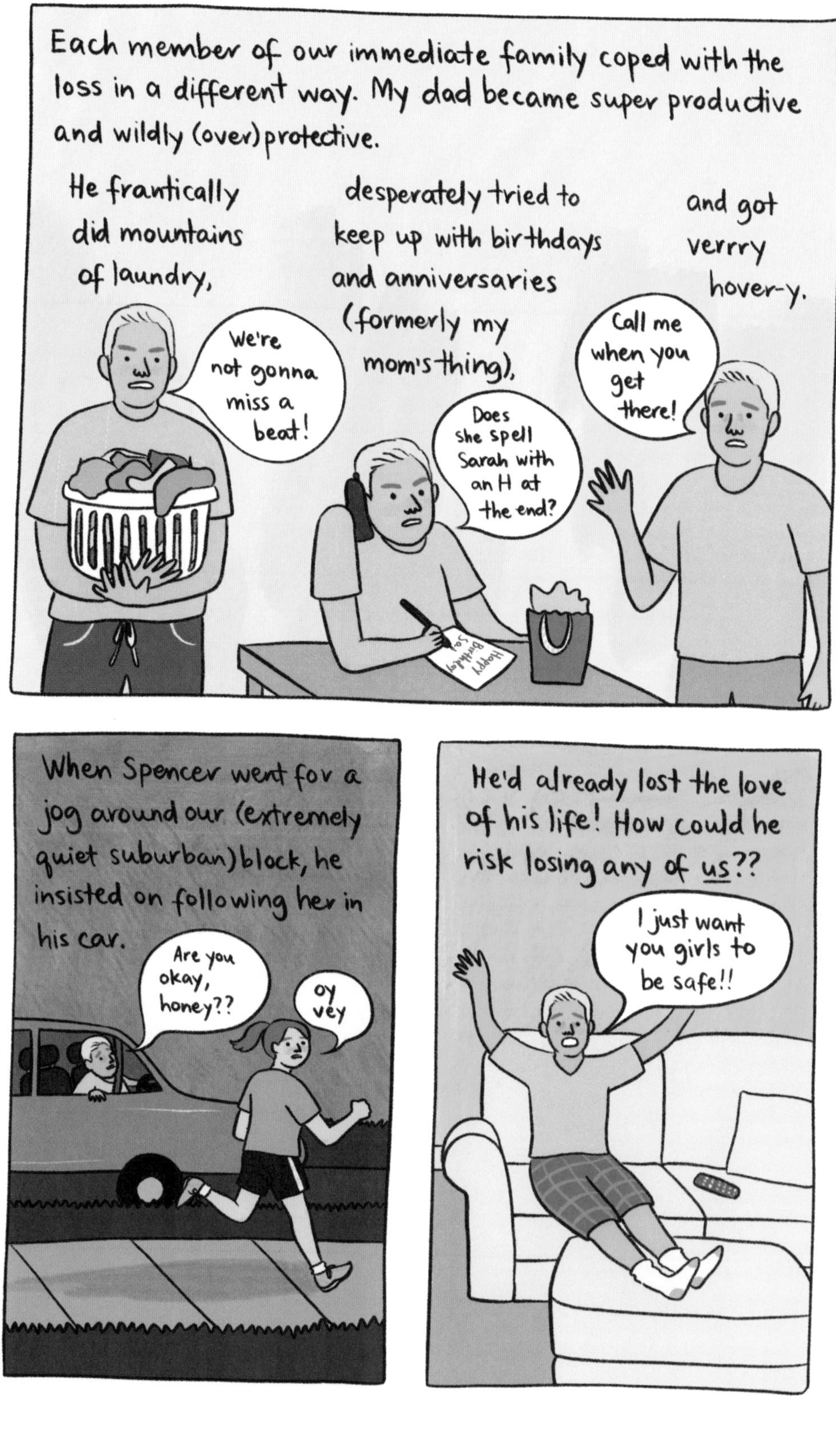
Each member of our immediate family coped with the loss in a different way. My dad became super productive and wildly (over)protective.
He frantically did mountains of laundry,
We're not gonna miss a beat!
desperately tried to keep up with birthdays and anniversaries (formerly my mom's thing),
Does she spell Sarah with an H at the end?
Happy Birthday
and got verrry hover-y.
Call me when you get there!
When Spencer went for a jog around our (extremely quiet suburban) block, he insisted on following her in his car.
Are you okay, honey??
oy vey
He'd already lost the love of his life! How could he risk losing any of us??
I just want you girls to be safe!!

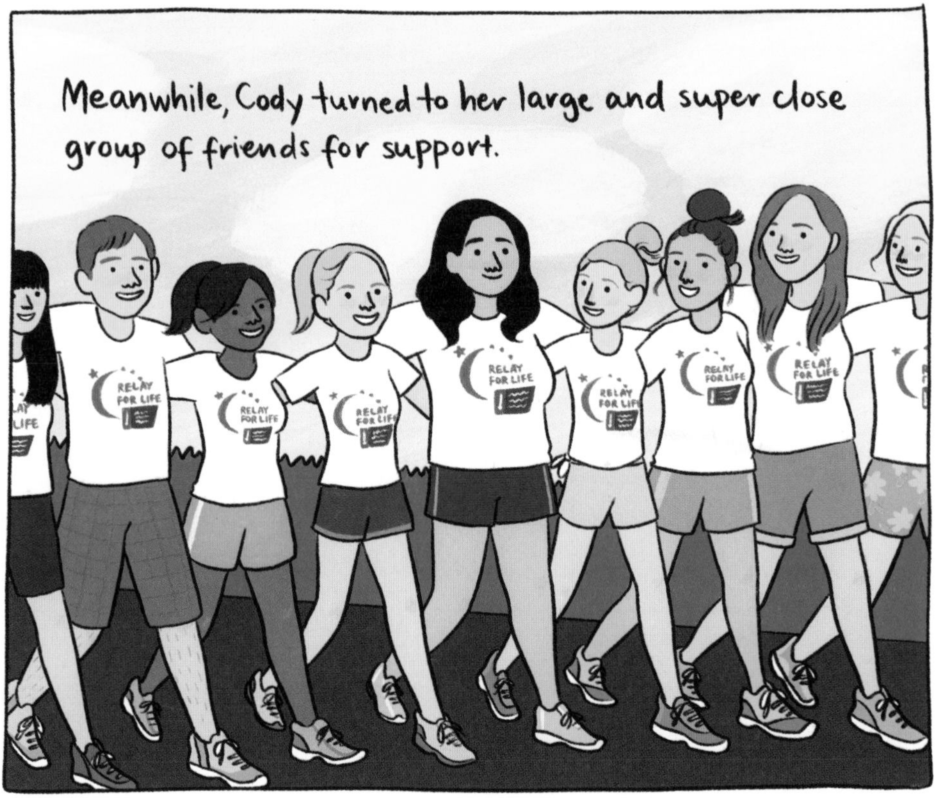
Meanwhile, Cody turned to her large and super close group of friends for support.
RELAY FOR LIFE

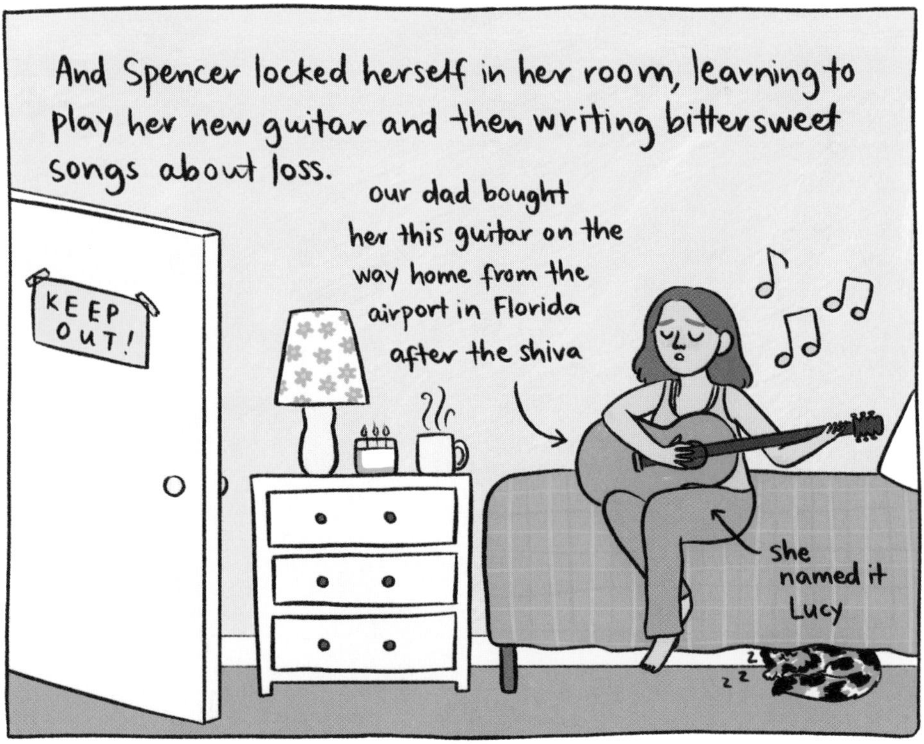
And Spencer locked herself in her room, learning to play her new guitar and then writing bittersweet songs about loss.
our dad bought her this guitar on the way home from the airport in Florida after the shiva
KEEP OUT!
she named it Lucy
z z z

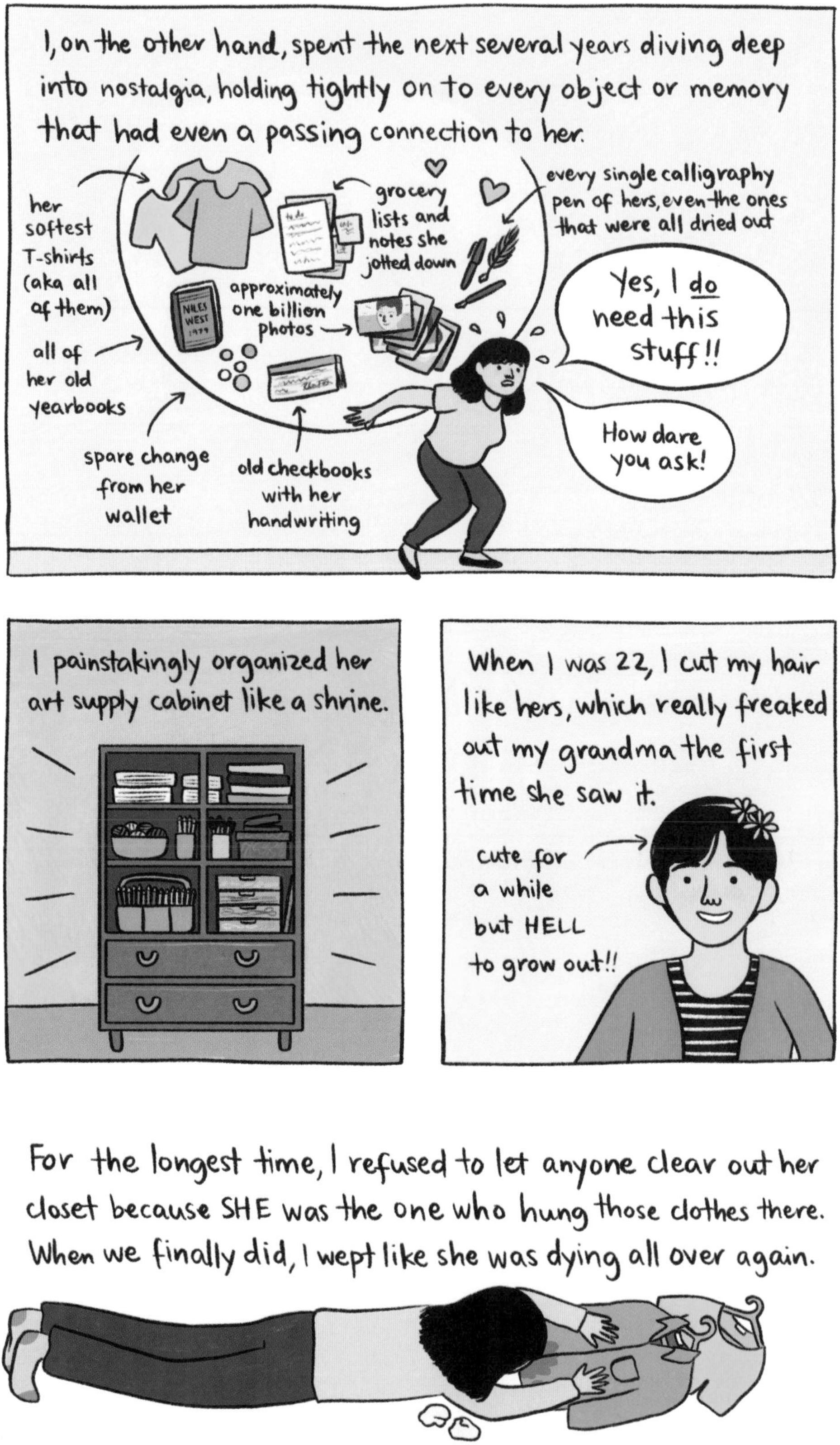

I, on the other hand, spent the next several years diving deep into nostalgia, holding tightly on to every object or memory that had even a passing connection to her.
her softest T-shirts (aka all of them)
grocery lists and notes she jotted down
every single calligraphy pen of hers, even the ones that were all dried out
approximately one billion photos
NILES WEST 1979
all of her old yearbooks
spare change from her wallet
old checkbooks with her handwriting
Yes, I do need this stuff!!
How dare you ask!
I painstakingly organized her art supply cabinet like a shrine.
When I was 22, I cut my hair like hers, which really freaked out my grandma the first time she saw it.
cute for a while but HELL to grow out!!
For the longest time, I refused to let anyone clear out her closet because SHE was the one who hung those clothes there. When we finally did, I wept like she was dying all over again.

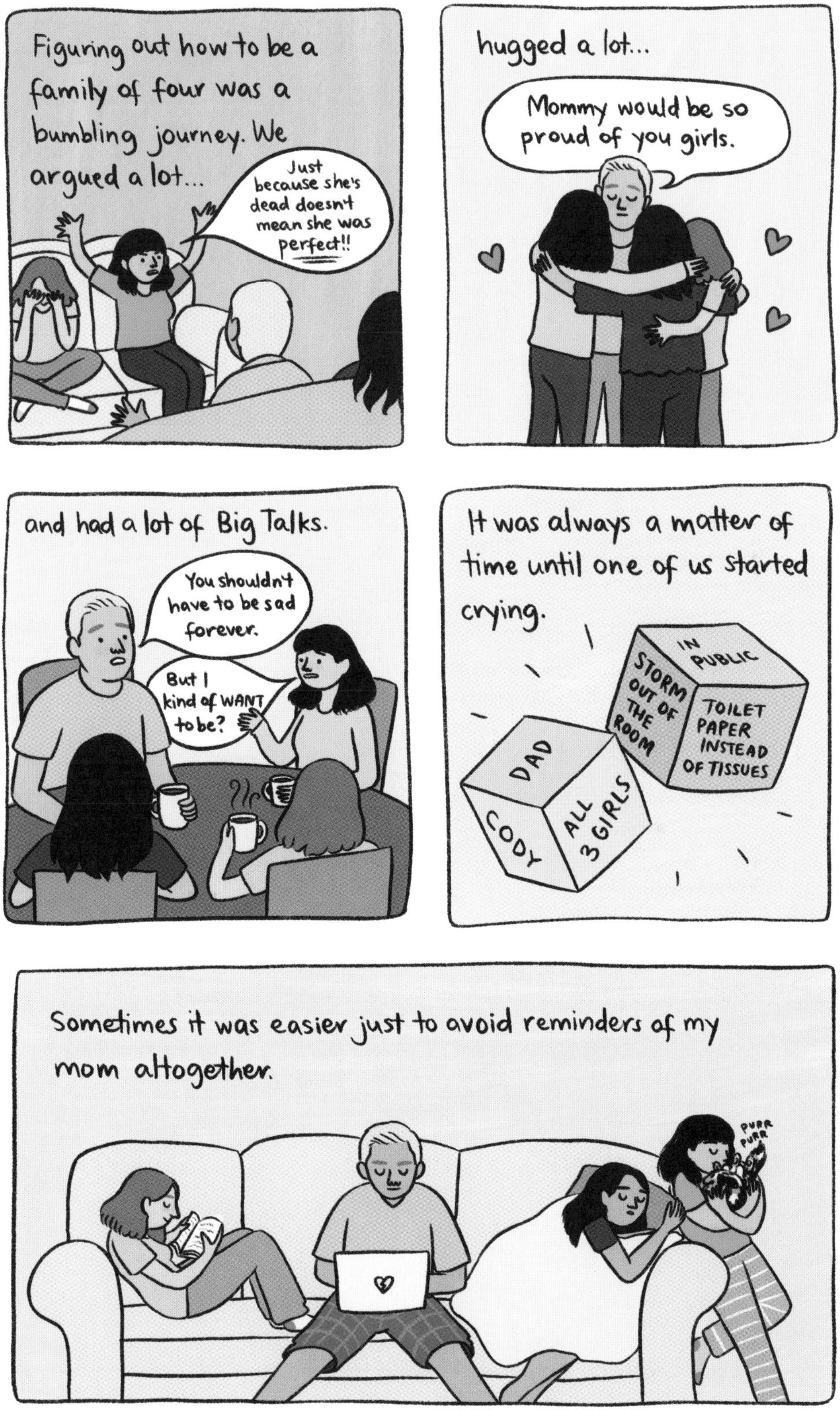
Figuring out how to be a family of four was a bumbling journey. We argued a lot...
Just because she's dead doesn't mean she was perfect!!
hugged a lot...
Mommy would be so proud of you girls.
and had a lot of Big Talks.
You shouldn't have to be sad forever.
But I kind of WANT to be?
It was always a matter of time until one of us started crying.
IN PUBLIC
STORM OUT OF THE ROOM
TOILET PAPER INSTEAD OF TISSUES
DAD
CODY
ALL 3 GIRLS
Sometimes it was easier just to avoid reminders of my mom altogether.
PURR PURR

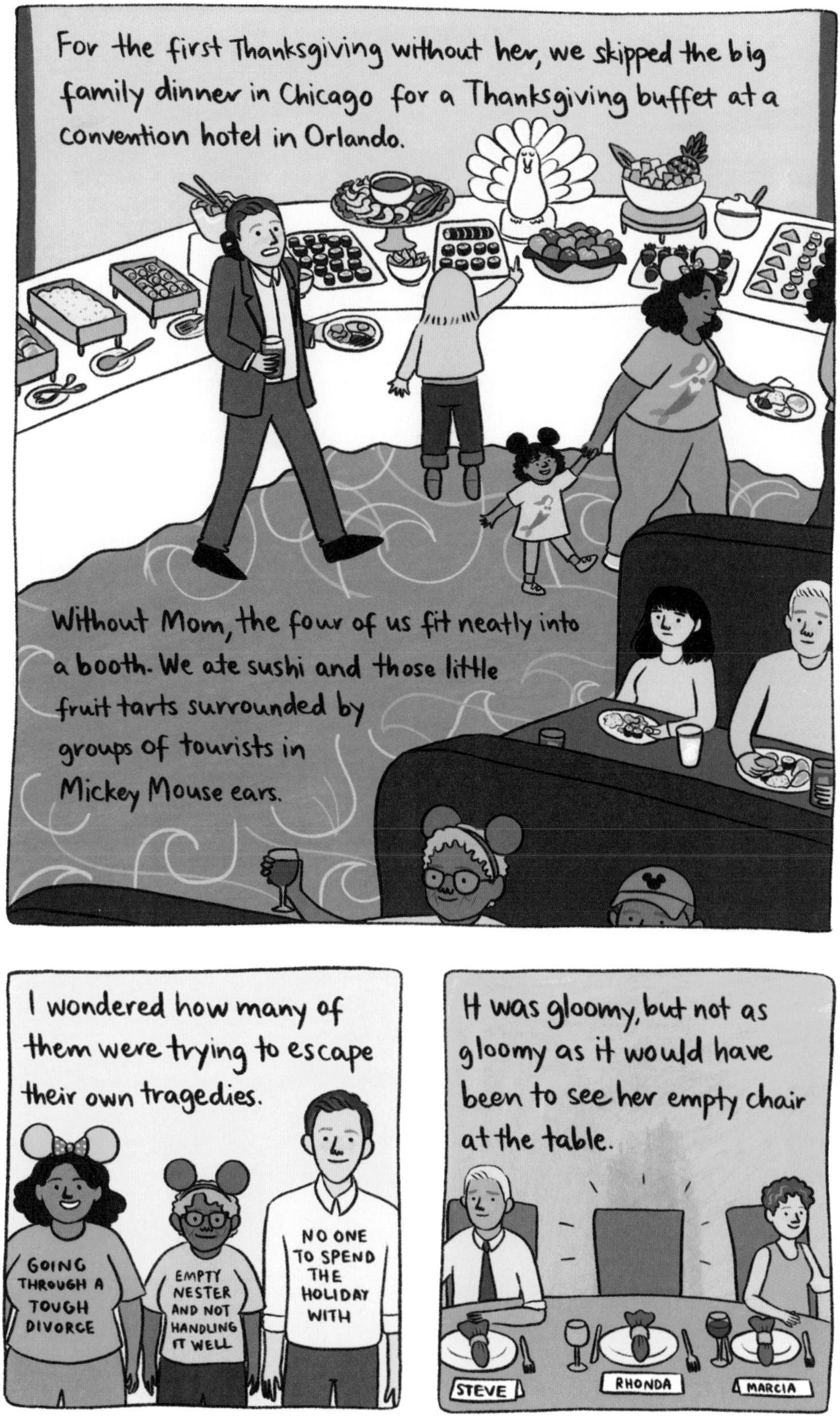
For the first Thanksgiving without her, we skipped the big family dinner in Chicago for a Thanksgiving buffet at a convention hotel in Orlando.
Without Mom, the four of us fit neatly into a booth. We ate sushi and those little fruit tarts surrounded by groups of tourists in Mickey Mouse ears.
I wondered how many of them were trying to escape their own tragedies.
GOING THROUGH A TOUGH DIVORCE
EMPTY NESTER AND NOT HANDLING IT WELL
NO ONE TO SPEND THE HOLIDAY WITH
It was gloomy, but not as gloomy as it would have been to see her empty chair at the table.
STEVE
RHONDA
MARCIA

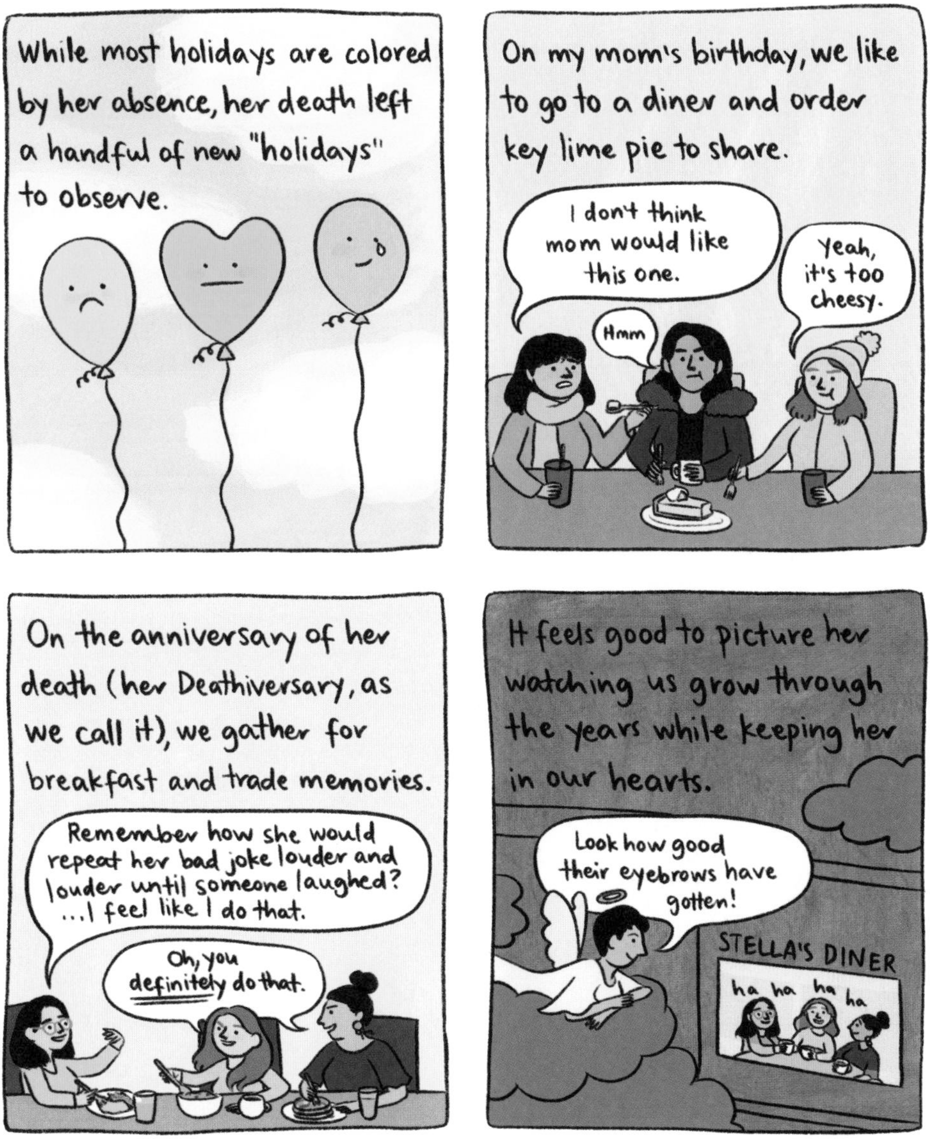
While most holidays are colored by her absence, her death left a handful of new "holidays" to observe.
On my mom's birthday, we like to go to a diner and order key lime pie to share.
I don't think mom would like this one.
Hmm
Yeah, it's too cheesy.
On the anniversary of her death (her Deathiversary, as we call it), we gather for breakfast and trade memories.
Remember how she would repeat her bad joke louder and louder until someone laughed? ...I feel like I do that.
Oh, you definitely do that.
It feels good to picture her watching us grow through the years while keeping her in our hearts.
Look how good their eyebrows have gotten!
STELLA'S DINER
ha ha ha ha

During those first few days in Florida after she died, we talked about the strangeness that all of this would eventually feel normal. As the months and years passed, it became clear:

This is THE NEW NORMAL™ (not really)

Hey! That's the name of this chapter!

The New Normal is like the old normal, except that everything is tinged with a secret sadness.

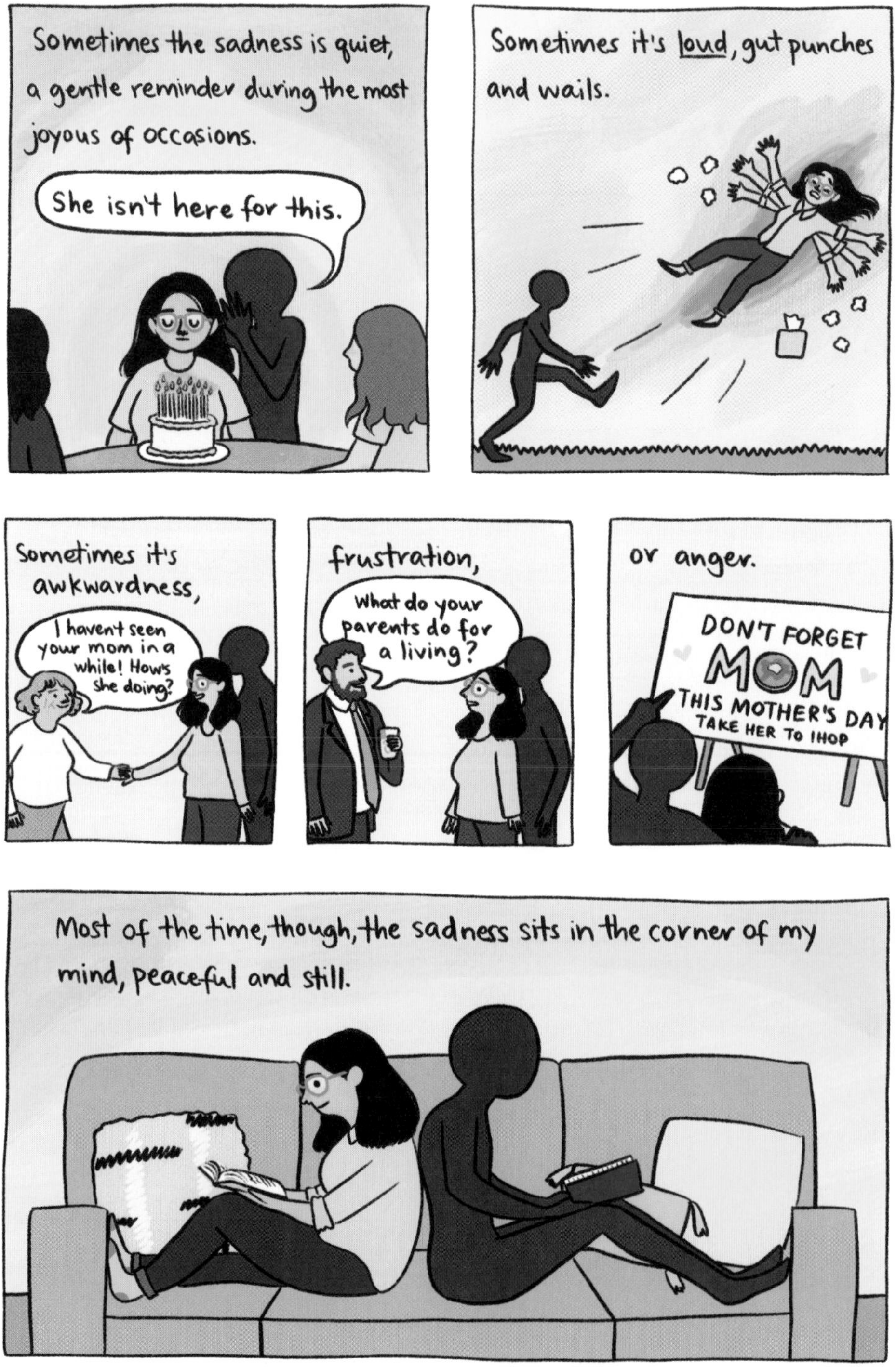

Sometimes the sadness is quiet, a gentle reminder during the most joyous of occasions.
She isn't here for this.
Sometimes it's loud, gut punches and wails.
Sometimes it's awkwardness,
I haven't seen your mom in a while! How's she doing?
frustration,
What do your parents do for a living?
or anger.
DON'T FORGET MOM THIS MOTHER'S DAY
TAKE HER TO IHOP
Most of the time, though, the sadness sits in the corner of my mind, peaceful and still.

# cliché grief remedies that actually work

## (for me, anyway)

**looking through old photos**

**listening to sad songs on repeat**

**spraying their perfume or cologne on one of their shirts and hugging it**

**looking in the mirror until you see their face in yours**

**dramatic jogging (leave your hair loose for maximum effect)**

**cooking recipes that they used to make**

**laughing with pals who get it**

**making angsty art about it**

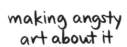

dancing
at the
PITY PARTY
a best mom graphic memoir

**a good cry (see page 39 for tips)**

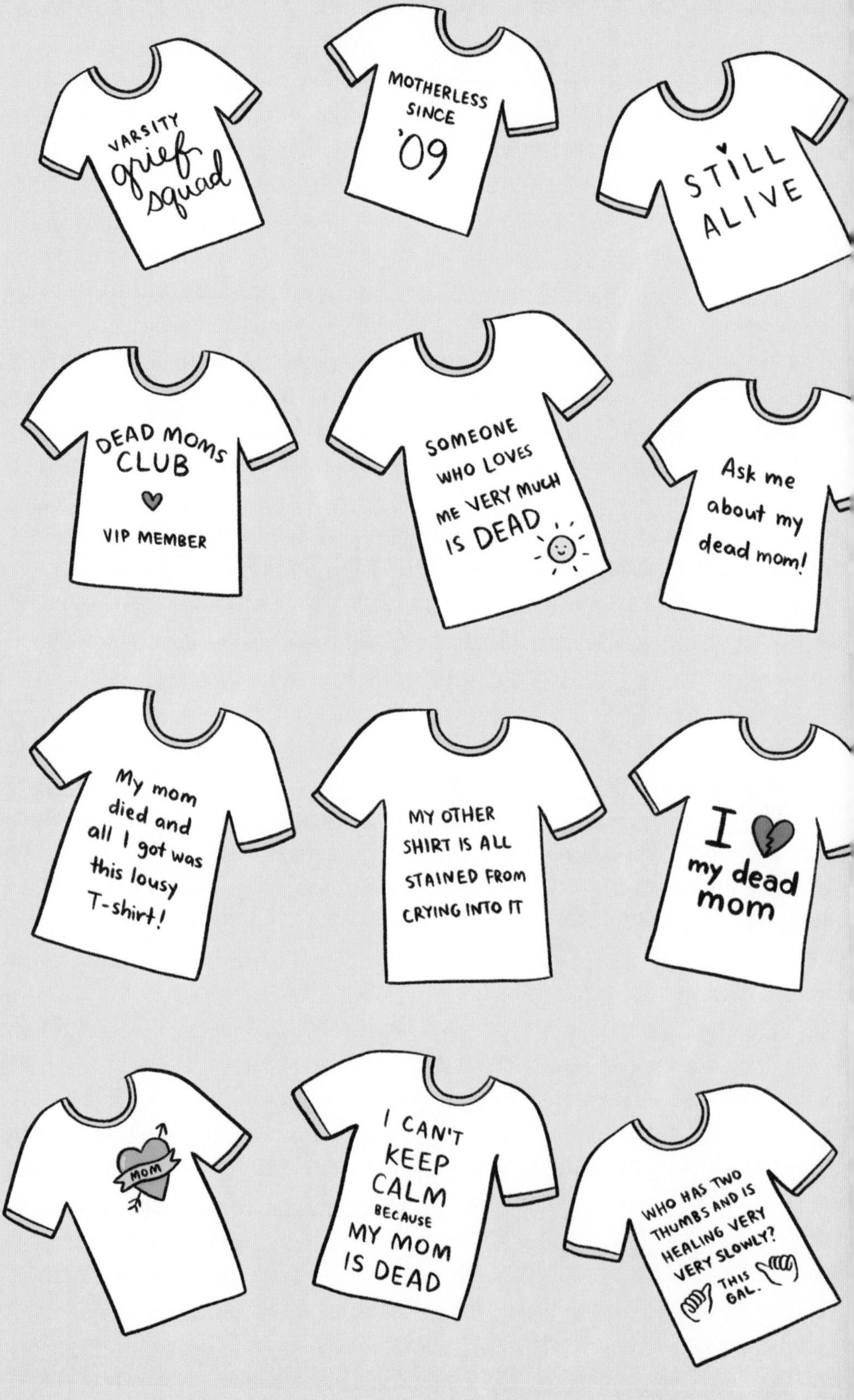

VARSITY grief squad
MOTHERLESS SINCE '09
STILL ALIVE
DEAD MOMS CLUB VIP MEMBER
SOMEONE WHO LOVES ME VERY MUCH IS DEAD
Ask me about my dead mom!
My mom died and all I got was this lousy T-shirt!
MY OTHER SHIRT IS ALL STAINED FROM CRYING INTO IT
I my dead mom
MOM
I CAN'T KEEP CALM BECAUSE MY MOM IS DEAD
WHO HAS TWO THUMBS AND IS HEALING VERY VERY SLOWLY? THIS GAL.

# chapter nine

## THE GOOD, THE BAD,
## and THE AWKWARD
### ( but mostly The Bad, if
### we're really being honest)

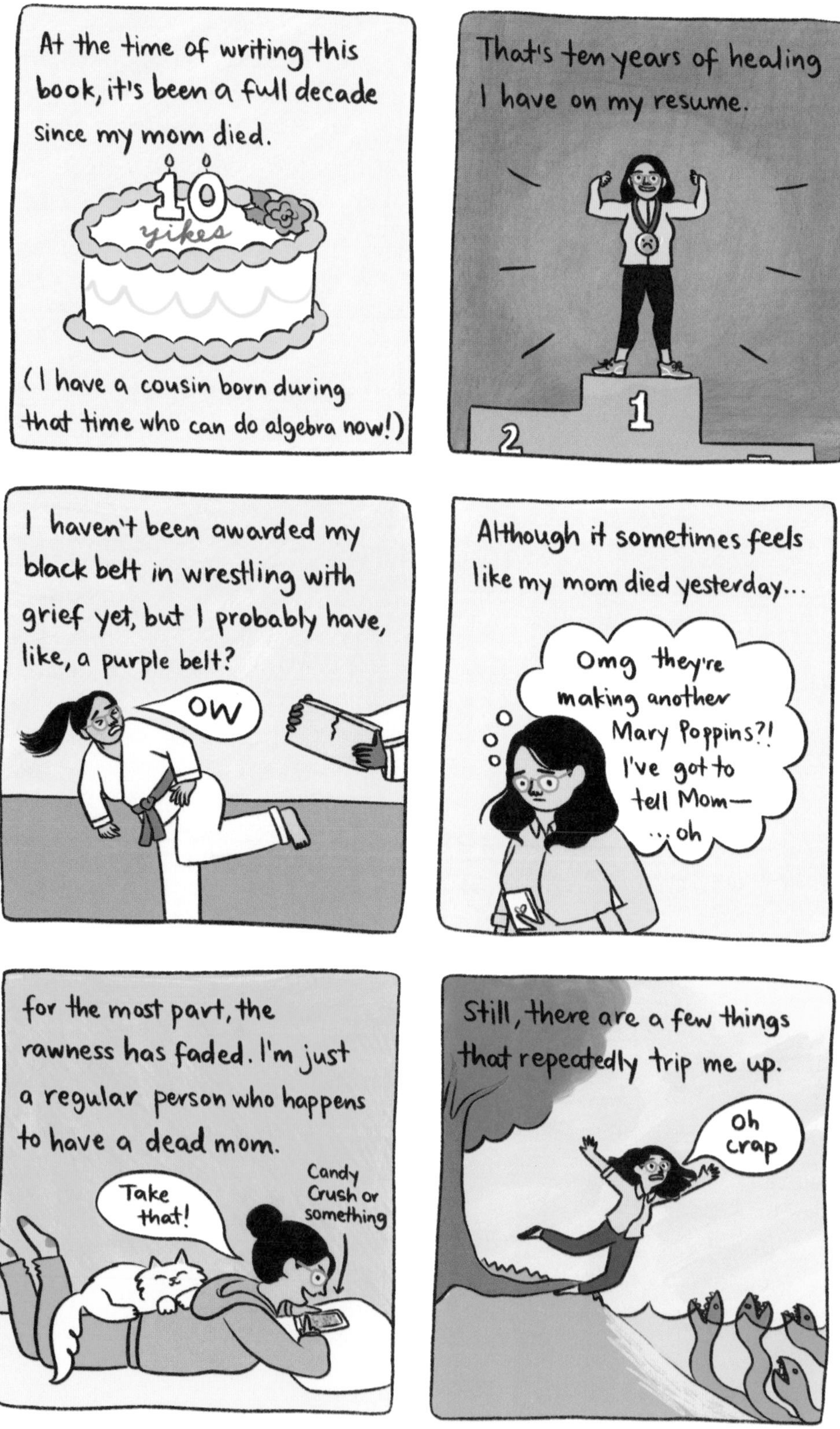
At the time of writing this book, it's been a full decade since my mom died.
10
yikes
(I have a cousin born during that time who can do algebra now!)
That's ten years of healing I have on my resume.
1
2
I haven't been awarded my black belt in wrestling with grief yet, but I probably have, like, a purple belt?
OW
Although it sometimes feels like my mom died yesterday...
Omg they're making another Mary Poppins?! I've got to tell Mom— ...oh
for the most part, the rawness has faded. I'm just a regular person who happens to have a dead mom.
Take that!
Candy Crush or something
Still, there are a few things that repeatedly trip me up.
Oh crap

Firstly, let's talk about a little thing called

DECOMPOSITION

AAAAHH

Look, I'm a big fan of science.

It's the circle of liiiife ♫

But there's still a SIGNIFICANT portion of my brain that feels like my mom is just on a long trip somewhere far away.

See ya later!

It's like that lie that some parents tell their kids when the family goldfish has to be flushed down the toilet, but I'm telling it to myself.

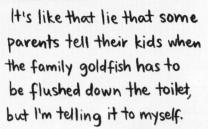

Mom just went to play mah-jongg with her friends for a while!

I know that she's GONE, but more "gone" like when a cutesy video game monster is defeated, vanishing into thin air with nothing but a few coins left behind.

POOF

Like the moment that I left the hospital room, her body simply stopped existing.

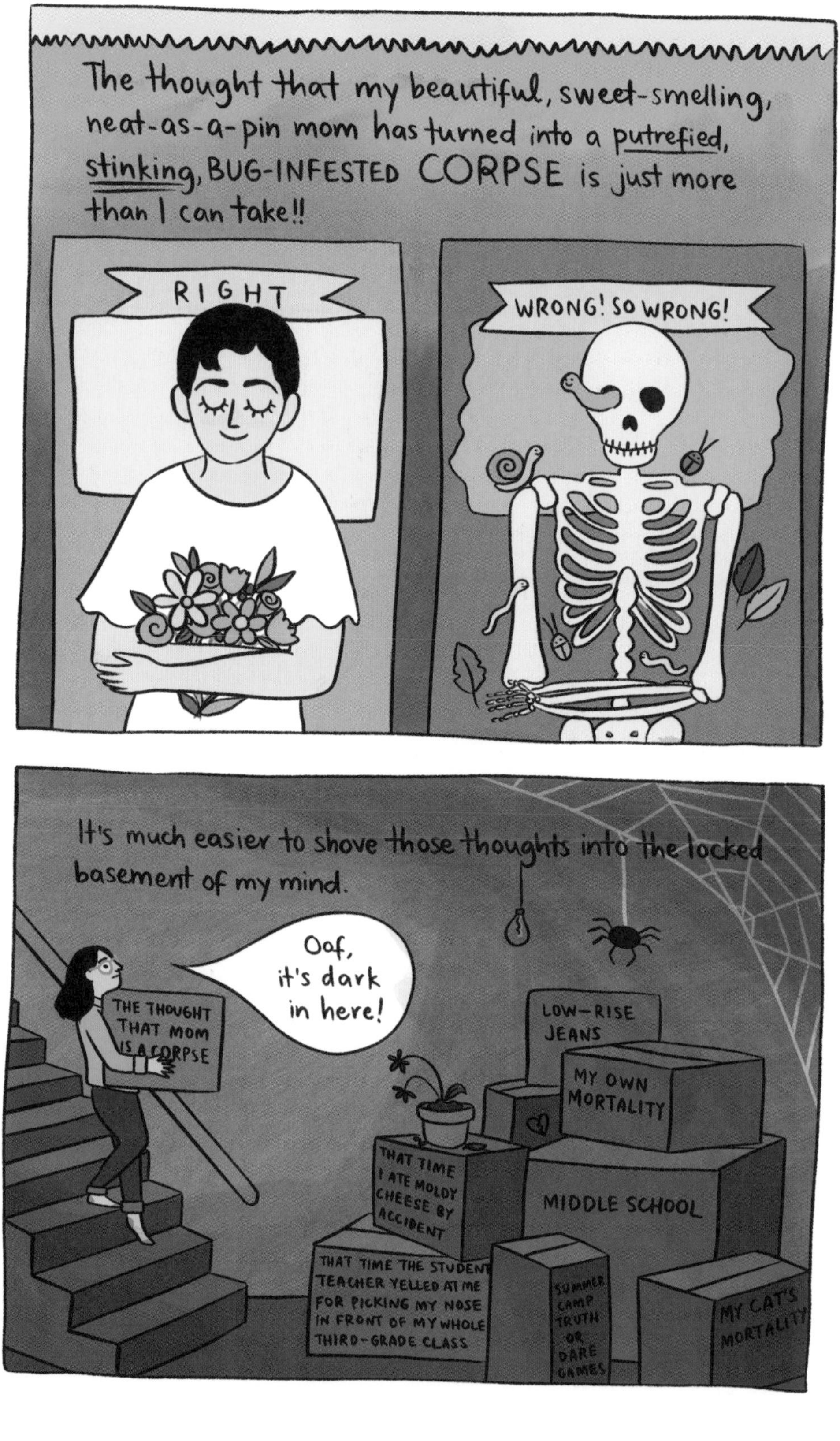

The thought that my beautiful, sweet-smelling, neat-as-a-pin mom has turned into a putrefied, stinking, BUG-INFESTED CORPSE is just more than I can take!!
RIGHT
WRONG! SO WRONG!
It's much easier to shove those thoughts into the locked basement of my mind.
Oof, it's dark in here!
THE THOUGHT THAT MOM IS A CORPSE
LOW-RISE JEANS
MY OWN MORTALITY
THAT TIME I ATE MOLDY CHEESE BY ACCIDENT
MIDDLE SCHOOL
THAT TIME THE STUDENT TEACHER YELLED AT ME FOR PICKING MY NOSE IN FRONT OF MY WHOLE THIRD-GRADE CLASS
SUMMER CAMP TRUTH OR DARE GAMES
MY CAT'S MORTALITY

Even more insidious than the thoughts of worms crawling through my mom's eye sockets is the guilt.

There's so much of it, in so many different forms.

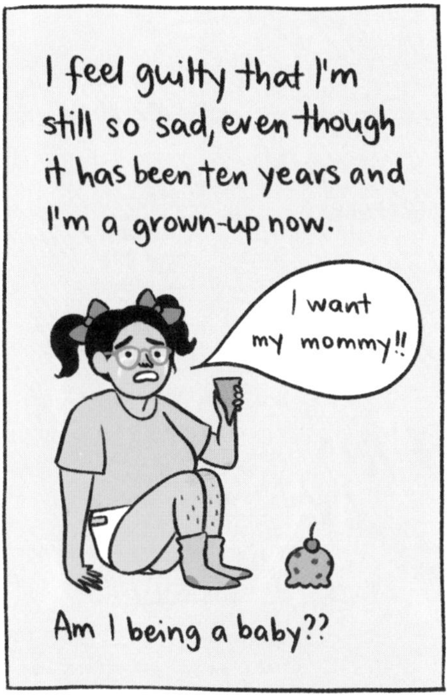
I feel guilty that I'm still so sad, even though it has been ten years and I'm a grown-up now.
I want my mommy!!
Am I being a baby??

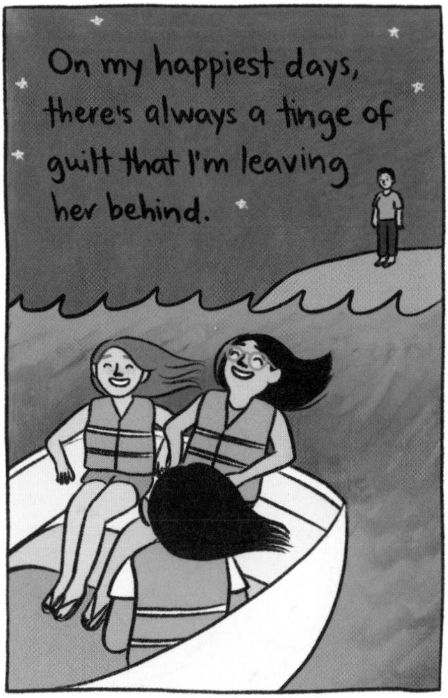
On my happiest days, there's always a tinge of guilt that I'm leaving her behind.

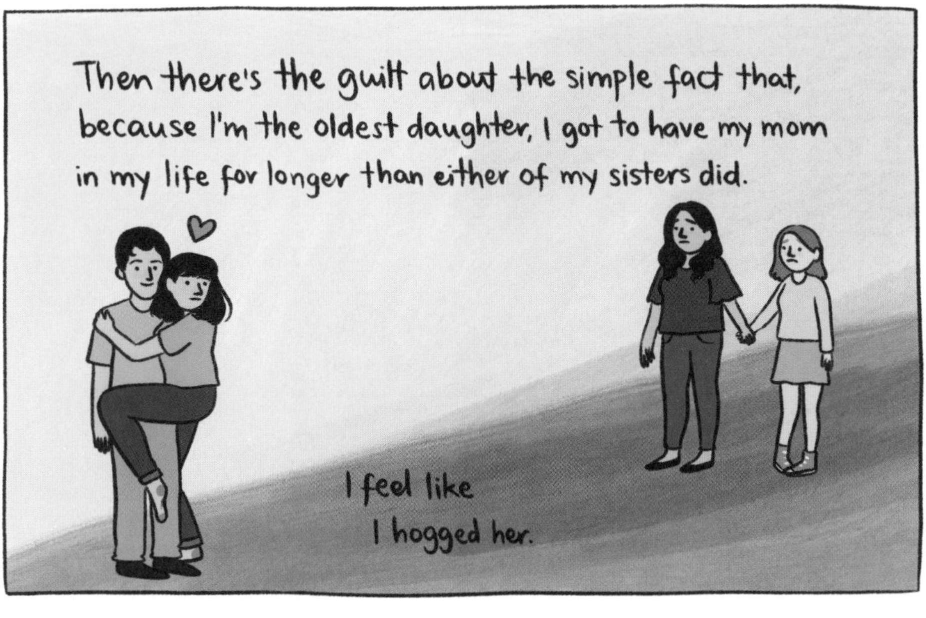
Then there's the guilt about the simple fact that, because I'm the oldest daughter, I got to have my mom in my life for longer than either of my sisters did.
I feel like I hogged her.

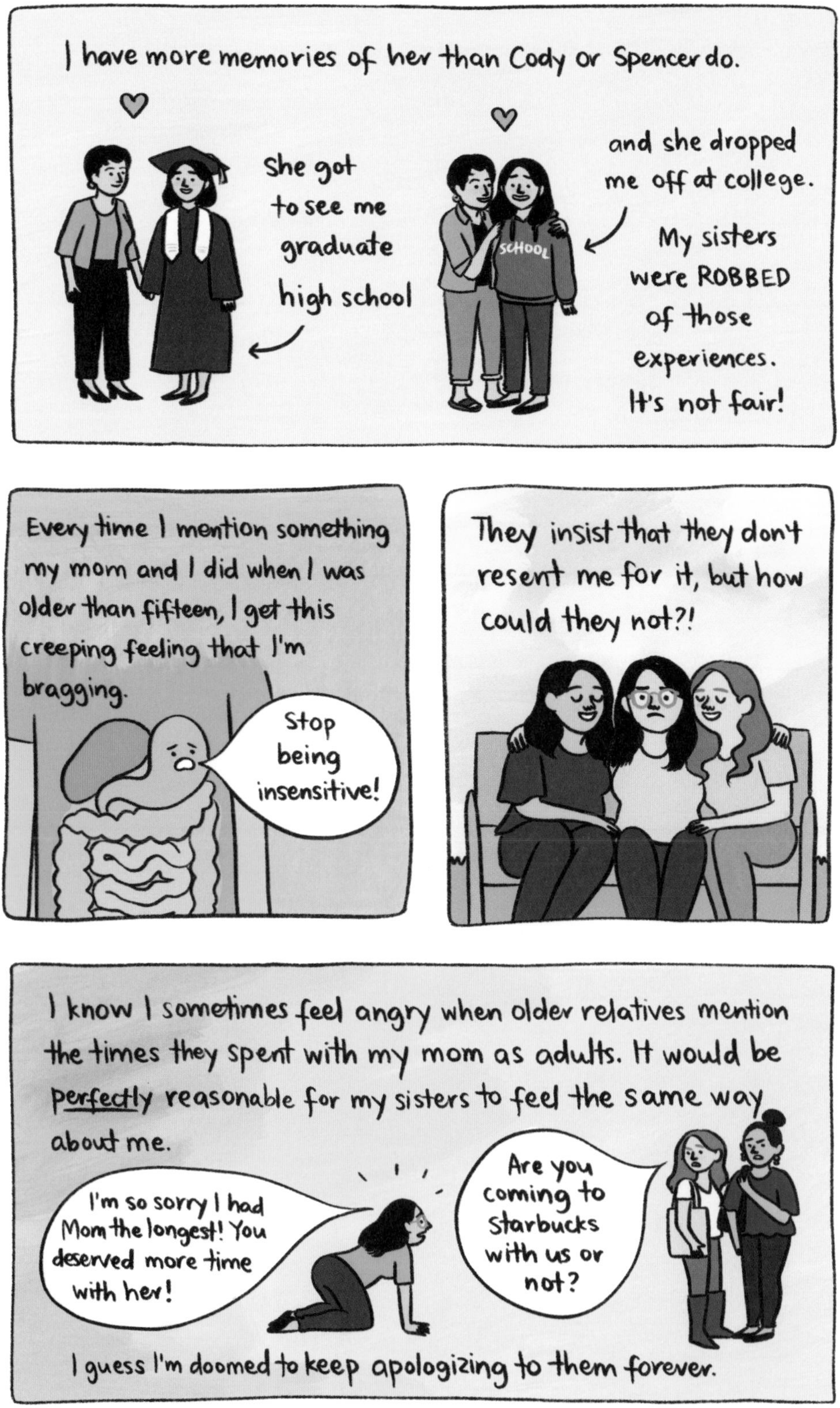
I have more memories of her than Cody or Spencer do.
She got to see me graduate high school
and she dropped me off at college.
SCHOOL
My sisters were ROBBED of those experiences. It's not fair!
Every time I mention something my mom and I did when I was older than fifteen, I get this creeping feeling that I'm bragging.
Stop being insensitive!
They insist that they don't resent me for it, but how could they not?!
I know I sometimes feel angry when older relatives mention the times they spent with my mom as adults. It would be perfectly reasonable for my sisters to feel the same way about me.
I'm so sorry I had Mom the longest! You deserved more time with her!
Are you coming to Starbucks with us or not?
I guess I'm doomed to keep apologizing to them forever.

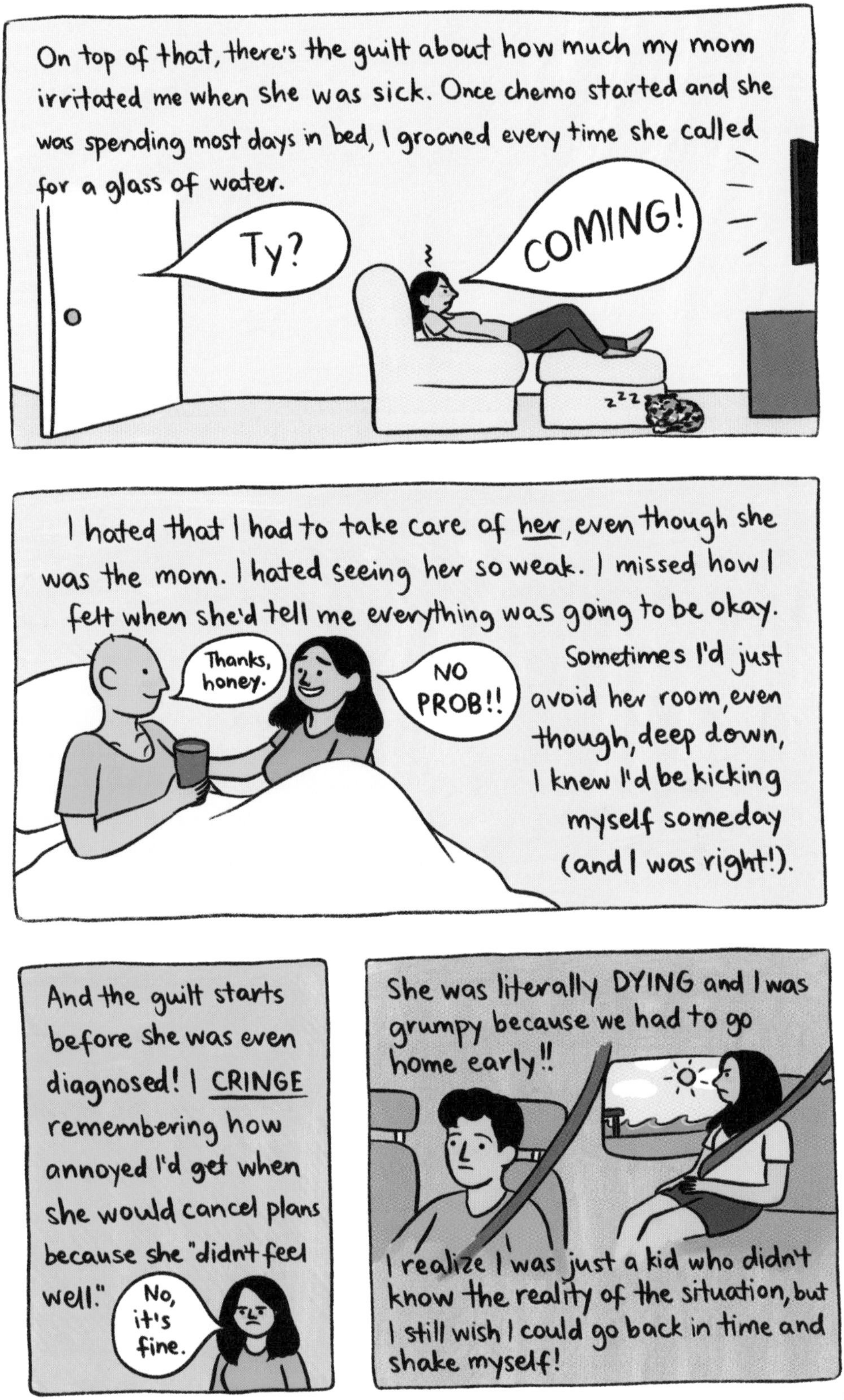

On top of that, there's the guilt about how much my mom irritated me when she was sick. Once chemo started and she was spending most days in bed, I groaned every time she called for a glass of water.
Ty?
COMING!
z z z
I hated that I had to take care of her, even though she was the mom. I hated seeing her so weak. I missed how I felt when she'd tell me everything was going to be okay.
Thanks, honey.
NO PROB!!
Sometimes I'd just avoid her room, even though, deep down, I knew I'd be kicking myself someday (and I was right!).
And the guilt starts before she was even diagnosed! I CRINGE remembering how annoyed I'd get when she would cancel plans because she "didn't feel well."
No, it's fine.
She was literally DYING and I was grumpy because we had to go home early!!
I realize I was just a kid who didn't know the reality of the situation, but I still wish I could go back in time and shake myself!

Every once in a while, I'm in a Target or somewhere, minding my own business, and I see a woman with this nightmare combination:

headscarf that is neither religious nor fashionable

no eyebrows

undereye bags

Every single time it's like a baseball bat to the back of the knee.

Noooooooooooooo

Even the word "chemo" makes me queasy.

Before my mom got sick, our culture's talk about cancer was just background noise, like commercials for products I didn't need or want. I didn't really pay attention.

CANCER

Could dark chocolate/sitting/happiness cause cancer???

EVERY WOMAN YOU KNOW will develop cancer in her lifetime!!

Do this 5k/have a bake so forward this e for cancer research

Amazing cancer survival story TED Talk!!

Get tested for HPV or else you'll definitely get cancer!

SAVE SECOND BASE

Okay but could dark chocolate PREVENT cancer??

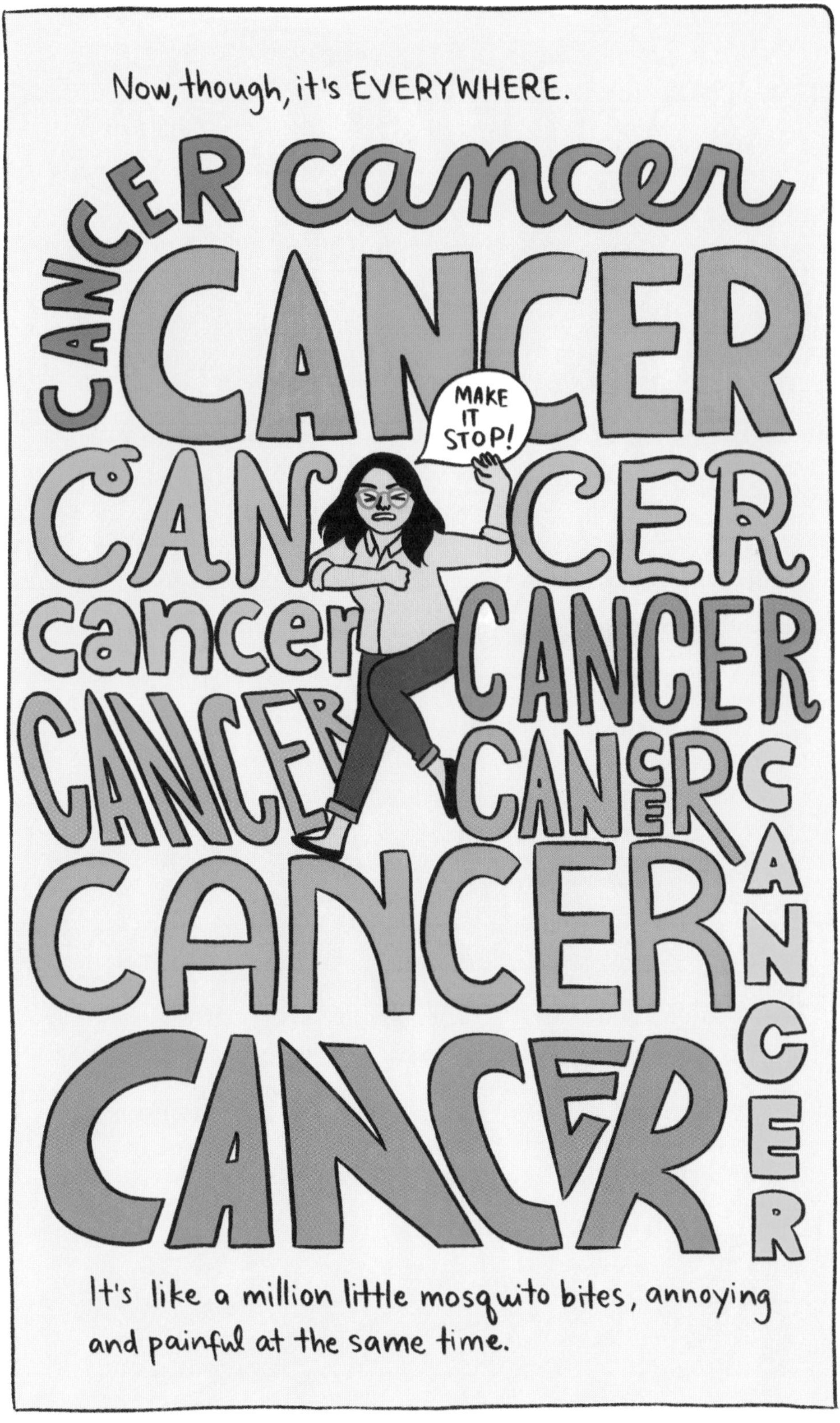
Now, though, it's EVERYWHERE.
CANCER
cancer
CANCER
MAKE IT STOP!
CANCER
cancer
CANCER
CANCER
CANCER
CANCER
CANCER
CANCER
It's like a million little mosquito bites, annoying and painful at the same time.

The fearmongering PSAs about "getting tested" make me panic and catastrophize.

Just one test can save a life.

Welp, I'm definitely going to get cancer, like Mom!!!

The sugarcoated commercials for medications, hospitals, and holistic cancer centers send the memories flooding back.

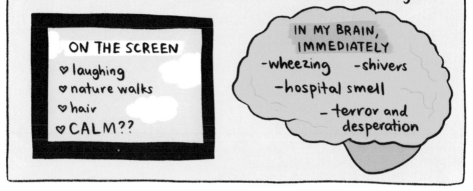

ON THE SCREEN
♡ laughing
♡ nature walks
♡ hair
♡ CALM??

IN MY BRAIN, IMMEDIATELY
-wheezing   -shivers
-hospital smell
- terror and desperation

Even though I know the people in the commercials are actors, I still find myself grieving for them and their families.

When I was diagnosed with metastatic lung cancer—

Oh GOD his kids aren't going to have a FATHER!

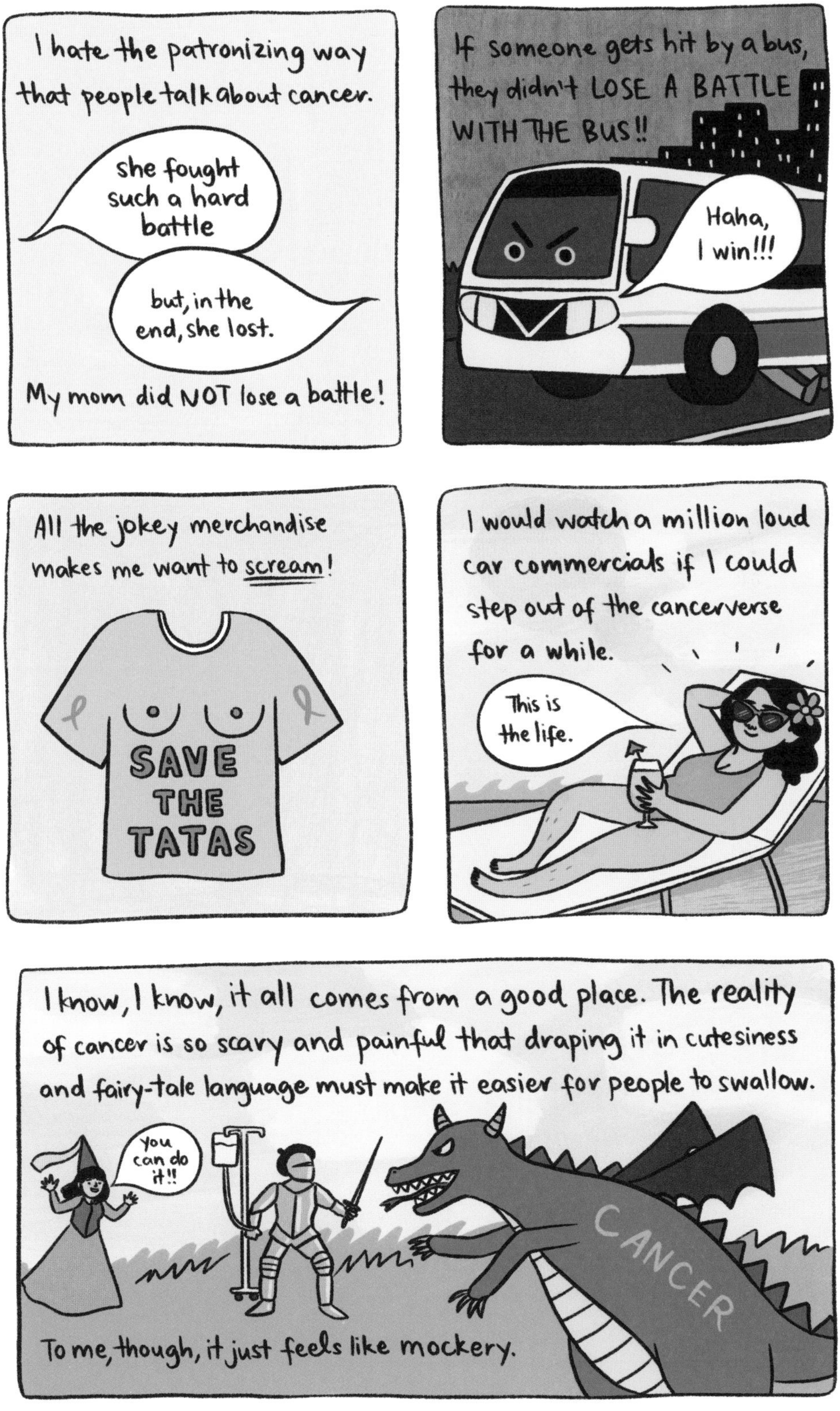
I hate the patronizing way that people talk about cancer.
she fought such a hard battle
but, in the end, she lost.
My mom did NOT lose a battle!
If someone gets hit by a bus, they didn't LOSE A BATTLE WITH THE BUS!!
Haha, I win!!!
All the jokey merchandise makes me want to scream!
SAVE THE TATAS
I would watch a million loud car commercials if I could step out of the canceverse for a while.
This is the life.
I know, I know, it all comes from a good place. The reality of cancer is so scary and painful that draping it in cutesiness and fairy-tale language must make it easier for people to swallow.
you can do it!!
CANCER
To me, though, it just feels like mockery.

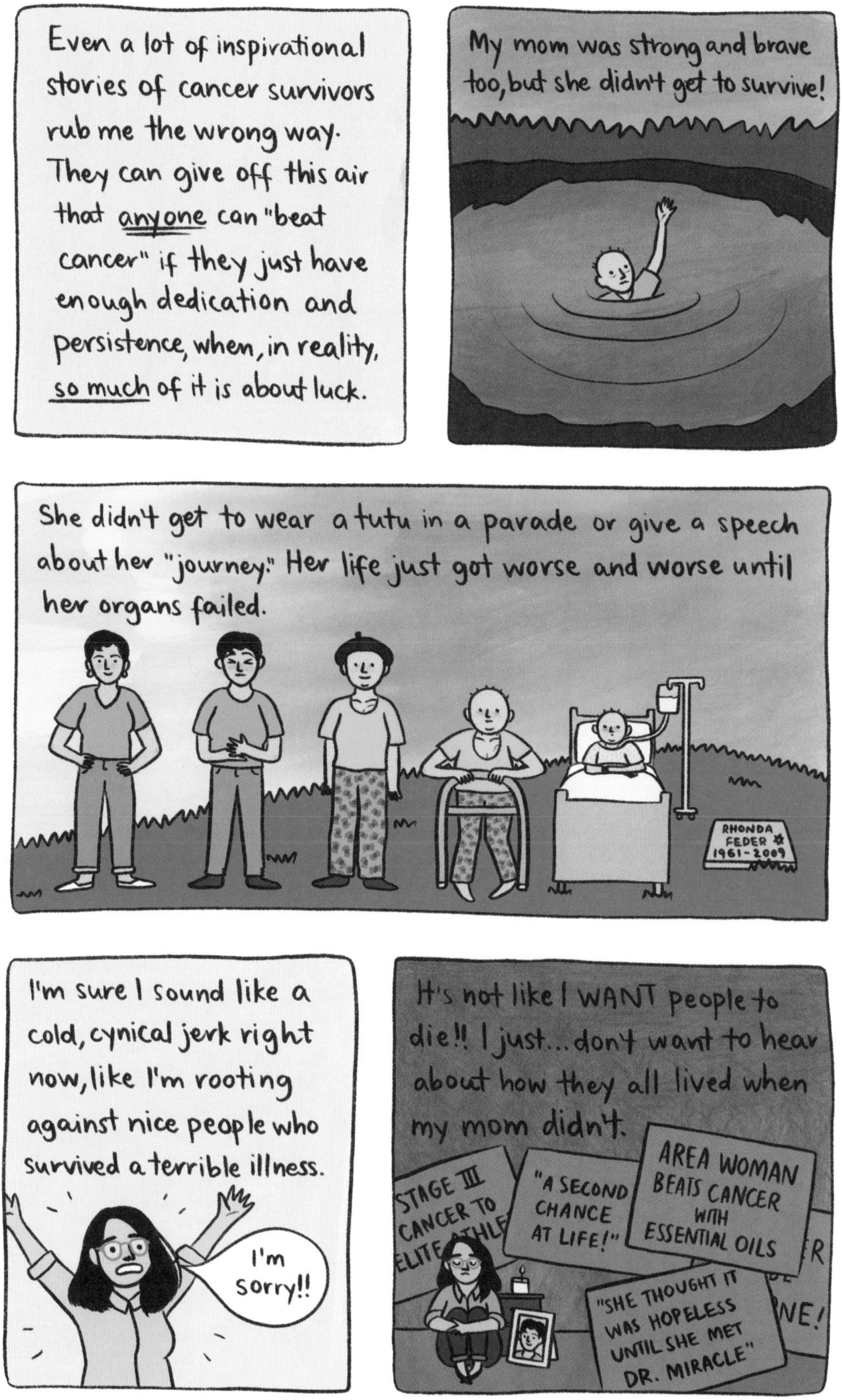
Even a lot of inspirational stories of cancer survivors rub me the wrong way. They can give off this air that anyone can "beat cancer" if they just have enough dedication and persistence, when, in reality, so much of it is about luck.
My mom was strong and brave too, but she didn't get to survive!
She didn't get to wear a tutu in a parade or give a speech about her "journey." Her life just got worse and worse until her organs failed.
RHONDA FEDER 1961-2009
I'm sure I sound like a cold, cynical jerk right now, like I'm rooting against nice people who survived a terrible illness.
I'm sorry!!
It's not like I WANT people to die!! I just... don't want to hear about how they all lived when my mom didn't.
STAGE III CANCER TO ELITE ATHLE
"A SECOND CHANCE AT LIFE!"
AREA WOMAN BEATS CANCER WITH ESSENTIAL OILS
"SHE THOUGHT IT WAS HOPELESS UNTIL SHE MET DR. MIRACLE"

And don't get me started on hearing people complain about their healthy, LIVING moms!*

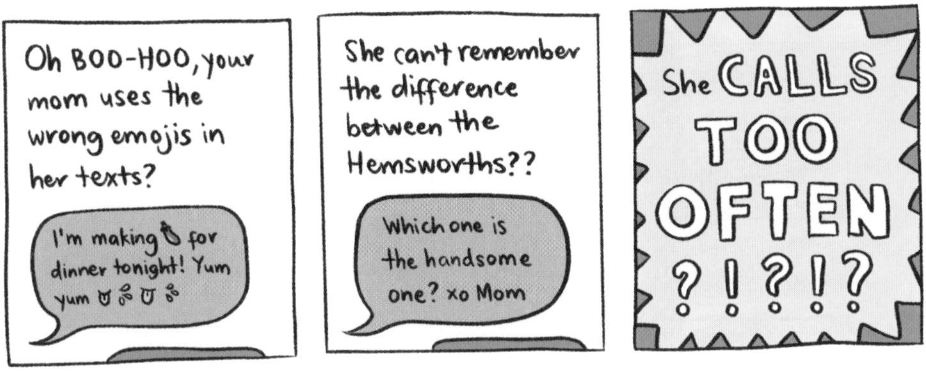
Oh BOO-HOO, your mom uses the wrong emojis in her texts?
I'm making for dinner tonight! Yum yum
She can't remember the difference between the Hemsworths??
Which one is the handsome one? xo Mom
She CALLS TOO OFTEN ?!?!?

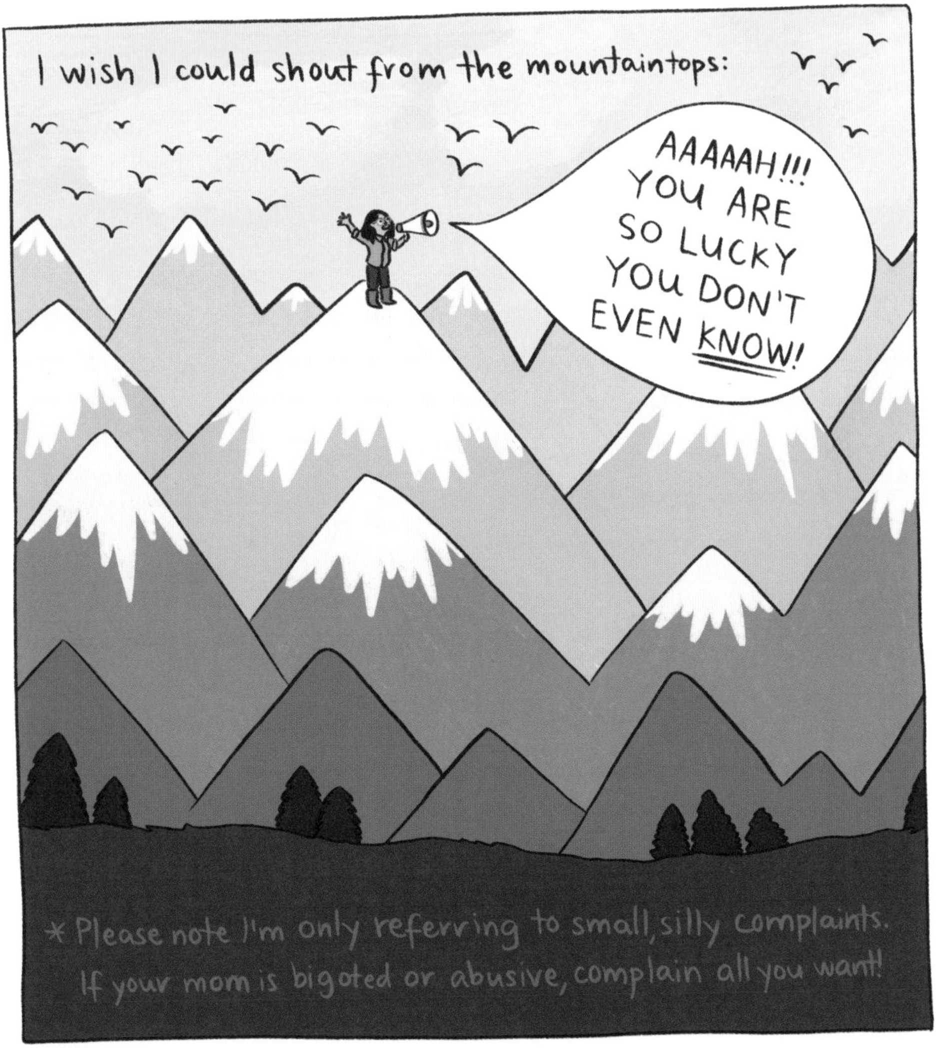
I wish I could shout from the mountaintops:
AAAAAH!!! YOU ARE SO LUCKY YOU DON'T EVEN KNOW!
* Please note I'm only referring to small, silly complaints. If your mom is bigoted or abusive, complain all you want!

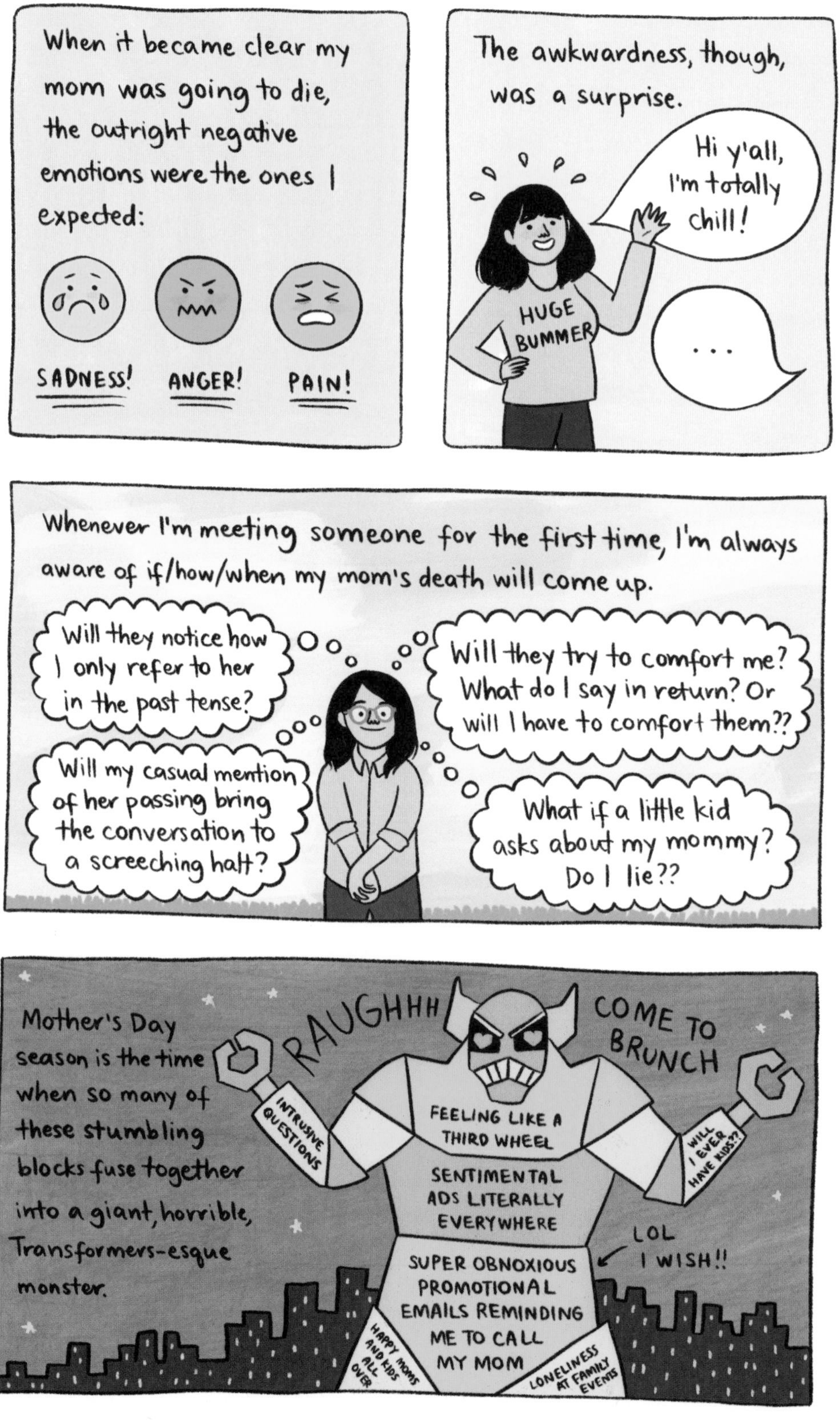
When it became clear my mom was going to die, the outright negative emotions were the ones I expected:
SADNESS!
ANGER!
PAIN!
The awkwardness, though, was a surprise.
Hi y'all, I'm totally chill!
HUGE BUMMER
...
Whenever I'm meeting someone for the first time, I'm always aware of if/how/when my mom's death will come up.
Will they notice how I only refer to her in the past tense?
Will my casual mention of her passing bring the conversation to a screeching halt?
Will they try to comfort me? What do I say in return? Or will I have to comfort them??
What if a little kid asks about my mommy? Do I lie??
Mother's Day season is the time when so many of these stumbling blocks fuse together into a giant, horrible, Transformers-esque monster.
RAUGHHH
COME TO BRUNCH
INTRUSIVE QUESTIONS
FEELING LIKE A THIRD WHEEL
WILL I EVER HAVE KIDS??
SENTIMENTAL ADS LITERALLY EVERYWHERE
LOL I WISH!!
SUPER OBNOXIOUS PROMOTIONAL EMAILS REMINDING ME TO CALL MY MOM
HAPPY MOMS AND KIDS ALL OVER
LONELINESS AT FAMILY EVENTS

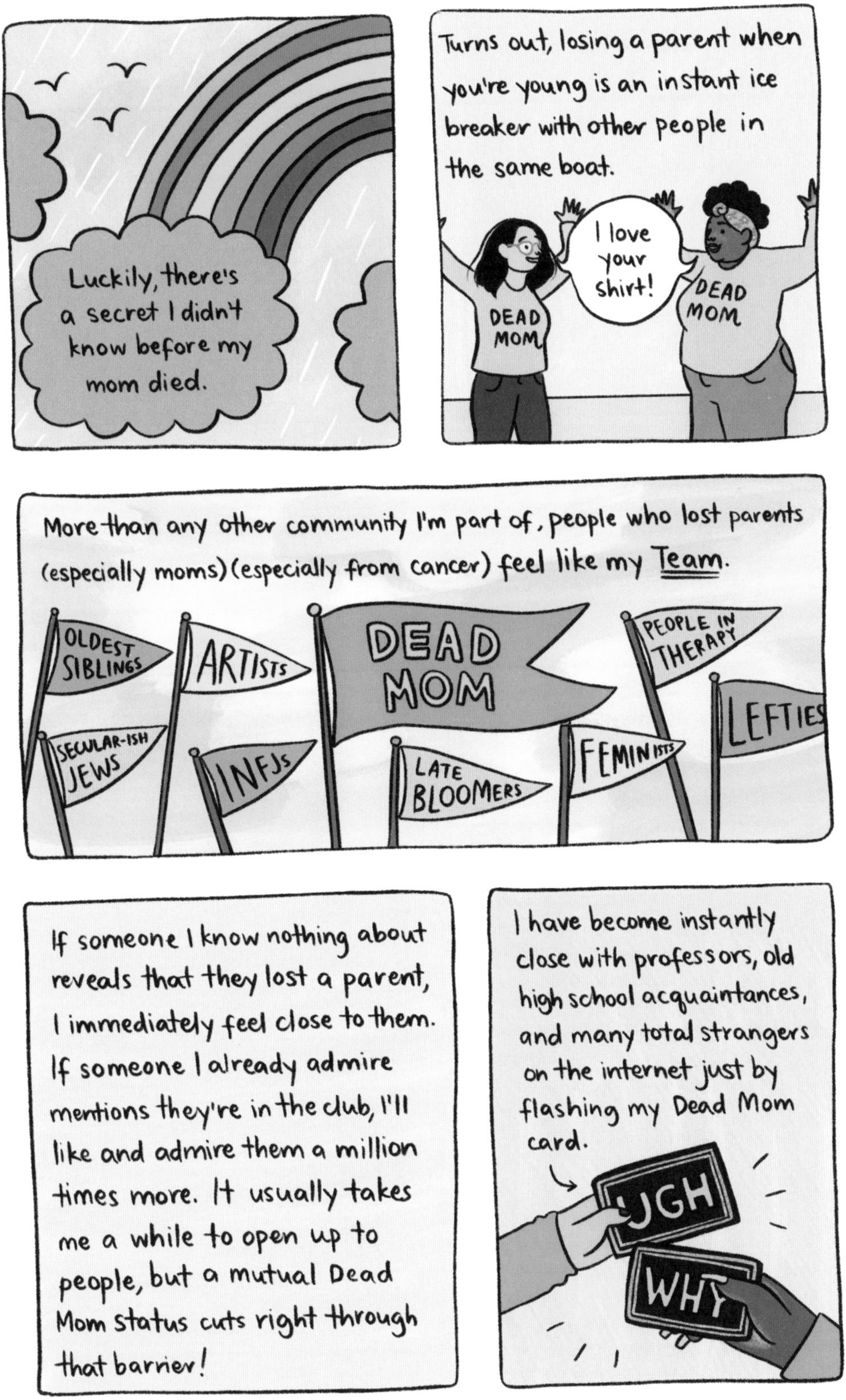
Luckily, there's a secret I didn't know before my mom died.
Turns out, losing a parent when you're young is an instant ice breaker with other people in the same boat.
DEAD MOM
I love your shirt!
DEAD MOM
More than any other community I'm part of, people who lost parents (especially moms) (especially from cancer) feel like my Team.
OLDEST SIBLINGS
ARTISTS
DEAD MOM
PEOPLE IN THERAPY
LEFTIES
SECULAR-ISH JEWS
INFJs
LATE BLOOMERS
FEMINISTS
If someone I know nothing about reveals that they lost a parent, I immediately feel close to them. If someone I already admire mentions they're in the club, I'll like and admire them a million times more. It usually takes me a while to open up to people, but a mutual Dead Mom status cuts right through that barrier!
I have become instantly close with professors, old high school acquaintances, and many total strangers on the internet just by flashing my Dead Mom card.
UGH
WHY

The Dead Moms Club comes with a lot of perks.

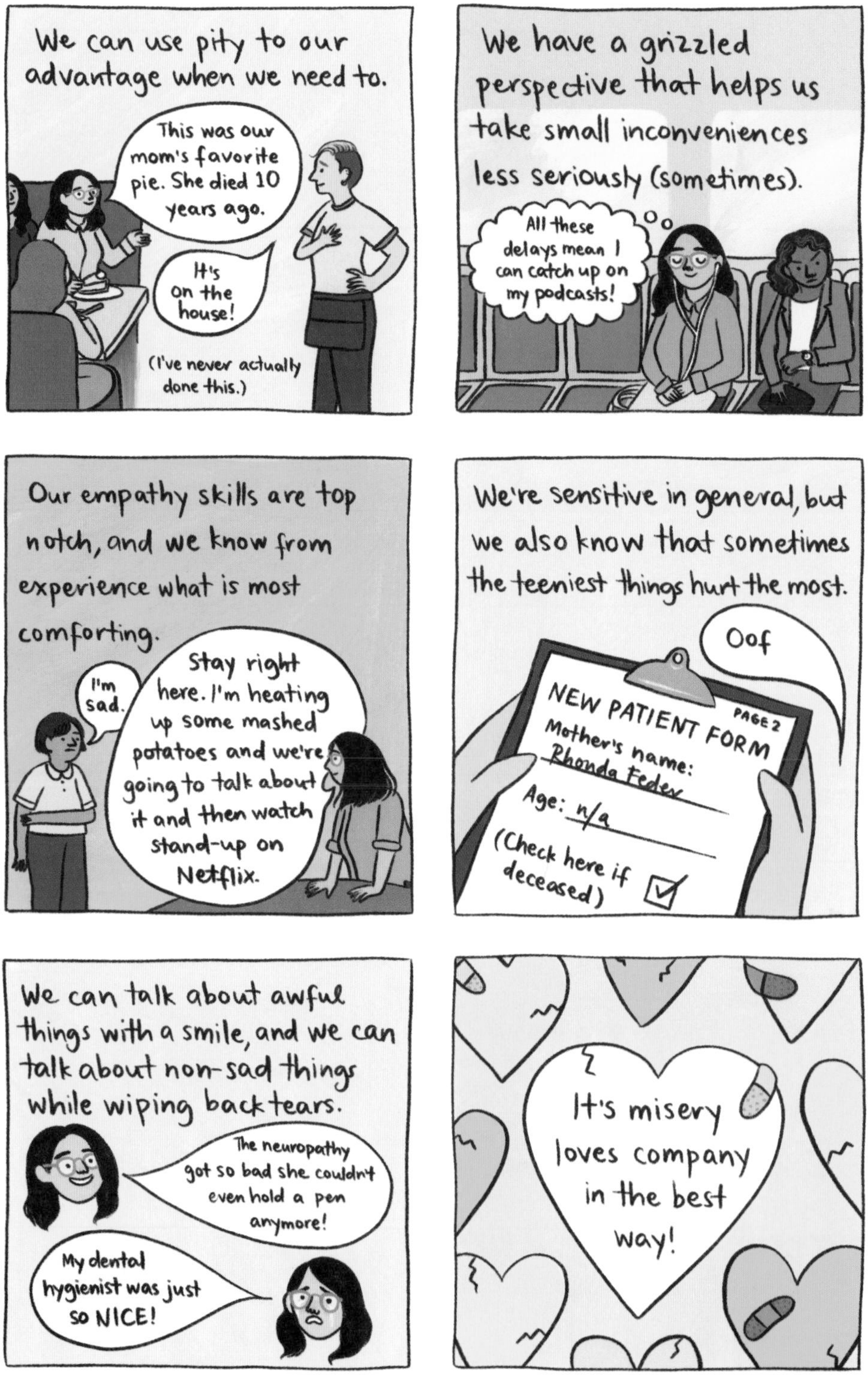
We can use pity to our advantage when we need to.
This was our mom's favorite pie. She died 10 years ago.
It's on the house!
(I've never actually done this.)
We have a grizzled perspective that helps us take small inconveniences less seriously (sometimes).
All these delays mean I can catch up on my podcasts!
Our empathy skills are top notch, and we know from experience what is most comforting.
I'm sad.
Stay right here. I'm heating up some mashed potatoes and we're going to talk about it and then watch stand-up on Netflix.
We're sensitive in general, but we also know that sometimes the teeniest things hurt the most.
Oof
NEW PATIENT FORM
PAGE 2
Mother's name: Rhonda Feder
Age: n/a
(Check here if deceased)
We can talk about awful things with a smile, and we can talk about non-sad things while wiping back tears.
The neuropathy got so bad she couldn't even hold a pen anymore!
My dental hygienist was just so NICE!
It's misery loves company in the best way!

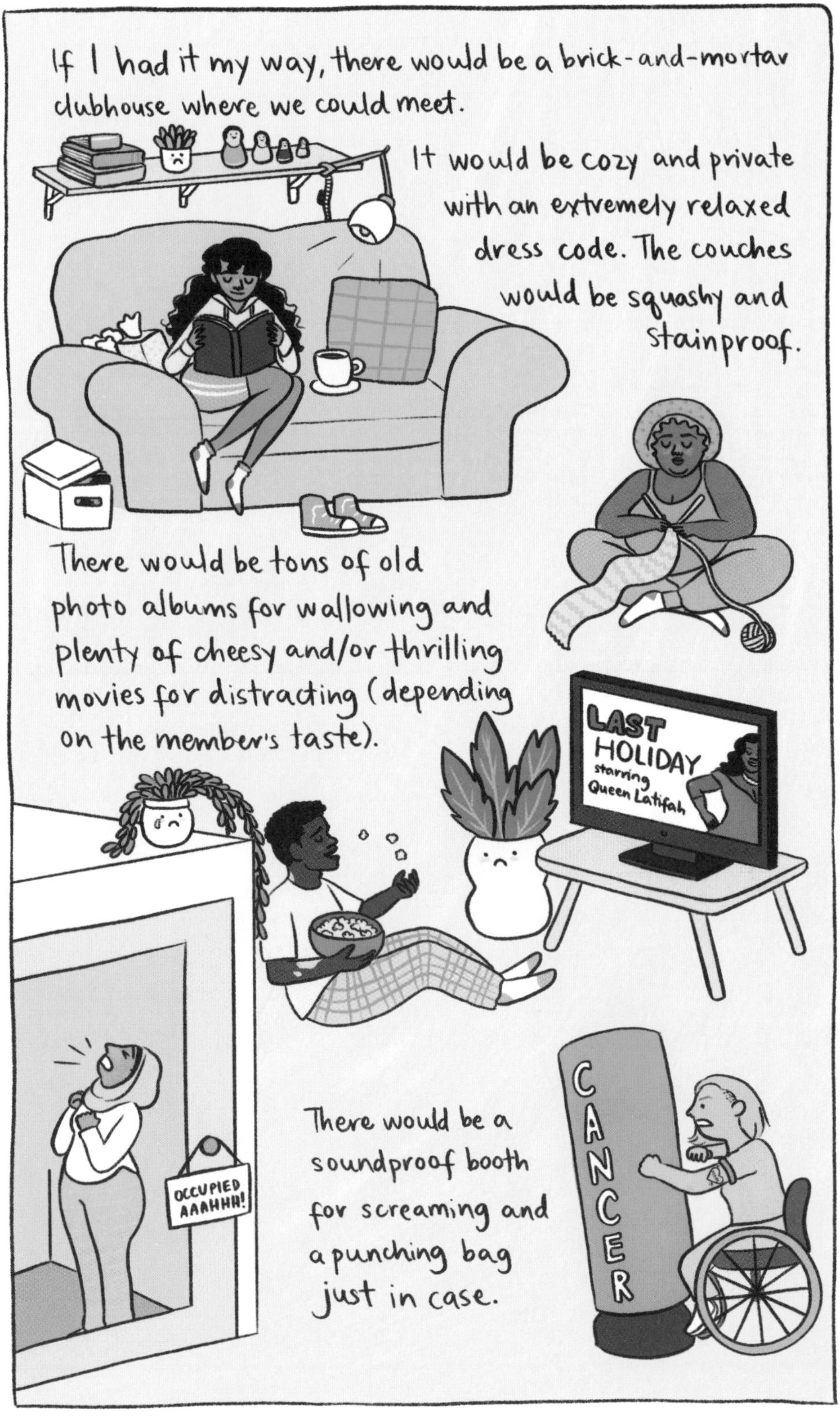
If I had it my way, there would be a brick-and-mortar clubhouse where we could meet.
It would be cozy and private with an extremely relaxed dress code. The couches would be squashy and stainproof.
There would be tons of old photo albums for wallowing and plenty of cheesy and/or thrilling movies for distracting (depending on the member's taste).
LAST HOLIDAY starring Queen Latifah
OCCUPIED AAAHHH!
There would be a soundproof booth for screaming and a punching bag just in case.
CANCER

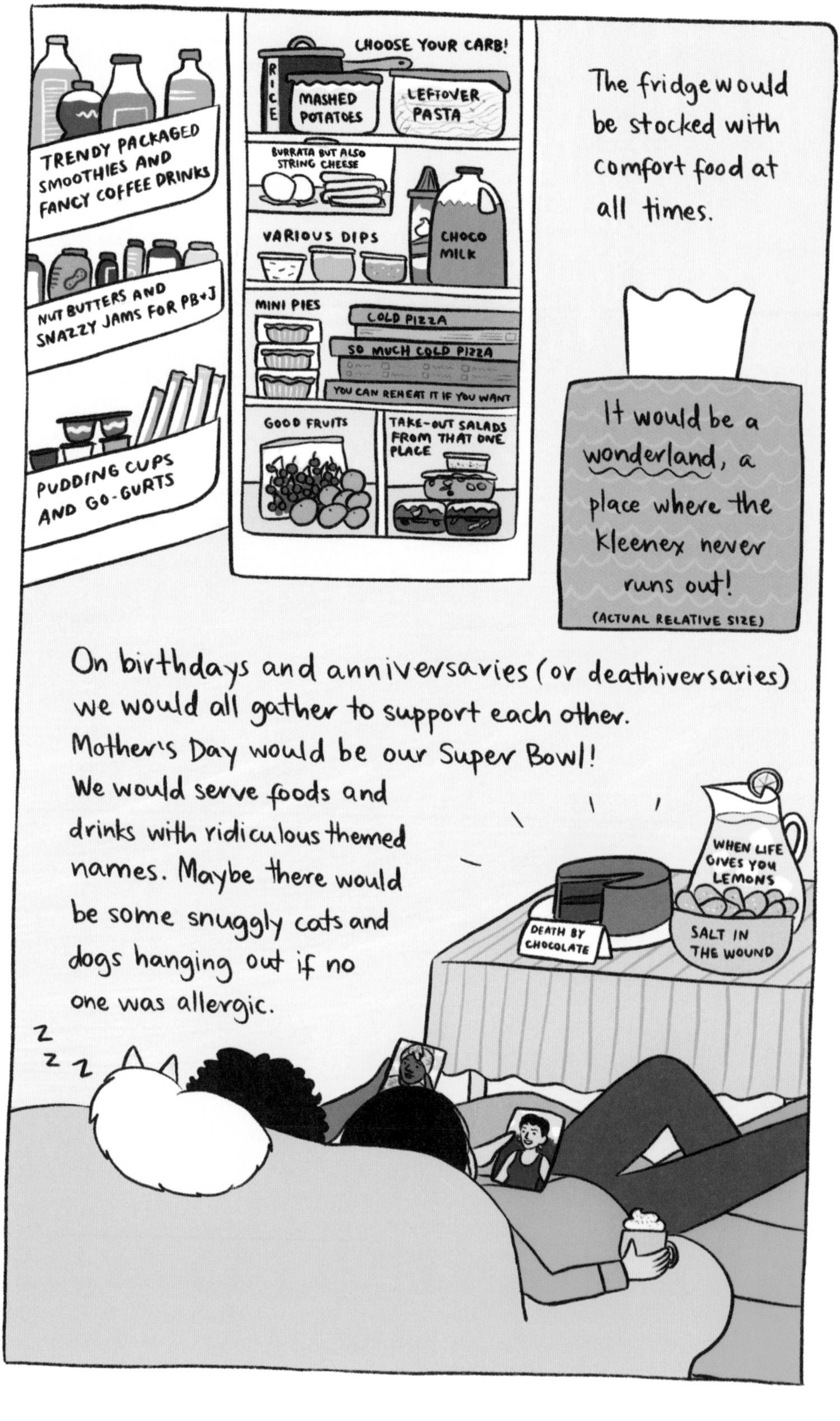
TRENDY PACKAGED SMOOTHIES AND FANCY COFFEE DRINKS
NUT BUTTERS AND SNAZZY JAMS FOR PB+J
PUDDING CUPS AND GO-GURTS
CHOOSE YOUR CARB!
RICE
MASHED POTATOES
LEFTOVER PASTA
BURRATA BUT ALSO STRING CHEESE
VARIOUS DIPS
CHOCO MILK
MINI PIES
COLD PIZZA
SO MUCH COLD PIZZA
YOU CAN REHEAT IT IF YOU WANT
GOOD FRUITS
TAKE-OUT SALADS FROM THAT ONE PLACE
The fridge would be stocked with comfort food at all times.
It would be a wonderland, a place where the Kleenex never runs out!
(ACTUAL RELATIVE SIZE)
On birthdays and anniversaries (or deathiversaries) we would all gather to support each other.
Mother's Day would be our Super Bowl!
We would serve foods and drinks with ridiculous themed names. Maybe there would be some snuggly cats and dogs hanging out if no one was allergic.
WHEN LIFE GIVES YOU LEMONS
DEATH BY CHOCOLATE
SALT IN THE WOUND
Z Z Z

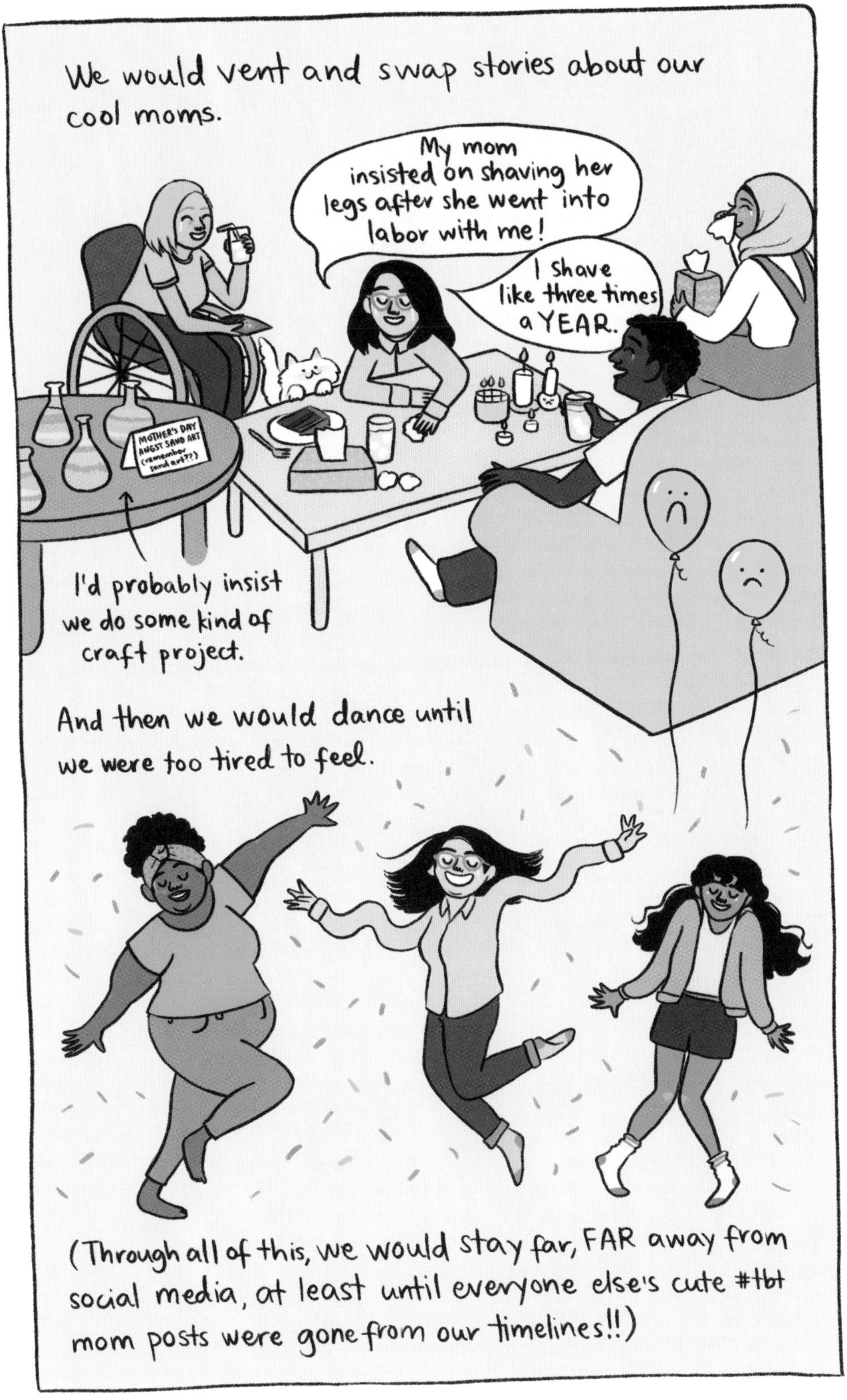
We would vent and swap stories about our cool moms.
My mom insisted on shaving her legs after she went into labor with me!
I shave like three times a YEAR.
MOTHER'S DAY ANGST SAND ART (remember sand art??)
I'd probably insist we do some kind of craft project.
And then we would dance until we were too tired to feel.
(Through all of this, we would stay far, FAR away from social media, at least until everyone else's cute #tbt mom posts were gone from our timelines!!)

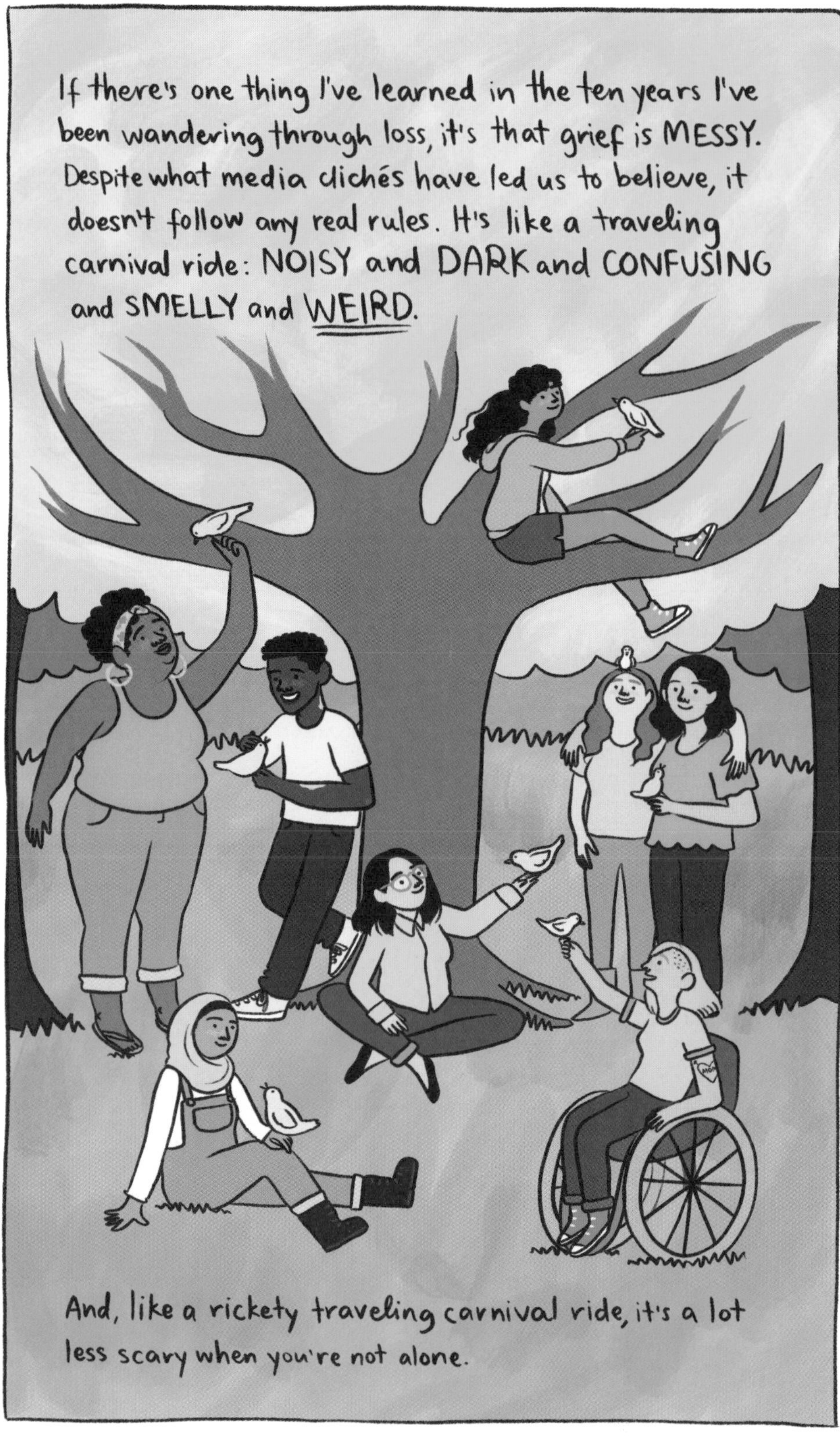
If there's one thing I've learned in the ten years I've been wandering through loss, it's that grief is MESSY. Despite what media clichés have led us to believe, it doesn't follow any real rules. It's like a traveling carnival ride: NOISY and DARK and CONFUSING and SMELLY and WEIRD.
And, like a rickety traveling carnival ride, it's a lot less scary when you're not alone.

the app i wish existed

# DEADMOM: THE APP

(It would probably end up being called, like, "Motherly" or something with a vowel cleverly removed.)

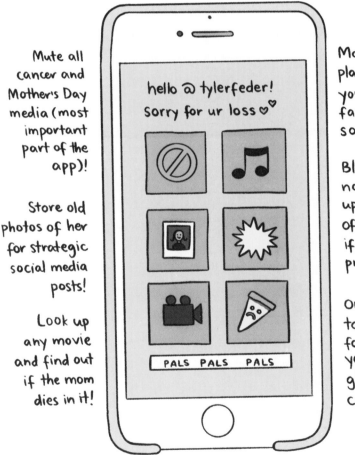

Mute all cancer and Mother's Day media (most important part of the app)!

Store old photos of her for strategic social media posts!

Look up any movie and find out if the mom dies in it!

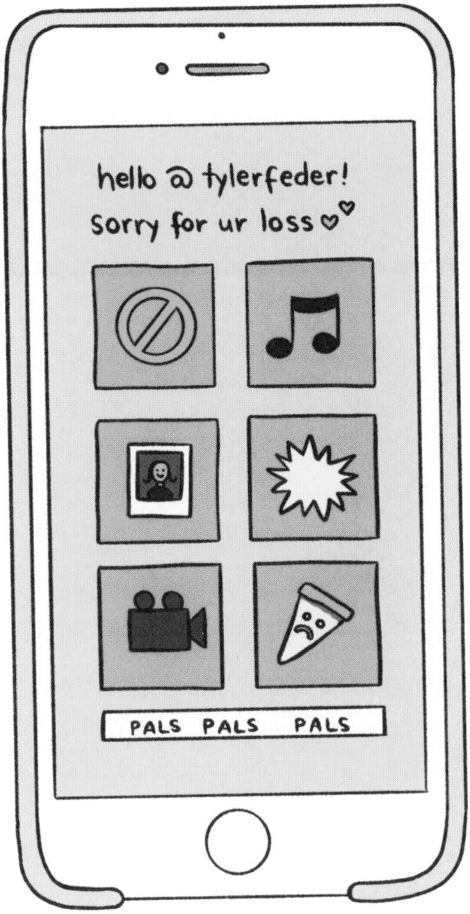

hello @tylerfeder!
sorry for ur loss
PALS PALS PALS


Make a playlist of your mom's favorite songs!

Blast white noise to cover up the sounds of your crying if you want privacy!

One-click takeout for when you're too gloomy to cook!

PLUS: connect and commiserate with other motherless folks!

# what i wish grief looked like

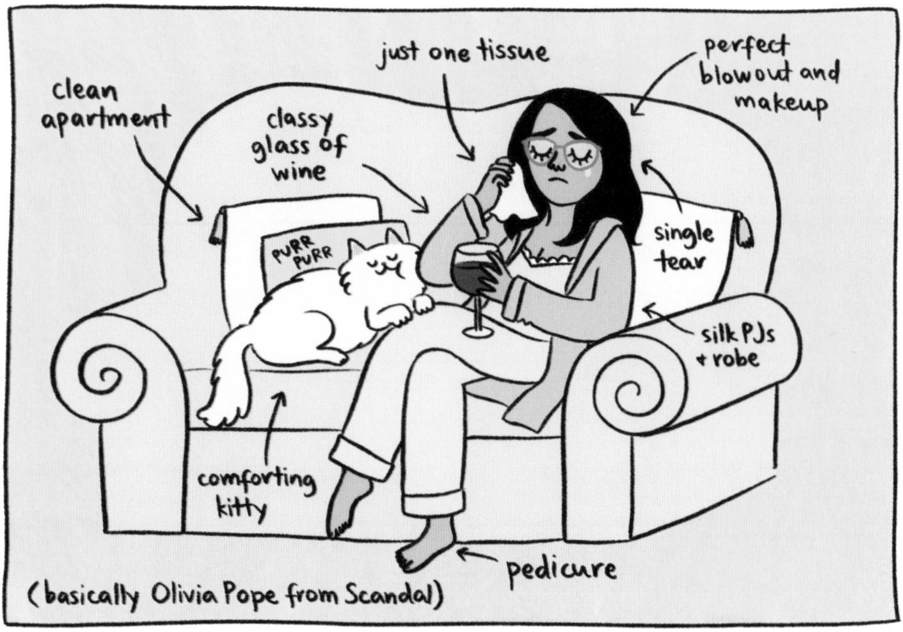


# what grief actually looks like

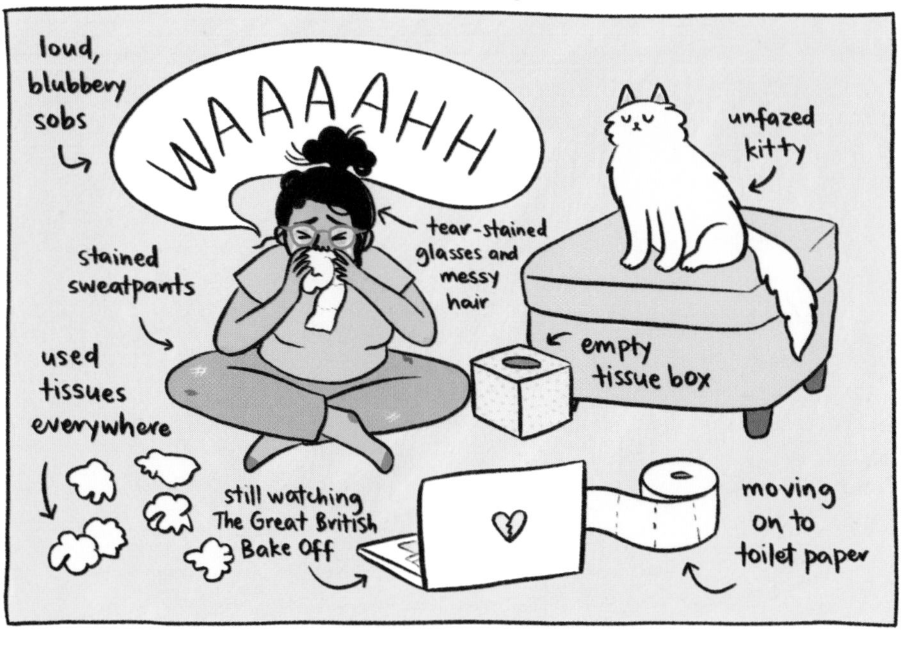

# chapter ten

MOTHERLESS 4EVER

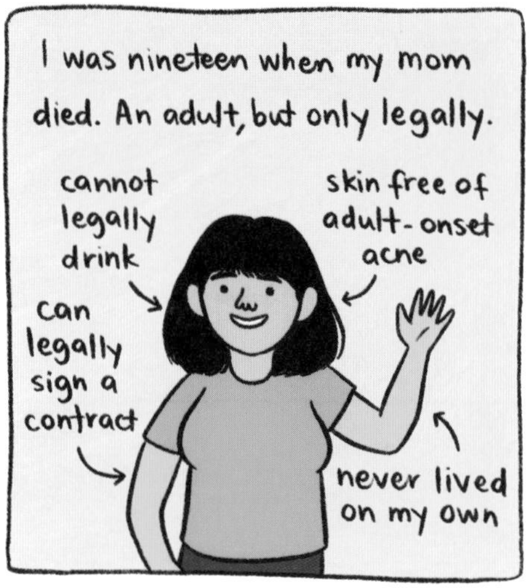
I was nineteen when my mom died. An adult, but only legally.
cannot legally drink
skin free of adult-onset acne
can legally sign a contract
never lived on my own

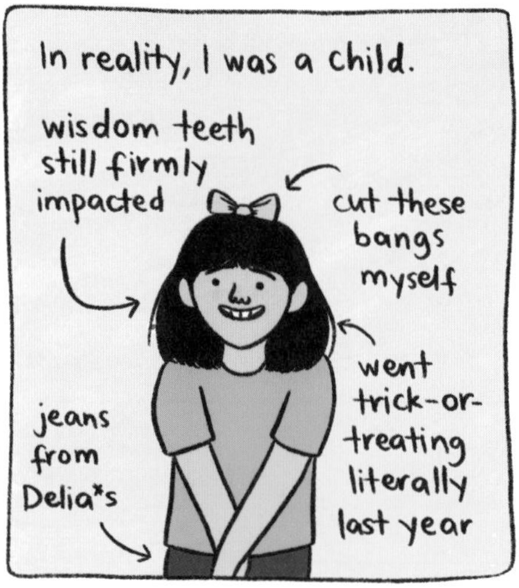
In reality, I was a child.
wisdom teeth still firmly impacted
cut these bangs myself
went trick-or-treating literally last year
jeans from Delia*s

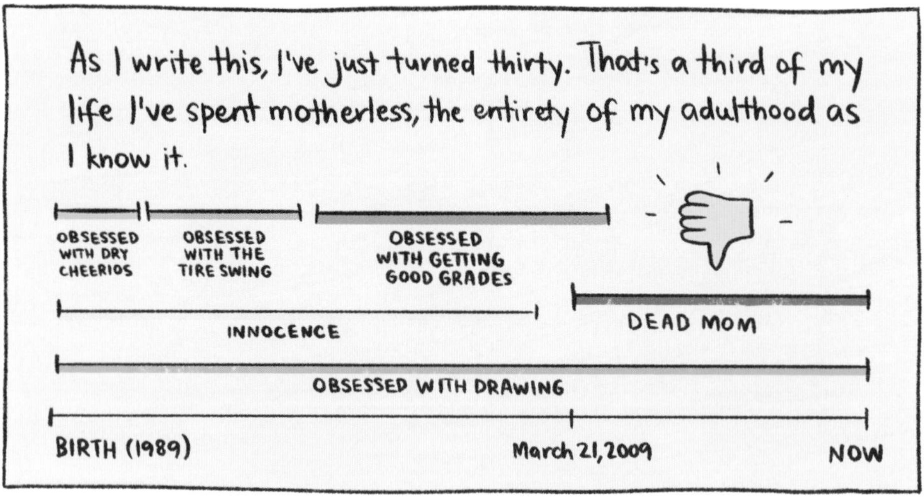
As I write this, I've just turned thirty. That's a third of my life I've spent motherless, the entirety of my adulthood as I know it.
OBSESSED WITH DRY CHEERIOS
OBSESSED WITH THE TIRE SWING
OBSESSED WITH GETTING GOOD GRADES
INNOCENCE
DEAD MOM
OBSESSED WITH DRAWING
BIRTH (1989)
March 21, 2009
NOW

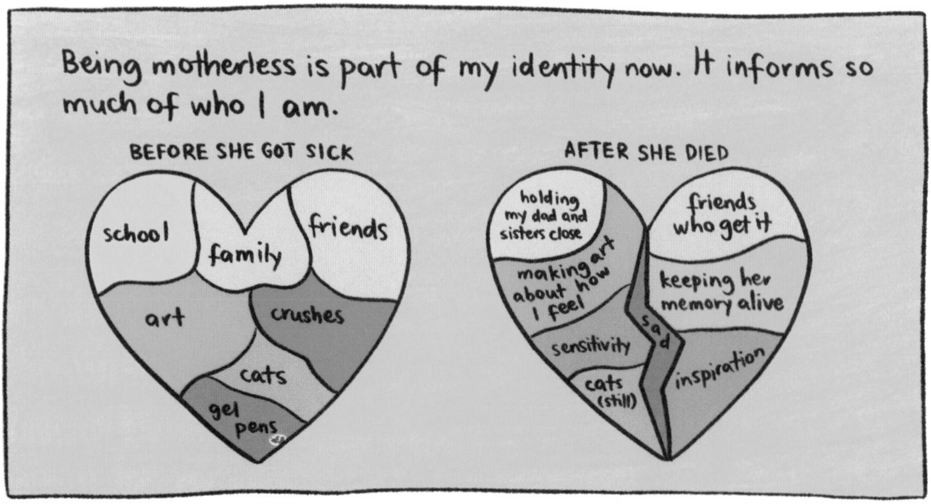
Being motherless is part of my identity now. It informs so much of who I am.
BEFORE SHE GOT SICK
school
family
friends
art
crushes
cats
gel pens
AFTER SHE DIED
holding my dad and sisters close
friends who get it
making art about how I feel
keeping her memory alive
sad
sensitivity
cats (still)
inspiration

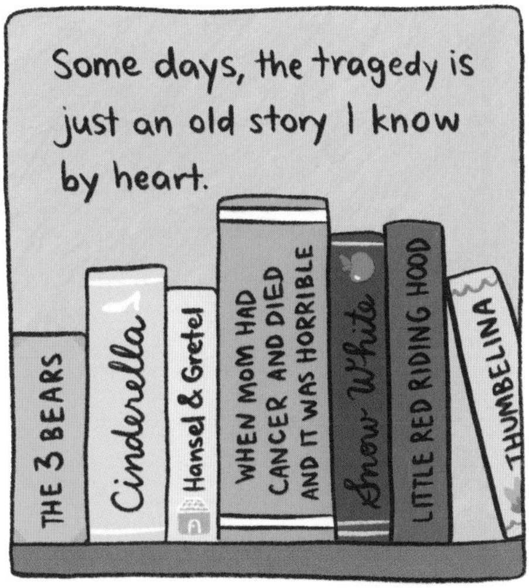
Some days, the tragedy is just an old story I know by heart.
THE 3 BEARS
Cinderella
Hansel & Gretel
WHEN MOM HAD CANCER AND DIED AND IT WAS HORRIBLE
Snow White
LITTLE RED RIDING HOOD
THUMBELINA

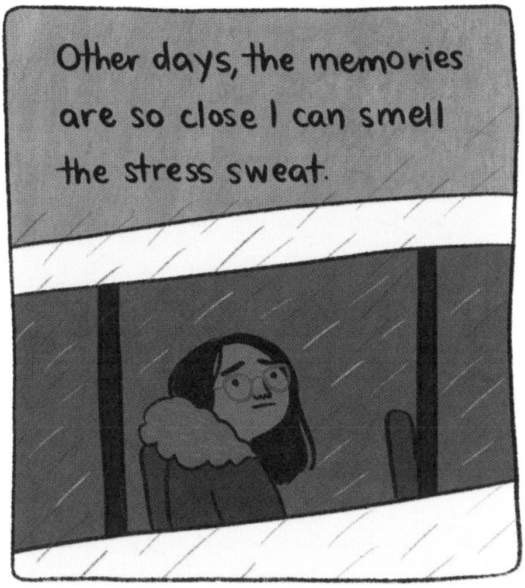
Other days, the memories are so close I can smell the stress sweat.

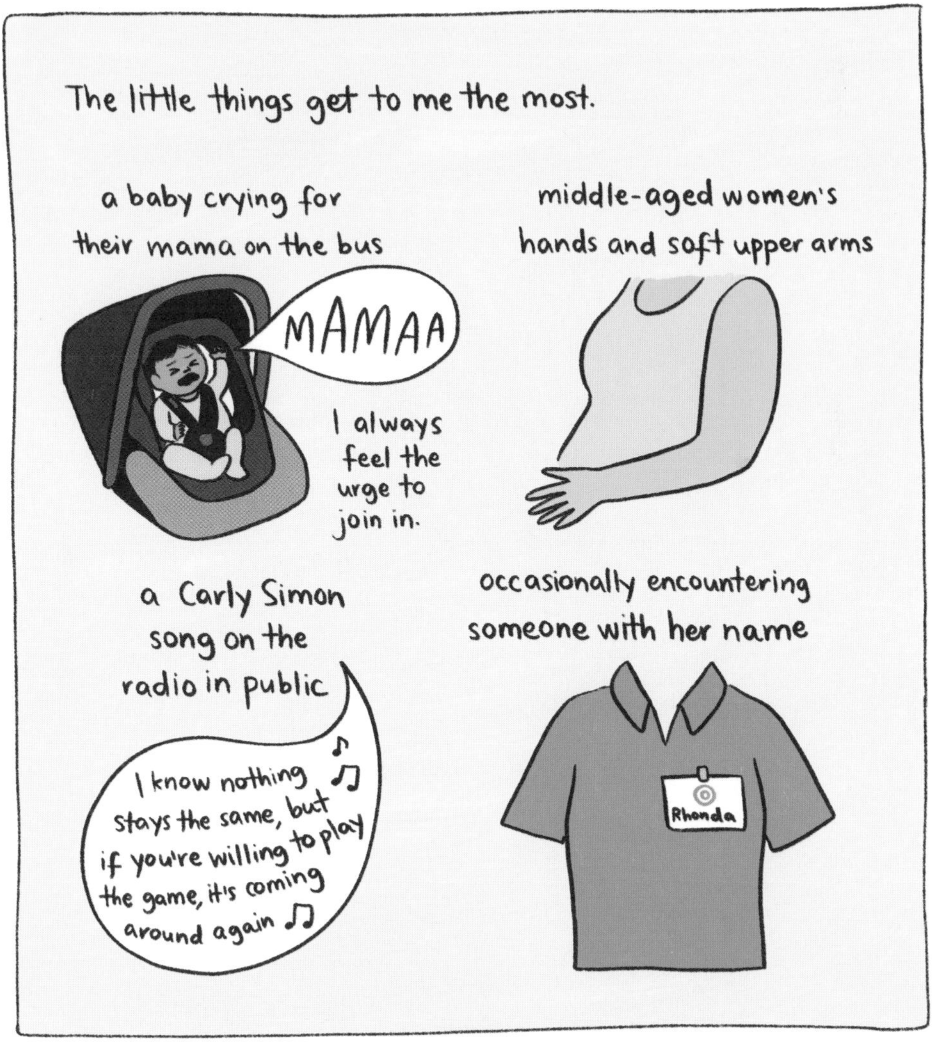
The little things get to me the most.
a baby crying for their mama on the bus
MAMAA
I always feel the urge to join in.
middle-aged women's hands and soft upper arms
a Carly Simon song on the radio in public
I know nothing stays the same, but if you're willing to play the game, it's coming around again ♫
occasionally encountering someone with her name
Rhonda

I ache for the experience of having a mom as an adult.

Sharing a pitcher of margaritas with her after a long day sounds like the most fun thing.

L'chaim!

I wish she could lie on my couch and bark directions at me while I decorate my new apartment.

Try putting the vase on THAT side.

FINE

...

Oh yeah, that does look good.

I wish I could tell her so many things, ask her about her life when she was my age, ask her if it's OK I write this book, ask her for advice (she would have given plenty, whether I asked or not).

I miss feeling like my family was complete, whole.

If I ever have kids, she won't get to meet them. No matter how many stories I tell them about her, they'll never know the softness of her excessively moisturized hands.

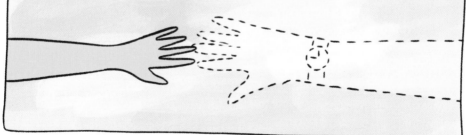

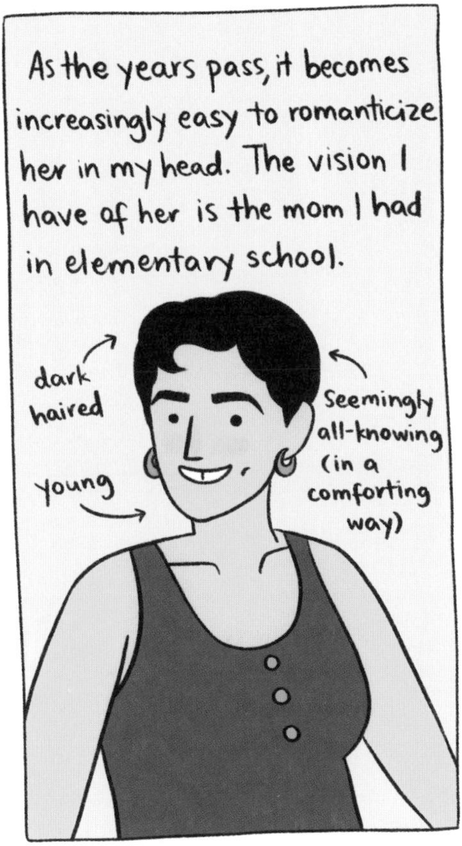
As the years pass, it becomes increasingly easy to romanticize her in my head. The vision I have of her is the mom I had in elementary school.
dark haired
young
Seemingly all-knowing (in a comforting way)

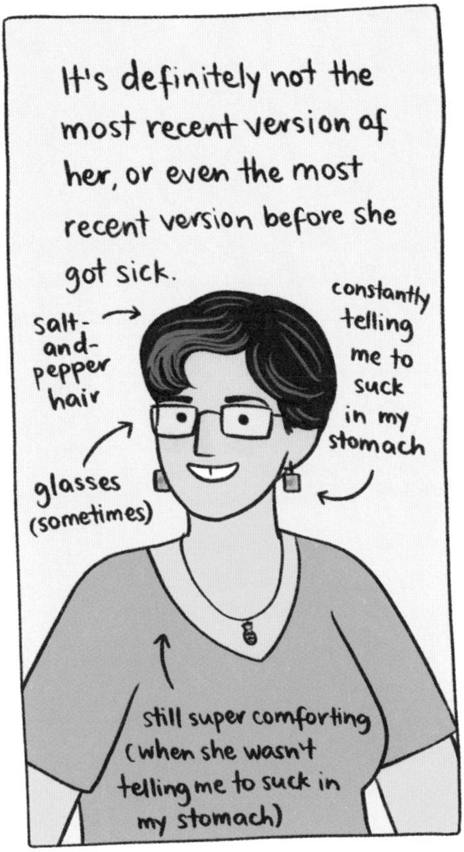
It's definitely not the most recent version of her, or even the most recent version before she got sick.
salt-and-pepper hair
glasses (sometimes)
constantly telling me to suck in my stomach
still super comforting (when she wasn't telling me to suck in my stomach)

It feels natural and good to focus only on the best memories I have of her and ignore the other stuff.

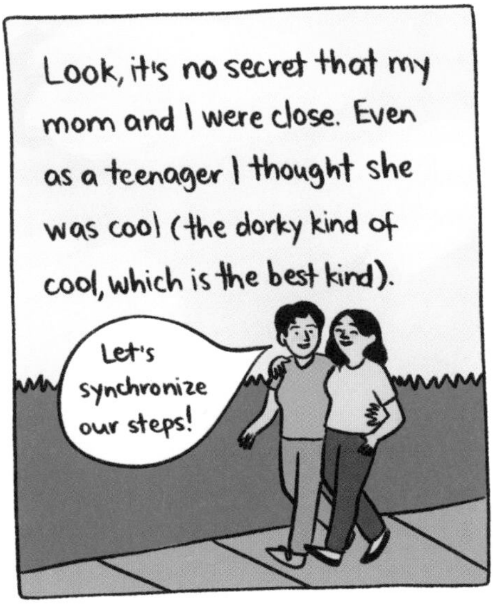
Look, it's no secret that my mom and I were close. Even as a teenager I thought she was cool (the dorky kind of cool, which is the best kind).
Let's synchronize our steps!

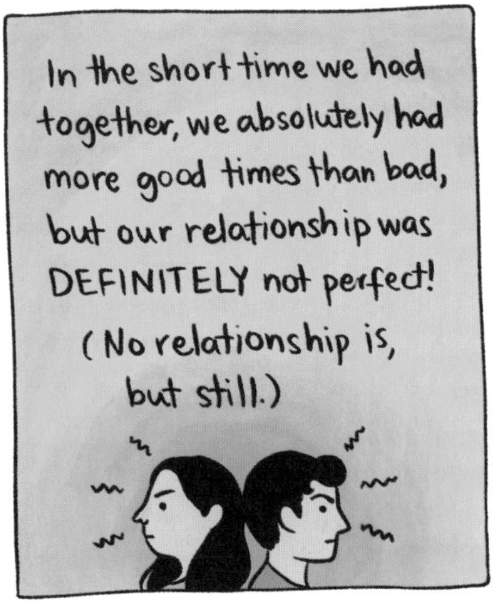
In the short time we had together, we absolutely had more good times than bad, but our relationship was DEFINITELY not perfect!
(No relationship is, but still.)

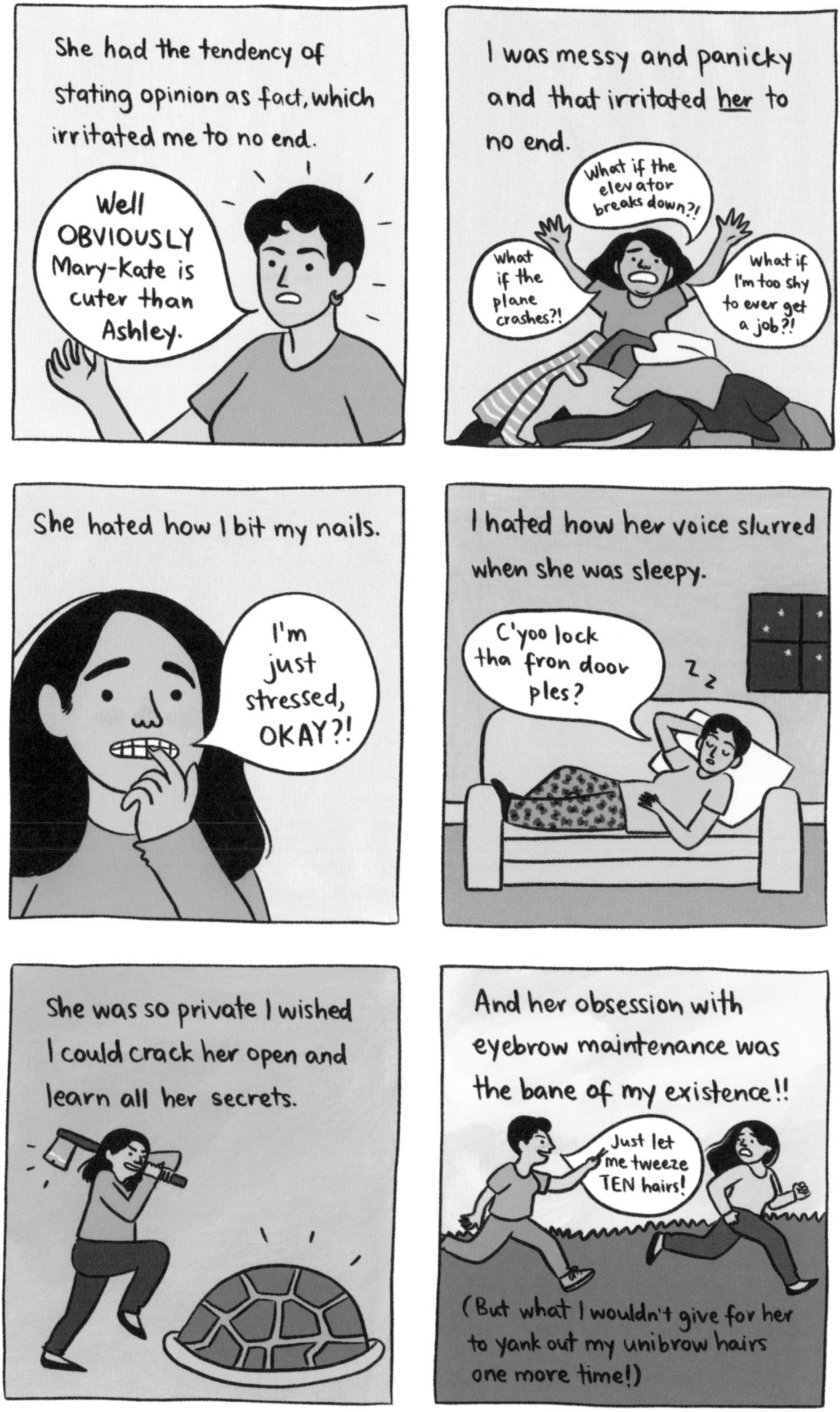
She had the tendency of stating opinion as fact, which irritated me to no end.
Well OBVIOUSLY Mary-Kate is cuter than Ashley.
I was messy and panicky and that irritated her to no end.
What if the elevator breaks down?!
What if the plane crashes?!
What if I'm too shy to ever get a job?!
She hated how I bit my nails.
I'm just stressed, OKAY?!
I hated how her voice slurred when she was sleepy.
C'yoo lock tha fron door ples?
Z z
She was so private I wished I could crack her open and learn all her secrets.
And her obsession with eyebrow maintenance was the bane of my existence!!
Just let me tweeze TEN hairs!
(But what I wouldn't give for her to yank out my unibrow hairs one more time!)

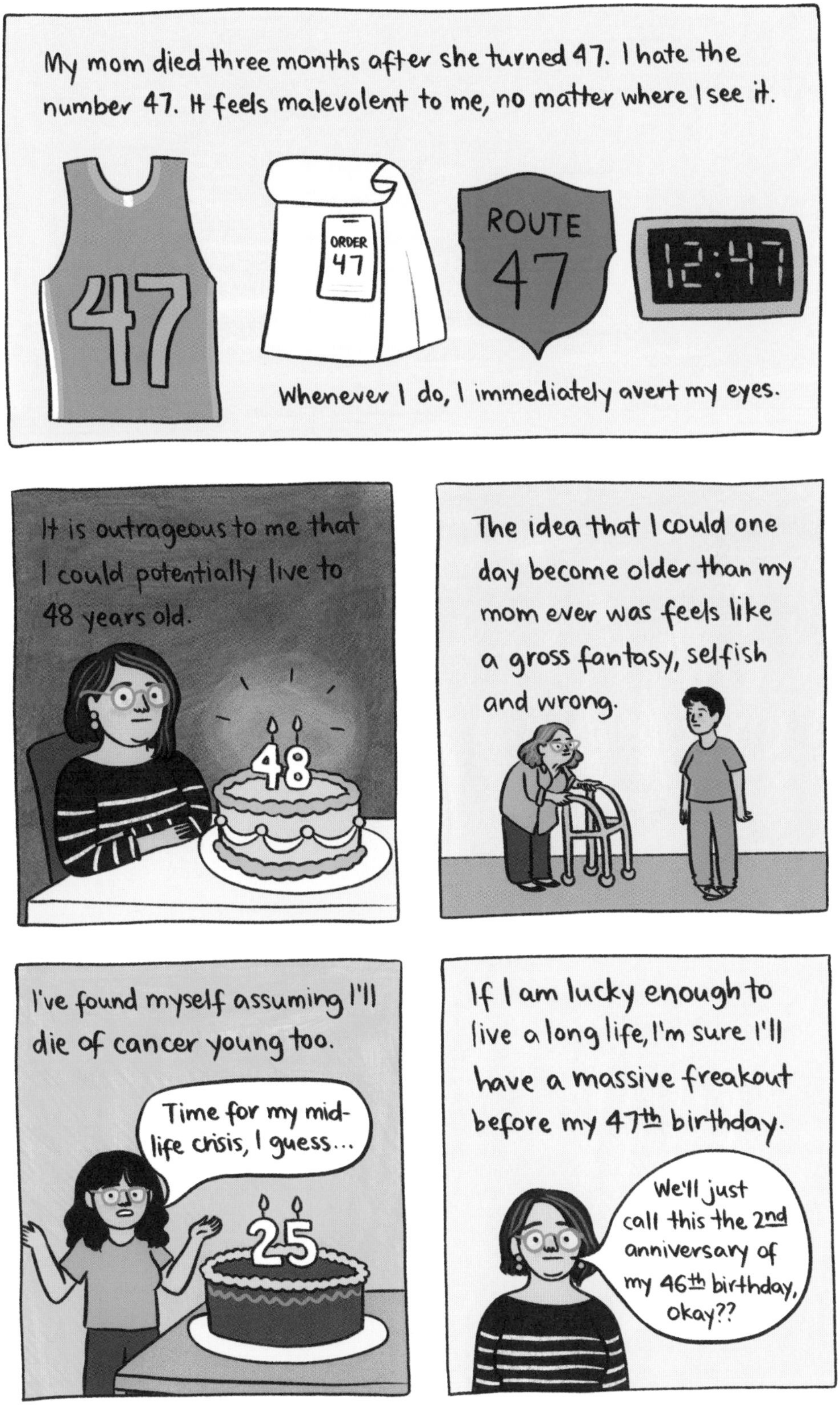
My mom died three months after she turned 47. I hate the number 47. It feels malevolent to me, no matter where I see it.
47
ORDER 47
ROUTE 47
12:47
Whenever I do, I immediately avert my eyes.
It is outrageous to me that I could potentially live to 48 years old.
48
The idea that I could one day become older than my mom ever was feels like a gross fantasy, selfish and wrong.
I've found myself assuming I'll die of cancer young too.
Time for my mid-life crisis, I guess...
25
If I am lucky enough to live a long life, I'm sure I'll have a massive freakout before my 47th birthday.
We'll just call this the 2nd anniversary of my 46th birthday, okay??

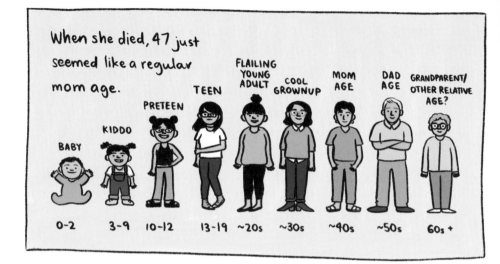

When she died, 47 just seemed like a regular mom age.

| BABY | KIDDO | PRETEEN | TEEN | FLAILING YOUNG ADULT | COOL GROWNUP | MOM AGE | DAD AGE | GRANDPARENT/ OTHER RELATIVE AGE? |
|---|---|---|---|---|---|---|---|---|
| 0-2 | 3-9 | 10-12 | 13-19 | ~20s | ~30s | ~40s | ~50s | 60s + |

As I get older, I have become increasingly shocked by how YOUNG that is.

47!!

0 — REGULAR LIFESPAN 80-something

You know who's OLDER THAN MY MOM EVER WAS??

J. LO!!!

THE HOT YOUNG TRIPLE-THREAT!!

what the hell??

Something else that's weird to think about is how my mom never experienced the world past early 2009.

The most recent cell phone she had looked like this →

- tiny screen
- number buttons only
- no texting

How strange it is that she only existed in a specific era.

Obama had just been elected president for the first time.

Twilight was MEGA POPULAR.

Instagram didn't exist at all!

A fun game my sisters and I like to play is guessing what our mom would be like now if she hadn't died in March 2009. What would her hair look like? How would she dress? What slang would she use?

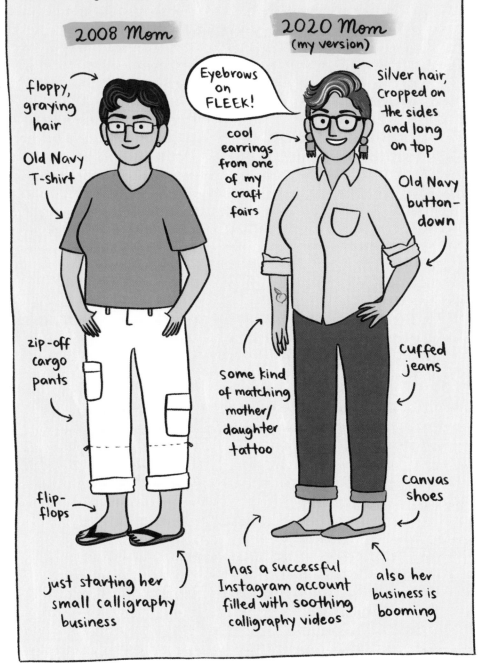

2008 Mom

2020 Mom
(my version)

Eyebrows on FLEEK!

floppy, graying hair

Old Navy T-shirt

zip-off cargo pants

flip-flops

just starting her small calligraphy business

cool earrings from one of my craft fairs

Some kind of matching mother/daughter tattoo

has a successful Instagram account filled with soothing calligraphy videos

Silver hair, cropped on the sides and long on top

Old Navy button-down

cuffed jeans

canvas shoes

also her business is booming

# THINGS MY MOM WOULD TOTALLY BE INTO *if she hadn't died in 2009*

how introversion is a thing people are talking about

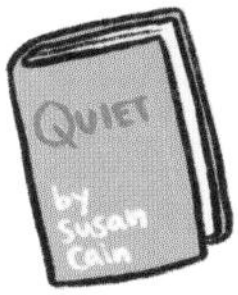
QUIET
by Susan Cain

being able to order her fav avocado toast at restaurants

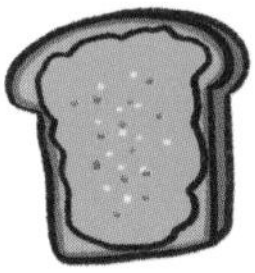

texting and emojis (especially this one)

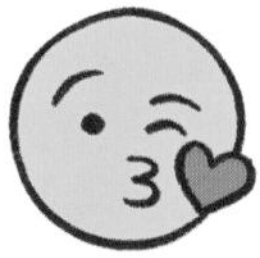

all the new flavors of LaCroix

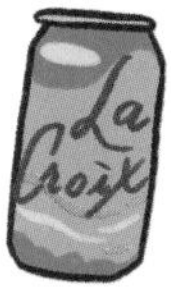
La Croix

comparing our family to the Kardashians

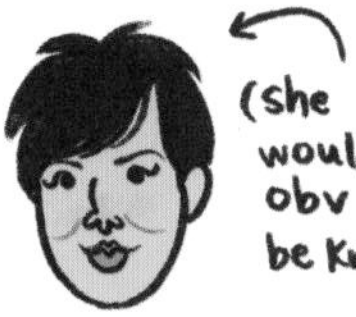

(she would obv be Kris)

"Smoother than a Fresh Jar of Skippy" from Uptown Funk

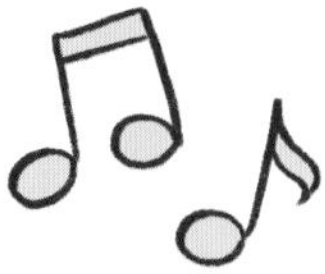

finding commercials from her childhood on YouTube and making me watch them

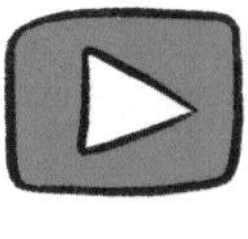

all things Marie Kondo

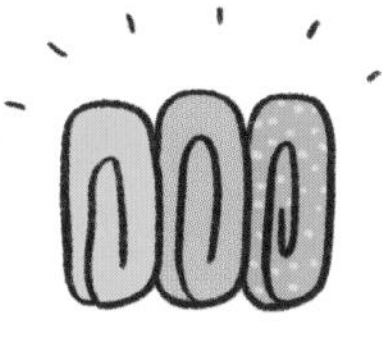

Haim (they're three sisters!!)

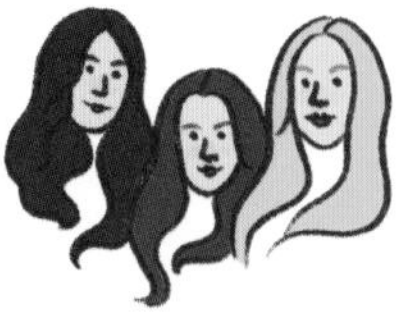

SO MANY iPhone games, especially Candy Crush and Words with Friends

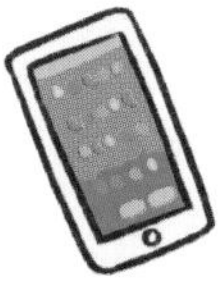

PODCASTS (omg she would be SO into podcasts)

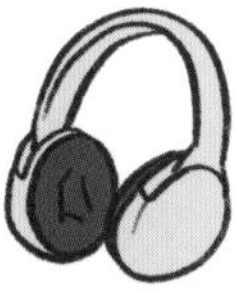

the rest of society joining in on her eyebrow obsession

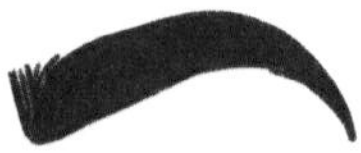

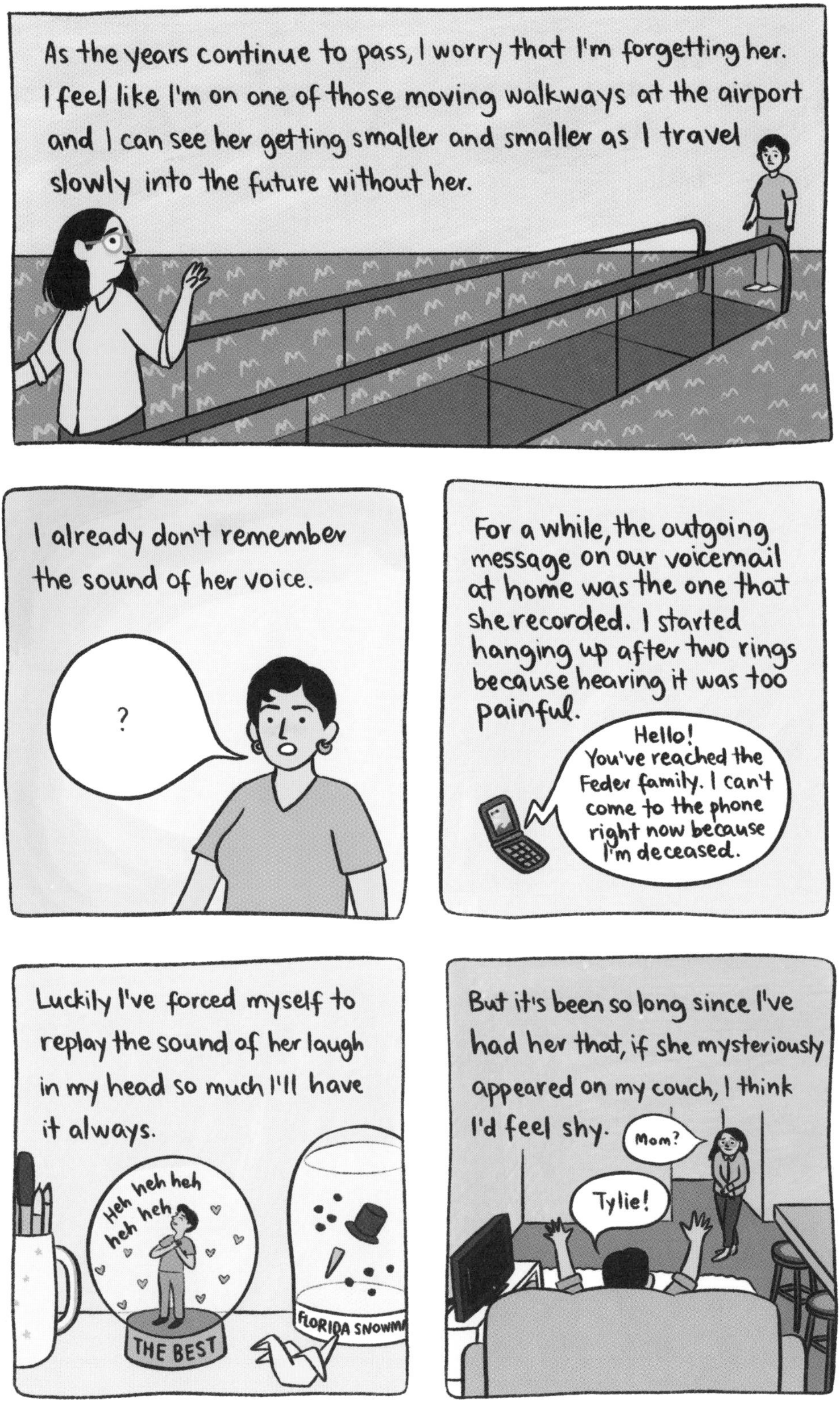

As the years continue to pass, I worry that I'm forgetting her. I feel like I'm on one of those moving walkways at the airport and I can see her getting smaller and smaller as I travel slowly into the future without her.
I already don't remember the sound of her voice.
?
For a while, the outgoing message on our voicemail at home was the one that she recorded. I started hanging up after two rings because hearing it was too painful.
Hello! You've reached the Feder family. I can't come to the phone right now because I'm deceased.
Luckily I've forced myself to replay the sound of her laugh in my head so much I'll have it always.
Heh heh heh heh heh
THE BEST
FLORIDA SNOWM
But it's been so long since I've had her that, if she mysteriously appeared on my couch, I think I'd feel shy.
Mom?
Tylie!

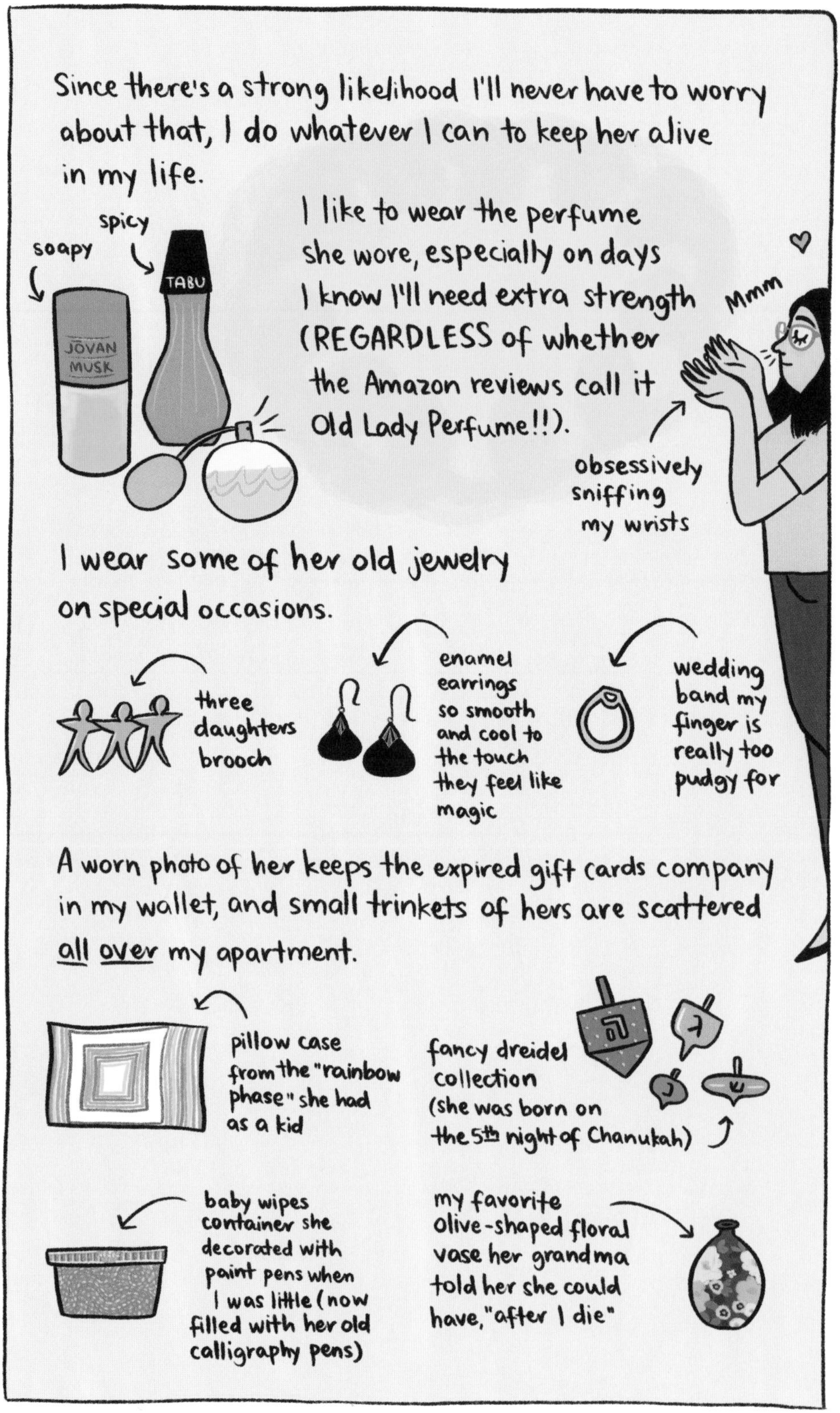
Since there's a strong likelihood I'll never have to worry about that, I do whatever I can to keep her alive in my life.
I like to wear the perfume she wore, especially on days I know I'll need extra strength (REGARDLESS of whether the Amazon reviews call it Old Lady Perfume!!).
soapy
spicy
TABU
JOVAN MUSK
Mmm
obsessively sniffing my wrists
I wear some of her old jewelry on special occasions.
three daughters brooch
enamel earrings so smooth and cool to the touch they feel like magic
wedding band my finger is really too pudgy for
A worn photo of her keeps the expired gift cards company in my wallet, and small trinkets of hers are scattered all over my apartment.
pillow case from the "rainbow phase" she had as a kid
fancy dreidel collection (she was born on the 5th night of Chanukah)
baby wipes container she decorated with paint pens when I was little (now filled with her old calligraphy pens)
my favorite olive-shaped floral vase her grandma told her she could have, "after I die"

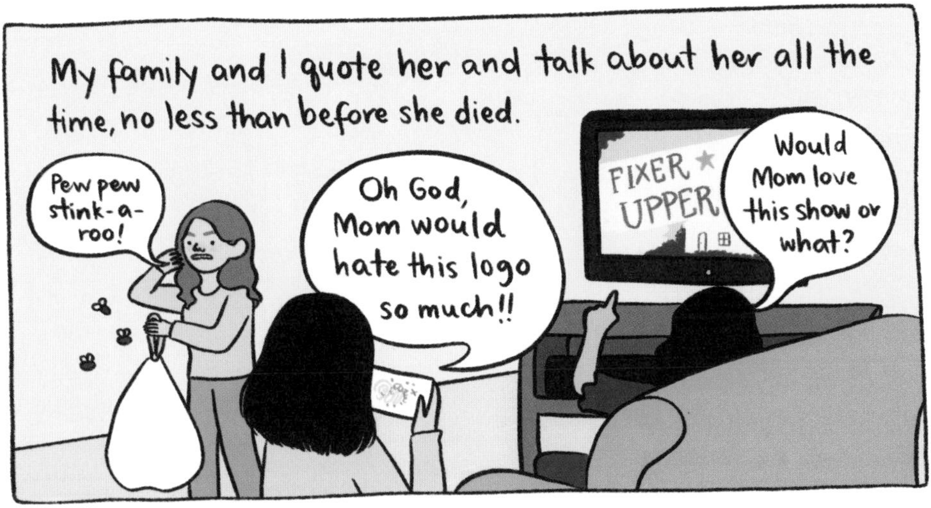
My family and I quote her and talk about her all the time, no less than before she died.
Pew pew stink-a-roo!
Oh God, Mom would hate this logo so much!!
FIXER ★ UPPER
Would Mom love this show or what?

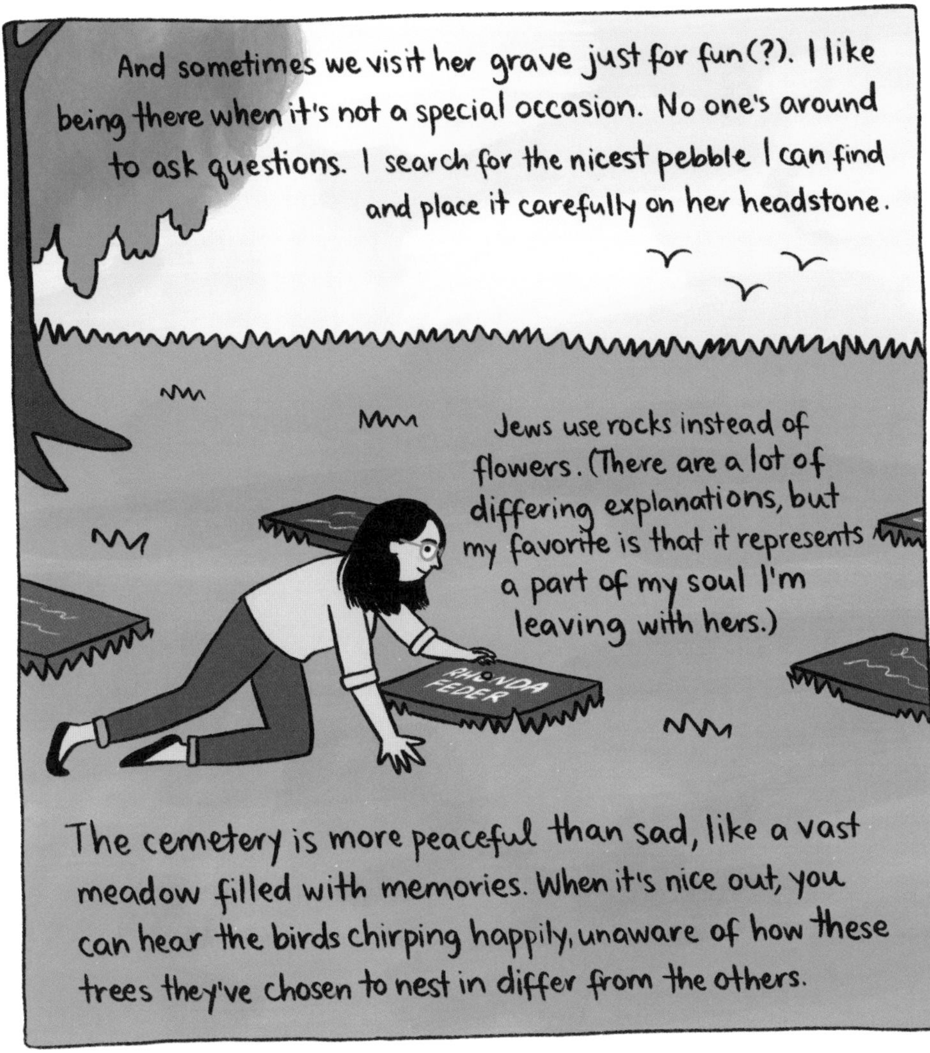
And sometimes we visit her grave just for fun(?). I like being there when it's not a special occasion. No one's around to ask questions. I search for the nicest pebble I can find and place it carefully on her headstone.
Jews use rocks instead of flowers. (There are a lot of differing explanations, but my favorite is that it represents a part of my soul I'm leaving with hers.)
RHONDA FEDER
The cemetery is more peaceful than sad, like a vast meadow filled with memories. When it's nice out, you can hear the birds chirping happily, unaware of how these trees they've chosen to nest in differ from the others.

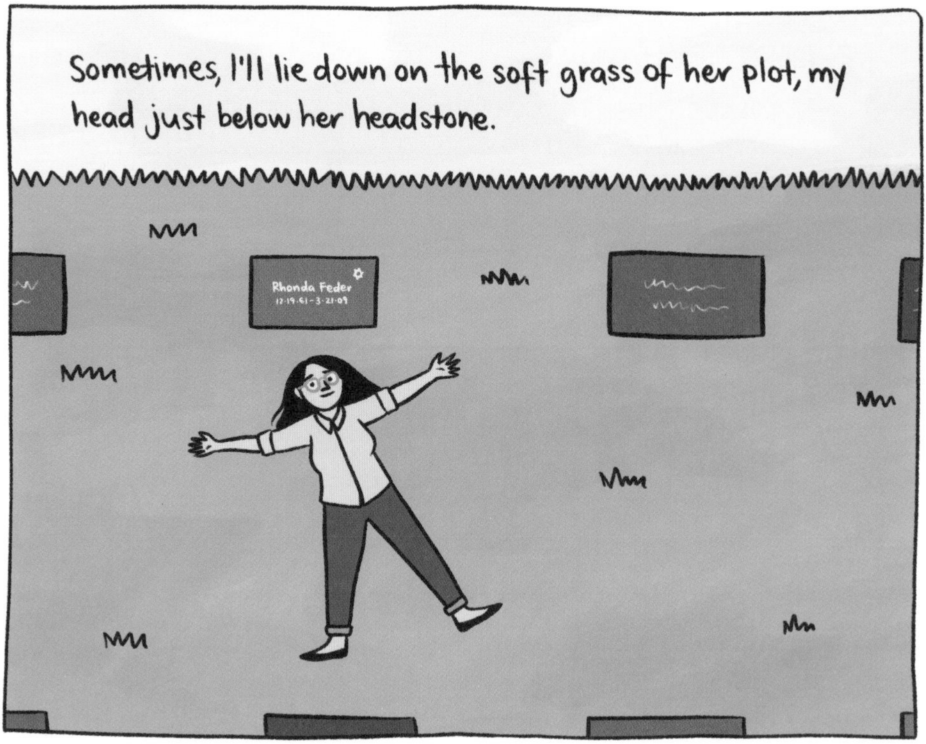
Sometimes, I'll lie down on the soft grass of her plot, my head just below her headstone.
Rhonda Feder
12·19·61 - 3·21·09

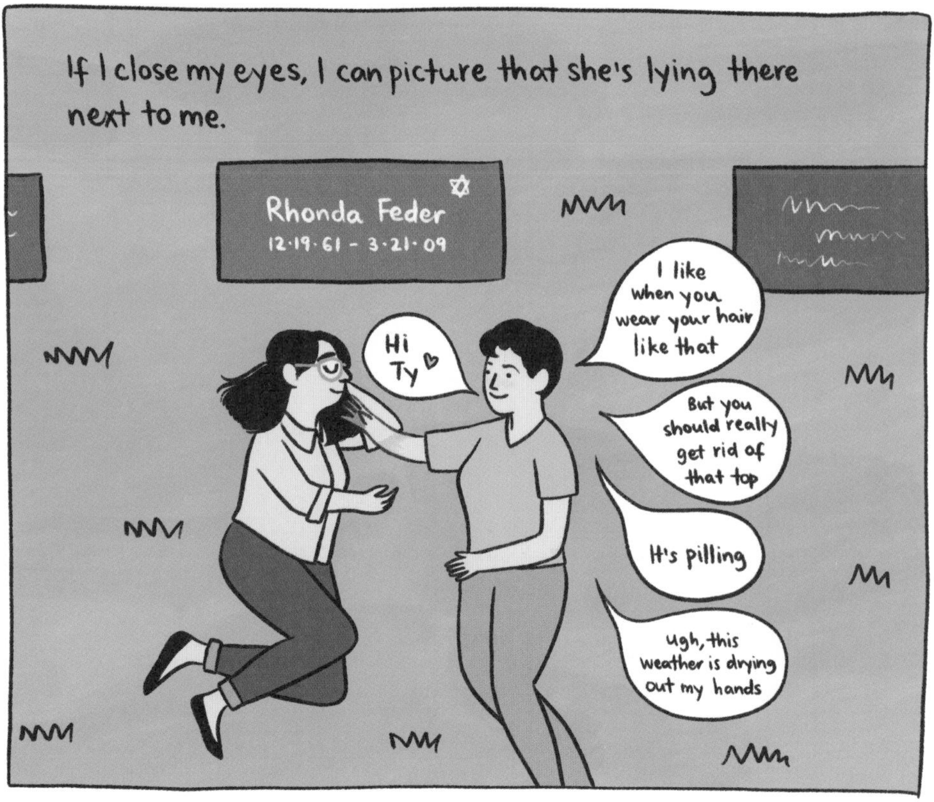
If I close my eyes, I can picture that she's lying there next to me.
Rhonda Feder
12·19·61 - 3·21·09
Hi Ty ♡
I like when you wear your hair like that
But you should really get rid of that top
It's pilling
Ugh, this weather is drying out my hands

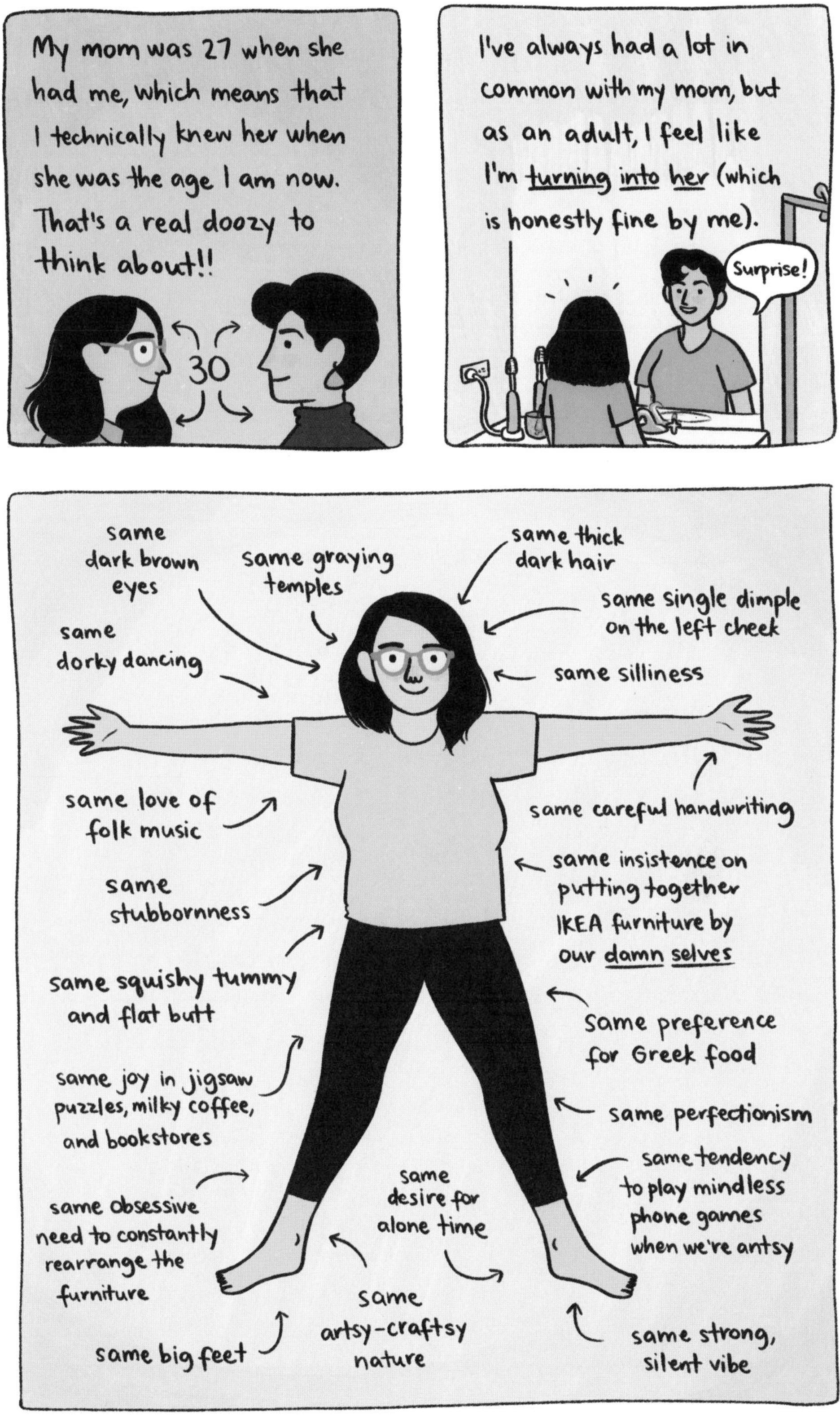
My mom was 27 when she had me, which means that I technically knew her when she was the age I am now. That's a real doozy to think about!!
30
I've always had a lot in common with my mom, but as an adult, I feel like I'm turning into her (which is honestly fine by me).
Surprise!
same dark brown eyes
same graying temples
same thick dark hair
same single dimple on the left cheek
same dorky dancing
same silliness
same love of folk music
same careful handwriting
same stubbornness
same insistence on putting together IKEA furniture by our damn selves
same squishy tummy and flat butt
same preference for Greek food
same joy in jigsaw puzzles, milky coffee, and bookstores
same perfectionism
same tendency to play mindless phone games when we're antsy
same desire for alone time
same obsessive need to constantly rearrange the furniture
same artsy-craftsy nature
same big feet
same strong, silent vibe

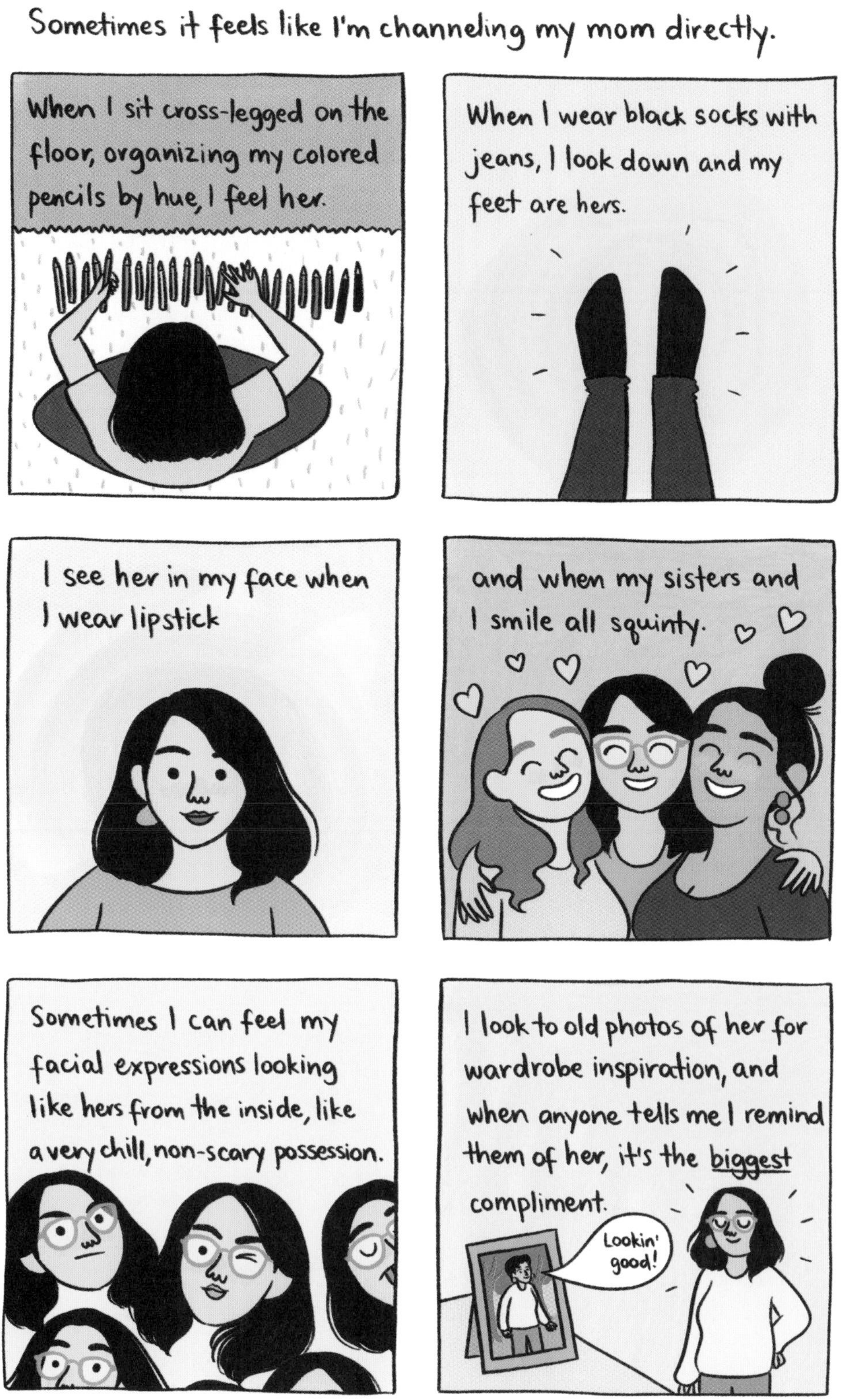
Sometimes it feels like I'm channeling my mom directly.
When I sit cross-legged on the floor, organizing my colored pencils by hue, I feel her.
When I wear black socks with jeans, I look down and my feet are hers.
I see her in my face when I wear lipstick
and when my sisters and I smile all squinty.
Sometimes I can feel my facial expressions looking like hers from the inside, like a very chill, non-scary possession.
I look to old photos of her for wardrobe inspiration, and when anyone tells me I remind them of her, it's the biggest compliment.
Lookin' good!

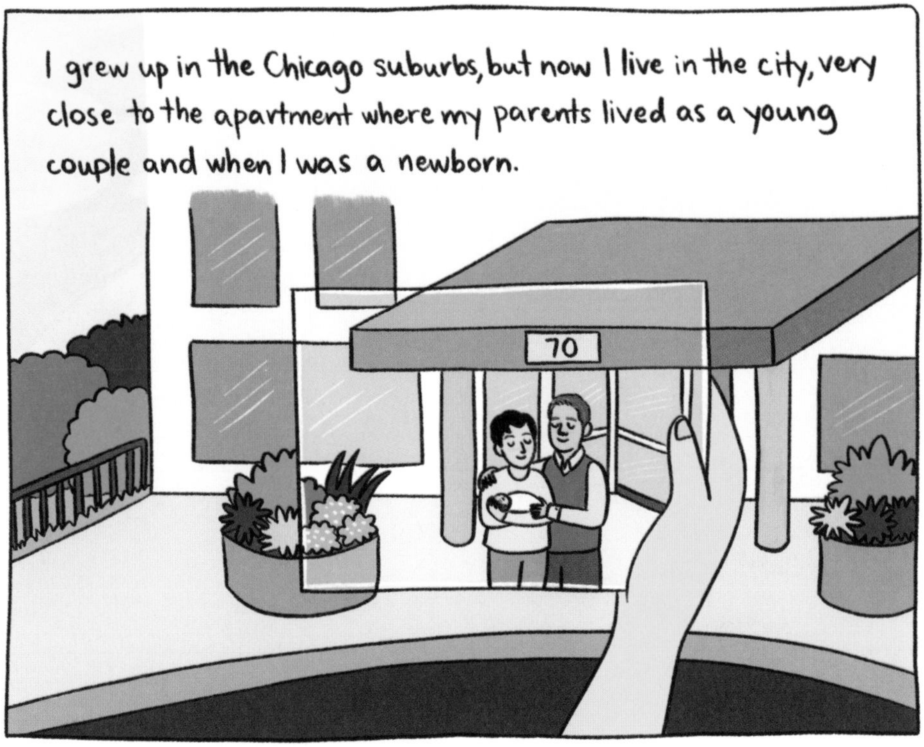
I grew up in the Chicago suburbs, but now I live in the city, very close to the apartment where my parents lived as a young couple and when I was a newborn.
70

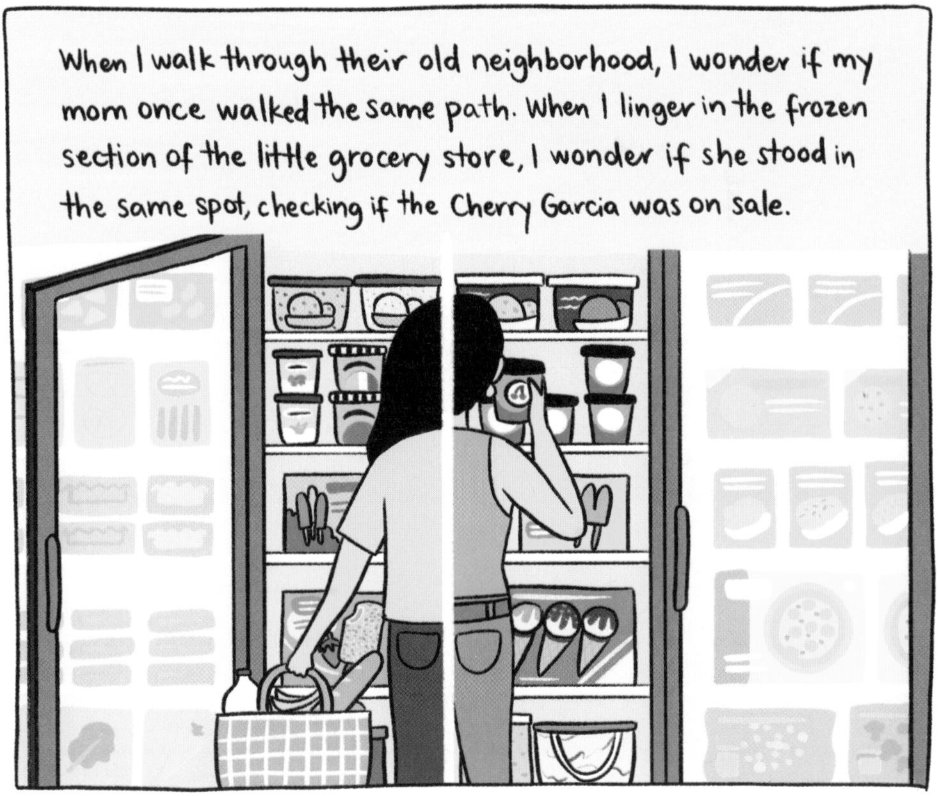
When I walk through their old neighborhood, I wonder if my mom once walked the same path. When I linger in the frozen section of the little grocery store, I wonder if she stood in the same spot, checking if the Cherry Garcia was on sale.

I don't know where my mom is now...

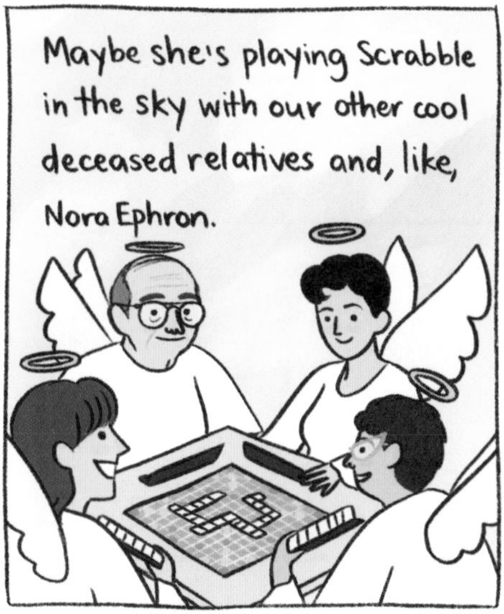

Maybe she's playing Scrabble in the sky with our other cool deceased relatives and, like, Nora Ephron.


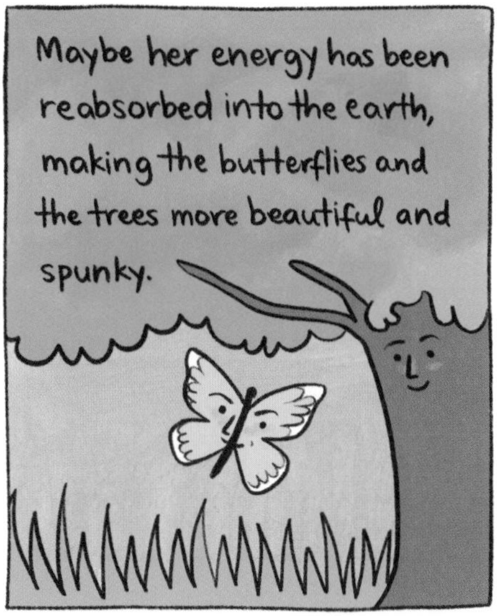

Maybe her energy has been reabsorbed into the earth, making the butterflies and the trees more beautiful and spunky.


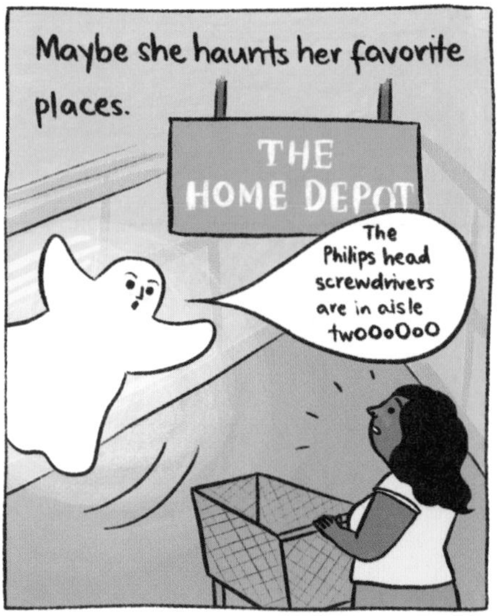

Maybe she haunts her favorite places.
THE HOME DEPOT
The Philips head screwdrivers are in aisle twoOoOoO


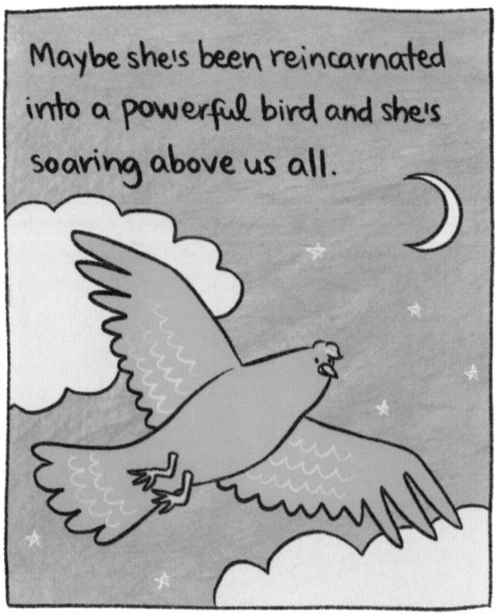

Maybe she's been reincarnated into a powerful bird and she's soaring above us all.


One thing's for sure, I wouldn't trade the nineteen years I had with her for a hundred with some other mom (especially [redacted]).

my childhood friend's mom from page 13, heh heh heh

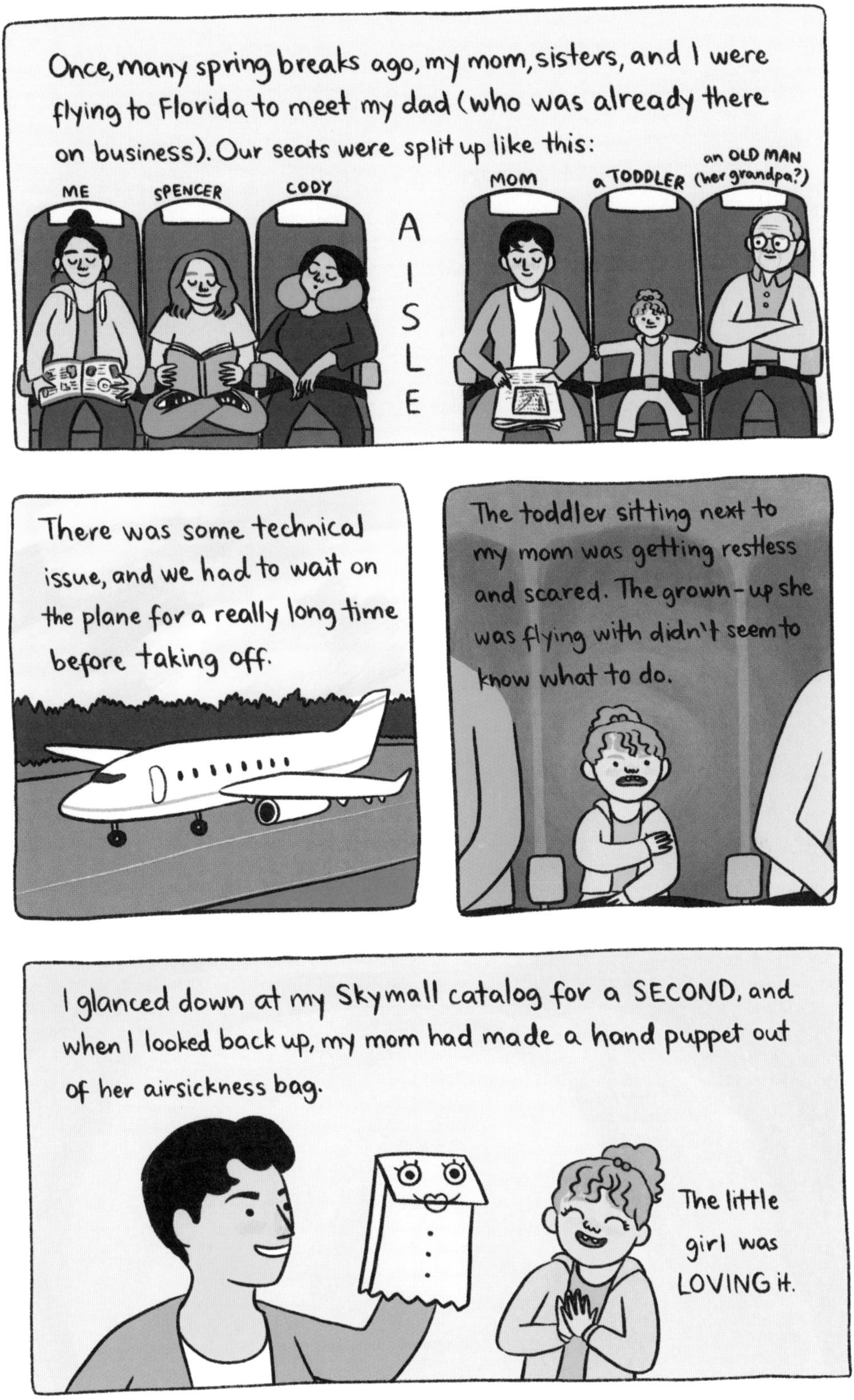
Once, many spring breaks ago, my mom, sisters, and I were flying to Florida to meet my dad (who was already there on business). Our seats were split up like this:
ME
SPENCER
CODY
AISLE
MOM
a TODDLER
an OLD MAN (her grandpa?)
There was some technical issue, and we had to wait on the plane for a really long time before taking off.
The toddler sitting next to my mom was getting restless and scared. The grown-up she was flying with didn't seem to know what to do.
I glanced down at my Skymall catalog for a SECOND, and when I looked back up, my mom had made a hand puppet out of her airsickness bag.
The little girl was LOVING it.

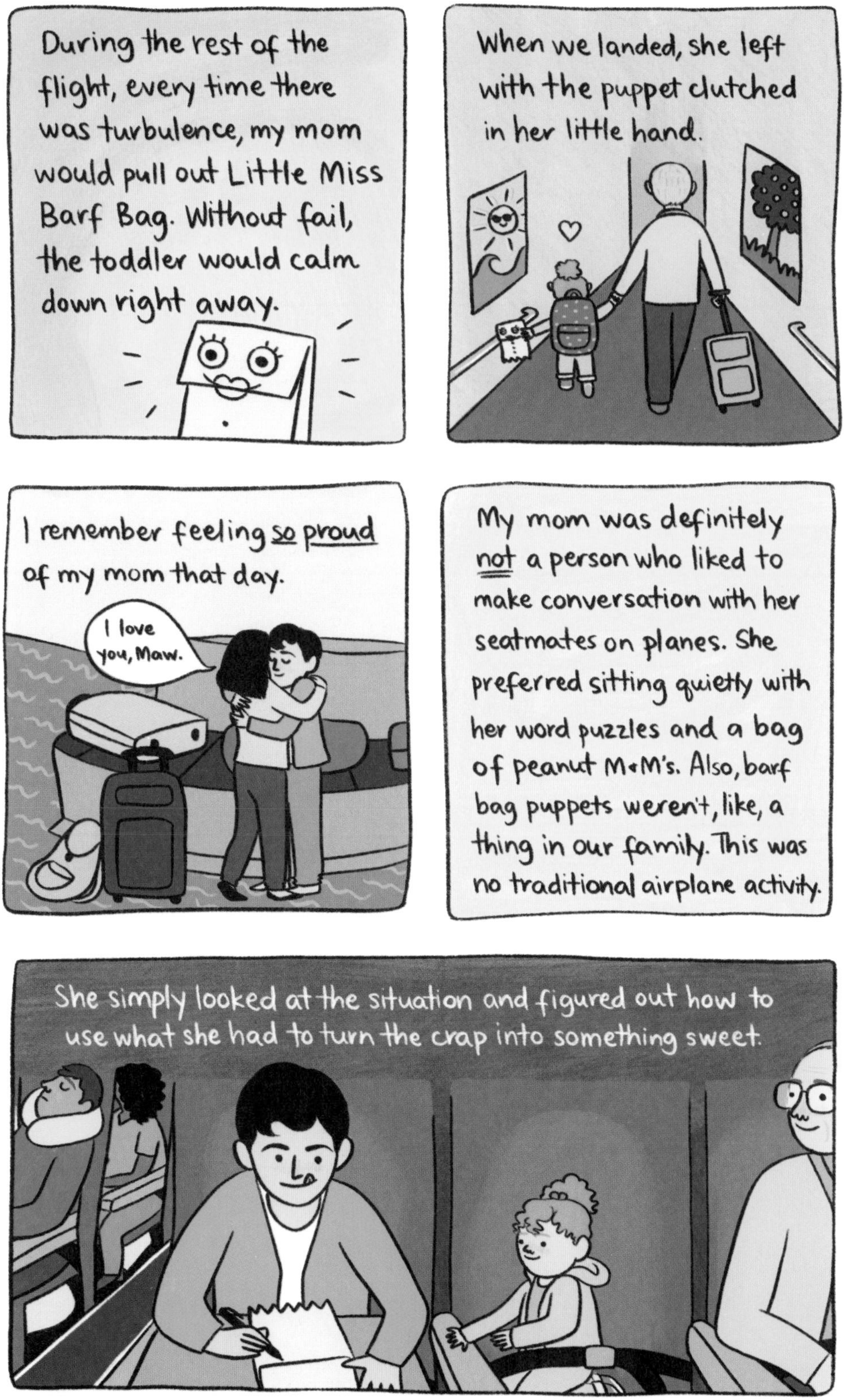
During the rest of the flight, every time there was turbulence, my mom would pull out Little Miss Barf Bag. Without fail, the toddler would calm down right away.
When we landed, she left with the puppet clutched in her little hand.
I remember feeling so proud of my mom that day.
I love you, Maw.
My mom was definitely not a person who liked to make conversation with her seatmates on planes. She preferred sitting quietly with her word puzzles and a bag of peanut M&M's. Also, barf bag puppets weren't, like, a thing in our family. This was no traditional airplane activity.
She simply looked at the situation and figured out how to use what she had to turn the crap into something sweet.

Long before my mom ever got sick, her death felt like the number one scariest thing that could ever happen. And then it happened. And it <u>was</u> the scariest thing that could ever happen.

But I survived.

Ten years later, I'm still here, trying to turn the crap into something sweet, just like she would.

my favorite photo of my mom

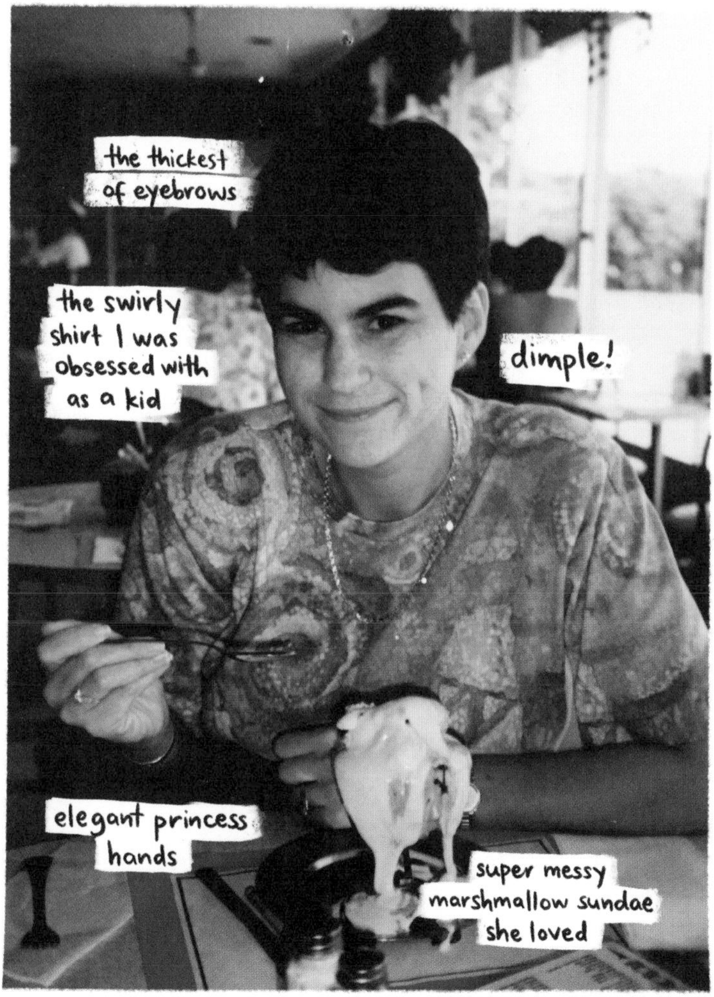
the thickest
of eyebrows
the swirly
shirt I was
obsessed with
as a kid
dimple!
elegant princess
hands
super messy
marshmallow sundae
she loved

# afterword

A WHOLE BUNCH OF PHOTOS

the first photo ever taken of us (I think)

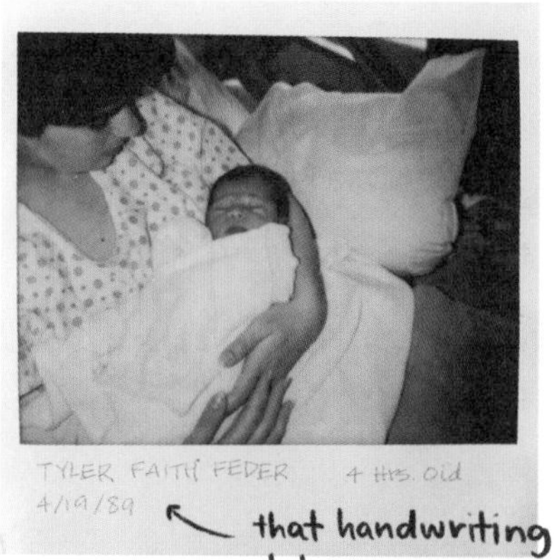
TYLER FAITH FEDER 4 HRS. Old
4/19/89

that handwriting I love so much

the last photo ever taken of us, probably a week after her diagnosis

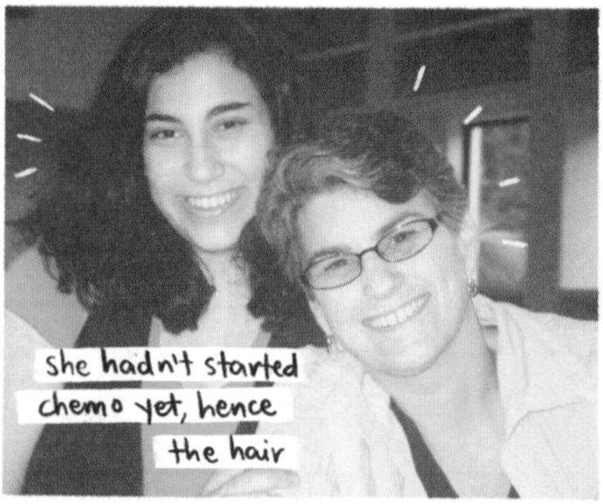
she hadn't started chemo yet, hence the hair

how I picture us in my head

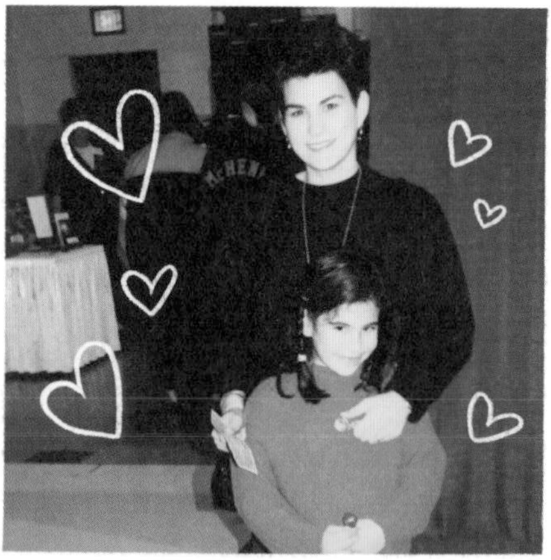

our general vibe

comforting

freaking

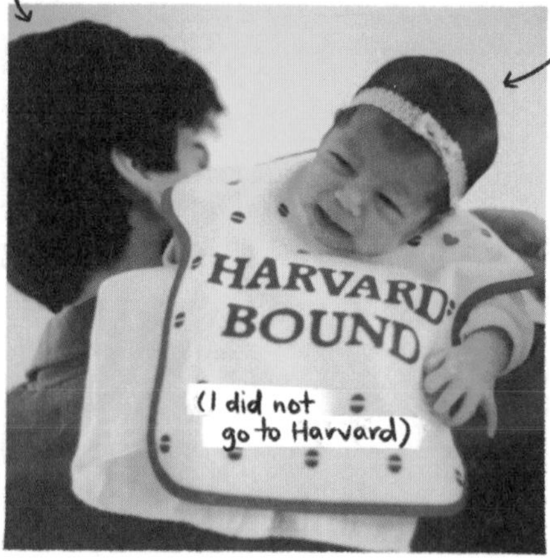
HARVARD BOUND
(I did not go to Harvard)

my mom shepherding me through my extreme dork phase

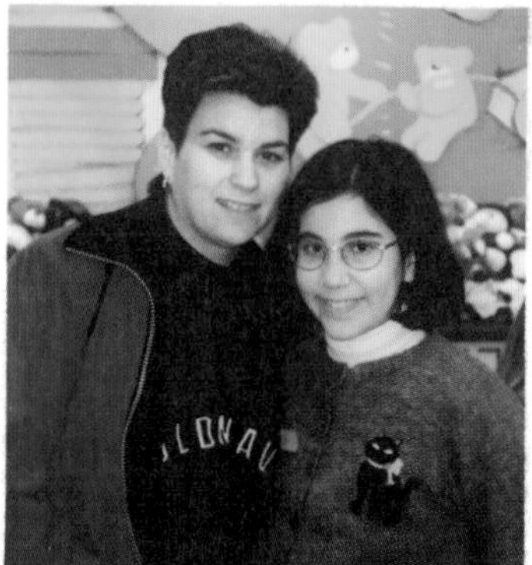

feeling super giggly that my mom let me "pick her up" in the swimming pool

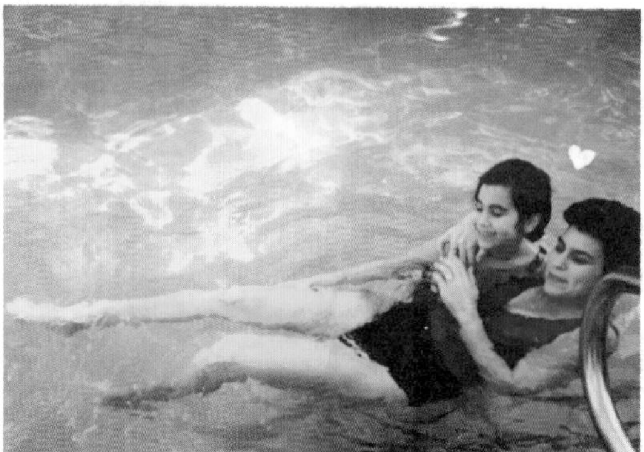

Spencer working on Cody's goofy/oddly poetic cake at the end of the shiva

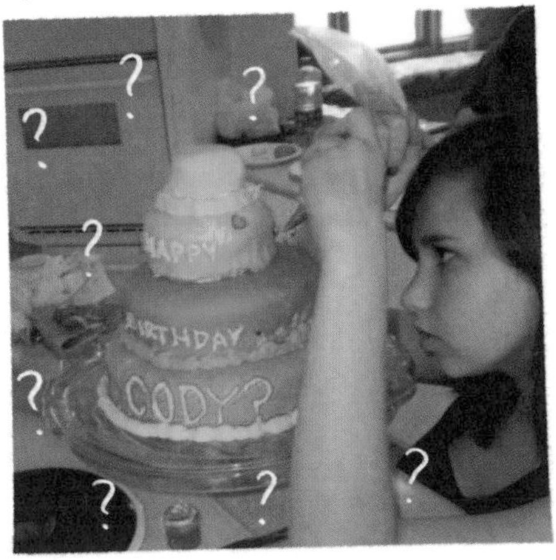
HAPPY
BIRTHDAY
CODY?

the three of us looking positively THRILLED at Cody's birthday "party"

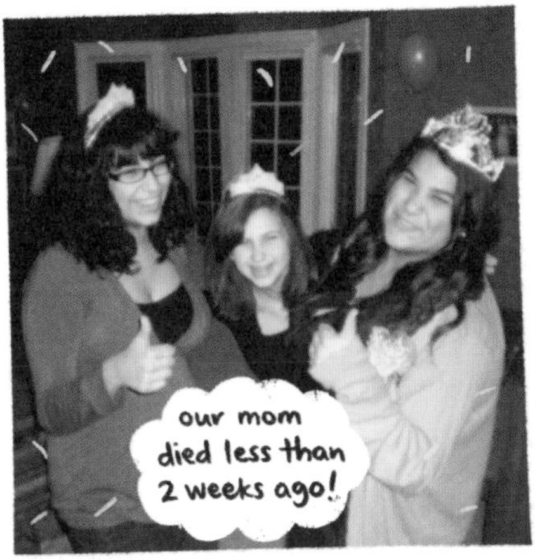
our mom died less than 2 weeks ago!

the Feder girls approximately 7 years before our mom died

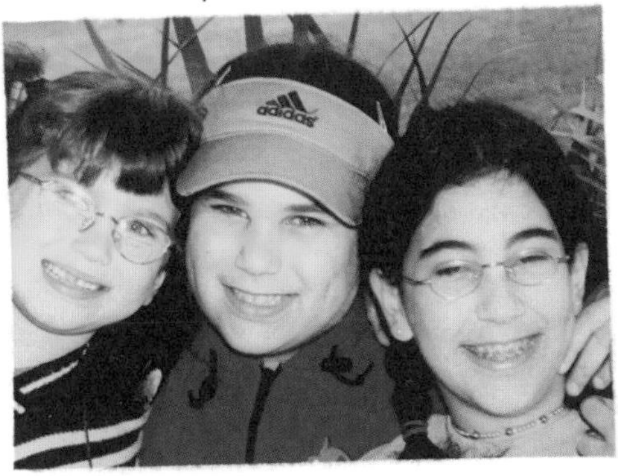
adidas

the Feder girls approximately 7 years after our mom died, closer than ever!

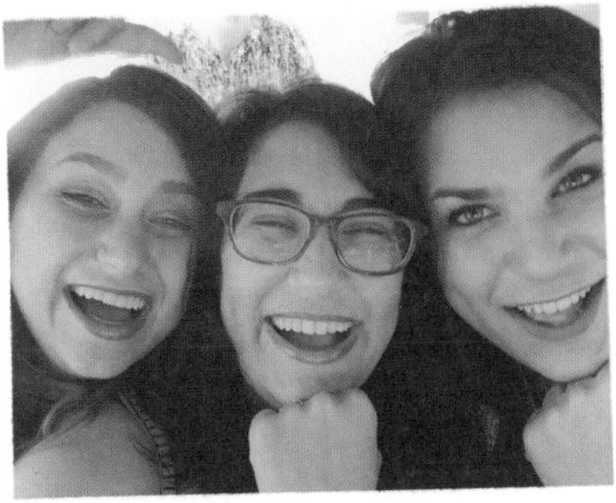

one of our first photos as a family of five

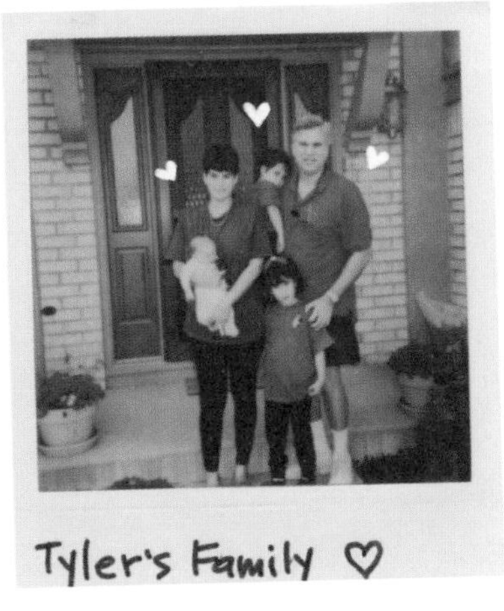
Tyler's Family ♡

one of our first photos as a family of four again

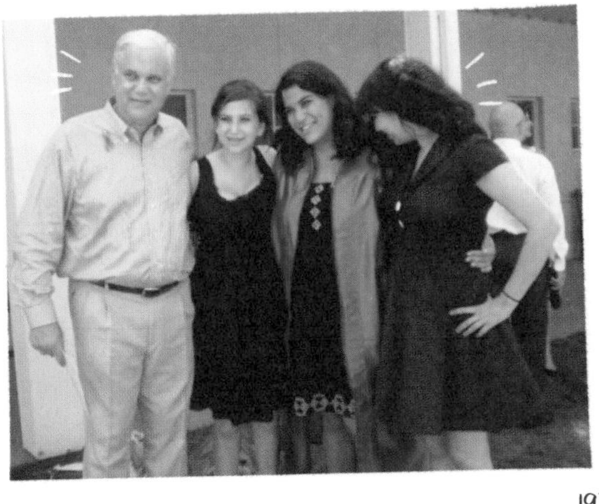

my Aladdin birthday party, aka the peak of my existence

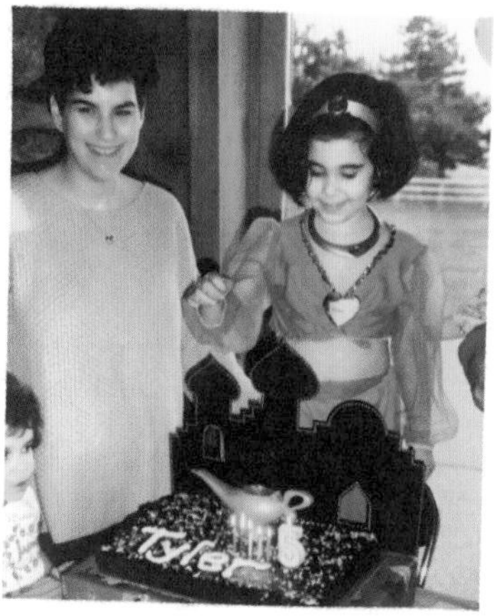
Tyler

showing off our mom-made Halloween costumes as a family (I was a butterfly, Cody was a bee, and Spencer was a ladybug)

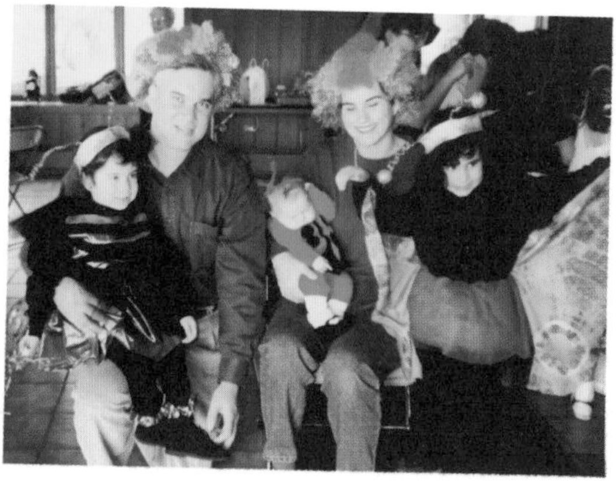

one of my mom's face-in-a-hole things at a springtime-themed birthday party

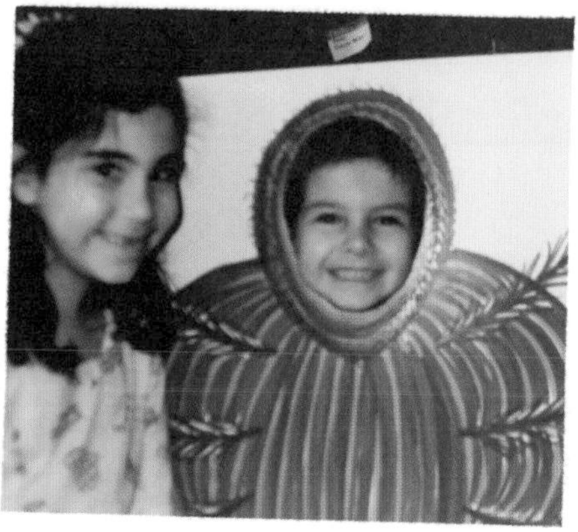

in action, making one of her classic masking tape hopscotch boards

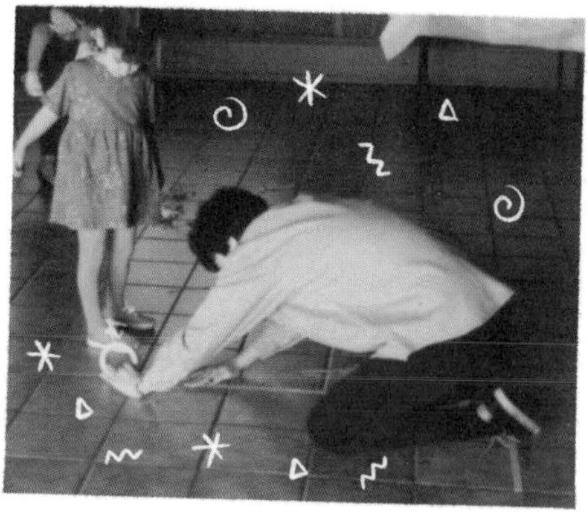

celebrating her last birthday at Disney World

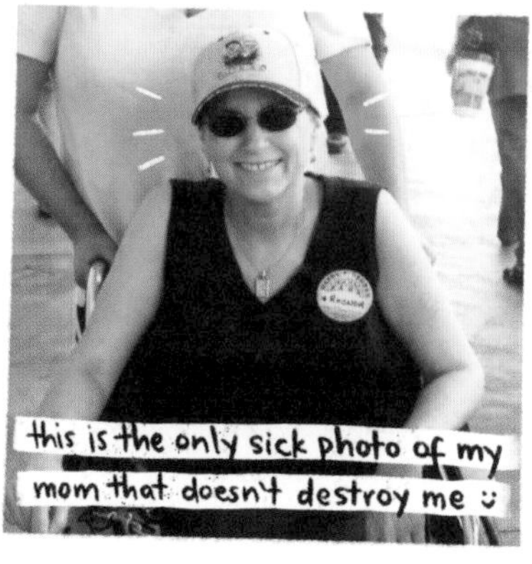
this is the only sick photo of my
mom that doesn't destroy me :)

I like this picture because my mom + I look great and everyone else looks ridiculous

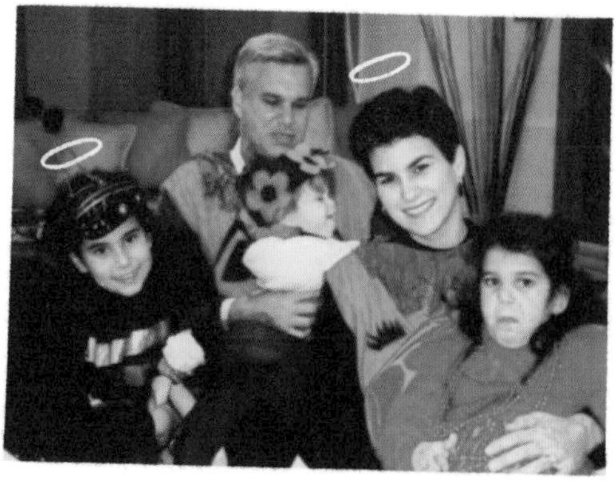

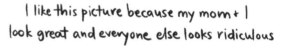

hanging out with my mom at an art fair where she was selling super '80s hair bows

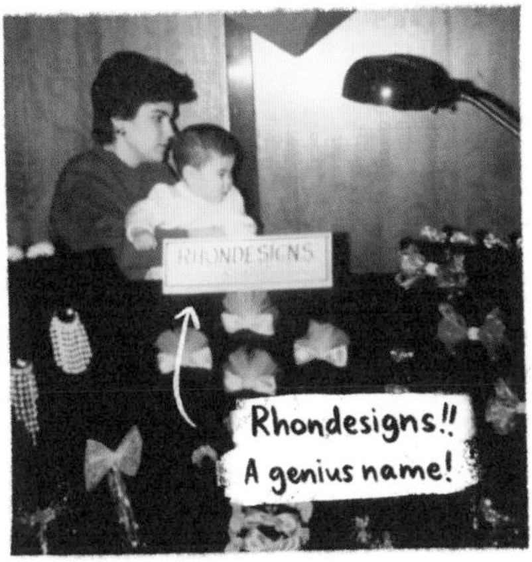
RHONDESIGNS
Rhondesigns!!
A genius name!

hanging out in the hospital in happier times (when Spencer was born)

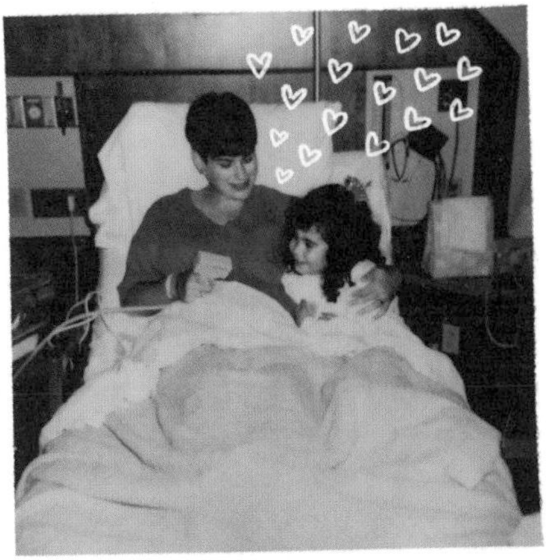

the most stoic mother/daughter twinning photo ever taken at a Chuck E. Cheese

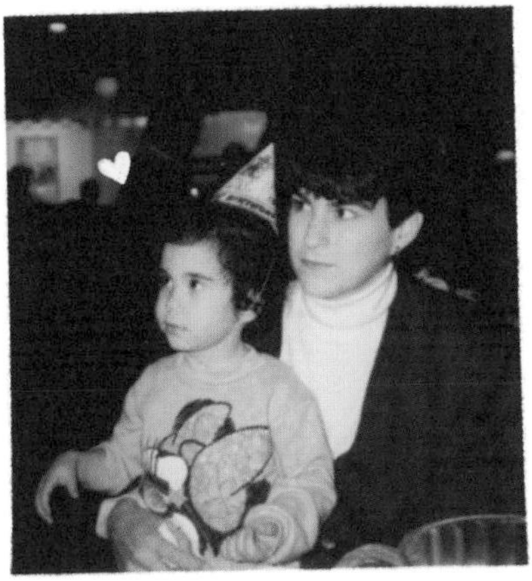

the candid photo that best portrays our essence

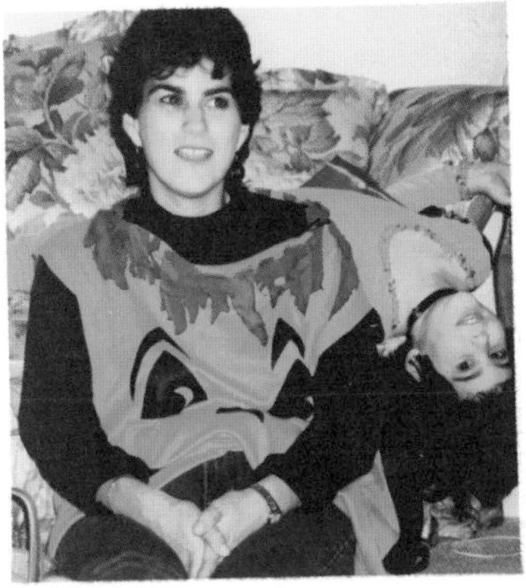

me hula hooping at my bat mitzvah

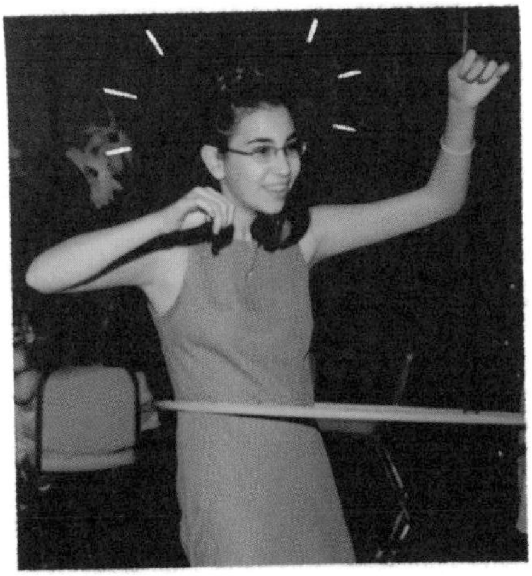

my mom hula hooping at a similar age, looking way cooler than I ever could

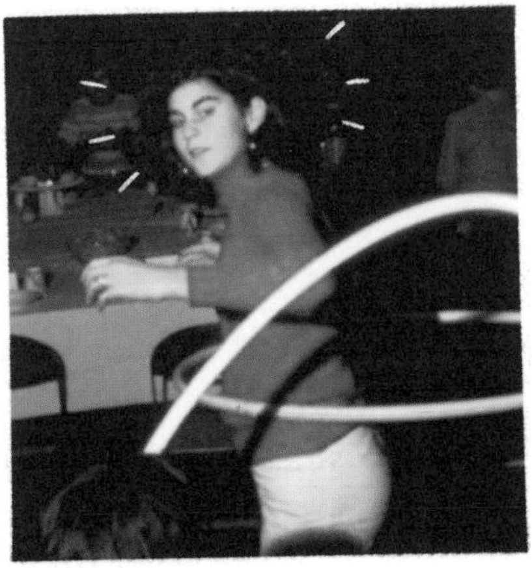

the last birthday card my mom ever gave me

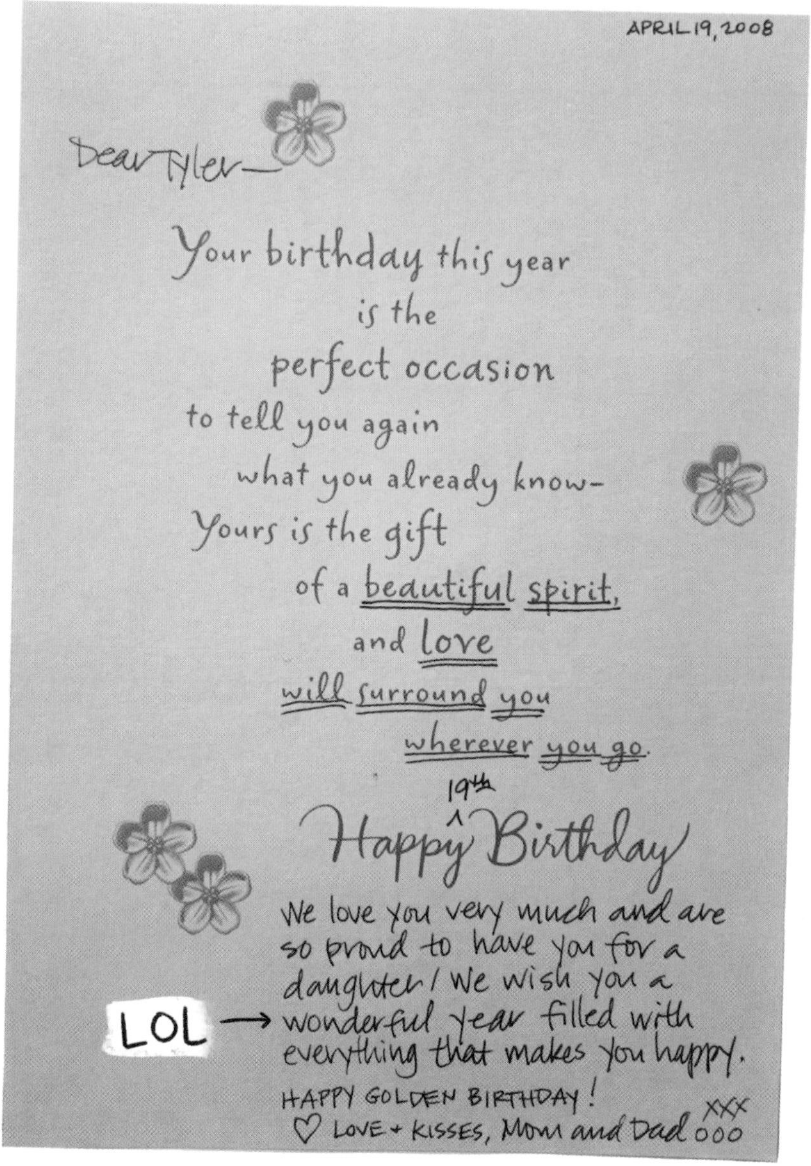

APRIL 19, 2008

Dear Tyler—

Your birthday this year
is the
perfect occasion
to tell you again
what you already know—
Yours is the gift
of a beautiful spirit,
and love
will surround you
wherever you go.

Happy 19th Birthday

We love you very much and are so proud to have you for a daughter! We wish you a wonderful year filled with everything that makes you happy.

LOL →

HAPPY GOLDEN BIRTHDAY!

♡ LOVE + KISSES, Mom and Dad XXX OOO

I have zero recollection of making this paper plate drawing as a kid, but somehow it encapsulates this whole book.

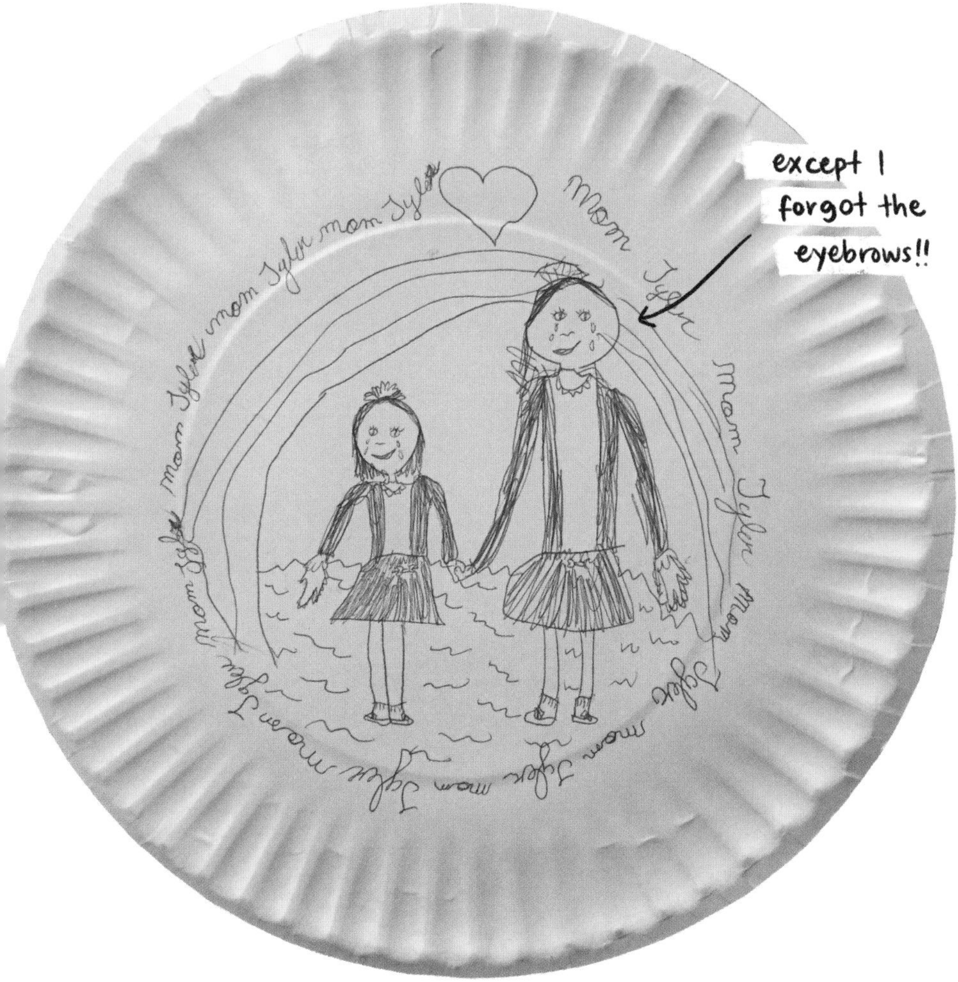
except I forgot the eyebrows!!

# acknowledgements

Thank you thank you thank you to my fearless agent and dear pal Monica Odom, a ray of sunshine in human form (if that ray of sunshine was whip-smart and had perfect curls). My cup overfloweth with love and gratitude for my publisher/editor/literary guardian angel Lauri Hornik, and the teams at Dial and Penguin Teen, without whom this book would still be a four-page essay for my creative nonfiction class in college. A million hugs to Jenny Kelly, a dream of an art director with an open mind and a heart of gold, who knows just how I like my emails: chock-full of exclamation points and smiley faces!! To my ever-patient therapist Dr. Kern, an unofficial but essential part of the Pity Party team: Because of you, I got through the book-making process without evaporating into a cloud of anxiety! Hooray!

A giant gold star to the many wonderful teachers that have encouraged my love of writing or art or both: Regina Stewart, Mia McCullough, Robert Gundlach, Eula Biss, Deb Sokolow, Bill Fritz, Doug Jennings, Donna Hickman, Patrick Fairchild, Joan Ackerman-Zimny, Judy Cooper, and Marcy Cohen. To the nice people of the internet, who have reblogged and retweeted and shared my art over the years, to the Etsy customers that turned into friends, to the internet pals that turned into IRL pals, and to the IRL pals that turned into internet pals because I was too busy working on the book to hang out: I literally could not have done this without you.

To Cody and Spino and Dad, who never stopped cheering me on even though I've been constantly ruining the mood by talking about cancer and death all year, you are my whole heart. I promise we can just talk about TV or something the next time we have lunch.

The tightest squeeze to Aunt Marcia, who reminds me of my mom in all the best ways. And, to the terrific, kind-hearted doctors and nurses at Sarasota Memorial Hospital, thank you for working tirelessly to keep my mom around.

Finally, thank you to my mom, for giving me life and for teaching me how to draw hands. I hope that, wherever you are, you can feel my love. ♥